FRISSON

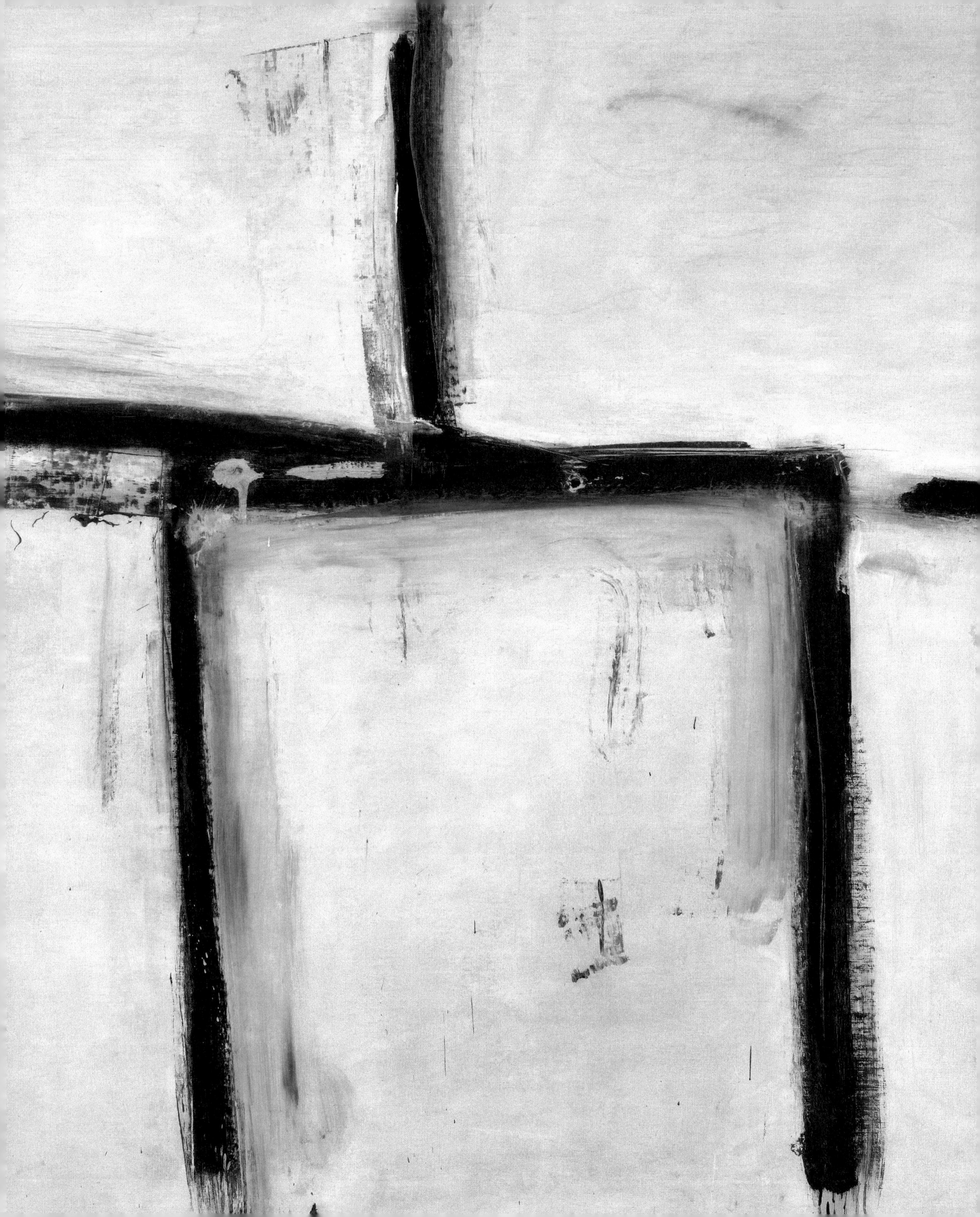

FRISSON

The Richard E. Lang and Jane Lang Davis Collection

Edited by
Catharina Manchanda

David Anfam
Michael Brenson
John Elderfield
Jack Flam
Carter E. Foster
Catherine Grenier
Bruce Guenther
Martin Harrison
Sanford Hirsch
Norman L. Kleeblatt
Eleanor Nairne
Amy Rahn
Elizabeth A. T. Smith
Robert Storr
Carol Vogel
Jeffrey Weiss

Seattle Art Museum

Distributed by the
University of Washington Press, Seattle

The Seattle Art Museum would like to acknowledge that we are on the traditional homelands of the Duwamish, and the customary territories of the Suquamish and Muckleshoot Peoples. As a cultural and educational institution, we honor our ongoing connection to these communities past, present, and future. We also acknowledge the many urban Native Peoples from many Nations who call Seattle their home.

CONTENTS

DIRECTOR'S FOREWORD

This catalogue is a cause for celebration, as it marks the Friday Foundation's landmark gift of nineteen iconic post-war American and European artworks in honor of collectors and former Seattle Art Museum (SAM) trustees Richard E. Lang and Jane Lang Davis. The publication appears on the occasion of the collection's inaugural exhibition at SAM. Distinguished by its artistic caliber and emphasis on leading members of New York's Abstract Expressionist circle, along with some important European contemporaries, the collection is evidence of the remarkable vision of Richard and Jane Lang, who acquired these works over the short span of twelve years. Their formidable aesthetic sensibility, careful research, and astute judgment can be discerned in each individual acquisition. Especially noteworthy is their selection of soaring works by three extraordinary female abstract painters, Helen Frankenthaler, Lee Krasner, and Joan Mitchell, fully recognizing the importance of their voices at a time when this was not as widely acknowledged as it is today. The gift of the Lang Collection is transformative for SAM. In a city known for its many dedicated art collectors, we hope—following the intentions of the donors—that this gift may inspire others to experience the joy of collecting and, ultimately, of giving works to the museum so that it will continue to flourish and grow.

In addition to the gift of the collection, the Friday Foundation is providing significant funding to augment SAM's conservation program, led by the newly named Jane Lang Davis Chief Conservator Nicholas Dorman. The museum will initiate a program of technical examination, care, and preservation of the Lang Collection itself, and the resources provided by the grant will also greatly enhance SAM's standing as a center for the conservation and study of modern and contemporary works of art more broadly. In addition, we are grateful for the Friday Foundation's substantial contributions to the museum's Closure Relief Fund and the creation of the Richard E. Lang and Jane Lang Davis Acquisition Fund for Global Contemporary Art, as well as its provisions of additional funds to enhance SAM's facilities to enrich our visitors' experience.

We are extraordinarily grateful to the directors of the Friday Foundation, Lyn Grinstein, Don Hussong, and George Steers, for their trust in SAM and their generosity toward the institution and, by extension, the city of Seattle. With deep appreciation, we would like to thank Jane Lang Davis's children, Lyn Grinstein and Don Hussong, whose commitment to SAM represents second-generation support by a family that has strengthened the institution for more than fifty years. Their largesse over so many decades has benefited not only SAM but also several cultural organizations across Seattle. Their pride in their city and sense of civic responsibility for its institutions is exemplary. We have also had the pleasure of a close collaboration with Pablo Schugurensky, the Friday Foundation's representative and adviser, as well as Laura Paulson, Friday Foundation adviser, who together shepherded this process.

The fulfilment of this gift was aided by the guidance and advice of several SAM trustees, including Stewart Landefeld, Jon Shirley, and Charles Wright. Former museum directors Mimi Gardner Gates and Kimerly Rorschach also supported this gift through their leadership during their respective tenures. We owe further thanks to attorneys Lorri Anne Dunsmore at Perkins Coie and Wendy Goffe at Stoel Rives, who worked closely with the directors of the Friday Foundation to help facilitate this exceptional donation.

A team of SAM staff worked diligently to arrange for the transfer of the works to the museum and to plan the collection's inaugural exhibition and this catalogue. Jon and Mary Shirley Curator of Modern and Contemporary Art Catharina Manchanda led the curatorial effort, editing the publication and organizing the exhibition. Special thanks go to Chief Financial Officer Cindy Bolton, Jane Lang Davis Chief Conservator Nicholas Dorman, Chief Development Officer Chris Landman, Senior Manager of Exhibitions and Publications Tina Lee, Director of Museum Services and Chief Registrar Lauren Mellon, Director of Design and Installation Nate Peek, Director of Legal Affairs and Legal Counsel Viviana Pitta, Kayla Skinner Deputy Director for Education Regan Pro, and Collections and Provenance Associate Elisabeth Smith.

Many hands played crucial parts in the realization of this exhibition and publication. For the catalogue's beautiful design and meticulous editing, we are indebted to Miko McGinty, Rita Jules, and Kristin Swan, whose careful eye and expertise make this publication shine. Proofreader Dianne Woo and indexer Kathleen Friello helped perfect the text with admirable skill. Spike Mafford's new photography brings to the fore each work's subtle details. Nicole Mitchell, director of the University of Washington Press, coordinated the publication's distribution, broadening the audience for the valuable new scholarship it presents.

This remarkable gift serves as a reminder that great institutions are built through the visionary leadership of true believers, and we are honored that the Friday Foundation has put its faith in us as stewards of Jane Lang Davis and Richard E. Lang's legacy.

Amada Cruz
Illsley Ball Nordstrom Director and Chief Executive Officer,
Seattle Art Museum

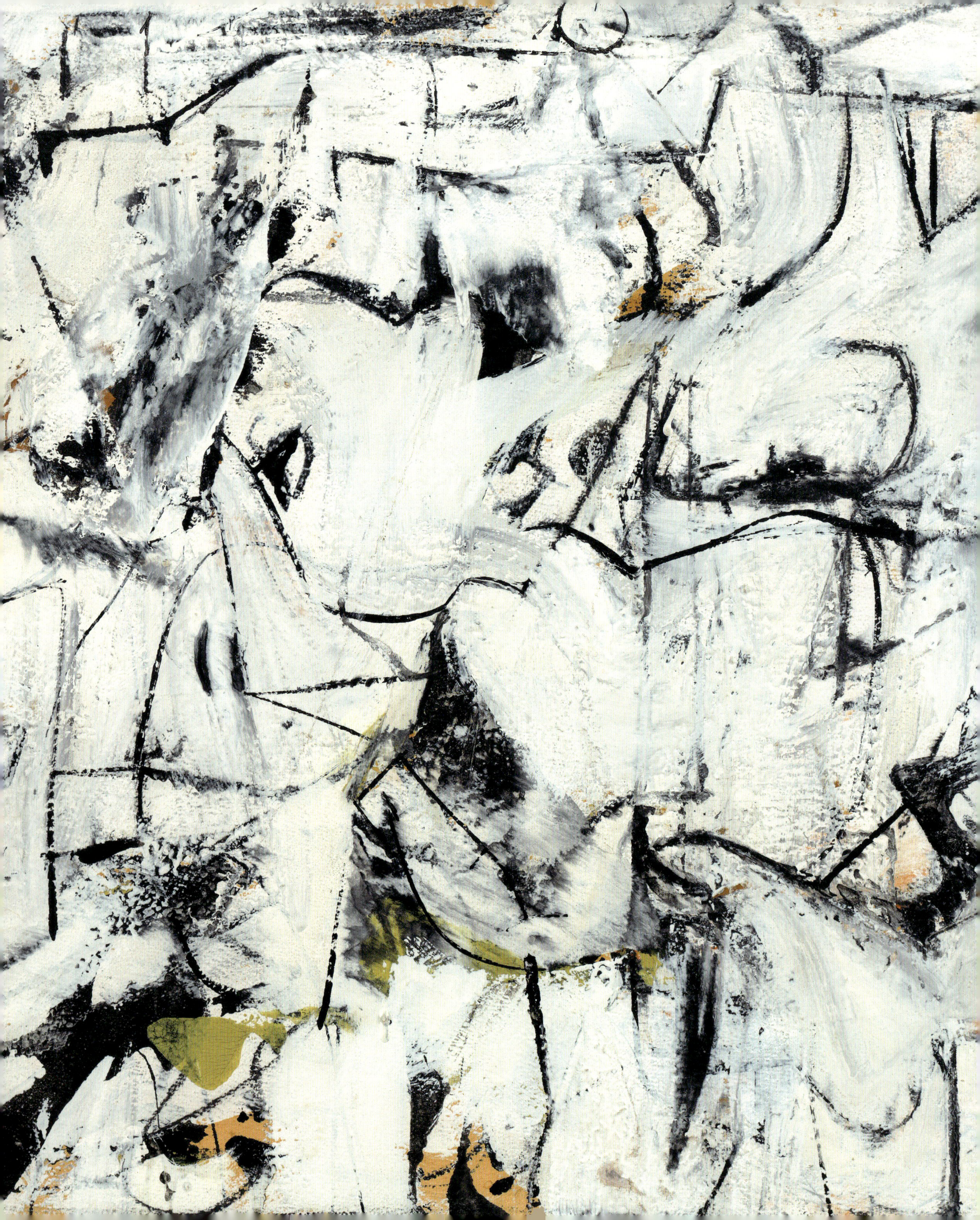

ACKNOWLEDGMENTS

Jane Lang moved to Seattle in 1966 when she married Richard Lang at a crucial moment in the city's cultural life, and when support of contemporary art, especially the Abstract Expressionists and their peers, was just starting to accelerate in the Pacific Northwest. Like members of the New York School, European artists who centered their practice on the figure, such as Francis Bacon and Alberto Giacometti, would have been unfamiliar to most Seattleites at the time. Private initiative played a pivotal role in the appreciation and understanding of contemporary art in the city. It was largely due to the ambition of collectors such as Richard and Jane Lang, and a cohort of like-minded collector friends, that the Seattle Art Museum, which had been founded as a museum of Asian art in 1933, was inspired to establish a department of modern and contemporary art in 1974. Within a few years of their acquaintance with the local art scene, the Langs became not only astute collectors of the most sophisticated abstract currents but pillars within the city's cultural community as well. Images of the Langs' former home serve as a reminder that the vanguard art they collected—daring and often large in scale—was selected to fit into the house, which required ingenuity and aesthetic finesse, as some paintings nearly touched the ceiling. Lyn Grinstein, daughter of Jane Lang Davis and president of the Friday Foundation, notes how the works of art became the very fabric of her family's everyday life.

In just twelve years, the Langs built an extraordinary case study of visionary directions in American and European postwar art. Individually, each painting and sculpture is an exquisite example of the artist's unique practice and style, marking important turning points and lifetime achievements. Collectively, the group's significance stems from the cross-references, aesthetic dialogues, and departures that can be traced from one work to the next as artists formulated new ideas and artistic solutions. This catalogue accompanies the inaugural exhibition of the Lang Collection at the Seattle Art Museum. The newly commissioned essays represent the most recent research of leading scholars in the field. Bruce Guenther, curator of modern and contemporary art at the Seattle Art Museum in the late 1970s and early 1980s, introduces us to Jane and Richard Lang as an eyewitness to their collecting and staunch support of Seattle's cultural institutions. Looking back upon the period between 1945 and 1976, when the artists created the works in the Lang Collection, David Anfam's rich introductory essay reminds us of the close-knit friendships between artists, writers, and critics and the intellectual capital they invested in the process. Additional scholarly essays by David Anfam, Michael Brenson, John Elderfield, Jack Flam, Carter E. Foster, Catherine Grenier, Martin Harrison, Sanford Hirsch, Norman L. Kleeblatt, Eleanor Nairne, Amy Rahn, Elizabeth A. T. Smith, Robert Storr, and Jeffrey Weiss provide nuanced information about each artist and individual work. We are deeply grateful for the extraordinary efforts of all these scholars, who navigated unprecedented and difficult research terrain during the COVID-19 crisis, which left many libraries and archives closed. The fact that they found ways around the many obstacles is in itself a testament to creative ingenuity. Organized chronologically by the date of each artwork, these texts start with Mark Rothko's *Untitled* (ca. 1945) and end with Philip Guston's epic 1976 canvas *The Painter*.

The catalogue also includes a chronology that allows readers to retrace how the Lang Collection grew over the years. We would like to express our special thanks to former *New York Times* art writer Carol Vogel, who interviewed many art insiders who remember a very different New York art world than the one we see today. This catalogue would not have been realized without the tireless advocacy of Friday Foundation advisers Laura Paulson and Pablo Schugurensky. We are deeply grateful for their vital contributions and support.

We hope the catalogue will provide rich opportunities for research and discovery for future scholars and entice readers to visit the museum and spend time with the works themselves. Above all, this publication is intended to honor Richard E. Lang and Jane Lang Davis, whose legacy will live on at the Seattle Art Museum to benefit future generations.

Catharina Manchanda
Jon and Mary Shirley Curator of Modern and Contemporary Art

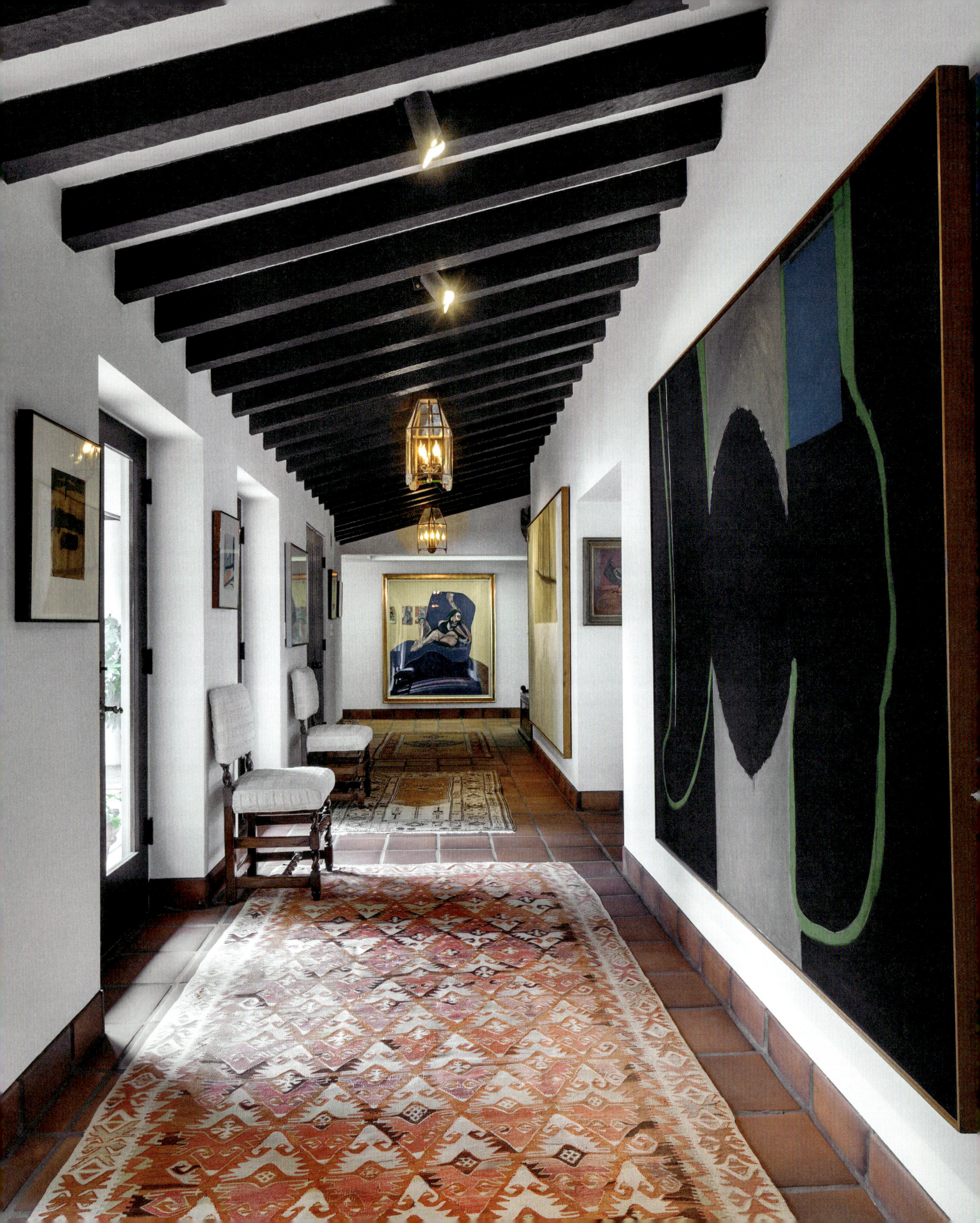

PRELUDE TO A GIFT

BRUCE GUENTHER

It was in early 1976 that I met Jane and Richard Lang because of a passing conversation with Robert Motherwell. During a symposium I had organized at the Washington State University Museum of Art in Pullman the preceding fall, Motherwell mentioned he would be stopping in Seattle to visit with some collectors he quite liked. They had recently bought a second great painting of his, *Irish Elegy* (1965, plate 14), and he thought I should see their collection. In a subsequent telephone call, Jane Lang breezily noted that Motherwell had spoken of our meeting and campus visit, and that she would be delighted to make a date "between Hawaii and New York" for me to see their collection. Arriving at the Langs' door on the appointed day, I was met by a vivacious and welcoming woman who quickly put aside all formality. We spent the two-hour visit talking enthusiastically about the artworks that commanded the walls of their elegant, light-filled home (fig. 1).

On that first viewing, the quality and impact of the collection, centered on a core of New York School painters, was exhilarating. Two powerful Motherwell paintings were indeed hanging in the company of singularly beautiful canvases by Franz Kline and Clyfford Still, along with the surprise of three important works by European artists Francis Bacon and Alberto Giacometti that signaled an independent, personal criterion at work. The strength of every work in the collection, coupled with the lack of the usual peripheral "filler" artworks, spoke volumes to me about the intention of these collectors. Richard Lang's appearance near the end of the visit clarified the joint nature of their collecting activity. Our conversation confirmed for me how much the balance of Jane's obvious knowledge and passion for art with Richard's rigor and clear distrust of the fashionably predictable drove their shared search for the very best. It was a visit and dialogue that I would relish and repeat again and again over the ensuing years as our relationship developed along with their collection.

Hired in the fall of 1979 as the curator of contemporary art and second head of the Modern Art Department of the Seattle Art Museum, I was able both to gain a better understanding of how this singular, focused collection began and to observe the Langs' collecting activities firsthand. The start of the collection was clearly rooted in who they were as individuals, their interest in contemporary art ignited by the people the couple had come to know in

Fig. 1 Richard and Jane Lang's home in Medina, Washington, 2018, with Robert Motherwell's *Irish Elegy* (1965, right foreground) and *Before the Day* (1972, right background); Francis Bacon's *Study for a Portrait* (1967) hangs at the end of the hall.

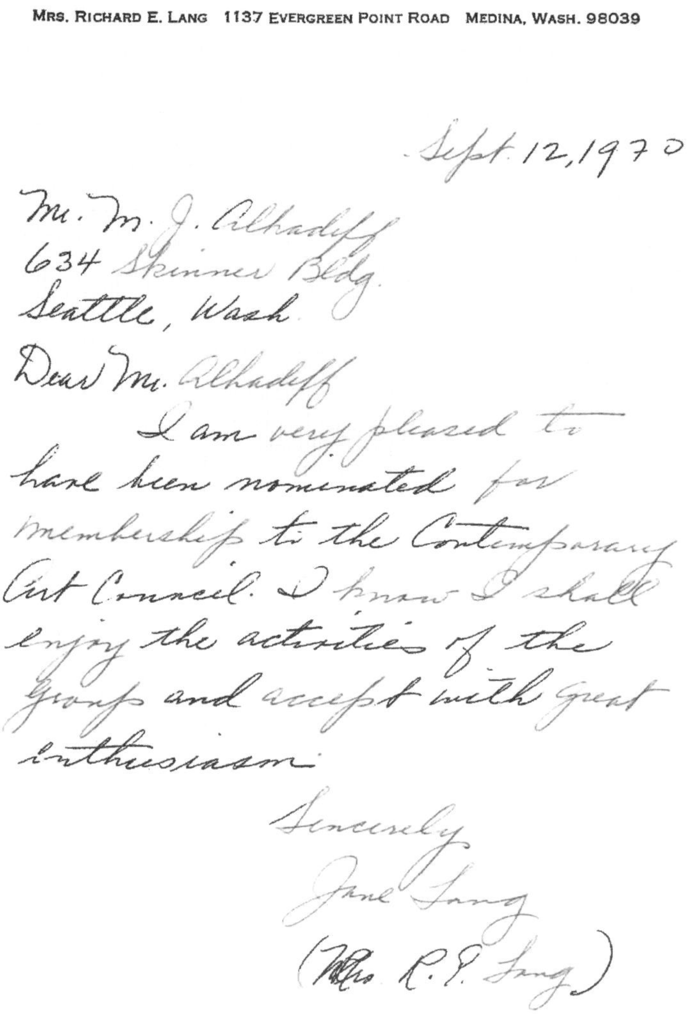

MRS. RICHARD E. LANG 1137 EVERGREEN POINT ROAD MEDINA, WASH. 98039

Sept. 12, 1970

Mr. M. J. Alhadeff
634 Skinner Bldg.
Seattle, Wash.

Dear Mr. Alhadeff

I am very pleased to have been nominated for membership to the Contemporary Art Council. I know I shall enjoy the activities of the group and accept with great enthusiasm.

Sincerely
Jane Lang
(Mrs. R. E. Lang)

Fig. 2 Letter from Jane Lang to Morris Alhadeff formally accepting membership in the Contemporary Art Council of the Seattle Art Museum, September 12, 1970. Seattle Art Museum Archives.

Seattle who drew them into an important transition period for the community and its museum.

Introduced in Hawaii in 1965, Jane (née MacGregor) and Richard Lang fell in love and would marry in 1966. After her move to Seattle, as was Jane's nature, she threw herself into exploring her new community and pulled Richard along into the city's rapidly evolving contemporary art scene. It was a community that had historically focused on the Northwest regional painters and its university-based artists. The city's museum—established and built primarily to house a private Asian art collection—was slow to expand its programming beyond the interests of its founder/director, Dr. Richard E. Fuller, and the limitations of its Volunteer Park building. The 1962 Seattle World's Fair—*Century 21 Exposition*—had literally introduced the region's citizens to the world, and one of its art exhibitions,

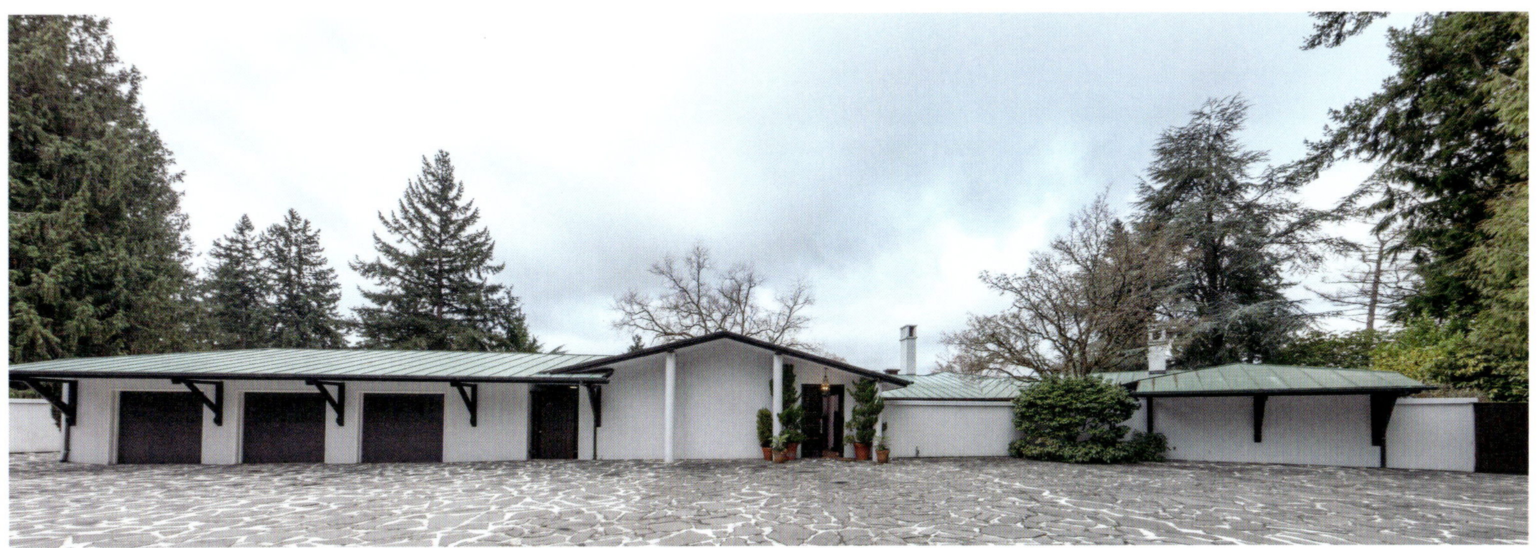

Fig. 3 Exterior of the Langs' home, 2018.

American Art since 1950, became a local cause célèbre in its presentation of challenging new abstract painting. A local group of early collectors of modern and contemporary art, including Saul Schluger, Anne Gerber, Bagley and Virginia Wright, Samuel Rubinstein, and John Denman, occasionally met socially in one another's homes to hear a visiting contemporary art dealer or share their latest acquisitions with like-minded people. Inspired by the World's Fair, they decided to formalize their activities in 1964 through incorporation as a private, by-invitation group under the aegis of the museum. The Contemporary Art Council (CAC) would sponsor lectures, symposia, and visiting artists for the education of their membership and the broader community, and would periodically sponsor or organize contemporary art exhibitions for the city as part of the museum's public program.

The Langs' involvement with the council, which Jane formally joined in 1970 (fig. 2), introduced them to this expanding community and gave them the opportunity to see and discuss the art being acquired in Seattle. CAC programming, through the national contacts of active collectors like Bagley and Virginia Wright, provided access to an impressive stream of prominent art dealers, artists, critics, and curators who opened up the latest contemporary art ideas and criteria, both in public appearances and in the council's private social evenings held in members' homes. Jane Lang described the impact of the discussions and events of those early days of camaraderie and discovery with the CAC. She credited the close friends that she and Richard made there, like the Wrights and Robert Dootson, with encouraging and emboldening them to collect. An astute businessman with a law degree from Stanford University, Richard Lang found learning the new language of art and the mechanics of the art marketplace stimulating. He was more than intrigued by the question of what constituted a great work of art, what defined a contemporary masterpiece. And so, inspired by their CAC activities and introductions to Gotham's art scene, the Langs' business and pleasure trips to New York began to change, with visits to galleries and museums added to the usual theater and ballet evenings on their itinerary.

With the construction of their new home on Lake Washington in 1970 (fig. 3), Jane recognized an opportunity to begin seriously collecting and proposed they look

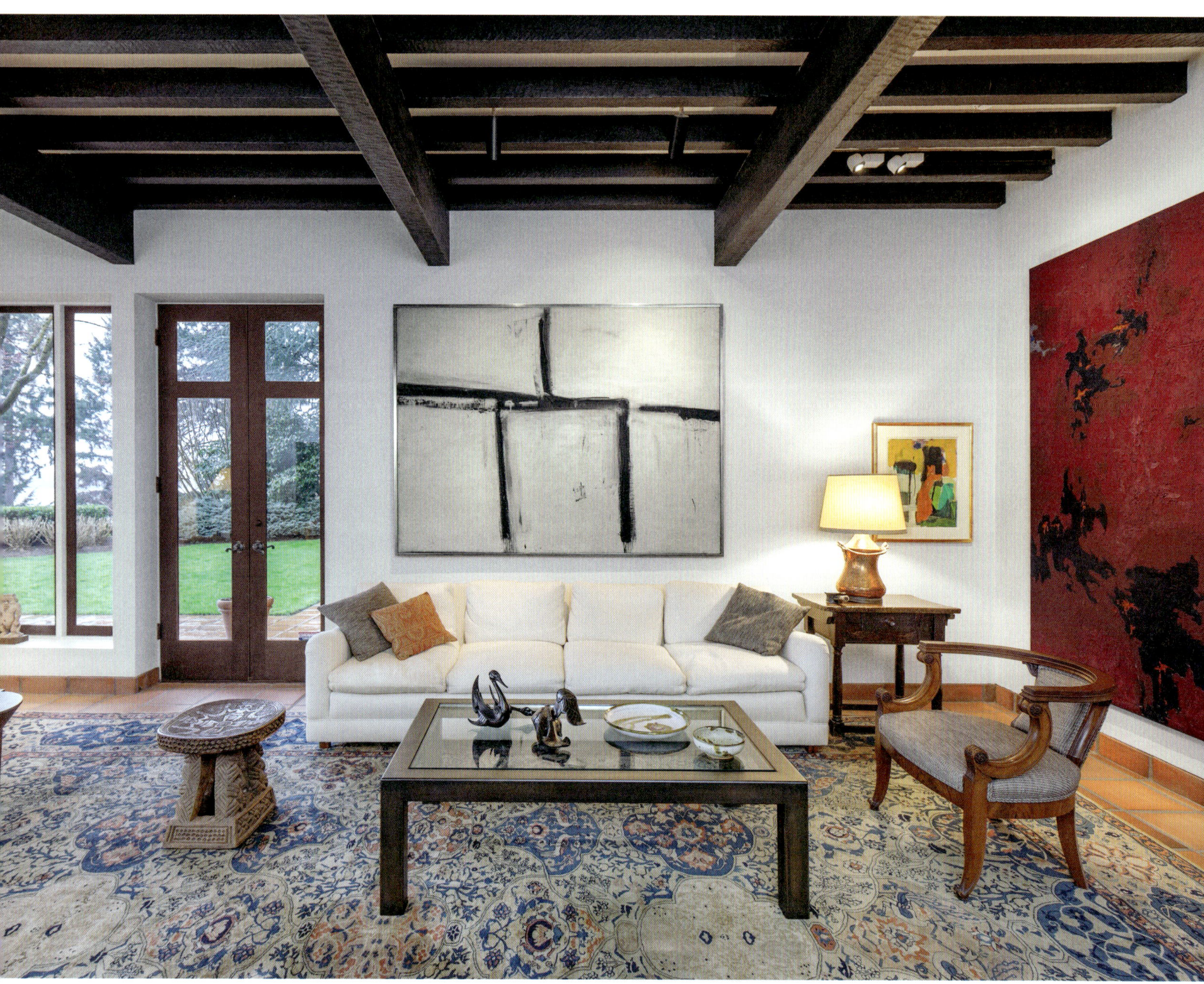

Fig. 4 Franz Kline's *Painting No. 11* (1951) hanging above the couch in the Langs' living room, with Clyfford Still's PH-338 (1949) at right, 2018.

around New York that fall and perhaps buy a "painting for over the couch." It was clear from things Richard said in the often-recounted story of their first purchase that a painting was a negotiated compromise from his vision for their new home as one with stylishly empty walls and a view of the water. Franz Kline's magisterial *Painting No. 11* (1951, plate 5) "for over the couch" (fig. 4) was a remarkable first purchase and a life-altering event, both setting a direction for the couple's collecting over the next twelve years and establishing an exceptional standard of quality for any work that would come into their home in the future. The Kline was Richard's choice, and it remained his favorite for the rest of his life. *Painting No. 11* is a powerful abstraction with a linear structure of black brushstrokes defining and containing white blocks of paint, which seem to have materialized in the artist's repeated campaigns with the brush across the surface. These dense slabs of white pigment reveal the pentimenti of their forming and the drips and shadows of the black line's struggle to limit the slabs. Richard once observed that until he saw that Kline canvas, he did not know a painting could affect him so physically, that it could wordlessly take over his imagination. He was enthralled by his experience with Kline, and the couple would go on eventually to acquire an additional eleven of the artist's works on paper and earlier paintings.

Over the next three years after purchasing the Kline, the Langs abandoned all thoughts of empty walls as they sought out and bought five major museum-quality works by exponents of American Abstract Expressionism, signaling to their Seattle friends and to the New York art world the couple's commitment to building a first-tier collection. The next two paintings they acquired, *Untitled* (1963, plate 13) by Mark Rothko and *Before the Day* (1972, plate 18) by Robert Motherwell, share a number of formal qualities with the Kline canvas—a severely restricted palette, a strong, clear composition, and an emotionally potent paint surface characteristic of each artist's mature style. Reputedly the last canvas sold by Marlborough Gallery from Rothko's estate before it was sealed in a legendary five-year legal battle, the large, signature Rothko canvas is darkly brooding and, like the Kline, is not an easy work for many people to approach. Rothko used shadowy gradients of transparent and translucent pigments applied with brush and paint-soaked rag to create a series of four stacked rectangles that optically recede and advance in perceptual space, slipping from solid to void. Its closed and somber austerity has always struck me as a surprisingly tough choice for these lively new collectors. The Rothko evokes the meditative, enveloping silences of the night, whereas the Motherwell, one of his Opens, purchased during a studio visit, is filled with bright possibility. In the reflected and refracted light from its brush-activated surface, warm and cool whites, sooty grays, and sharp black lines animate both the field and an aperture rich with associations.

In close succession in the fall of 1972, the Langs then purchased a graphically dynamic Adolph Gottlieb canvas from his Burst series, *Crimson Spinning #2* (1959, plate 10). The expansive canvas's white field barely contains its two stacked orbs—a compressing, optically pulsing alizarin crimson oval over an explosive black frenzy of spattering brushstrokes challenging the work's balance. Its hieratic power is like a sharp cracking sound on the wall compared to the enveloping silence of Rothko's 1963 masterpiece.

The collection's early chromatic austerity shifted in 1973 with the acquisition of two works that revel in color and extend the painterly vocabularies represented among the Langs' holdings. An important early Clyfford Still canvas, PH-338 (1949, plate 3), presents a rich record of the artist's brush and palette knife caressing and cutting across the canvas's expanse in a continuous, densely brushed, impastoed field of smoldering red paint. Eruptions of an earthy sienna and deep black, highlighted by molten notes of a sharp yellow or vermilion, fracture the surface. This compelling painting embodies both vast distances and an intimate immediacy in its horizonless sweep. A rarity in private collections due to the artist's early withdrawal from the marketplace, this beautifully mysterious painting is a singularly important work within the Lang collection. In contrast to the Still's opaque physicality, the graceful Helen Frankenthaler work chosen by the Langs, *Dawn Shapes* (1967, plate 16; fig. 5), is a fluid, directly worked composition of brushed and dragged washes of transparent and opaque acrylic. Pooling pigments tease out shapes and lead the viewer's eye across a coral-framed threshold into the canvas center with its roiling, circling ochre overtaking a shadowing sage green. Balancing the spontaneous with the deliberate,

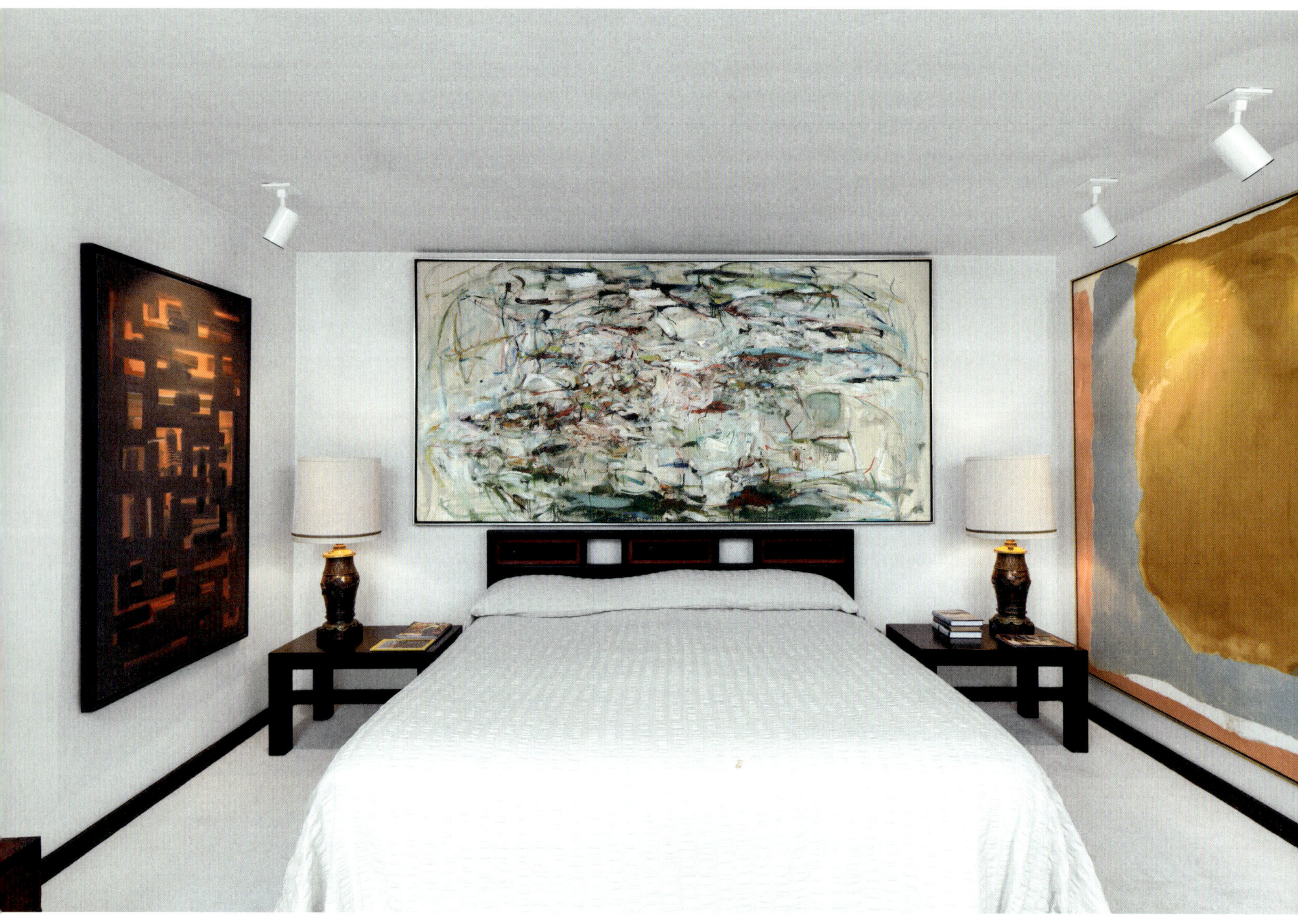

Fig. 5 The Langs' bedroom with (left to right) Ad Reinhardt's *Painting, 1950* (1950), Joan Mitchell's *The Sink* (1956), and Helen Frankenthaler's *Dawn Shapes* (1967), 2018.

the Frankenthaler is a vital open work that brings her pioneering direct-action methodology into the dialogue. Auspiciously anchoring the collection's focus and future, these six massive works represent artists at the center of Abstract Expressionism in New York. Taken together, the canvases evince the Langs' confidence as collectors and their willingness to risk waiting for works of the finest quality that embodied the essence of an artist's contribution to the movement's development.

In just four short years, the Lang Collection was on the art world's must-see list in Seattle, and Richard had agreed to join the Seattle Art Museum Board of Trustees. Thanks in many ways to the CAC activities that introduced them to artists and ideas, Jane and Richard had developed a comfortable process for identifying and evaluating artists with whom they both connected emotionally. They were also finding the people in New York who could help them further refine their eye and hone their choices to realize the couple's vision. Their twice-annual trips to New York had taken on a more complex character as the search for artworks plunged them headlong into the New York scene where they would become virtual fixtures (fig. 6). As a couple, Jane and Richard thrived on the insider world of attending gallery and museum openings and gala parties, meeting artists, and interacting with museum professionals and other committed collectors with whom they could share their new passion. A warmly gregarious and outgoing person, Jane quickly made friends across the art scene through galleries, museum events, and travel.

The Langs joined the International Council of the Museum of Modern Art (MoMA) in 1973 and became founding members of the National Committee of the Whitney Museum of American Art in 1980. In recounting their New York visits, Jane once shared that Richard was such an inveterate competitor, so energized by their encounters with dealers and fellow collectors, that he would want to spend hours at the end of the evening discussing and comparing what they had seen with their own works. He had become an avid collector, using every opportunity to deepen his knowledge of art and the marketplace to sharpen his judgments.

The growth of the collection shows the clear imprint of those spring and fall sojourns in New York, with the dates that artworks entered the collection closely mirroring the Langs' trips to the East Coast. I always relished the first phone call with Jane when she returned from New York, as did many people in Seattle, for the generous, ebullient tumble of exhibitions seen, theater tips, and art-world news and gossip. We would then get down to the discussion of which dealers had shown them what paintings, what she and Richard had thought of them, and what work would be finding its place on the walls of their Seattle home. Like a pebble dropped in a quiet pool, Jane would share her enthusiasms and most recent discoveries with a swath of people across the broader art scene—ballet, theater, music, and visual arts—to inspire and challenge them. Those calls from Jane had a surprisingly tangible effect on the community, frequently sparking new discussions and projects with the Langs' support. And then, when each new work arrived, Jane would issue a much-coveted invitation to a few close art friends for a first viewing to celebrate and discuss the latest arrival.

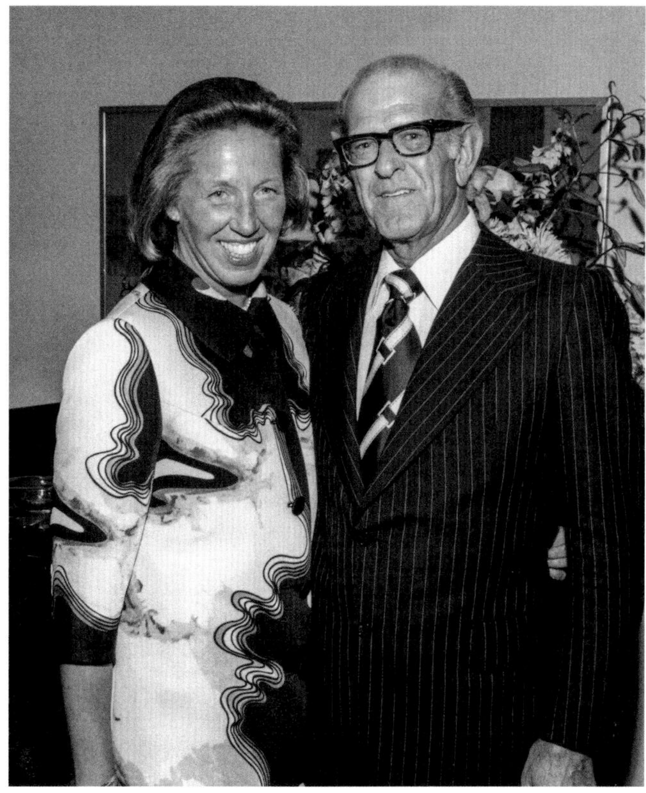

Fig. 6 Jane and Richard Lang at an event in New York in 1973. Lang Family Collection.

The Langs' criteria for collecting only works that expressed a strong, individual vision to which they both responded brought the addition of figurative works to the collection's core of Abstract Expressionist paintings in the mid-1970s. New acquisitions from two of the most eminent postwar European artists—Francis Bacon and Alberto Giacometti—introduced specific subject matter, enriching the experience and understanding of expressionism offered by the collection. Richard was particularly moved by Bacon's power to communicate the emotional emanations of personality in his often-radical rendering of the figure, the peeling away of decorous signifiers to suggest underlying psychological truths in paint. Offered an opportunity to acquire *Portrait of Man with Glasses I* (1963, plate 12) at auction and then *Study for a Portrait* (1967, plate 17) from his dealer friend David McKee, Richard acted, the deals were struck, and the works found their

July 15th 1974

Sidney Janis Gallery
6 W. 57th
New York, New York

Attention: Carroll Janis

Gentlemen:

In May when Mrs. Richard E. Lang was with you in the gallery she commented on the Giacometti sculpture which was in a corner. It was a female with a long skinny neck and approximately 4 feet high. As Mrs. Lang told you this is exactly what she is looking for and was advised at the time that you did not know if your Father would sell it or not.

Mrs. Lang is now looking at several other Giacometti's which, frankly, she does not like as well as the one she saw in your gallery. If you would please advise if the one you have is for sale and, if so, price and full description (provenance etc.) it would be greatly appreciated.

Thanks in advance for your cooperation in this matter.

Yours truly,

Veronica Whittaker
Secretary to Mrs. Lang.

P.S. As Mrs Lang has a hold on another Giacometti we would appreciate a wire response if yours is for sale.

Above and opposite: Figs. 7, 8 Correspondence between Veronica Whittaker, Richard Lang's secretary, and the Sidney Janis Gallery securing the Langs' purchase of the Giacometti bronze in July 1974.

way to Seattle—causing quite a stir at the time as the first Bacon paintings in the Northwest. When Jane saw a cast of Giacometti's epochal *Femme de Venise II* (1956, plate 9) in the back room at Sidney Janis Gallery in May 1974, she was convinced its evocative surface and timeless presence had to be part of their lives and the collection; the task of convincing Janis to relinquish his personal bronze fell to Richard in a series of letters and calls that prompted a swift affirmative when Jane's secretary formally requested the work in July (figs. 7, 8). His success brought this beautiful example of Giacometti's most important series of female figures to Washington (fig. 9). Memorably, after

SIDNEY JANIS GALLERY · NEW YORK janis6W57

July 17, 1974

Veronica Whittaker
Secretary to Mrs. Lang
4521 Seattle-First National Bank Building
Seattle, Washington 98154

Dear Ms Whittaker:

In Carroll's absence (vacation), his father replies to your kind letter of July 15th.

The Giacometti standing in the corner, which Mrs. Lang liked, is as follows:

Femme de Venise II 1956 Bronze 6/6 48" high

from the collection of Aime Maeght, Maeght Fondation,
St Paul de Vence, France A/M
and was included in the following exhibitions at our gallery:
"Giacometti-Dubuffet" exhibition, November '68
"European XXth Century Masters", February '70
"XXth Century European Art", December '72

As you know, I am most hesitant to part with it, but since Mrs. Lang remains so intrigued by it, I am tempted to let her have it.

It is my belief that the sculpture, which is one of Giacometti's best of the famous Venise series, will fetch in 1975 a figure far above the value I am now quoting: $185,000.00

I simply could not wire all this information, and trust this letter reaches you in ample time.

Yours sincerely,

SIDNEY JANIS

SJ:meg

installing and living with the work a while, Jane noticed to her delight one afternoon that the setting sun transformed the attenuated figure's normally pencil-thin shadow into a voluptuous avatar stretched across the wall behind it. A story she enjoyed recounting for visitors to the collection, it was also an example of why I loved giving art groups tours of the Lang Collection with Jane over some thirty years. The directness of her response to the works, coupled with the personal, anecdotal context of discovering them, was so refreshingly immediate and informed. And she never tired of my drawing ever-larger art historical circles around groups of works and methods,

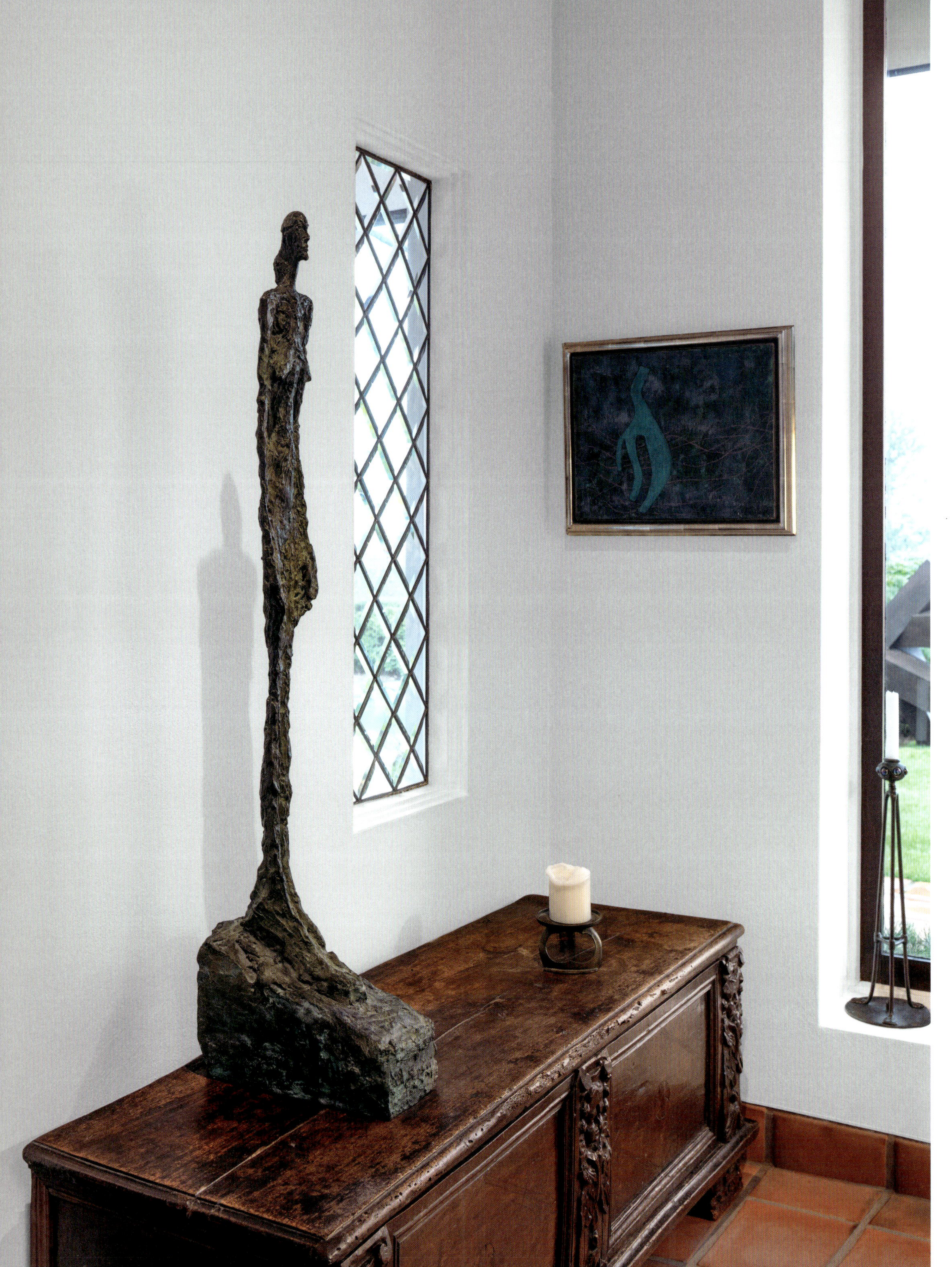

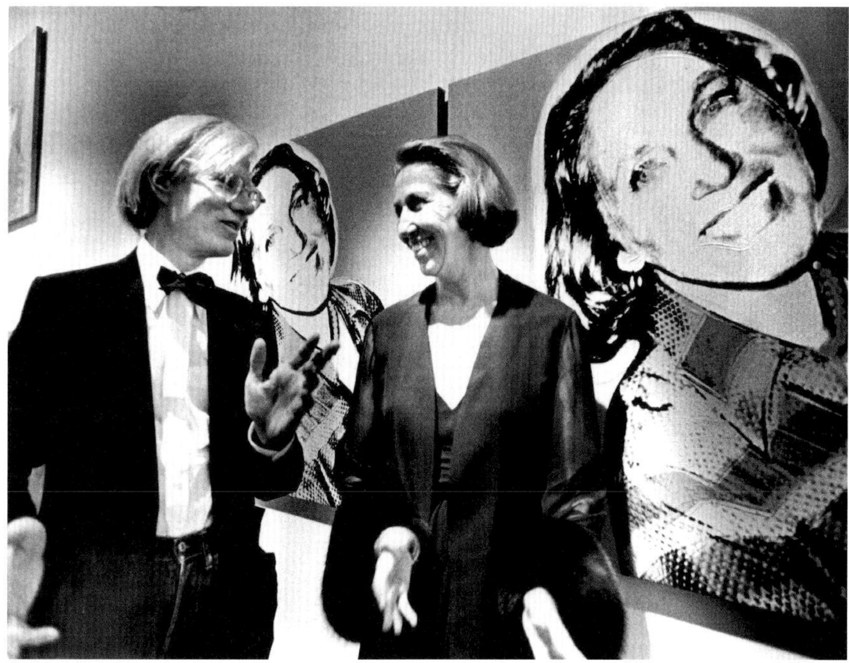

Fig. 10 Jane Lang and Andy Warhol at the opening reception for the exhibition *Andy Warhol: Portraits*, Seattle Art Museum, 1976. Seattle Times Photo Archives.

illuminating the through lines of ideas that connected the works.

Thanks to the programming and growth of the CAC over the preceding decade, the Seattle Art Museum established its Modern Art Department in 1974 with the council's support, designating its Seattle Center facility as the Modern Art Pavilion and announcing the hiring of Charles Cowles as the museum's first curator of modern art. Though without actual curatorial experience, Cowles brought to Seattle his network of connections as the publisher of *Artforum*, a who's who of the New York art world, to kick-start the program; his presence energized the community with the promise of future possibilities. As a collector himself, Cowles was a generous and eager collaborator for the Langs. He proved to be particularly helpful in 1976, when Richard decided to surprise Jane for her birthday with her portrait by Andy Warhol, whom they had met in 1973 in San Francisco. Cowles was negotiating one of the major acquisitions of his tenure at SAM—Warhol's *Double Elvis* (1963)—with the intention of staging an exhibition around his purchase, and he was delighted to assist a museum trustee while enhancing his position with the Warhol studio. The exhibition concept would expand to incorporate a group of Warhol's recent works and society portraits, including the special birthday surprise for Jane that Cowles was helping to arrange. In gratitude to the museum for the enterprise's success, the Langs donated one panel of the portrait following the exhibition (fig. 10; see page 27).

As a ploy to engineer the necessary Polaroid sitting at Warhol's studio in New York to capture Jane's likeness for her portrait, Richard told her *he* was the portrait subject.[1] So it was no surprise when, a few months after the unveiling of her portrait, Jane brought up commissioning an actual portrait of Richard. The Langs then discussed the Warhol portrait idea with their friend David McKee, who responded, "Dick's too ornery to be painted by Warhol.

Fig. 9 Alberto Giacometti's *Femme de Venise II* (1956) installed in the Langs' home, 2018.

You need somebody who can really catch him."[2] Richard revealed his long-held dream of having Francis Bacon do his portrait. McKee, who had a relationship with Bacon going back to his days at the Marlborough Gallery, rather quickly disabused Richard of the possibility of Bacon taking on the commission. Instead, he suggested the American painter Alice Neel, who after a 1974 Whitney Museum retrospective was becoming more prominent for her tough, uncompromising portraits. Intrigued, the Langs did some research, met the artist, and chose to have her paint the portrait of Richard in 1978 (see page 29), which brilliantly captures the man and the dynamic encounter between sitter and artist. "Jane took a chance," McKee recalled, "and she loved the portrait. And Dick loved Alice Neel. They were two ornery people who got along famously." Together, the Lang portraits in the context of the collection both provide a vibrant reflection of the collectors' personalities and illuminate the poles of formal invention, from expressionist abstraction to the flat, mechanical surface of Pop Art, represented in the collection.

In 1976, while the subterfuge around the commissioning of Jane's portrait played out, the Langs added Bacon's *Study for a Portrait* to the collection, along with a quietly enticing monochromatic Willem de Kooning painting. *Town Square* (1948, plate 2) was purchased from Ben Heller, an early and influential collector of Abstract Expressionism and fellow member of MoMA's International Council, who had become an adviser and friend to Richard; similar personalities, both were tough businessmen, curious, and opinionated. Part of a seminal group of late-1940s paintings that launched de Kooning's career, *Town Square* is a work in continuous visual flux. De Kooning played a bold, brushed line off of elusive shapes as they coalesce into momentary forms that open and close the field, suggesting motion and the passage of time in both method and the resulting painting. It is a work that foreshadows the powerful gestural paintings that changed the course of American abstraction and assured de Kooning's place in its pantheon.

The de Kooning presaged the Langs' engagement with artists who attacked the canvas directly—exploring, putting down, and removing paint in the battle to discover the spirit and inscribe the form of the work. Jane led the acquisition of major mature works by Joan Mitchell and Lee Krasner for the collection, buoyed in part by the emerging scholarship in the late 1970s on these women's contributions to Action Painting. The fluid trails and swirling knots of spontaneously brushed oil paint set into motion Mitchell's *The Sink* (1956, plate 8), a lyric painting filled with the echo of observations and memories of places in the artist's past, which have taken form in a deeply personal vocabulary of mark and color, gesture and surface. It often elicited from Richard a comparison to his beloved view of Lake Washington. Lee Krasner's monumental *Night Watch* (1960, plate 11) is a masterpiece of gestural abstraction in which the full-arm strokes that define and animate the surface create a powerful, mysterious place. Engaged by Jungian theory and the view that painting is an act of discovery and revelation, Krasner opens imagination's door to a nocturnal place of all-seeing eyes. The Krasner and Philip Guston's heroic self-portrait *The Painter* (1976, plate 19)—for me, one of the great works of Guston's long career—were the last paintings that Jane and Richard would buy together. As I witnessed it, they were complicated pictures for Richard to embrace emotionally, even as he understood their importance intellectually and finally agreed they should be in the collection. Writing to David McKee to secure the Guston, Richard noted, "Frankly [Jane] is very excited about it," and conceded, "I must admit that in the daylight, it is a terrific painting" (fig. 11). The two paintings came to live on opposite walls in Jane's office (fig. 12), where they never failed to stop even the most sophisticated visitors in their tracks with the power and intensity emanating from those canvases.

By the late 1970s, even as they continued to make judicious acquisitions for their own collection, the Langs found ways to integrate art into their philanthropy beyond Seattle. In 1979, in an act of generosity that anticipated later gifts, they supported the acquisition of an Alexander Calder sculpture for the campus of Richard's alma mater, Stanford, and commissioned a painting by Robert Motherwell to celebrate their endowment of the university's Richard E. Lang Law Chair (fig. 13). The spring of 1982 brought an important opportunity for the Langs to share their collection when MoMA's International Council visited Seattle and Vancouver, British Columbia. Virginia Wright and Jane Lang organized the council's crowded tour itinerary of public and private arts venues, including a collection tour and special luncheon at the Langs' home.

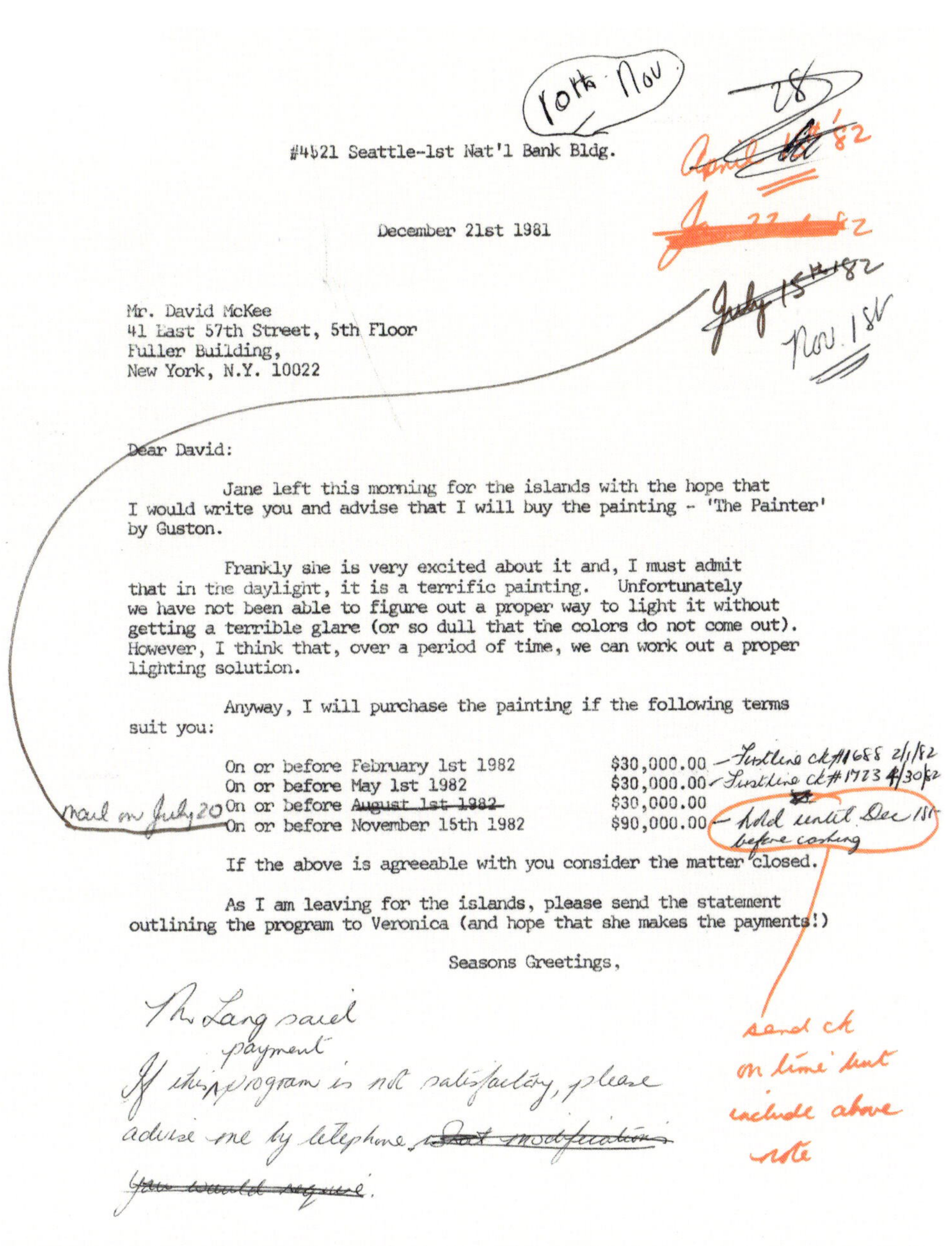

#4521 Seattle-1st Nat'l Bank Bldg.

December 21st 1981

Mr. David McKee
41 East 57th Street, 5th Floor
Fuller Building,
New York, N.Y. 10022

Dear David:

Jane left this morning for the islands with the hope that I would write you and advise that I will buy the painting - 'The Painter' by Guston.

Frankly she is very excited about it and, I must admit that in the daylight, it is a terrific painting. Unfortunately we have not been able to figure out a proper way to light it without getting a terrible glare (or so dull that the colors do not come out). However, I think that, over a period of time, we can work out a proper lighting solution.

Anyway, I will purchase the painting if the following terms suit you:

On or before February 1st 1982	$30,000.00
On or before May 1st 1982	$30,000.00
On or before ~~August 1st 1982~~	$30,000.00
On or before November 15th 1982	$90,000.00

If the above is agreeable with you consider the matter closed.

As I am leaving for the islands, please send the statement outlining the program to Veronica (and hope that she makes the payments!)

Seasons Greetings,

Fig. 11 Letter from Richard Lang to David McKee arranging for the Langs' final purchase together, Philip Guston's *The Painter* (1976).

The council members were awestruck by the focus and quality of the collection they discovered inside the plain white stucco walls of the modest-looking house. Adjourning to the yellow-and-white-striped tent set up on the lawn with perfectly framed views of the lake and of David Smith's sculpture *Cubi XXV* (1965, plate 15) set against a wall of evergreens, the sixty attendees were feted with a spectacular Northwest seafood buffet. It was Lang hospitality at its finest—lovingly characterized by one of the attendees as "a feast to end all feasts."[3]

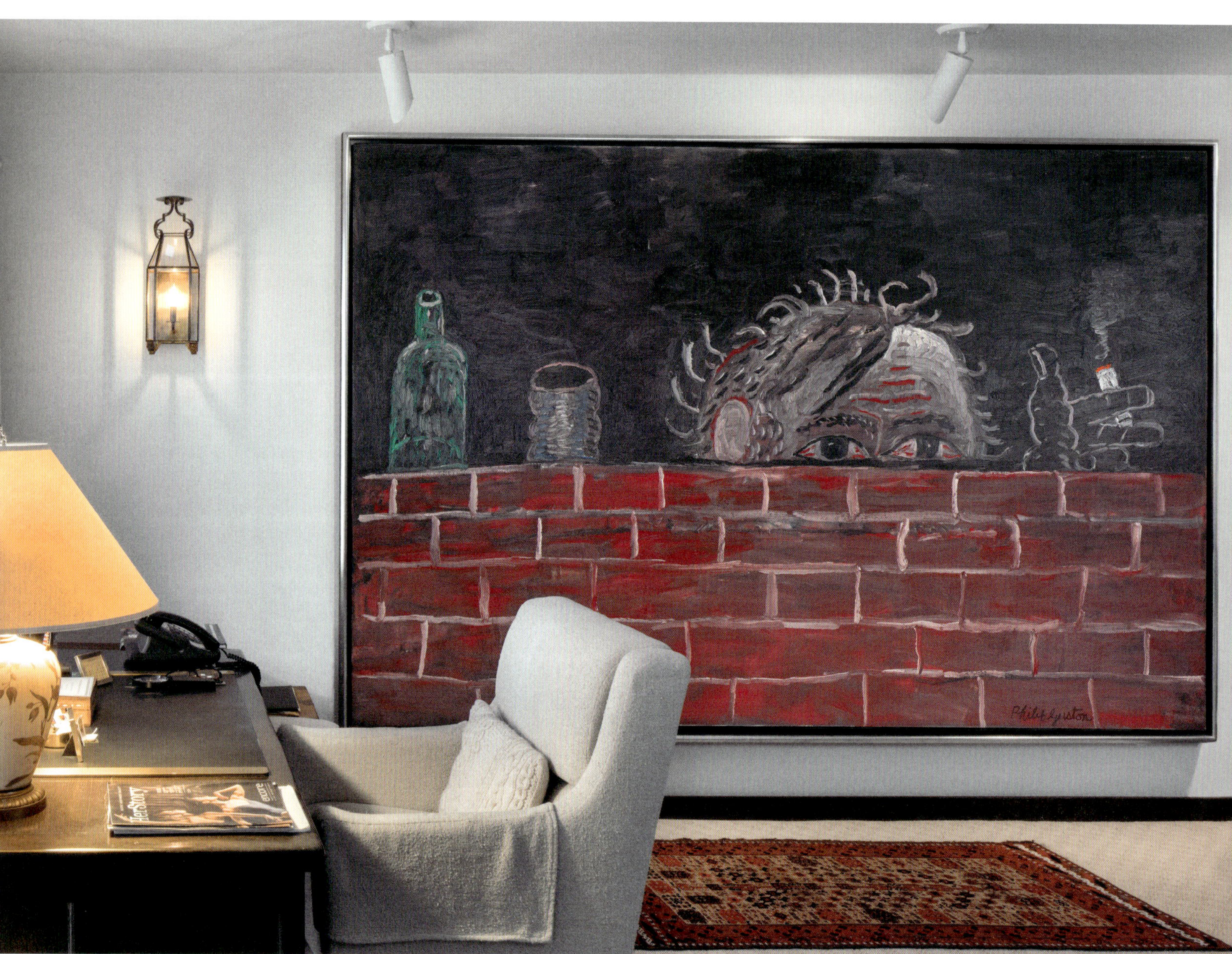

Fig. 12 Jane Lang's office with Philip Guston's *The Painter* (1976), 2018.

Richard Lang died in November 1982 as we were planning the first public exhibition of the collection, at the Seattle Art Museum, for early 1984. The exhibition was the outgrowth of over five years of conversations I had had with Richard and Jane about the future of their growing collection and the part it could play in the Seattle Art Museum's projected new building in the heart of downtown Seattle. Before Richard died, we had agreed to a preliminary checklist and assigned the exhibition a slot on the museum's schedule, with the mutual understanding that the exhibition was part of the concerned parties' desire to forge a plan for the future public life of the collection. I worked with Jane to finish the exhibition, which showcased a selection of forty-four works. It opened to acclaim and surprise in the region, which had not realized the depth and quality of the collection, even though the Langs had generously lent works to museums throughout their collecting lives. The exhibition and publication celebrated the collection, which encompassed works by fourteen first- and second-generation Abstract Expressionists, as well as two European contemporaries, with seven artists represented by small clusters of important works from across their careers.[4] As Jane explained to a member of the press at the opening, they had chosen to live with their collection and only buy as many works as their home in Seattle could accommodate; this led the Langs to focus early, remodel twice, and continually broaden and deepen the collection with additional fine examples of each artist's work. Their passion for quality was what most distinguished the Langs' acquisitions and separated theirs from larger private collections. As was clear in the 1984 exhibition and remains true in the present one, virtually every work is an aesthetic summary of the artist's contribution to the course of postwar contemporary art as we understand it today.

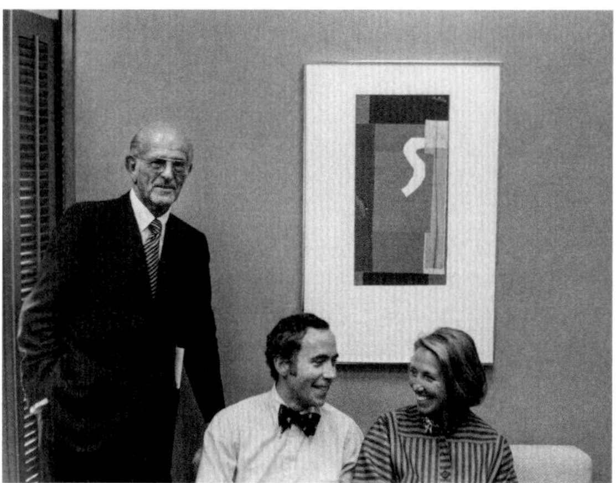

Fig. 13 Richard and Jane Lang with Tom Ehrlich (center), dean of Stanford Law School, 1979.

Serious, passionate collectors, the Langs assembled a rare trove of art to enhance their life together, to live with beauty and greatness, and to enrich their community's cultural resources. The transformative gift to the Seattle Art Museum of nineteen remarkable works from the Richard E. Lang and Jane Lang Davis Collection is a fitting legacy for this extraordinary couple and their love of Seattle.

NOTES

1 For more on the Warhol portrait commission, see p. 26 of this volume.

2 David McKee, in conversation with Carol Vogel, January 2021.

3 Carol Coffin, executive director of the International Council of the Museum of Modern Art, in conversation with Carol Vogel, January 2021.

4 Bruce Guenther and Barbara Johns, *The Richard and Jane Lang Collection* (Seattle: Seattle Art Museum, 1984). In addition to works by the artists represented in the Friday Foundation's 2021 gift to the Seattle Art Museum, the exhibition, which was on view February 2–April 1, 1984, presented works from the larger corpus of the collection, including a major late painting by Hans Hofmann and the Lang portraits by Andy Warhol and Alice Neel.

PORTRAITS OF THE COLLECTORS

BRUCE GUENTHER

ANDY WARHOL, *JANE LANG*, 1976

When Richard Lang wished to celebrate Jane Lang's birthday with a surprise portrait commission from Andy Warhol in 1976, he sought the aid of Charles Cowles, curator of modern art at the Seattle Art Museum. After initially trying to use existing photographs of Jane for the silkscreen-based portrait, the Warhol studio insisted on a sitting in the Factory using their Polaroid Big Shot camera. To preserve the surprise, Richard and Cowles devised an elaborate ruse in which Richard announced he was considering having Warhol do *his* portrait, explaining that the couple would have to visit the artist's studio for the requisite Polaroid photography session on their early October trip to New York.

Warhol's portrait sittings always began with a catered studio lunch to give him a chance to meet and watch the subject prior to the photography session, and to ensure the patron felt at ease going into the studio. The convivial lunch went well, and subsequently Warhol took a dozen Polaroids of Richard that he declared usable before turning to Jane and insisting that since he still had film left, she absolutely must let him photograph her as well; he took almost forty Polaroids in quick order. Flattered, Jane happily accommodated him and thought nothing more about it. The double-panel portrait was promptly finished—along with a third panel (now in a private collection), as was often Warhol's practice with comparable commissions. The Lang diptych was secretly shipped to the museum for unveiling at the mid-November exhibition *Andy Warhol: Portraits*, which opened with a gala dinner for Warhol organized by a committee on which Jane served (see fig. 10). Seattle's museum patrons and art collectors turned out en masse to meet the famous Andy Warhol. It was a great evening for Cowles and the modern art program, a genuine "speechless" surprise for Jane, and a triumph for Richard.

The portrait captures the beauty and confident vitality of Jane Lang in both pose and palette. Varying the left-to-right placement of the silkscreened torso on the two canvases, Warhol accentuates the dynamic quality of her pose. While underlining the photomechanical source of the image, this gesture emphasizes the importance of the artist's hand in the compositional and color choices. The palettes of the portraits of Jane are rendered in progressive color variants inspired by her patterned blouse, with each background color a different solid hue while her hair, lips, and eyes remain the same. Viewed within Warhol's portrait production of the 1970s, the Lang portraits are among the most successful in glamour, composition, and use of color. Effectively the court painter for international society, Warhol produced over one thousand portraits of public and private personalities in the period from 1970 until his untimely death in 1987.

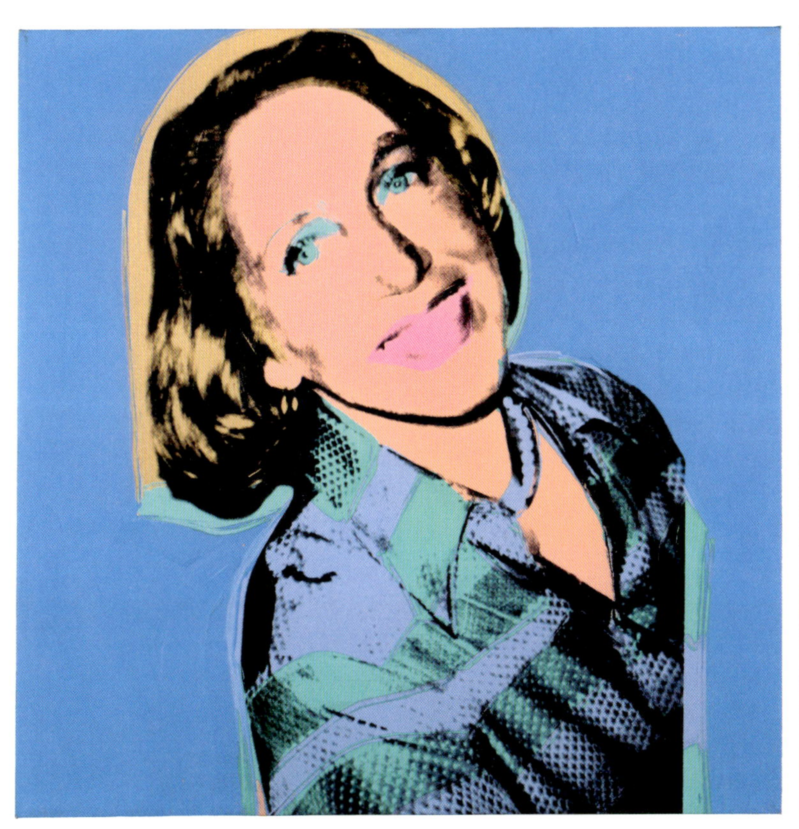

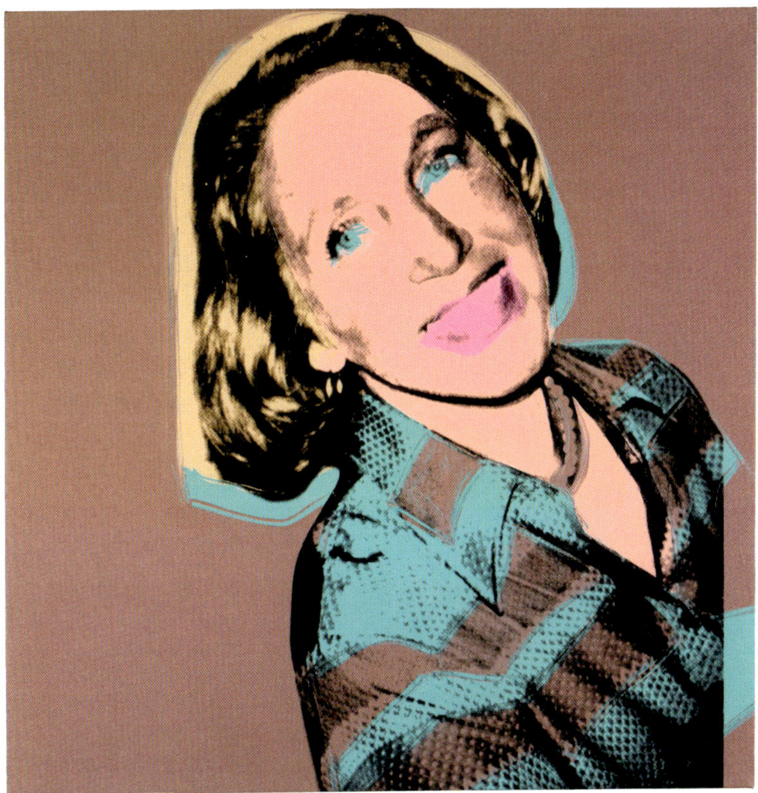

Andy Warhol, *Jane Lang*, 1976, acrylic and silkscreen ink on linen, diptych, each panel 40 × 40 in. (101.6 × 101.6 cm).
Seattle Art Museum, Gift of Mr. and Mrs. Richard E. Lang, 76.47 (left); and Gift of Lyn and Jerry Grinstein, 2020.19 (right).

ALICE NEEL, *RICHARD LANG*, 1978

American painter Alice Neel was a septuagenarian in the 1970s when her career took off and the Graham Gallery in New York finally began representing her. Neel had chosen to work as a figurative painter against the currents of abstraction, instead exploring issues of race, class, and sexuality in her portrait-driven work from apartment studios in Spanish Harlem and, later, the Upper West Side. Having lived a politically engaged, ribald bohemian life on the fringes of the New York art scene for much of her creative life, the ebullient Neel was really just moving into its center following her 1974 retrospective exhibition at the Whitney Museum of American Art when David McKee boldly suggested Neel as the artist to paint his friend and client Richard Lang. Neel, a political activist sensitive to class distinctions, rarely took on commissioned portraits, preferring instead to paint people she selected, like fellow artists, art-world denizens, and neighbors. While Richard and Jane researched her work and tested the idea on art-world friends, McKee contacted Neel and the Graham Gallery to make certain she would welcome the invitation. Following a meeting and the Langs' studio visit with the artist, it was decided: the 78-year-old Neel, who only painted from life, would come to the couple's Lake Washington home and make Richard's portrait.

Close to Richard Lang in age, with just as strong a personality, Alice Neel was known for the insightful psychological tension of her portraits that captured the alchemy of the moment between artist and sitter. Richard traveled to New York for several studio sessions as a warm-up before Neel went to Seattle. Having arranged accommodations for her at the Sunset Club (Seattle's historic ladies' social club) and with a large rented easel in place, the Langs welcomed her lakeside. Neel sittings were famously encounters between two people—with lively, wide-ranging conversations and interrogations on life and politics as she verbally and visually sought to uncover how her sitters physically manifested their tension and emotion. One can easily imagine the spirited back-and-forth exchanges during the sittings between Richard and the lifelong Communist, feisty feminist painter as they passed the days. The choice of Neel resulted in a brilliant portrait that captures the visage and the spirit of the man in situ with his beloved Franz Kline painting behind him (plate 5). The expressively charged canvas records Richard with a glint in his eye and a slight smile, seemingly in mid-conversation, making his point and raising the stakes through hand gesture and self-assured posture. Jane Lang donated the portrait to the Seattle Art Museum in 1987.

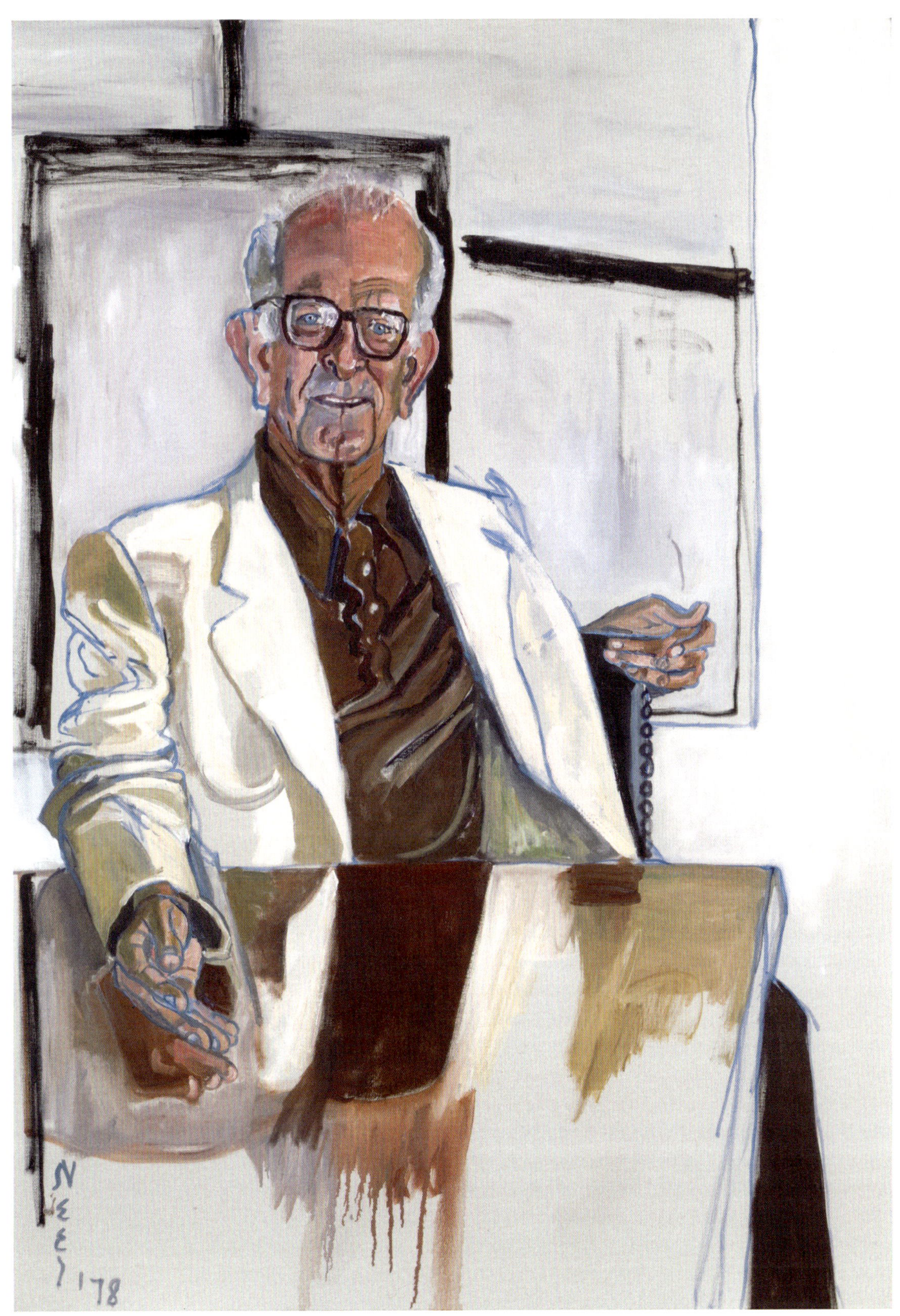

Alice Neel, *Richard Lang*, 1978, oil on canvas, 50 × 35 in. (127 × 88.9 cm).
Seattle Art Museum, Gift of Jane Lang Davis, 87.46.

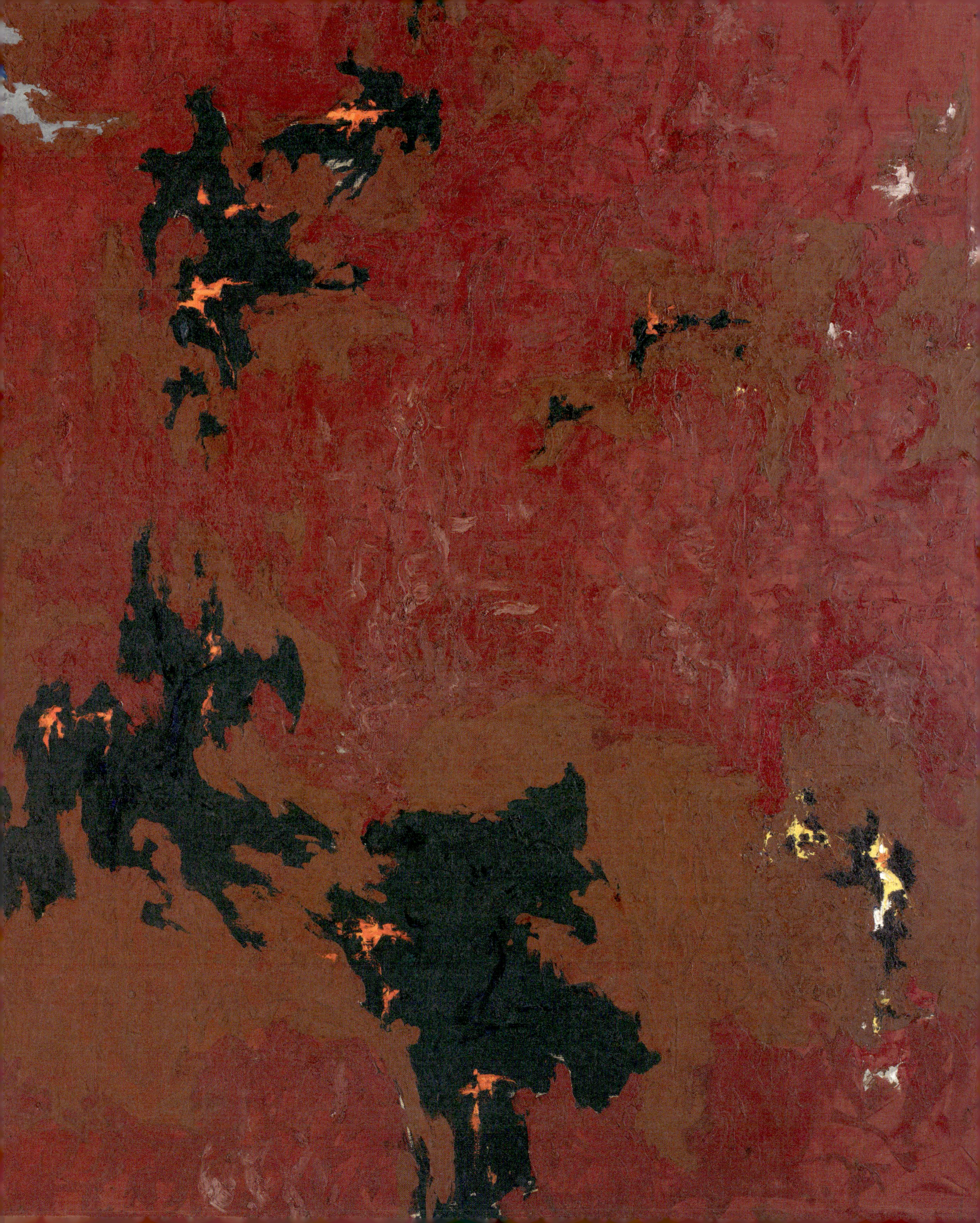

ART OF EXTREMES

DAVID ANFAM

In a dark time, the eye begins to see.
—Theodore Roethke

I. THE TIMES

The signature styles associated with the American artists commonly known as the Abstract Expressionists, alongside those of select European contemporaries, have by now become iconic—vivid to the point where they might dazzle us into overlooking the history, culture and people underlying them decades ago. Here a ready comparison arises with a successive American icon, Andy Warhol. Take his Marilyn series from the 1960s (fig. 14). Behind the starstruck gilded showiness, the real Marilyn Monroe, not to mention Andy himself, tends to fade from sight. As for the preceding generation, the showstoppers include Francis Bacon's visceral portraits, Willem de Kooning's formidable Women, Alberto Giacometti's attenuated personages, Adolph Gottlieb's spectacular Bursts, Mark Rothko's tinted veils, David Smith's climactic *Cubi*, Clyfford Still's coruscating abstractions . . . the list could continue apace. Indeed, it will—because the Richard E. Lang and Jane Lang Davis Collection includes these names, and more besides: Helen Frankenthaler, Philip Guston, Franz Kline, Lee Krasner, Joan Mitchell, Robert Motherwell, Jackson Pollock and Ad Reinhardt. From a biographical angle, this constellation covers a century or so (Rothko was born in 1903; Frankenthaler died in 2011) and, counting the collectors, 114 years from start to finish (Jane Lang Davis passed at the age of 97 in 2017). Even more consequentially, the timespan encompasses very different epochs, disparities that the eminent British historian Eric Hobsbawm justly took to define an "Age of Extremes."[1] Hobsbawm's model fits much of the art that sprung from it.

When Warhol silkscreened the then–Jane Lang in 1976[2] in a diptych format (as though a single focus were insufficient to catch her outsize charisma; see page 27), even the movement that he had spearheaded, Pop Art, had already segued to other, dissimilar tendencies such as Minimalism, Earthworks and Process art. To recall Bob Dylan, the times they were a-changin' fast. Hobsbawm has another relevant rubric: the "Short Twentieth Century." Using the outbreak of the First World War and the Soviet

Detail, plate 3

Fig. 14 Andy Warhol, *Gold Marilyn*, 1962, silkscreen ink and acrylic on canvas, 83¼ × 57 in. (211.4 × 144.7 cm). The Museum of Modern Art, New York, Gift of Philip Johnson, 316.1962.

Union's collapse as bookends, Hobsbawm reckoned the swift Short Twentieth Century lasted from 1914 to 1991.[3] Give or take some, the dates prove handy to further bracket Abstract Expressionism. Pollock was born in 1912, Guston and Reinhardt in 1913, Motherwell died in 1991 and Mitchell in 1992. Exact years aside, Abstract Expressionism's overall trajectory paralleled Hobsbawm's apocalyptic Age of Extremes—eight decades or so riven by world historical catastrophe. Its grim roster may be familiar yet always bears repeating. Before the First World War ended, the Russian Revolution erupted. Next the Great Depression, then the Spanish Civil War (1936–1939)—so key for Motherwell's imagination—phased straight into the Second World War. Barely had the latter reached its unimaginably devastating close before the Cold War struck. Throughout the 1950s, the ever-present threat of nuclear extinction rubbed shoulders in the United States with a conflicted sociological mix. Naturally, the Abstract Expressionists—beholden to their time while liable to defy it—were not immune to the zeitgeist.

On the one hand, America's imperial "golden age"[4] of newfound abundance, consumerism and military/technological heft seemed to confirm the nation's post-war claims to exceptionalism, the *Pax Americana*, an updated descendant from the nineteenth century's Manifest Destiny doctrine.[5] On the other hand, during the Truman and Eisenhower administrations the political home front witnessed McCarthyism and liberalism (rarely, in practice, as liberal as it sounded, especially given the ongoing prevalence of racial repression, male chauvinism and ubiquitous social pressures to conform). They spawned what a trenchant historian has described as an outrageous machinery of repression in American life.[6] In short, from 1945 onward, America's so-called Age of Anxiety—a phrase coined by the transatlantic British poet W. H. Auden[7]—vied with another of heady affluence. Inevitably, these extremes and their implications percolated into Abstract Expressionism,[8] albeit morphing into symbol, allusion, metaphor, withdrawl as resistance and so on.

For example, Abstract Expressionism has long been linked to the intellectual climate that came to prominence in the United States and Europe during and after the Second World War—a nexus combining trauma, fear, uncertainty, inwardness and similar states that falls under the convenient umbrella of existentialism.[9] Probably de Kooning best exemplified this edgy outlook. However, his "existentialism" owed less to obvious contemporary European types such as those associated with Jean-Paul Sartre, Albert Camus and Paul Tillich than it did to older and/or homegrown strains.

Simply put, space—equated with anxiety, absurdity and the void—preoccupied de Kooning from around 1945 onward. As he despaired in 1951, "There seems to be no end to the misery of the scientists' space. All that it contains is billions and billions of hunks of matter, hot or cold, floating around in darkness according to a great design of aimlessness."[10] Despite the nod to modern science—its wonders and often terrible consequences were an important part of the period's paradigm that also affected Gottlieb, Kline, Mitchell, Pollock and the sculptor David Smith[11]—de Kooning's sentiment sounds closer to the seventeenth-century French existentialist *avant la lettre*, Blaise Pascal.[12] His desperation mirrored Pascal's oft-cited aperçu regarding humankind's place in the infinite scheme of things: "The universe knows none of this. . . . The eternal silence of these infinite spaces fills me with dread."[13] The monochromes[14] that culminated in *Excavation* (1950, Art Institute of Chicago) and include *Town Square* (1948, plate 2) addressed this spatial phobia. These tumults, wherein jagged semihumanoid fragments teem to bursting point, embody a dire *horror vacui*. Analytical Cubism's all-over ordonnance might look like their primary source,[15] yet a more venerable precedent lies with de Kooning's fellow countrymen, the Netherlandish old masters Hieronymus Bosch and Pieter Bruegel the Elder.[16]

Adopting an eye-in-the-sky viewpoint, Bosch and Bruegel depicted carnal human absurdity as a maelstrom teeming with bodies.[17] In such nightmarish tableaux as *Dark Pond* and *Asheville* (both 1948, Frederick R. Weisman Art Foundation and Phillips Collection), the latter-day Dutchman propelled his Low Countries' artistic forebears into an abstract idiom that mingles the past with the present in a painterly stream of consciousness. A third factor completes the formula. In short, the artist doubtless knew the native existentialist brew conjured by his near-contemporary William Faulkner: he chose the American novelist's title *Light in August* (1932) for a seminal 1946 canvas. In a passage where a character recalls the death of his grandfather in a cavalry raid, Faulkner evokes the sound and fury that is mortal existence:

> Then they sweep into sight, borne now upon a cloud of phantom dust. They rush past, forwardleaning in the saddles, with brandished arms, beneath whipping ribbons from slanted and eager lances; with tumult and soundless yelling they sweep past like a tide whose crest is jagged with the wild heads of horses and the brandished arms of men like the crater of the world in explosion.[18]

Could there be a better ekphrasis for de Kooning's savage pictorial eruptions in the late 1940s? Hardly. If the comparison sounds fanciful, earlier in the same book the nouns "town," "square" and "noon"—the title of another de Kooning, from 1946—occur in close succession.[19] The artist once characterized content as a "glimpse": glimpses are exactly what the novelist envisages and syntactically impacts.[20] Speed, of hand and mind, reigns.

In another vein, de Kooning could be up-to-the-minute hip. "Today, some people think that the light of the atom bomb will change the concept of painting once and for all. The eyes that actually saw that light melted out of sheer ecstasy. . . . It made angels out of everybody."[21] Atomic fission, Netherlandish old masters, modern American existentialist parables—this medley conflating old and new, obscurity and topicality, presents just one among innumerable instances of the far-flung polarities running throughout Abstract Expressionism's every level. They underpin both its complexity (which engages specialists) and its brute force or magnetism (which attracts the layperson). Thus, the Friday Foundation's gift to the Seattle Art Museum in honor of Richard and Jane Lang—a self-sufficient microcosm of the broader phenomenon that is Abstract Expressionism—holds something for everyone. And the movement possesses a referential range that makes it somewhat like a mid-twentieth century's semantic analogue to today's hypertexts. We can attend to the surfaces, depths, or both at once. Whichever, the élan still thrills.

Within its layerings, Abstract Expressionism also signals the tragic events, writ large in blood and suffering, that stained the past century. Make no mistake, humanity's worst sides dominated that strife-riven age. Suffice it for Hobsbawm, in his introductory "Bird's Eye View," to first quote the philosopher Isaiah Berlin: "I have lived through most of the twentieth century without, I must add, suffering personal hardship. I remember it only as the most terrible century in Western history";[22] and second, the Anglo-American violinist Yehudi Menuhin: "If I had to sum up the twentieth century I would say that it raised the greatest hopes ever conceived by humanity, and destroyed all illusions and ideals."[23] World wars, genocide and nuclear destruction made their marks on Abstract Expressionism and also farther afield. In Europe, Bacon and Giacometti scrutinized the human condition, twisted by the passions or eroded by emptiness.[24] Come the stage when the Nazi death camps were liberated and atomic bombs had razed Hiroshima and Nagasaki, this predicament had been exposed in extremis as perhaps never before. Despite dating from the relatively calmer mid-1950s, the Swiss sculptor's *Femme de Venise II* (1956, plate 9) retains an affrighted rigidity, rigor mortis atremble.

Significantly, Bacon's mature imagery began to gel in earnest with his *Three Studies for Figures at the Base of a Crucifixion* (1944, Tate) as the full shock of the carnage grew clearer once the Second World War drew to its hideous denouement.[25] The anatomical distortions and screaming mouths in that triptych established an evolving template for his subsequent heads and bodies wracked and wrecked by unspeakable emotions, such as *Portrait of Man with Glasses I* (1963, plate 12) and *Study for a Portrait* (1967, plate 17). To recall the words of Hamlet, when "the time is out of joint," so literally are those who endure it. As the American historian Teofilo F. Ruiz has written about angst in general, "The terror of history is all around us, gnawing endlessly at our sense of, and desire for, order. It undermines, most of all, our hopes."[26] Such bleakness informs Bacon's sensibility as well as the youthful de Kooning's (though it drove their creativity too, since Ruiz adds that terror explains "why we often have such an inexhaustible desire to make and have meaning"[27]). Each found their personal shape for alienation and violence in pigment's convulsions and the hand's fleetness, as did Giacometti in clay.

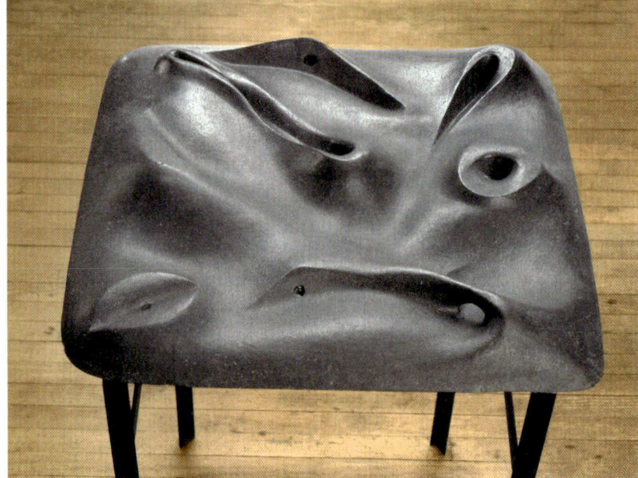

Fig. 15 Isamu Noguchi, *This Tortured Earth*, 1942–43 (cast 1963), bronze, 3 × 28⅛ × 29 in. (7.6 × 71.4 × 73.7 cm), edition 1/6 (2 realized). Fabricated by Fonditori Artistici, Rome. The Isamu Noguchi Foundation and Garden Museum, New York, 195B-1/6.

Bacon's slicing brushstrokes emulate lacerations, while de Kooning renders comparable effects even more tangible by the added cut-and-thrust inherent to collage. Two leading commentators on Abstract Expressionism, the critics Clement Greenberg and Thomas B. Hess, wrote, respectively, about de Kooning's "savage dissections" and "Procrustean" methods.[28] Their remarks could as well have been tailor-made for Bacon. In fact, if de Kooning had remained in Europe and Bacon lived in New York, which would posterity deem the Abstract Expressionist? The film director David Lynch understood the porous transnational framework when he paired Bacon with Pollock.[29] Doubtless the commonality stems from a shared historical matrix. Ever the tricky savant, de Kooning habitually covered his tracks by exalting ambiguity: "That's what fascinates me—to make something I can never be sure of, and no one else can either."[30] In contrast, Bacon exposed his sources.[31] "Swimming through a sea of images,"[32] he referenced Nazism, gruesome medical photographs (a subject lent new relevance in his prime by the concentration camps' atrocities) and the cinematic coup par excellence for the century's shock-fractured mindset, the screaming nurse shot through the eye in Sergei Eisenstein's *Battleship Potemkin* (1925).[33] Ambiguous or explicit, direct or implicit, the modern age's fearful road map guided both artists' expressive paths.

The Second World War cast such a long shadow over self and society that it permeated every creative medium from painting and sculpture to literature, poetry, photography and film.[34] In sculpture, the Japanese American Isamu Noguchi's *This Tortured Earth* (1942–43, fig. 15) ranks as one set piece among many where wrenching distortion and ruptures transform warfare's impact into a formal vocabulary.[35] By sheer happenstance, it does for terrain what Bacon did for the human physiognomy. Both become tortuous fields (the double entendre counts). In 1943, Pollock painted a *Burning Landscape* (Yale University Art Gallery) and a few years later drew *War* (1947, fig. 16) in ink and colored pencil, a semiabstract hecatomb of the kind he would revisit when old figurative elements resurfaced, once his "classic" pourings stopped after 1950. Unlike the serendipitous Bacon-Noguchi conjunction, the resemblance between Pollock's 1951 work on paper from the Lang Collection (plate 6) and *War*, which it changes into a ghostly residue, may be purposeful.[36] Along similar lines, the Holocaust informed Guston's iconography. Children who are watchers and watched—the wistful stand-ins for death camp prisoners—people the lugubrious *If This Be Not I* (tellingly, from 1945, fig. 17).[37] Thirty-one years hence, Guston reverted to a watcher who is watched (why else hide behind the brick wall?) in the klutzy "Kilroy was here" ideogram, *The Painter* (1976, plate 19). The piled corpses seen in documentary photographs and newsreels informed the jumbled bric-a-brac of Guston's ensuing canvases. Note that Pollock tended to atomize or splinter, whereas Guston agglomerates. Faced with doom or superhuman forces, the human presence may, airbound or earthbound, go either way. Or, through temporality, it can turn into memory.

Memory speaks in works by someone not represented in the Seattle Art Museum gift, Arshile Gorky. Whether by choice or chance, Gorky's omission from the Lang Collection—like Hans Hofmann's—could be a *felix culpa*

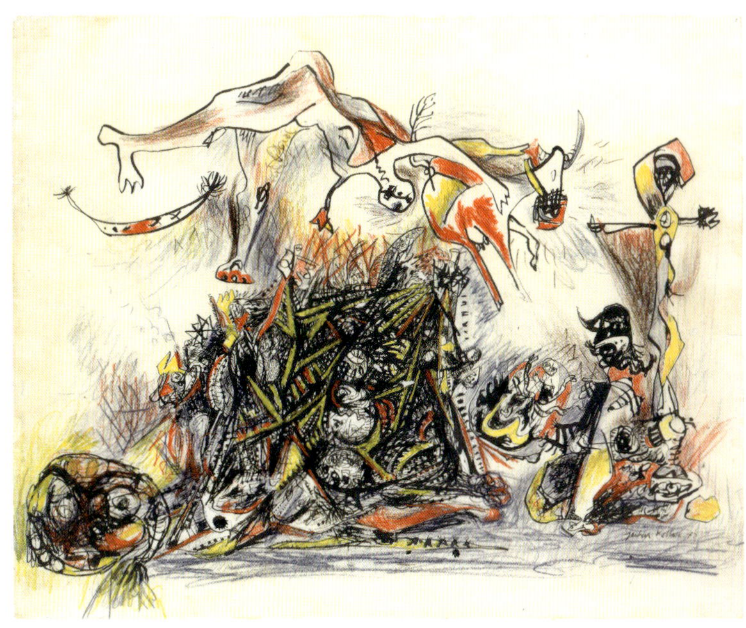

Fig. 16 Jackson Pollock, *War*, 1947, ink and colored pencil on paper, 20⅝ × 26 in. (52.4 × 66 cm). The Metropolitan Museum of Art, New York, Gift of Lee Krasner Pollock, in memory of Jackson Pollock, 1982, 1982.147.25.

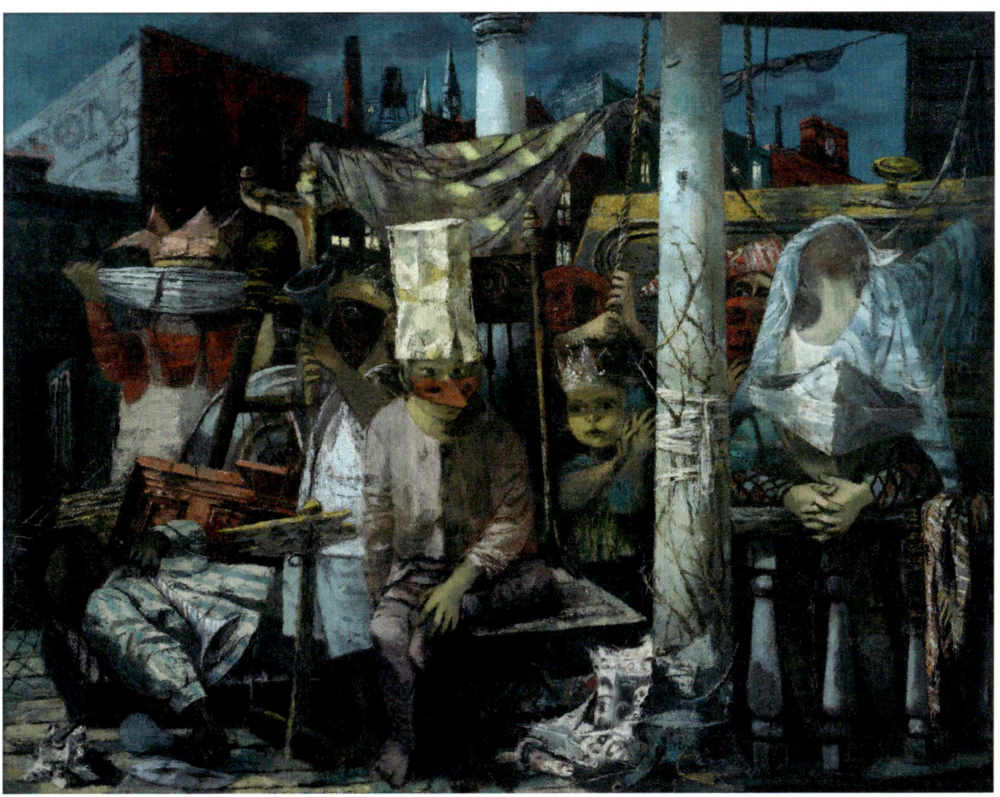

Fig. 17 Philip Guston, *If This Be Not I*, 1945, oil on canvas, 42¼ × 55¼ in. (107.3 × 140.3 cm). Mildred Lane Kemper Art Museum, St. Louis, University purchase, Kende Sale Fund, 1945, WU 3766.

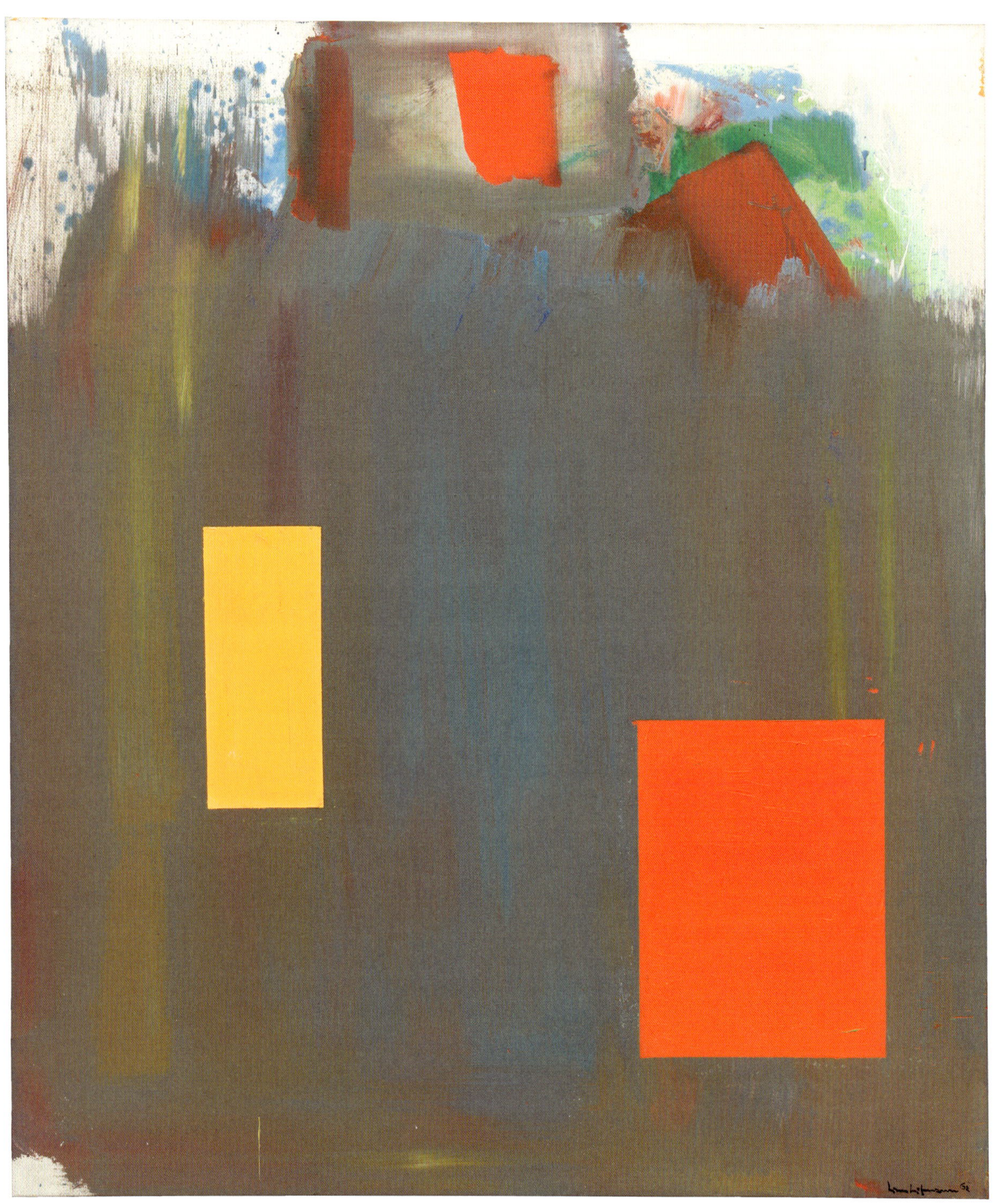

Fig. 18 Hans Hofmann, *Memoria in Aeternum*, 1962, oil on canvas, 84 × 72⅛ in. (213.3 × 183.2 cm). The Museum of Modern Art, New York, Gift of the artist, 399.1963.

insofar as both stood nearer the periphery than the center of whatever territory Abstract Expressionism demarcates.[38] Chronologically, too, Gorky's imaginative reach was distinct—backward to his native Armenia—while his premature suicide in 1948 after a car accident perforce excluded him from the movement's heyday. Nevertheless, he was a walking art history lesson who synthesized two earlier movements pivotal to its development, Cubism and Surrealism. Analogously, Hofmann, born in central Bavaria in 1880, worked as a longtime teacher, becoming a mentor to numerous younger students, including Krasner, Mitchell and Frankenthaler.[39] As a painter, Hofmann only came into his own with a triumphant pictorial endgame in the 1960s. Yet to regard Hofmann as a card-carrying Abstract Expressionist risks mistaking formalism—his final brilliant amalgam melding color fields and gestural passages (fig. 18)—for thematics. At root, Hofmann's tenor was exuberant, hedonistic. As such, it countered Abstract Expressionism's stress on interiority, symbolism[40] and romantic Sturm und Drang,[41] which in his hands tended to become pure panache. Nor is the foregoing meant to banish Gorky and Hofmann, as it were, into art historical exile (though the German's birth date does distance him further from midcentury Manhattan). Rather, it attests to how any core requires perimeters for its very definition.

Defining the movement's reach—a compass destined to remain a signifier shifting in the eyes of beholders[42]—also needs to be supple enough to accommodate the mood swing that soon saw war-inflicted traumas recede into the past. Again, another player absent from the current gift helps clarify it from without.[43] When war's ghastly pall still hung in the air, Barnett Newman sounded a challenge: "We now know the terror to expect. Hiroshima showed it to us. . . . We are living, then, through a Greek drama. . . . Let us rather, like the Greek writers, tear the tragedy to shreds."[44] Despite Newman's prescience, in 1948 nobody could foresee the future. With hindsight, we can. Soon Abstract Expressionism would move with the times into fresh energies, epic scale, chroma incarnate, vitality and light—not to mention its being invigorated by a younger set, notably led by women artists. But extremes depend on one another. The American poet Theodore Roethke knew this existential truth and, thus, what agent must first hone bright vision: "In a dark time, the eye begins to see."[45] Or, as the French language has it, "les extrêmes se touchent" (opposites meet). That Roethke taught at the University of Washington in Seattle from 1947 until his death in 1963 adds a nice grace note, a touch of poetic justice in the present context.[46]

II. THE PEOPLE

> **Some say it was art**
> **Killed Jackson Pollock**
> **As if that could be.**
> **In fact his car failed to take a bend**
> **And he drove into a tree.**
>
> **—Anonymous[47]**

Shaped by their times, Abstract Expressionism's movers and shakers themselves now demand a short, sharp look.[48] While the membership of earlier avant-gardes, such as the Italian Futurists and Dresden's *Die Brücke*, had a comparatively clear-cut makeup, no matter how we juggle whoever should be lumped into or out of the Abstract Expressionists' ranks, the result will never cohere without bending facts to fiction. The latter is precisely what Nina Leen's 1950 *Irascibles* photograph for *Life* magazine contrived (fig. 19). Any unity among the photo shoot's fifteen participants was not internal but externally motivated—a common protest against the Metropolitan Museum of Art's aesthetic conservatism, which ultimately helped put their work in museums.[49] Substitute canny individualism for inept nervousness and it is a serious version of Lewis Carroll's comical band of brothers on their quixotic hunt for the Snark:

> But the valley grew narrow and narrower still,
> And the evening got darker and colder,
> Till (merely from nervousness, not from good will)
> They marched along shoulder to shoulder.[50]

Not too long after the photograph's publication, Newman, Reinhardt, Rothko and Still had all bitterly—and permanently—split from one another. Jimmy Ernst had no artistic reason to be in the assembly anyway, whereas Guston, Kline, David Smith and Aaron Siskind did but were missing (neither abstract sculpture nor

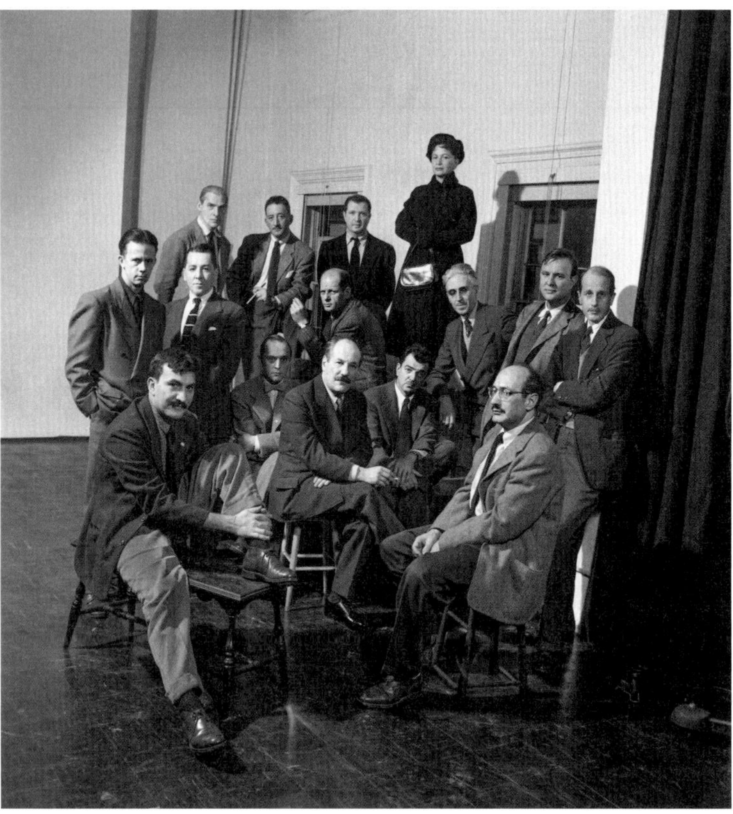

Fig. 19 Nina Leen, *The Irascibles*, 1950, left to right, from back row: Willem de Kooning, Adolph Gottlieb, Ad Reinhardt, Hedda Sterne; Richard Pousette-Dart, William Baziotes, Jackson Pollock, Clyfford Still, Robert Motherwell, Bradley Walker Tomlin; Theodoros Stamos, Jimmy Ernst, Barnett Newman, James Brooks, Mark Rothko. Published in *Life*, January 15, 1951.

photography enjoyed the fine art status then that it later acquired).[51] Bradley Walker Tomlin's untimely death came a year after Guston's 1952 tribute to him, *To B.W.T.* (plate 7), lending that gesture a special poignancy. De Kooning was on the bottle, while Pollock, too, had reverted to drink and within five years would perish in a semi-suicidal car crash that confounded reality with mythmaking (invoked/debunked in the doggerel of the epigraph, above); Kline died prematurely from heart disease at the age of 52 in 1962; and Rothko took an overdose, then cut through the artery in his right arm in 1970. The art world would not see the likes of this somber bohemianism again.[52] Politically, Newman and Rothko were anarchists. Still approached the margins of an anarchist libertarianism that defies neat categories and was an absolute outsider in every respect.[53] Despite a wealthy background, Motherwell was left-leaning, writing in 1947–48 that "the deadly political position exerts an enormous pressure,"[54] and his *Elegies to the Spanish Republic* (the sister series to the Lang Collection's *Irish Elegy*, 1965, plate 14) represent if not quite an engagé's retort to Francoism then surely a humanist's.[55] Politically and personally, Smith took a similar, though more committed stance.[56] Early on, Pollock lamented that his classmates thought he was "a rotten rebel from Russia."[57] As for Reinhardt, he was doubtless a socialist and arguably a Communist.[58] To some extent, then, these ideologies upheld an older American tradition of speaking truth to power, decency to oligarchy.[59] If the CIA co-opted some of these radicals during the Cold War, it was still a complete clash of minds and hearts (at least the artists had theirs in the right place).[60] Like it or not, the Abstract Expressionists had plenty to gain by international recognition/promotion; so did American politicians and elites who wanted to cosmeticize their country on the world stage as the land of the free.

Leen's *Irascibles* photograph also opens a window onto the period's prejudices. Again, extremism is in play: placing one diminutive woman standing on a table amid fourteen males (in front of a female photographer, too) was not a moderate strategy. Worse, these men openly resented Hedda Sterne's inclusion in the group portrait: "They all were very furious that I was in it because they all were sufficiently macho to think that the presence of a woman took away from the seriousness of it all."[61] A fortiori, Krasner's predicament summarized everything because she was not even a contender for Leen's lens.[62] A painter friend observed of Krasner, "She didn't get anywhere, until her husband died," to which the former Mrs. Jackson Pollock, who effaced her signature during the 1940s and 1950s to "L. K.," added, "It was like I wasn't there"—and by "there" she did not just mean the studio where the *Life* session happened.[63] That at last women's stake in the Abstract Expressionist milieu is being recorded by women themselves promises that the tables have begun turning.[64] Noteworthy, too, is the foresight that led to the strong contingent formed by Frankenthaler, Krasner and Mitchell in the Lang Collection in the 1970s.

Moreover, as with women, accolades have come late to Black and homosexual artists, as well as those with other gender identities, of this generation. [65] The Abstract Expressionists were as susceptible to doxa—established or unchallenged beliefs in a given social system—as the next man (pun intentional). Truth to tell, some have gone so far as to typecast Abstract Expressionism as aggressively masculinist. Of late, Norman Lewis, a Harlem-born Abstract Expressionist of Bermudan parentage, has been rediscovered; he should never have been invisible.[66] Similarly, William T. Williams deserves mention for progressing his idiosyncratic take on Color Field painting,[67] and recent scholars have drawn attention to how second-generation Black women such as Betty Blayton, Howardena Pindell and Alma Thomas expanded abstract horizons from around the 1960s onward.[68] "Relations," as Henry James pointedly opined, "stop nowhere."[69] Likewise, the sexual identities of the dealer Betty Parsons and the painters Tomlin and Theodoros Stamos were long elided in accounts of the period, as were those of the major patron/collector of Abstract Expressionism Alfonso Ossorio and Peggy Guggenheim's curator/dealer Howard Putzel.[70] And despite the hypermasculine mythos around Pollock, his leading biographers suggest he was bisexual.[71] The historical literature divulges almost nothing about these workaday facts. Nowadays, this omission appears another societal extreme.[72] As for photographers such as Siskind, Harry Callahan, Barbara Morgan and Minor White, even art historians committed to broadening the canon seem reluctant to revise their criteria to include them among Abstract Expressionism's ranks, where they belong.[73] Analogously, action photography had a substantial influence on Pollock, and it shortchanges Pousette-Dart, Smith and Still to overlook their judicious activities with the camera, while Reinhardt's cartoons are a smart didactic genre in their own right. The movement's men and women could span "the tragic and the timeless" (Gottlieb and Rothko's 1943 phrase),[74] humor (Reinhardt's wit and de Kooning's bons mots still raise many a smile) and the baseball field (Still was a passionate fan of the game, discerning artful sightlines in its performative displays) and could weather a season in hell (to borrow the title of Arthur Rimbaud's 1873 poem, which held a special magic for Krasner). Frankenthaler spoke as well as anyone might for her fellow contrarians: "I follow the rules until I go against them all."[75]

III. THE ART

Between extremities
Man runs his course

—W. B. Yeats[76]

Interpreting the art's "what?" means interrogating its "where?" A tendency to replace "Abstract Expressionism" with the geographic label "New York School"—which Motherwell introduced in two lectures (1949, 1950)—risks pushing critical vocabulary from the frying pan to the proverbial fire.[77] Why? First, because Motherwell hailed from the small city of Aberdeen in Washington State. This distance could have encouraged him to regard New York from a remoteness that, telescope-like, magnified its artistic centrality—which is not to deny Gotham's extraordinary cosmopolitanism or its formative influence on Abstract Expressionism as well as on its veritable de facto think tanks, such as The Club.[78] Second, one of the earliest cohesive exhibitions to feature Abstract Expressionists who would become canonical—de Kooning, Gottlieb, Motherwell, Pollock, Rothko and Still—bore the title *The School of New York*.[79] The venue? The Frank Perls Gallery in Beverly Hills.[80] Again it took the West Coast to put the East on a pedestal.[81] Third, the movement was multitudinous and mercurial. To confine it to a single spot slights others. Decisive action often happened elsewhere from New York and/or was what Still called "a testing of men and minds in the shadows."[82]

Still spent only twelve years in Manhattan out of a career that spanned six decades. He and Rothko first met not in New York but in San Francisco's Bay Area, and both reached a watershed while teaching at the California School of Fine Arts in the late 1940s, when Still sparked Rothko's breakthrough into abstraction with the latter's so-called Multiforms (fig. 20). In any case, Still was as much a man of the West as Pollock, who came from Wyoming and never forgot it. Similarly, Sam Francis and Mark Tobey—alike major figures associated with Abstract Expressionism—had long-standing West Coast ties.[83] Francis was active in San Francisco and Los Angeles early and late in his career, while Tobey did much of his work in Seattle. Moreover, Francis spent the 1950s in Paris, and Tobey (a lifelong global wanderer) emigrated in the early 1960s to Basel,

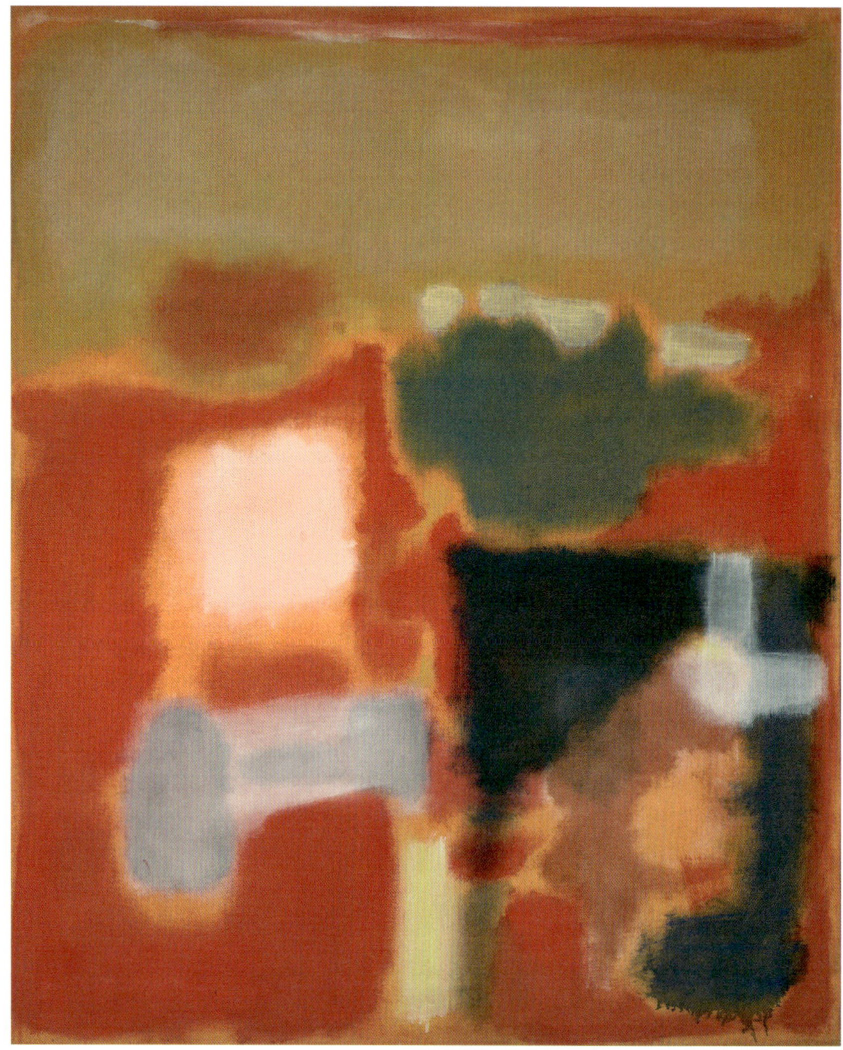

Fig. 20 Mark Rothko, *No. 1 (No. 18, 1948)*, 1948–49, oil on canvas, 67¹¹⁄₁₆ × 55⅞ in. (171.93 × 141.92 cm). Frances Lehman Loeb Art Museum, Vassar College, Gift of Mrs. John D. Rockefeller 3rd (Blanchette Hooker, class of 1931), 1955.6.6.

Switzerland. Farther afield, Bacon, Giacometti (whose disconcerting women invite immediate comparison with de Kooning's)[84] and other European or Canadian artists, such as Pierre Soulages and Jean-Paul Riopelle, shared various themes and ideas with their American coevals. All of this tends to decenter the assumption that New York was the exclusive site of a "School" for Abstract Expressionism and its soulmates.[85] Lastly, when the American Academy in Rome awarded Guston a Prix de Rome, he left the United States for Europe in 1948, toured Italy and also visited Spain and France. This was an all-important juncture for the artist because his work had reached an impasse before the sojourn.[86] Admiring the old masters on their native ground made him "want to paint again."[87] So Guston canceled the remainder of his two-year fellowship, returned to the States and swiftly erased any vestigial mimetic traces. The outcome, by the early 1950s, was a group of richly tapestried palimpsests, albeit with a whiff of Freudian "screen memories" about them, fragile constructs masking depths from long ago and far away (perhaps his brother's untimely death in the early 1930s or the Holocaust thereafter), as well as losses more recent, as in *To B.W.T.* Whatever, the "New York School" per se is a misnomer for Abstract Expressionism's center of gravity. As such, it begs a question, What's in a name?

De Kooning zapped the name game outright in 1950: "It is disastrous to name ourselves."[88] Nevertheless, language names the world into existence. Like all intellectual disciplines, art history requires taxonomies (even if artists themselves might reject labels) to instill structure into what may well be unruly or inchoate.[89] Terminologically, "Abstract Expressionism" has one cardinal virtue: it identifies the poles to which the art extends. To cite a clear face-off, consider Guston's resurgent figuration through the 1970s ("crapola") versus Reinhardt's drive toward the absolute ("negation") from the 1950s on.[90] *Painting, 1950* (1950, plate 4) itself stands on a cusp, its two-color slabs midway between pattern (which Reinhardt admired in Islamic ornament) and timeless monochrome.[91] One commentator has gone so far as to discern a "dualism present in all his work."[92] These antitheses, themselves unstable—as Guston approached the 1960s his motifs courted recognition and Reinhardt knowingly stopped short of ultimate blackness—constitute the one constant in an equation that otherwise eludes fixity.[93] Polarities are nothing if not extremes, Yeats's poetic "antinomies of day and night."[94] No wonder the second-generation Abstract Expressionist painter Pat Passlof described her peers as all "so extreme in their personal and national traits and philosophies."[95] Most were also dialecticians in one way or another.[96] As with artists, so with the art.

The cosmic buzz emanating from Pollock's classic poured compositions (1947–50)—they hum with innumerable filigrees, whorls and flecks[97]—had a prior flip side. Namely, the youth who confessed, "People have always frightened and bored me. . . . [C]onsequently I have been within my own shell and have not accomplished anything materially."[98] From small formats in the 1930s, Pollock switched to epic dimensions with the landmark *Mural* (1943, University of Iowa Museum of Art).[99] The self-enclosed "shell" broke, so to speak, spilling myriad lemniscates (∞) that twist and coil hither and thither upon themselves. In 1951, though, the dialectical pendulum swung back. "I've had a period of drawing on canvas in black," Pollock explained, "with some of my early images coming through."[100] Whereas the previous pourings exploited enamel paint's utter liquidity, Pollock instead now talked "drawing." Liquids flow and expand. By definition, the hand's reach and the pencil's precision delimit drawing.[101] Put another way, a mellifluous technique changed into staccato or abbreviated pulses, just as obscured imagery (Pollock used the verb "veil") during 1947–50 yielded to the return of the repressed: a phantasmagoric figuration. Apart from the dialectic at stake—abstraction/image, line/mass, finesse/forcefulness, and so forth—Pollock's meteoric trajectory and early demise meant that he reached an exploratory late style prematurely, performing a radical volte-face compared to the total control that distinguishes his classic mode.[102]

The German philosopher Theodor W. Adorno attributed specific traits to "late style." They include sparseness, retrospection, discontinuities, fracture and the like.[103] The 1951 drawing manifests all these qualities. Furthermore, Adorno mentioned "emptiness turned outward,"[104] a trope that matches certain elements throughout Pollock's concluding work in general. Think of the face that seems to stare from the other side of the canvas in *Portrait and a Dream* (1953, Dallas Museum of Art) and the yawning black void in *The Deep* (1953, fig. 21),[105] as well as the unblinking eyes that glare from within Krasner's *Night Watch* (1960, plate 11).[106] Soaking, central to Pollock's output in the 1951 paintings in black on raw canvas, itself entails surface planarity projected into the ground's physical depth so that material flatness and virtual dissolution commingle.

In the same breath, distinctive textures—auratic touch by any other name—rank among Abstract Expressionism's hallmarks. Witness Still's fierce palette-knife troweling that writhes throughout the animistic PH-338 (1949, plate 3), Pollock's sheeny aluminum enamels and additives such as sand or a door key in his pigment layers,[107] Kline's raw facture that injects grittiness into *Painting No. 11* (1951, plate 5) and the haptic contrasts that range from svelte to rugged between the two motifs composing Gottlieb's sundry Bursts. At the other end of the scale, Rothko stated that his scrims should look as though "breathed" onto the canvas.[108] For all her muscular gesturalism, Mitchell could evince a feather-light touch, strokes tracing memories of more tactile, somatic experiences that she had managed to internalize. Hence her credo: "I carry my landscapes around with me."[109] Ripples, refractions and choppy rhythms fill *The Sink* (1956, plate 8), testimony to Mitchell's perennial attachment to water: the common thread between her native Chicago alongside Lake Michigan, a Brooklyn studio in the late 1940s bordering the East River, and the Seine at Vétheuil, her final destination.[110] Pushed to the furthest limits from liquidity, Reinhardt developed a method akin to *peinture à l'essence* in reverse. He diluted tubes of oil paint in turpentine, mixed the emulsion in a jar like a cocktail until it homogenized, then waited for it to decant—until the oil rose to the top—so that the majority could be poured away, and finally used the sediment that had settled. This singular substance was both responsive to the brush's pressure and resistant to overly recording the selfsame pressure.[111] In short, brinkmanship: hand-painted non-painterly painting. Could anything be more subtly extreme? Probably not, unless it be Reinhardt's rival, Rothko.

Rothko invented his own technical niceties. He mixed powder pigments with whole eggs (an unorthodox variant of the traditional tempera method) plus a thinner into an amalgam that did not completely homogenize. This fragile concoction was then layered onto unprimed canvas in successive scrims, creating a unique, sometimes friable impalpability. Despite the impressive dimensions Rothko frequently adopted, he applied these layers with relatively small brushes.[112] Hence the hypnotic Rothko "look"—big engulfing fields ruffled by the merest edgings and inflections. In *Untitled* (1963, plate 13), the uppermost white quivers while the rectangle under it stands firm and the lowermost brown field masks a subliminal maroon glow. Silent polyphony. By this means, the rectangles become "facades"—to quote Rothko verbatim[113]—brimming with a chromatic plenitude that fills our gaze yet hints that more lies beneath the hovering apparitions than meets the eye. Revelation and reticence, magnitude and minuteness, marry. In an unusually frank tête-à-tête, Rothko once bared his intentions to a fellow artist while visiting England in 1959: "Look again. I am the most violent of all the new Americans. Behind the color lies the cataclysm."[114] Behind the oxymoron lies the eighteenth-century aesthetician Edmund Burke's characterization of the sublime: "tranquility tinged with terror."[115]

Although Still's often-brutal signature style stands at the opposite end of the spectrum to Rothko's, his art also pits immediacy against concealment. The pigment may rise to scabrous bas-relief intensified by an oil-rich gloss, yet tiny fissures and halos to the tectonic masses—sometimes in the most improbable tints such as pink, violet or lemon yellow[116]—imply phantasmal agencies concealed below the incandescent or nocturnal surfaces. A kindred duality is Still's identification with the vertical as a signifier of sentient being amid the imploded, cliff-like expanses. Doubtless this dialectic stemmed from the artist's youthful experiences on the Canadian prairies where the upright figure denoted life ascendant against the landscape's vast horizontal vistas. However, Still studiedly interiorized these perceptions to the point that, around the early to mid-1940s, they became abstract vectors—a cartography, as it were, of inner consciousness.[117] The ubiquitous clashes throughout Still's pictorial dramaturgy between light and darkness articulate an existential dualism analogous to the horizontal/planar versus vertical/linear coordinates. Regardless of the feelings that Still chose to explore in individual paintings, the uncanny awesomeness remains combative, a reflection of their creator's intransigence. This also explains his notion that the works are at root self-portraits.

An edifying aspect to the Lang Collection is how the nineteen pieces gifted to the Seattle Art Museum (a tally neither inconsequential nor dauntingly monumental)[118] form an ensemble that contains enough variety to offer at least two rejoinders to Rothko's rectangles and Still's chthonic mindscapes. The first is Krasner's strikingly original *Night Watch*, which brings to the fore a fresh formal alternative to each man's indelible leitmotifs. Krasner's arcs and ovoids derived from a long-standing involvement with circles.[119] The eyes in *Night Watch* not only advert to the body's manifold role in Abstract Expressionism but also must constitute a quiet homage to Pollock's *Eyes in the Heat* (1946, Peggy Guggenheim Collection, Venice). Reprising Pollock, Krasner became her own woman. What matters most, though, for the present purpose is that these eyes, umbers and slivers form an all-over field.[120] In turn, the field recurs over and over again in Abstract Expressionism. But to what end? The answer is straightforward. The field—whether predominantly linear as treated by Krasner, de Kooning and Pollock or colorful as with Rothko, Still and

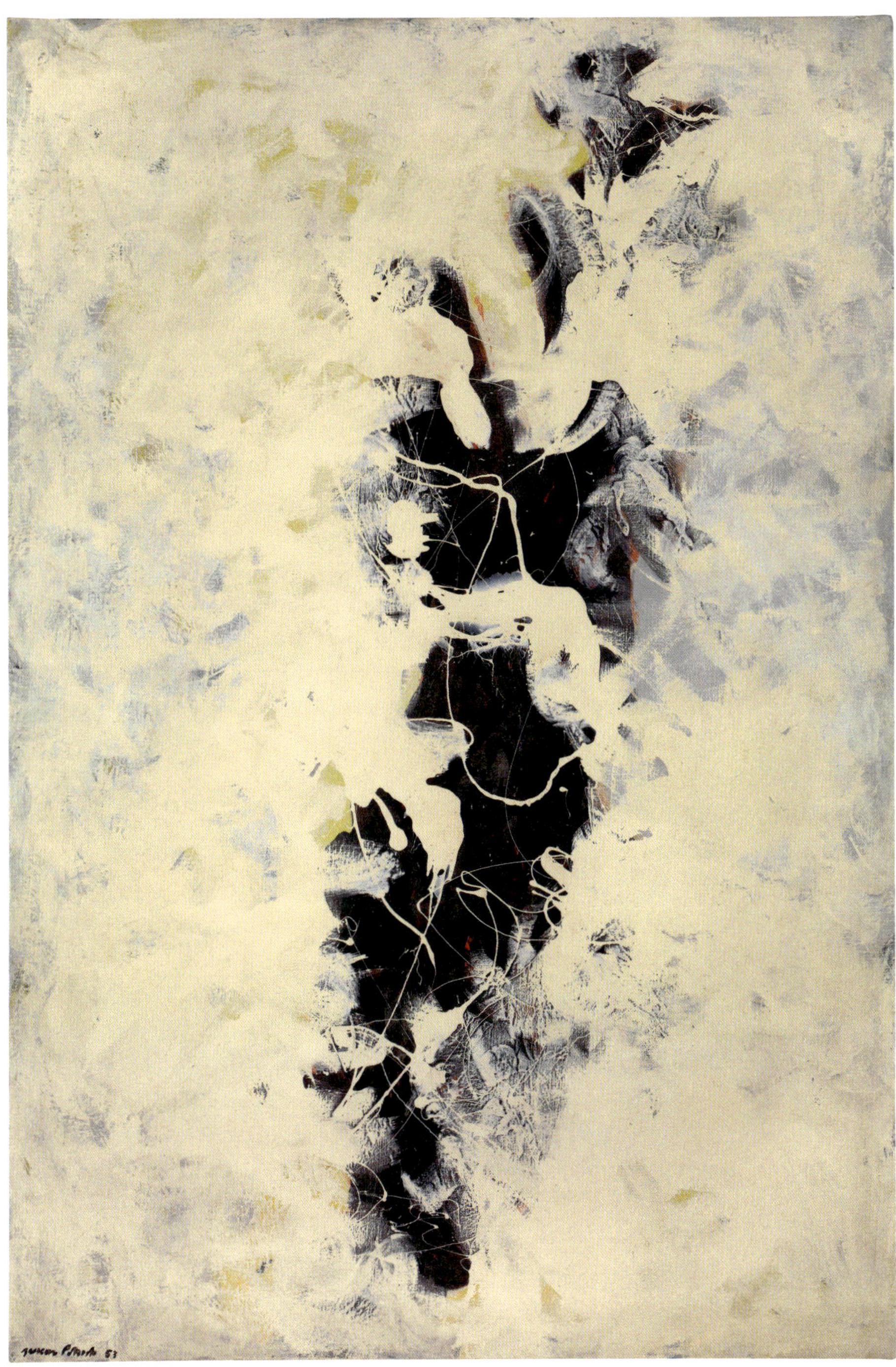

Fig. 21 Jackson Pollock, *The Deep*, 1953, oil and enamel on canvas, 86¾ × 59⅛ in. (220.4 × 150.2 cm). Musée National d'Art Moderne, Centre Georges Pompidou, Paris, France, Given in memory of Jean de Menil by his children and by the Menil Foundation, 1976, AM 1976-1230.

Reinhardt's eschatological gambits—fuses extremes into a whole. If painting offers insufficient evidence for this assertion, then the wider period culture confirms it. Listen to a poetic bellwether for the times, Wallace Stevens:

> Everything comes to him
> From the middle of his field . . .
> There he touches his being. There as he is
> He is.[121]

Forget the cliché that the subject is male. Remember that selfhood was Abstract Expressionism's mantra, and Stevens's ethos makes perfect sense. The field attains the goal for which modernist art ever strives, the suspension of time into an epiphany that momentarily superimposes Being upon Becoming.[120] Auden knew this metaphysical-cum-experiential verity; otherwise, he would not have written in "New Year Letter" (significantly, dating from the year after he arrived in the United States) about "a field that never closes" and, crucially, "the field of Being."[123] To him, as well as to other artists at that time, the field's possibilities waxed limitless. Even its precursors had preternatural ramifications. The three bands in Rothko's *Untitled* (ca. 1945, plate 1) connote deep time as much as they do a fledgling landscape format, an evolutionary matrix for the filament-thin, primordial organisms. They gyrate; their matrix is an unmoved mover. Subsequently, the field blossomed pictorially into felt time, "expanding and quickening in the eyes of the sensitive observer."[124] Duration is intrinsic to being.[125]

The second counterweight to the first generation's full-throttle gravitas is a group of two or three paintings and one sculpture keyed to a novel register—the exuberance and lightness that beckoned as the Age of Anxiety ceded to the Beat generation, the "culture of cool" and the Swinging Sixties.[126] Gottlieb's breakthrough Bursts vibrate with cosmic energies anticipating president-elect John F. Kennedy's "new frontier" speech (1960) that suggested illimitable futures stretching into outer space. They also echo contemporary science and technology's delving into the microscopic and the infinite, now understood as benign or reparative compared to earlier collective neuroses—physical and psychic equations or balances rather than a route to nuclear catastrophe.[127] A prophetic subtext to *Crimson Spinning #2* (1959, plate 10) are notes that Gottlieb penned in 1956 and titled "Polarities"—the word says it all—which ponder on psychology and science as though thought were at a new crossroads. That Frankenthaler moved into the acrylic medium spoke for her seizing the optimistic angle to Pollock's pictorial fluency.[128] Instead of bringing forth archetypal specters from the Jungian unconscious, Frankenthaler's washes possess a breezy ease that allows color to rise aloft, billowing and translucent, as in *Dawn Shapes* (1967, plate 16). The titular "Dawn" hardly requires explication. Even Motherwell's *Irish Elegy* exudes a calculated crispness closer to 1960s Color Field painting than to the previous decade's loose gesturalism. His *Before the Day* (1972, plate 18) replaces the lowering oppressiveness of the Elegies with uplift. In David Smith's *Cubi XXV* (1965, plate 15), the gesture grew architectonic, precise and geometric—a syntax parsed, like grammar, in space. As a series, the sculptures are heroes that never lose their stainless steel's "cool" demeanor. Fresh ideas of order and hedonism had crystallized in place of the old abandonment to risk and nervousness. One could speak of existence in easier, measured cadences.

But the big, universal themes of Abstract Expressionism in its glory days will endure, testaments to a particular age, its places and complex ideologies, as well as emotive depth charges for new audiences—significantly, the movement has percolated into cinema and television, a bellwether for popular feelings[129]—provided they are grasped in context rather than lionized as just transcendent, timeless mythologies. I have in mind such exemplary declarations as Still's 1950 note that his images targeted "life and death merging in fearful unison";[130] Rothko's ethos, "I'm interested only in expressing basic human emotions—tragedy, ecstasy, doom and so on";[131] Pollock's avowal that his goal was "energy and motion made visible—memories arrested in space";[132] Guston's late meditations on temporality, the banality of evil and the individual's fate;[133] and Motherwell's epic engagements with modern history conceived as an abstract threnody in the Elegies. Compact in number and expansive in spirit, the Friday Foundation's donation to the Seattle Art Museum encapsulates a rich array of the art and extremes that people can muster when rising to face their changeful times.

NOTES

Epigraph Theodore Roethke, "In a Dark Time" (1964), in *Theodore Roethke: Collected Poems* (London: Faber and Faber, 1985), 231.

1 Eric Hobsbawm, *Age of Extremes: The Short Twentieth Century 1914–1991* (London: Abacus, 1995).

2 Jane Lang married David Davis in 1985, following Richard Lang's death in 1982. Warhol did the silkscreen to celebrate the Seattle Art Museum's *Andy Warhol: Portraits* exhibition that year.

3 Hobsbawm, *Age of Extremes*, ix. Hobsbawm's counterweight was the "Long Nineteenth Century," beginning with the French Revolution.

4 Also Hobsbawm's term.

5 American exceptionalism is at least as old as the writings of the French political philosopher Alexis de Tocqueville (1805–1858), if not the Pilgrim fathers' messianism. The term *Pax Americana* was coined after the American Civil War. Ripples of the Manifest Destiny syndrome, aesthetically figured, inform Clement Greenberg's teleological criticism.

6 David Caute, *The Great Fear: The Anticommunist Purge under Truman and Eisenhower* (London: Secker and Warburg, 1978). To be fair, Harry S. Truman himself was relatively liberal in the best meaning of the word.

7 Auden moved to the United States in 1939 and wrote his poem "The Age of Anxiety" in 1947.

8 In the context of lectures and seminars, I have long used the abbreviation "Ab Ex" for a term that is, frankly, a mouthful. However, for the sake of consistency within this volume, the full phrase appears here. Hopefully, the reader will not find it overly repetitive.

9 A solid account is George Cotkin, *Existential America* (Baltimore: Johns Hopkins University Press, 2003).

10 Willem de Kooning, "What Abstract Art Means to Me" (1951), in *The Collected Writings of Willem de Kooning*, ed. George Scrivani (New York: Hanuman Books, 1988), 59.

11 Science underlies America's engineering feats. *Mutatis mutandis*, Kline and Smith had a fascination with the railroad, as Mitchell did with the Brooklyn Bridge. Smith's *Medals for Dishonor* (1937–40) offers a biting critique of the science that led to aerial bombing and poison gas. Still considered his age to be one of science and death.

12 As with Abstract Expressionism, there is no consensus as to where existentialism begins and ends.

13 Blaise Pascal, *Pensées*, trans. A. J. Krailsheimer (London: Penguin, [1670] 1966), 95. The Modern Library in New York published an English translation in 1941.

14 For accuracy's sake, some are not quite monochromatic. However, the small color accents intensify the overall starkness.

15 However, de Kooning's monochromes have a stronger affinity with Max Beckmann's crowded interiors, especially *The Night* (1919). That de Kooning is more likely to have known the black-and-white lithographic version of that work (published early in the literature) than the painting chimes with his grisaille in the late 1940s. See David Anfam, "Beckmann and Abstract Expressionism: The Space of Existence," in *Beckmann & Amerika*, ed. Jutta Schütt (Ostfildern: Hatje Cantz Verlag, 2011), 262–69.

16 John Elderfield, *De Kooning: A Retrospective* (New York: Museum of Modern Art, 2011), 183, referencing Thomas Hess, rightly adds Willem van de Velde's seventeenth-century Dutch naval prints.

17 David Anfam, "De Kooning, Bosch and Bruegel: Some Fundamental Themes," *Burlington Magazine* 145 (October 2003): 705–15.

18 William Faulkner, *Light in August* (London: Vintage, [1932] 2000), 370.

19 Faulkner, *Light in August*, 38–39. That the context is a house on fire clinches the reference, because scholars have identified burning as a leitmotif in de Kooning's repertoire during these years. See, for example, Charles F. Stuckey, "Bill de Kooning and Joe Christmas," *Art in America* 68 (March 1980): 66–79; and Martin Ries, "De Kooning's *Asheville* and Zelda's Immolation," *Art Criticism* [SUNY Stonybrook] 20, no. 1 (2005), http://www.martinries.com/article2005DK.htm.

20 The interwoven, nonlinear structure of Faulkner's most radical book, *The Sound and the Fury* (1929), offers a particularly audacious kaleidoscope of glimpses.

21 Willem de Kooning (1951), in Scrivani, ed., *The Collected Writings*, 60. He continued, "A truly Christian light, painful but forgiving." Is there a memory here of a notable Christian dualism, the loss (of earthly life) and gain (of eternal life)? The proposition known as "Pascal's wager" hinges upon this turn.

22 Isaiah Berlin, quoted in Hobsbawm, *Age of Extremes*, 1.

23 Yehudi Menin, quoted in Hobsbawm, *Age of Extremes*, 2.

24 Manifestly, Jean Dubuffet joins their company with his *Corps de dame* series.

25 Although, of course, overshadowed by the huge subsequent body of scholarship, John Russell, *Francis Bacon* (London: Thames and Hudson, 1979) remains a lucid, eloquent introduction to its subject.

26 Teofilo F. Ruiz, *The Terror of History: On the Uncertainties of Life in Western Civilization* (Princeton, NJ: Princeton University Press, 2011), 9.

27 Ruiz, *Terror of History*, 4.

28 Clement Greenberg, "'American-Type' Painting" (1955), in *Clement Greenberg: The Collected Essays and Criticism: Volume 3*, ed. John O'Brian (Chicago: University of Chicago Press, 1993), 222. Thomas B. Hess, "De Kooning Paints a Picture," *Art News* 52 (March 1953): 31. Here was a rare occasion when these otherwise steadfast adversaries agreed.

29 Martha P. Nochimson, *The Passion of David Lynch: Wild at Heart in Hollywood* (Austin: University of Texas Press, 1997), 21.

30 Harold Rosenberg, "Interview with Willem de Kooning," *Art News* 71 (September 1972): 58. In very different fashion, the key narrator, Benjy, in *The Sound and the Fury* is also a so-called idiot savant, uncovering the other protagonists' true motivations.

31 A signal exception is one source that I have long thought Bacon to have known: specifically, the police photograph of Jack the Ripper's last victim, Mary Jane Kelly, butchered beyond recognition. Too terrible to reproduce here, the image would have provided a topos for Bacon's recurrent, often horrifying, figures reclining on a bed/couch. According to various reports, Kelly's entrails had been tin-tacked around the walls of her room. This is the exact detailing seen, swag-like, at the top of Bacon's *Painting 1946* (1946, Museum of Modern Art, New York). Interestingly for the present context, MoMA acquired the Bacon before "any paintings by Pollock, Rothko, or other examples of nascent Abstract Expressionism" (Martin Harrison and Rebecca Daniels, eds., *Francis Bacon: Catalogue Raisonné, Volume II, 1929–57* [London: Estate of Francis Bacon, 2016], 172).

32 Peter Beard to Francis Bacon, October 15, 1985, citing "ideas we talked about," reproduced in "The Diary," Ordovas website, http://www.ordovasart.com/diary-entry/wild-life-04/.

33 An excellent account of these subjects is Martin Harrison, *In Camera: Francis Bacon. Photography, Film and the Practice of Painting* (London: Thames and Hudson, 2005).

34 For an art historical survey that glues everything to war and its transformation into myth and archetype, see Stephen Polcari, *Abstract Expressionism and the Modern Experience* (Cambridge: Cambridge University Press, 1991). An academic antitype to this approach is Michael Leja, *Reframing Abstract Expressionism: Subjectivity and Painting in the 1940s* (New Haven, CT: Yale University Press, 1993). The latter's master narrative is "Modern Man" discourse, which actually predates Abstract Expressionism by a long stretch. This "subjectivity" trope makes its decisive entrance into American literature at least as early as Stephen Crane's *The Red Badge of Courage* (1895), wherein the anti-hero Henry Fleming is buffeted by emotions and experiences from the *inside out*.

35 With hindsight, Noguchi appears neither an insider nor an outsider to Abstract Expressionism. Rather, he is a superb asider.

36 In both works, note the horizontal lines running along the lower edge, the hurled arcing humanoid that becomes a similarly configured strand of drips in the later drawing, and the crucified-type vertical presence at right in *War* whose counterpart is the similarly positioned heavy black motif in the upper-right quadrant of the 1951 sheet.

37 Though the title stems from a nursery rhyme, it also memorializes the erasure of human identity in the camps. See David Anfam, "Guston's Trauma: Ideal/Abject," in *Go Figure! New Perspectives on Guston*, ed. Peter Benson Miller (New York: American Academy in Rome and New York Review of Books, 2014), 83–93.

38 A good reference source for the literature is Ellen G. Landau, ed., *Reading Abstract Expressionism: Context and Critique* (New Haven, CT: Yale University Press, 2005). In David Anfam, ed., *Abstract Expressionism* (London: Royal Academy of Arts, 2015) and the exhibition it accompanied, my aim, among other things, was to update the definitions and constituencies of the subject.

39 Alongside Reinhardt and the still-underestimated Fritz Bultman (whose great-grandfather emigrated from Lower Saxony to New Orleans in 1845), Hofmann was the only other main figure associated with Abstract Expressionism who was of German, non-Jewish descent.

40 "Symbolism" understood with both a small and a capital *S*; the nineteenth-century movement's recourse to color as expression and correspondences between inner/outer reality anticipated Abstract Expressionism.

41 Exemplified, in a nutshell, by such titles as Kline's *Wotan* and *Siegfried*.

42 To take a most recent instance, we are told that Barbara Guest was "a poet who wrote the way Abstract Expressionists painted"—although quite how this is so remains a trifle unclear. See Tim Keane's article of that title, *Hyperallergic*, December 5, 2020, http://hyperallergic.com/605184/a-poet-who-wrote-the-way-abstract-expressionists-painted/?utm_campaign=Weekend&utm_content=20201205&utm_medium=email&utm_source=Hyperallergic%20Newsletter.

43 There may be a practical explanation for Barnett Newman's absence. His oeuvre numbers a mere 118 paintings; while he did not always enjoy the most canonical status as a painter rather than as an artist-thinker, he does so now.

44 Barnett Newman, "The New Sense of Fate" (1948), in *Barnett Newman: Selected Writings and Interviews*, ed. John P. O'Neill (New York: Alfred A. Knopf, 1990), 169.

45 Two critics summarize what poets such as Roethke shared with the Abstract Expressionists: "Rarely has plumbing of the self as a metaphor for life in the world reached so deeply" (Richard Ruland and Malcolm Bradbury, *From Puritanism to Postmodernism: A History of American Literature* [New York: Penguin, 1991], 405).

46 Of course, Jane and Richard Lang's philanthropy in Seattle benefited, among various other institutions, the University of Washington's Henry Art Gallery.

47 This wry, doggerel jingle's source, known since my postgraduate student days, now eludes me.

48 Despite its age, a good personal approach is still Dore Ashton, *The Life and Times of the New York School* (Bath, England: Adams and Dart, 1972).

49 Bradford R. Collins, Manuel Fontán del Junco, Inés Vallejo, and Beatrix Cordero, eds., *The Irascibles: Painters against the Museum, 1950* (Madrid: Fundación Juan March, 2020).

50 Lewis Carroll, "The Hunting of the Snark" (1874–76), in *The New Oxford Book of Victorian Verse*, ed. Christopher Ricks (Oxford: Oxford University Press, 1987), 204.

51 In sculpture, Constantin Brancusi and Henry Moore were among the main exceptions to this rule. Other worthy Abstract Expressionist sculptors included Herbert Ferber, Ibram Lassaw, Richard Lippold and Theodore Roszak. De Kooning, Newman, Pollock, Pousette-Dart and Still all made significant sculptures at some stage in their careers.

52 I am reliably told by a friend who knew Guston that smoking and alcohol hastened his death, as was also, of course, the case for more than a few of his fellow artists who died otherwise natural ones.

53 See Alan Antliff, "Clyfford Still on the Margins of Anarchy," *Modernism/modernity* 27 (September 2020): 491–517; David Anfam,

"Still's Journey," in *Clyfford Still: The Artist's Museum*, ed. David Anfam and Dean Sobel (New York: Skira-Rizzoli, 2012), 57–112.
54 Robert Motherwell, "Editorial Preface to *Possibilities I*" (Winter 1947–48), in *The Collected Writings of Robert Motherwell*, ed. Stephanie Terenzio (Oxford: Oxford University Press, 1992), 45. In October 1947, Congress created a committee to investigate Communism in the United States—a harbinger of things to come.
55 A thought-provoking coda to Motherwell's position is Jeremy Treglown, *Spanish Culture and Memory since 1936* (London: Chatto and Windus, 2014). It argues that Spain is a metaphorical edifice haunted by memories of the Civil War that it cannot forget.
56 Smith and his then-wife Dorothy Dehner (a distinguished sculptor in her own right) toured the Soviet Union in June 1936. Gorky's nephew was named Karlen after Karl Marx and Vladimir Lenin.
57 Jackson Pollock, letter to Charles and Frank [Pollock] (October 22, 1929), in *American Letters 1927–1947: Jackson Pollock and Family*, ed. Sylvia Winter Pollock (Cambridge, MA: Polity Press, 2011), 16.
58 Michael Corris, *Ad Reinhardt* (London: Reaktion, 2008), argued for the artist's substantive affiliation with the American Communist movement, causing some controversy.
59 Steve Fraser, *The Age of Acquiescence: The Life and Death of American Resistance to Organized Wealth and Power* (New York: Little, Brown, 2015). Hence, for instance, Rothko's nostalgia late in life about listening to the anarchist orator and activist Emma Goldman while he was still in grade school.
60 A fundamental issue sidestepped by Serge Guilbaut, *How New York Stole the Idea of Modern Art: Abstract Expressionism, Freedom, and the Cold War*, trans. Arthur Goldhammer (Chicago: University of Chicago Press, 1983). For an excellent critique of this interpretative trend, see Andreas Huyssen, "Degeneration Gap," *London Review of Books* 26 (October 2004): 31–33.
61 Hedda Sterne, quoted in Phyllis Tuchman, Oral history interview with Hedda Sterne, December 17, 1981, Archives of American Art, Smithsonian Institution, Washington, DC. Sterne's solo debut in Britain did not happen until her show at Victoria Miro, London, in 2020.
62 We should not miss the irony that *Life*'s photographer was a woman; ditto the magazine's art editor Dorothy Seiberling, who sent Nina Leen to do the shoot.
63 Anne M. Wagner, "Lee Krasner as L. K.," *Representations* 25 (Winter 1989): 42–57. Lee Krasner, quoted in Gail Levin, *Lee Krasner: A Biography* (New York: William Morrow, 2011), 318. See Krasner's characterization of herself as "irascible," as quoted in Eleanor Nairne, "Lee Krasner: *Night Watch*, 1960," in this volume, 60.
64 For example, Mary Gabriel, *Ninth Street Women* (New York: Back Bay Books, 2018). A precursor helping to establish the theoretical framework for inclusiveness was Ann Eden Gibson, *Abstract Expressionism: Other Politics* (New Haven, CT: Yale University Press, 1997).
65 Beauford Delaney, Black and homosexual, typified the exodus of outsiders by emigrating to Paris in 1953.
66 Given my own highly diverse family tree, I was especially heartened to write on Lewis: David Anfam, "The Music of Invisibility," in *Norman Lewis: Pulse. A Centennial Exhibition* (New York: Michael Rosenfeld Gallery, 2009), 3–21. For more on Lewis, see Norman Kleeblatt, "Ad Reinhardt, *Painting, 1950*, 1950," in this volume.
67 Perhaps significantly, Williams has received a Joan Mitchell Foundation Award (1996).
68 See Erin Dzeizic and Melissa Messina, eds., *Magnetic Fields: Expanding American Abstraction 1960s to Today* (Kansas City, MO: Kemper Museum of Contemporary Art, 2017).
69 Henry James, preface to *Roderick Hudson* (New York: Charles Scribner's Sons, 1907), vii.
70 An influential member of Guggenheim's circle, the homosexual Putzel played an early role in advancing Abstract Expressionism. See Melvin Lader, "Peggy Guggenheim's Art of This Century: The Surrealist Milieu and the American Avant-Garde, 1942–1947" (PhD diss., University of Delaware, 1981), 141–91.
71 Steven Naifeh and Gregory White Smith, *Jackson Pollock: An American Saga* (New York: Harper Perennial, 1989).
72 "Gender" as we understand it today was simply not in the period's ideological episteme. As for Latinos, only the Mexican Rufino Tamayo and the Cuban Wifredo Lam got near Abstract Expressionism's margins.
73 White (who was a homosexual) even taught alongside Still at the California School of Fine Arts in the late 1940s.
74 Mark Rothko and Adolph Gottlieb, quoted in Edward Alden Jewell, "The Realm of Art: A New Platform and Other Matters," *New York Times*, June 13, 1943.
75 Frankenthaler, quoted in Eric Gibson, "Breaking the Rules," *Washington Times*, April 16, 1993.
76 W. B. Yeats, "Vacillation" (1933), in *The Collected Poems of W. B. Yeats* (Ware, England: Wordsworth Editions, 1994), 213.
77 Terenzio, *Collected Writings of Robert Motherwell*, 76–84.
78 Jed Perl, *New Art City: Manhattan at Mid-century* (New York: Alfred A. Knopf, 2005) is a major scholarly achievement on this topic. See also Valerie Hellstein, "Grounding the Social Aesthetics of Abstract Expressionism: A New Intellectual History of the Club" (PhD diss., Stony Brook University, 2010).
79 Other fine Abstract Expressionists in the show who fall beyond my purview here are William Baziotes, James Brooks, Richard Pousette-Dart, Stamos, Sterne and Tomlin. Jack Tworkov, inter alia, also deserves a very honorable mention.
80 It traveled only to the Santa Barbara Museum of Art—New York packaged for California.
81 History repeated itself with the exhibition *New York School* (1965) at—guess where?—the Los Angeles County Museum of Art.
82 Clyfford Still (1963), typed manuscript, "An Open Letter to an Art Critic," Clyfford Still Museum Archives, Denver.

83 On Abstract Expressionism in relation to the concept of the "classic" as westward-bound and changeful, see David Anfam, "Abstrakter Expressionismus und Europa—Über den Atlantik hinweg," in *Es war einmal in Amerika: 300 Jahre US-Amerikanische Kunst* (Cologne: Wallraf-Richartz Museum and Fondation Corboud, 2018). The significance of Tobey's homosexuality has also gone under the radar. See David Anfam, "Intimate Immensities," in *Mark Tobey: Tobey or Not To Be?* (Paris: Gallimard, 2020), 52–71.

84 As with de Kooning, Giacometti regarded his women—partly based on prostitutes—as simultaneously attractive and repulsive. They also originally related to a wartime atmosphere of "terror"; Yves Bonnefoy, *Giacometti*, trans. Jean Stewart (Paris: Flammarion, 2001), 340.

85 A publication (and the accompanying exhibition) that did wonders in opening new geographic vistas in the discourse is Kay Heymer, Susanne Rennert, and Beat Wismer, *Le grand geste! Informel und Abstrakter Expressionismus, 1946–1964* (Düsseldorf: Museum Kunst Palast and DuMont, 2010).

86 The latest biography is Robert Storr, *Philip Guston* (London: Laurence King, 2020), now joined by the artist's daughter Musa Mayer's second book of reminiscences, published in 2021, making three in toto.

87 Philip Guston, annotation on a manuscript of Dore Ashton's book *Yes, but . . . A Critical Study of Philip Guston* (1976), quoted in Storr, *Philip Guston*, 292.

88 Willem de Kooning, in response to a question from the former director of the Museum of Modern Art, Alfred H. Barr Jr.; "Excerpts from Artists Sessions at Studio 35" (April 21–23, 1950), in Landau, *Reading Abstract Expressionism*, 164.

89 This is basically the view taken by medieval Nominalism. Cf. also the philosopher Ludwig Wittgenstein's thesis to the effect that "the limits of my language mean the limits of my world." Wittgenstein, *Tractatus Logico-Philosophicus*, trans. C. K. Ogden (London: Kegan Paul, Trench, Trubner [1922]), 5.6, 74. See also Ann Gibson, "Abstract Expressionism's Evasion of Language," *Art Journal* 47 (1988): 208–14.

90 For "crapola," see Philip Roth, *Why Write? Collected Nonfiction 1960–2013* (New York: Library of America, 2017), 289; on negation, see Reinhardt, "[On Negation]," in *Art as Art: The Selected Writings of Ad Reinhardt*, ed. Barbara Rose (Berkeley: University of California Press, 1975), 102–3. Reinhardt anticipated Theodor W. Adorno's *Negative Dialectics* (1966), which insists, as did the artist, on the limits of knowledge. Hence Reinhardt's ubiquitous "almost-ness" in his paintings and thoughts.

91 Lucy R. Lippard, *Ad Reinhardt* (New York: Harry N. Abrams, 1981), 63.

92 Lippard, *Ad Reinhardt*, 97.

93 Alfred Leslie, the last surviving major second-generation Abstract Expressionist—still active at the age of 93—was alert enough to have reproached me a while ago for wearing only one hearing aid rather than two!

94 Yeats, "Vacillation," 213.

95 Pat Passlof, quoted in Perl, *New Art City*, 5.

96 Cf. Perl, *New Art City*, chapter 2, "The Dialectical Imagination."

97 "Buzz" is not fantastical onomatopoeia, given titles that have auditory allusions—*Night Sounds, Sounds in the Grass, Croaking Movement*, *Echo*, and so forth—allied to Pollock's "ear" for nature's cadence: "You can hear the life in the grass, hear it growing" (Jackson Pollock, quoted by the dealer Julian Levy, in Ellen G. Landau, *Jackson Pollock* [New York: Harry N. Abrams, 1989], 159). Lawrence Kramer, *The Hum of the World: A Philosophy of Listening* (Oakland: University of California Pess, 2018), offers a thought-provoking framework for this proposition.

98 Jackson Pollock (1929), quoted in Winter Pollock, *American Letters 1927–1947*, 16.

99 Although I am reluctant to foreground my own writings, the essential study is David Anfam, *Jackson Pollock's 'Mural': Energy Made Visible* (London: Thames and Hudson, 2015).

100 Jackson Pollock (1951), quoted in Francis V. O'Connor and Eugene V. Thaw, eds., *Jackson Pollock: A Catalogue Raisonné of Paintings, Drawings, and Other Works, Vol. 4* (New Haven, CT: Yale University Press, 1978), 261.

101 Deanna Petherbridge, *The Primacy of Drawing: Histories and Theories of Practice* (New Haven, CT: Yale University Press, 2010), contains many insights relevant to draftsmanship in Abstract Expressionism.

102 *Pace* Rosalind Krauss, it was Pollock's final period, not his classic 1947–50 years, that saw him nearing the "formless." See Yve-Alain Bois and Rosalind E. Krauss, *Formless: A User's Guide* (New York: Zone Books, 1997).

103 Theodor W. Adorno, "Late Style in Beethoven," in *Essays on Music*, trans. Susan H. Gillespie, ed. Richard Leppert (Berkeley: University of California Press, 2002).

104 The title is almost an oxymoron.

105 Adorno, "Late Style in Beethoven," 11.

106 The following explores a very similar, intriguing theme: Charles F. Stuckey, "Another Side to Jackson Pollock," *Art in America* 65 (November–December 1977): 80–91.

107 Pollock embedded a key in the impasto of *Full Fathom Five* (1947), glass shards are visible in *Blue Poles* (1952), and so on.

108 James E. B. Breslin, *Mark Rothko: A Biography* (Chicago: University of Chicago Press, 1993), 316. Breslin omits the precedent for Rothko's "breathed" effects: Henry James quoted James Abbot McNeill Whistler back to himself by saying that "his manner of painting is to breathe upon the canvas." Henry James, "London Pictures and London Plays" (1882), in *Henry James: Essays on Art and Drama*, ed. Peter Rawlings (Aldershot, England: Scolar, 1996), 347–48.

109 Joan Mitchell, quoted in Irving Sandler, "Mitchell Paints a Picture," *Art News* 56 (October 1957): 45.

110 Titles iterate the aqueous tale: *Harbor December*, *Hudson River Day Line* and *George Went Swimming at Barnes Hole, But It Got Too Cold* are a few among a multitude.

111 Carol Stringari, ed., *Imageless: The Scientific Study and Experimental Treatment*

of an Ad Reinhardt Black Painting (New York: Guggenheim Museum, 2008), 13.

112 Photographs taken by Hans Namuth in Rothko's studio in 1964 show these modest-size brushes.

113 Mark Rothko, "Address to Pratt Institute, November [*sic*] 1958," in *Writings on Art: Mark Rothko*, ed. Miguel López-Remiro (New Haven, CT: Yale University Press, 2006), 125.

114 Mark Rothko, quoted in Chris Stephens, *Mark Rothko in Cornwall* (St. Ives, England: Tate Gallery St. Ives, 1996), 10.

115 Edmund Burke, *A Philosophical Enquiry into the Origin of Our Ideas of the Sublime and Beautiful* (1757). See Robert Rosenblum, "The Abstract Sublime" (1961), in Landau, *Jackson Pollock*, 239–44. Like the gothic, the sublime aestheticizes angst.

116 Contrary to stereotypical perceptions of Still as a heavyweight macho type, he admired one of the most refined European painters, Jean-Auguste-Dominique Ingres. It took someone who could draw to know one. Furthermore, the archives at the artist's museum in Denver indicate that perhaps he also had an otherwise surprising penchant for Pierre-Auguste Renoir. An explanation may be that Still much appreciated Renoir's acutely calibrated touch and sophisticated colorism. Like Still, Renoir drew in color.

117 Hence Still's ubiquitous insistence on the paramount importance of "ideas."

118 An immediate comparison looms with the Muriel Kallis Steinberg Newman donation to the Metropolitan Museum of Art, New York, which numbers a formidable sixty-three works.

119 *The Eye Is the First Circle* (1960, Private Collection) is a good contender for Krasner's magnum opus and refers to Ralph Waldo Emerson's essay "Circles" (1841). See David Anfam, "Mood Umber," in Anfam, Richard Howard, and Barbara Novak, *Lee Krasner: The Umber Paintings 1959–1962* (New York: Paul Kasmin Gallery, 2018), 9–15. Ellen G. Landau, *Lee Krasner: A Catalogue Raisonné* (New York: Harry N. Abrams, 1995), 186.

120 The arcs, ovoids and similar volumetric configurations may have gendered overtones insofar as they occur early in Krasner's studies of nudes that are mostly, though not exclusively, female. See Landau, *Lee Krasner*, 28–29, 46–54.

121 Wallace Stevens, "Yellow Afternoon" (1942), in *The Collected Poems of Wallace Stevens* (New York: Alfred A. Knopf, 1954), 237.

122 The distinction between Being and Becoming is as old as Western philosophy itself and was revived in the Abstract Expressionist era by Jean-Paul Sartre, Martin Heidegger and many other thinkers.

123 W. H. Auden, "New Year Letter" (1940), in *W. H. Auden: Collected Poems*, ed. Edward Mendelson (London: Faber and Faber, 1976), 208, 201.

124 Mark Rothko, "Ides of Art" (1947), in López-Remiro, *Writings on Art*, 44.

125 Hence Heidegger's magnum opus, *Sein und Zeit* (*Being and Time*) (1927). Since the German was an unrepentant Nazi sympathizer, I hesitate to introduce his name into Abstract Expressionist discourse with its plethora of Jewish artists. Nevertheless, Heidegger's ontological ideas are apposite, particularly to Newman's.

126 See Daniel Belgrad, *The Culture of Spontaneity: Improvisation and the Arts in Postwar America* (Chicago: University of Chicago Press, 1998); Thomas Frank, *The Conquest of Cool: Business Culture, Counterculture, and the Rise of Hip Consumerism* (Chicago: University of Chicago Press, 1997); and Arthur Marwick, *The Sixties: Cultural Revolution in Britain, France, Italy, and the United States, c. 1958–c. 1974* (Oxford: Oxford University Press, 1998).

127 On the multiple dimensions implicit in the Bursts, see Sanford Hirsch, "The Art of Adolph Gottlieb," in *Adolph Gottlieb: A Survey Exhibition* (Valencia, Spain: IVAM Centre Julio González, 2001), 29ff. The following—kindly submitted to the author for review—also delves interesting themes, science among them: Mary Davis MacNaughton, "Alchemy and the Inner Drama of Transformation in the Art of Adolph Gottlieb" (unpublished typescript, 2013).

128 Susan Cross, ed., *After "Mountains and Sea": Frankenthaler 1956–1959* (Berlin: Deutsche Guggenheim, 1998), chronicles the artist as a pioneer of what best happened after Abstract Expressionism's full-blooded, masculinist "triumph" (to recall the storied title of Irving Sandler's reading of what he saw, following Clement Greenberg's seminal "'American-Type' Painting" text, as a nationalistic movement).

129 Apart from the biopic *Pollock* (2000; dir. Ed Harris), Abstract Expressionism's incursions range from *Contraband* (2012; dir. Baltasar Kormákur), in which a Pollock canvas plays a dramatic role, to the black comedy *American Hustle* (2013; dir. David O. Russell), which ends with its scheming crooks' decision to open an art gallery, saying, "Let's do Abstract Expressionism." Rothkos feature in the television series *Mad Men* (2007–16) and a recent episode of the ongoing Netflix series *Ozark* (2017–).

130 Clyfford Still, unpublished typescript associated with his 1950 show at the Betty Parsons Gallery, Archives, Clyfford Still Museum.

131 Mark Rothko, "Notes from a Conversation with Selden Rodman, 1956," in López-Remiro, *Writings on Art*, 119.

132 Jackson Pollock (late 1950), handwritten notes, in *Jackson Pollock: Interviews, Articles, and Reviews*, ed. Pepe Karmel (New York: Museum of Modern Art, 1999), 24.

133 Cf. Adorno on Beethoven's late music, which he described as "unabashedly primitive" and "a catching fire between extremes, which no longer allow for any secure middle ground or harmony"; Adorno, "Late Style in Beethoven," as cited in *On Late Style: Music and Literature against the Grain*, by Edward W. Said (London: Bloomsbury, 2006), 10. Guston's late, risky leap into storytelling and figuration redux went equally "against the grain" of the various contemporary avant-gardes. Indeed, it was he who helped foster the rise of New Image art, wherein the abstract became expressionist again.

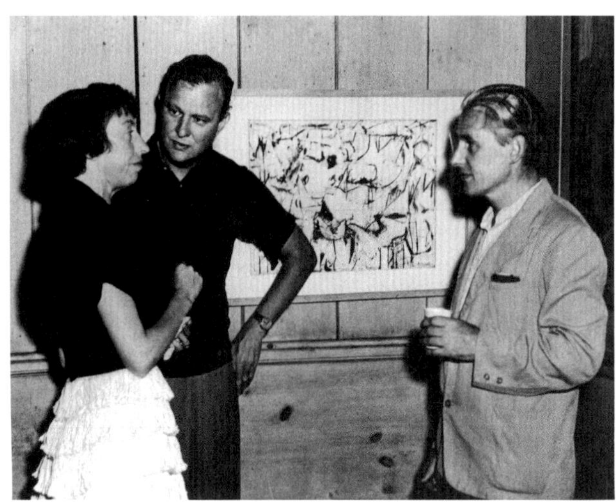

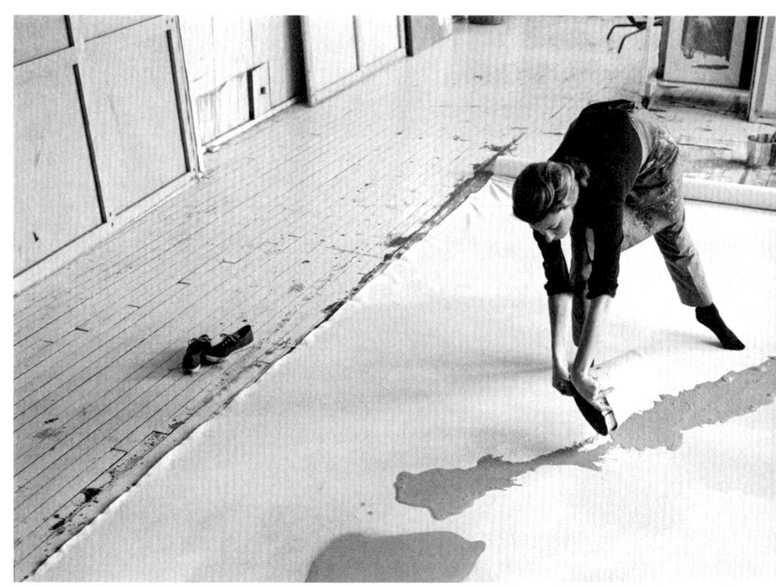

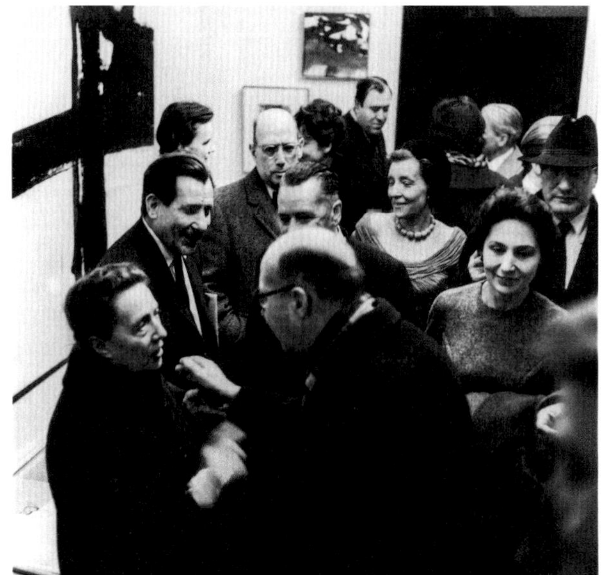

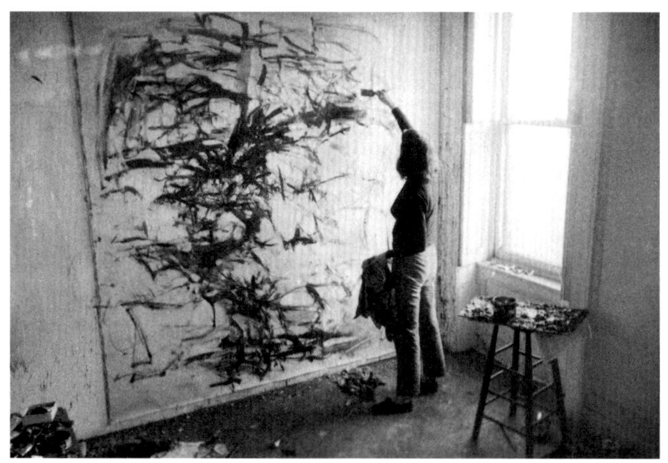

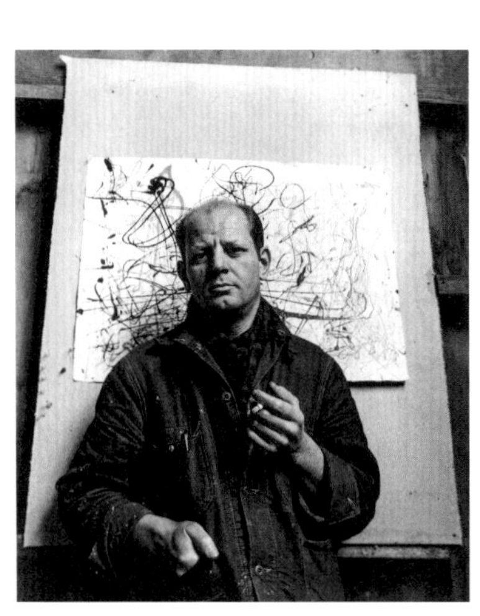

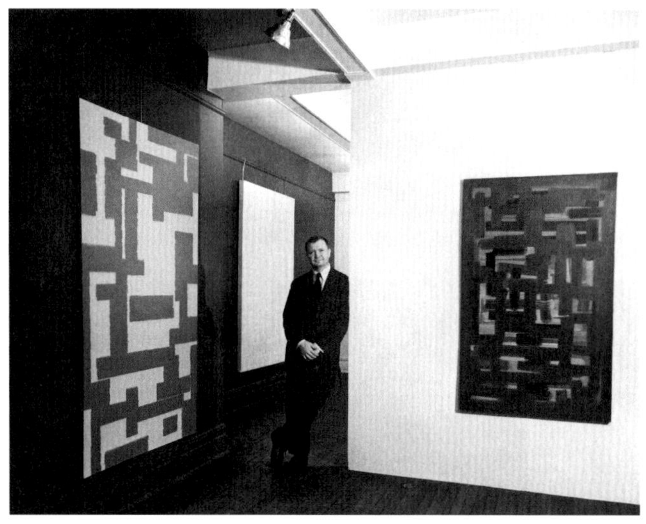

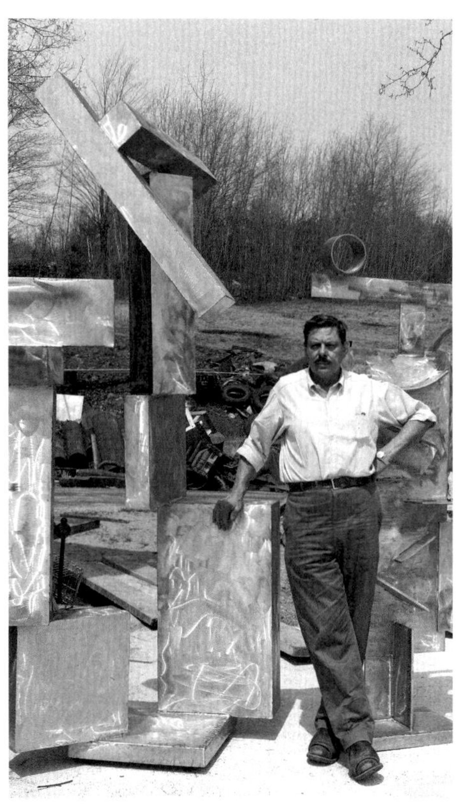

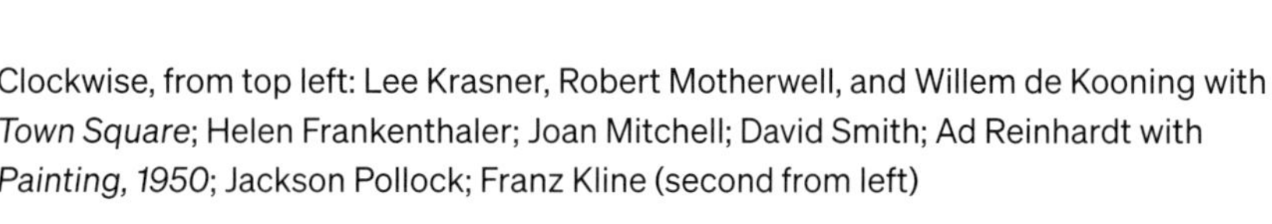

Clockwise, from top left: Lee Krasner, Robert Motherwell, and Willem de Kooning with *Town Square*; Helen Frankenthaler; Joan Mitchell; David Smith; Ad Reinhardt with *Painting, 1950*; Jackson Pollock; Franz Kline (second from left)

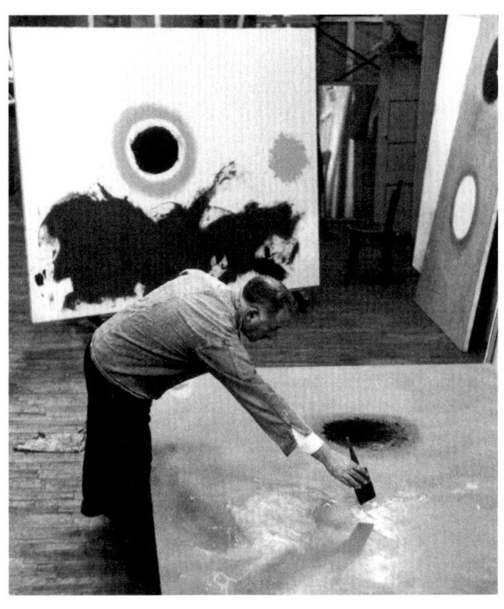

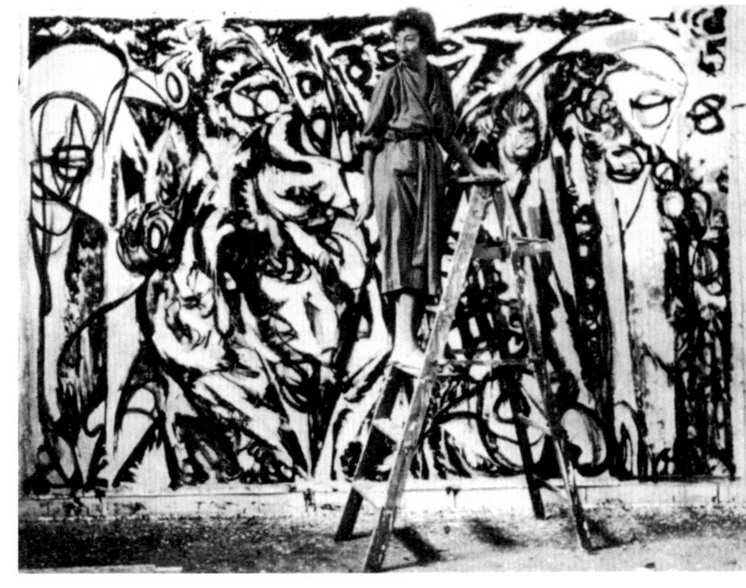

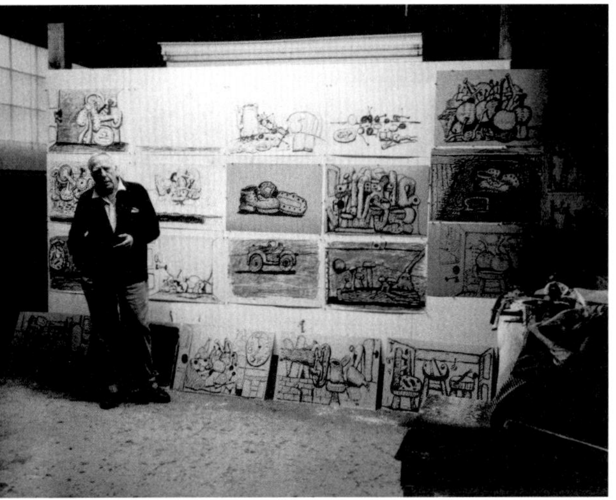

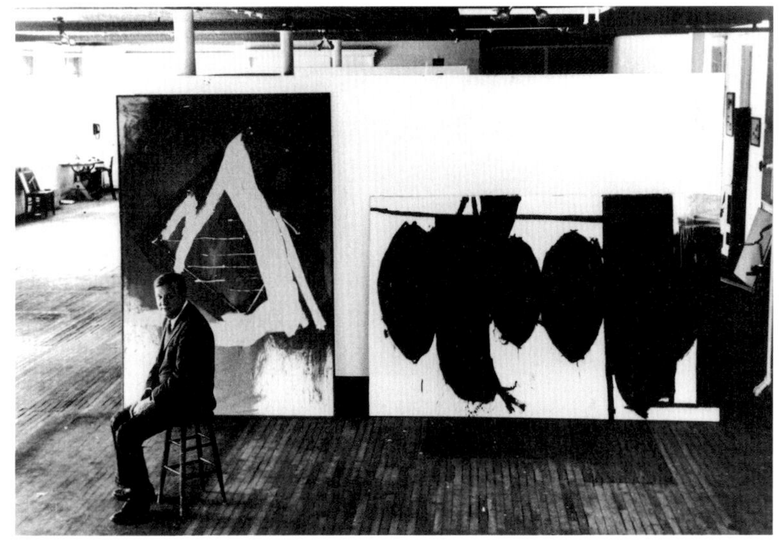

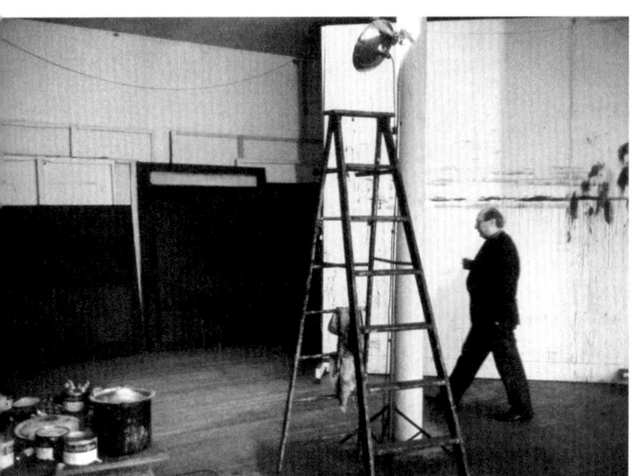

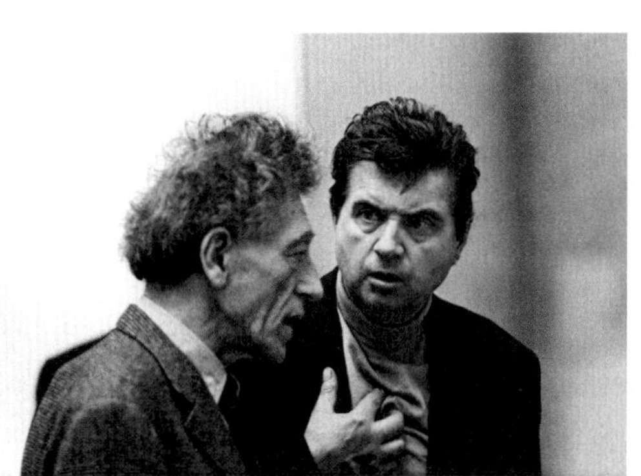

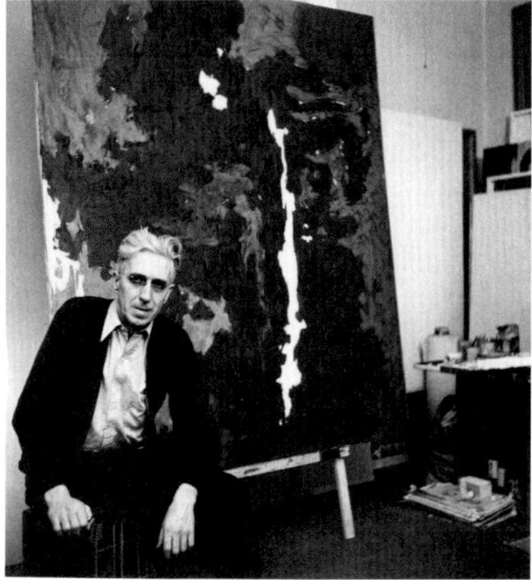

Clockwise, from top left: Adolph Gottlieb; Lee Krasner; Robert Motherwell; Clyfford Still; Alberto Giacometti (left) and Francis Bacon; Mark Rothko; Philip Guston

CATALOGUE

MARK ROTHKO
UNTITLED
CA. 1945

JEFFREY WEISS

According to David Anfam, author of the catalogue raisonné of Mark Rothko's paintings, the untitled Lang Collection painting of ca. 1945 (plate 1) is one of "three small oils at $150" recorded in a handwritten checklist of the artist's exhibition at the Betty Parsons Gallery in 1947.[1] (The others belong, respectively, to the collection of Christopher Rothko, the artist's son, and the National Gallery of Art, Washington, DC.) Together, the three works form an obvious group: identical in size, they all display a division of the pictorial field into three horizontal bands that alternate in value such that the center one is lighter than those on the top and bottom. The other two paintings are cool gray-blue in tonality, while the palette of the Lang Collection painting is warm—rosy gray in the center and dark gray-black in the upper and lower areas. Otherwise, the works share a repertoire of biomorphic glyphs that typify Rothko's work during the early to mid-1940s, although here they are smaller and more delicate than usual in relation to the composition overall, making the three paintings distinctively fragile and refined.

This repertoire comes from an inventory of images and motifs that occur throughout paintings of the forties by Rothko and his New York School contemporaries (and can be traced into the fifties in works by artists of the New York School's second wave). As a quasi-abstract manner, biomorphism derived from the example of Surrealism in Europe, especially visible in the New York gallery scene (and elsewhere across the country, including the West Coast and the desert Southwest) thanks to the emigration of a number of artists from Europe to the United States during World War II. Biomorphism was spawned by automatism, the cursive drawing style developed in Surrealist circles in Paris during the 1920s, which was understood to reflect, almost seismographically, the shifts and tremors of subconscious thought—a presumably free play of associations literally drawn from the depths of the subject's psyche. Transformed into the decidedly conscious underpinning for a new form of advanced painting by André Masson and Joan Miró, among others, this organic linearity generated a variety of forms that analogize the human subconscious to growth and change in the natural world. In postwar New York, this body of images came to be linked to what was characterized in certain anthropological and literary circles of the time as the metaphysical recesses of prehistoric, archaic, and tribal imagination—presumably, the domain of the premodern, precivilized mind. In that context,

Plate 1 Mark Rothko, *Untitled*, ca. 1945, oil on canvas, 22½ × 30⅜ in. (57.1 × 77 cm). Seattle Art Museum, Gift of the Friday Foundation in honor of Richard E. Lang and Jane Lang Davis, 2020.14.3.

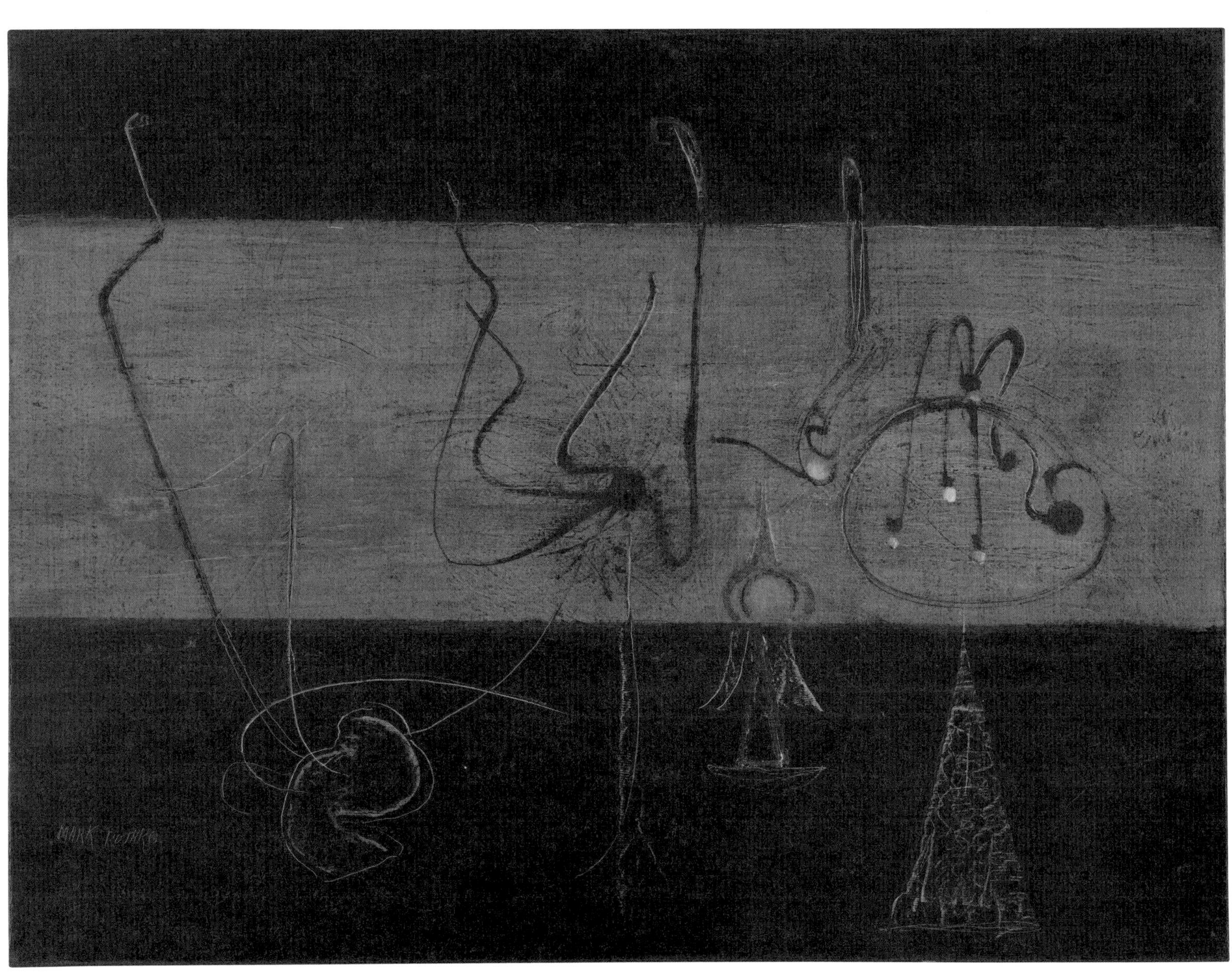

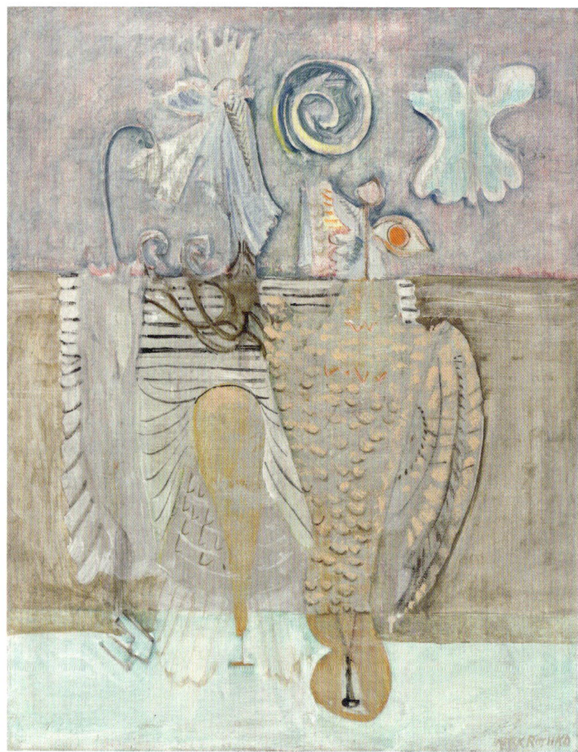

Fig. 22 Mark Rothko, *Hierarchical Birds*, 1944, oil on canvas, 39 5/8 × 31 11/16 in. (100.7 × 80.5 cm). National Gallery of Art, Washington, DC, Gift of the Mark Rothko Foundation, Inc., 1986.43.20.

biomorphic imagery, both abstract and representational, signified a pseudoprimeval mythography through which matter and spirit are shown to merge. In the wake of the war, painters in search of forms of meaning that circumvent the belief systems of the modern world awarded particular significance to Carl Jung's theories of the collective unconscious. With Jung's model in mind, biomorphic forms share iconographical space in their work with the schematic representation of other things—hieratic birds, floating eyes, gates, portals, and cosmological signs as well as masks, totems, and other tribal artifacts of the Pacific Northwest—that are taken to signify rituals and ceremonies of procreation, sacrifice, and death, which were said at the time to compose the primal underpinnings of Greek myth.[2]

Rothko's work on canvas and paper took this form throughout the early to mid-forties. These pictures often possess evocative titles featuring phrases such as archaic fantasy, primeval landscape, votive figure, hierarchical birds (fig. 22), and the like, as well as references to specific figures from history, myth, and religion including Lilith, Antigone, and Tiresias. By late 1946, his approach had begun to shift: titles were dropped and shapes became increasingly abstract, ultimately spreading across the surface in a long sequence of paintings of 1947–48 known as Multiforms.[3] It would be wrong, however, to ascribe purely iconographical interest to the earlier works. To begin with, their symbolic ambitions remind us that the paintings of the fifties and sixties were themselves claimed by Rothko to encompass themes belonging to the history of myth and psyche in Western culture, although the artist's means had, by then, dramatically changed. Moreover, Rothko's pictures of the post-Surrealist period also show the origin of formal and technical devices that served his pursuit of a more radical, absolute kind of painting.

So much of Rothko's work of the early mid-forties, including the untitled Lang Collection painting, demonstrates a consistent division of the pictorial surface into two or three horizontal areas or zones before, within, or across which his motifs are lodged. In most instances, the paintings show a distinct figure-ground relation between the motifs and the divided space. Yet the "ground"—the horizontal bands—clearly anticipates the turn that Rothko's work took in 1949: the emergence of two or three "stacked" rectangular forms. Those forms rarely extend from edge to edge the way the early bands do, but they often almost fill the surface, replacing the figure-ground relation of the earlier works with fields in which figure and ground almost merge. Even so, the resemblance between the bands of the forties and the stacked forms of Rothko's work of the following two decades is noteworthy. Its early application is intermittent, but it represents one solution to a pictorial problem—the noncompositional animation of the plane—to which Rothko would return.

While the division of the picture plane into two or three horizontal bands was a chief formal device in Rothko's work of the forties, it possessed clear symbolic value. Quite apart from the iconography of life forms, totems, and glyphs, the division in and of itself implicates strata, in the geological and/or archeological sense. In this way, it figures formation in time. (The idea was shared among many disciplines. The psychoanalytic writings of Sigmund Freud, for example, are filled with metaphors of

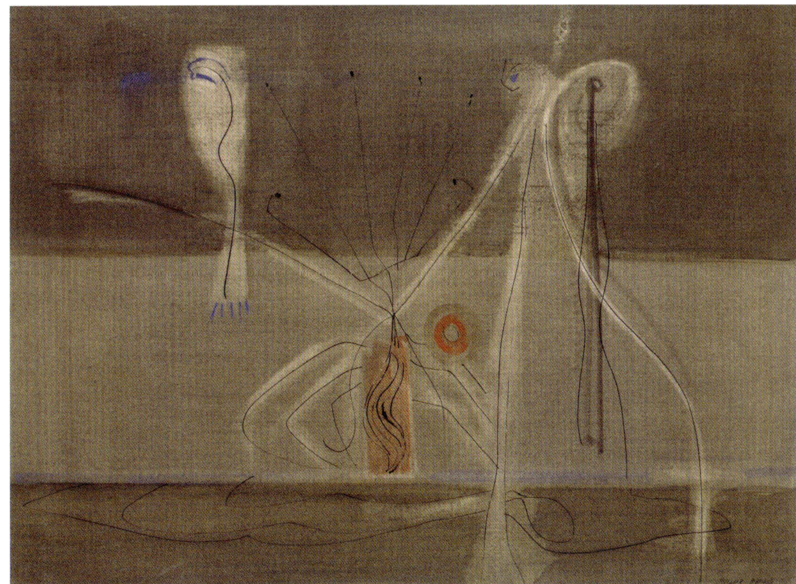

Fig. 23 Mark Rothko, *Tentacles of Memory*, ca. 1945–46, ink and watercolor on paper, 21¾ × 30 in. (55.25 × 76.2 cm). San Francisco Museum of Modern Art, Albert M. Bender Collection, Albert M. Bender Bequest Fund purchase.

stratification drawn from geology and archeology.[4]) We can, therefore, identify planar partition as a kind of symbolic form, an idea that has a direct bearing on Rothko's work after 1949, by which time biomorphic imagery had been abandoned and content was solely borne by multiple liminalities of form, color, value, and pictorial space. In the artist's later paintings, the metaphorical connotations of the early format are not eliminated but absorbed. At stake, in this regard, is the temporal significance of stratification: its allusion to that which lies below and comes before, and its intimations of gravity and space—of phenomena that are heavy, deep, hidden, or obscure.

Other qualities of the Lang Collection painting include separate factors of importance to the development of Rothko's work. For example, the painting demonstrates an extremely subtle deployment of luminous grays, which suffuse the image with a soft, smoky half-light, a quality that anticipates the optical nuances of works to come. The flatness of Rothko's partition of the plane supports a second, equally significant element: a material distillation of means. Simply put, during this period Rothko first began applying paint in thin layers. In certain works, including the Lang Collection painting, some areas are conspicuously wash-like in their transparency, others scraped down. These methods in oil are closely related to works of this kind in watercolor and gouache on paper, for which the medium is already inherently thin: there, Rothko can be seen experimenting with the spread of medium on and within the sheet. It is worth noting that the "three small oils" at the Parsons gallery resemble various works on paper of exactly the same dimensions and, almost certainly, the same date (fig. 23), suggesting an open equivalence between paper and canvas in this regard. The equivalence is not to be underestimated, for, notwithstanding the relatively small dimensions of the early works on both supports, this process of paint application was fundamental to the diaphanous surface qualities and expansive breadth of the paintings of Rothko's so-called classic period.

NOTES

1 David Anfam, *Mark Rothko: The Works on Canvas* (New Haven, CT: Yale University Press, 1998), cat. no. 269.

2 For an exhaustive overview of Rothko's early thematic concerns in the context of New York School painting in general, see Stephen Polcari, *Abstract Expressionism and the Modern Experience* (Cambridge: Cambridge University Press, 1991). See also in Anfam, *Mark Rothko*, chapter 2, "The Years of Transition, 1940–1950."

3 For the dropping of evocative titles, see Anfam, *Mark Rothko*, 57.

4 See Ernest S. Wolf and Sue S. Nebel, "Psychoanalytic Excavations: The Structure of Freud's Cosmography," *American Imago* 35, no. 1–2 (Spring–Summer 1978): 178–202.

WILLEM DE KOONING
TOWN SQUARE
1948

JOHN ELDERFIELD

Willem de Kooning's rapid development in the second half of the 1940s—roughly speaking, from *Pink Angels* in 1945 to *Excavation* in 1950—belongs among the greatest short periods of radical change in modern art. Moreover, his invention over these years was not only *continual*, always going on—as was, for example, Henri Matisse's transformation of his art from 1905 Fauvism to 1910 high decoration. De Kooning's was among the few such transformations that were also *continuous*, uninterrupted in time and sequence, comprising not the replacement of one style by another but an unbroken process of revising a personal vocabulary with ever more ambitious results.[1]

In this respect, de Kooning's richly productive period corresponds to that of his peer Jackson Pollock over roughly the same span of time: from works like *Mural* of 1943–44 to his all-over abstractions in 1948–50. They differ, though, in two important ways. First, de Kooning found that canvases of a relatively small size better served to maintain the momentum of his experimentation, given his meticulous, time-consuming methods; he only moved on to make large paintings at the end of this period, in 1949–50.[2] By contrast, Pollock's full-arm sweeps of paint in his canvases of the mid-1940s, and then his pouring it in layers, allowed and demanded large canvases; and he, in fact, opened this period with the very largest of its paintings, *Mural*, then worked back to something approaching its enormous size in 1950. The fact that de Kooning was able to work at a Pollock-like scale at that same time—in consciously summative works of 1949–50, *Attic* and especially *Excavation*—is testimony to the plateau of his extraordinary achievements in 1948–49, to which the Lang Collection painting *Town Square* (plate 2) belongs.

The second difference between Pollock's and de Kooning's developments over these years is simply that Pollock's paintings were abstract, whereas the course that de Kooning charted at mid-decade is unique in encompassing both abstract and figurative paintings. And it is more complicated than that: technical examination shows that some of de Kooning's works began as abstractions and became figurative.[3] Body parts depicted in some figurative works are little different from difficult-to-describe parts of abstract works; for example, the shape of the torso of *Woman* (1949, fig. 24) is similar to the shapes at the center of the roughly contemporaneous *Town Square*. And while paintings like *Town Square* caused de Kooning to be dubbed by the critic Clement Greenberg "an outright

Plate 2 Willem de Kooning, *Town Square*, 1948, oil on paper mounted on Masonite, 17⅜ × 23¾ in. (44.2 × 60.3 cm). Seattle Art Museum, Gift of the Friday Foundation in honor of Richard E. Lang and Jane Lang Davis, 2020.14.2.

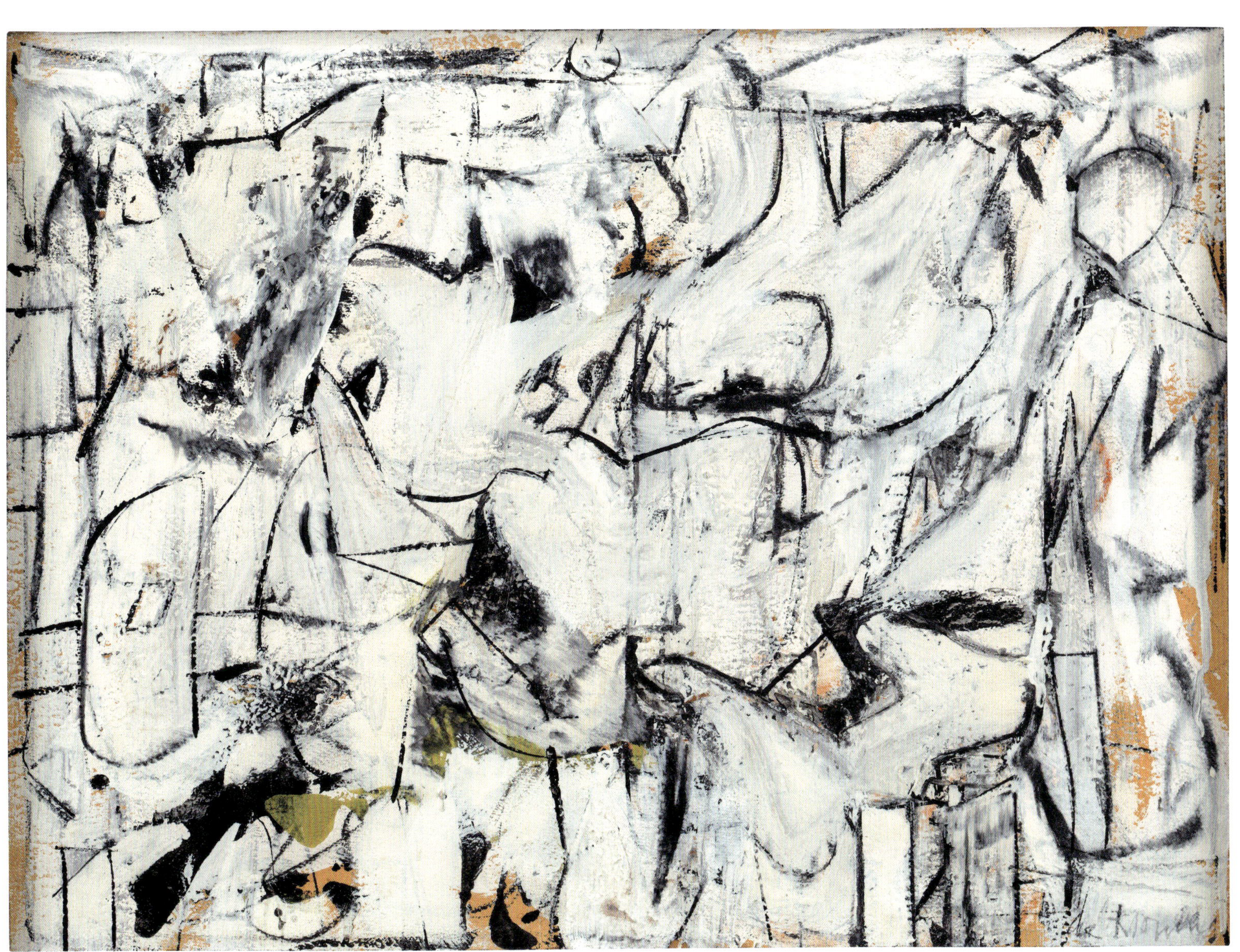

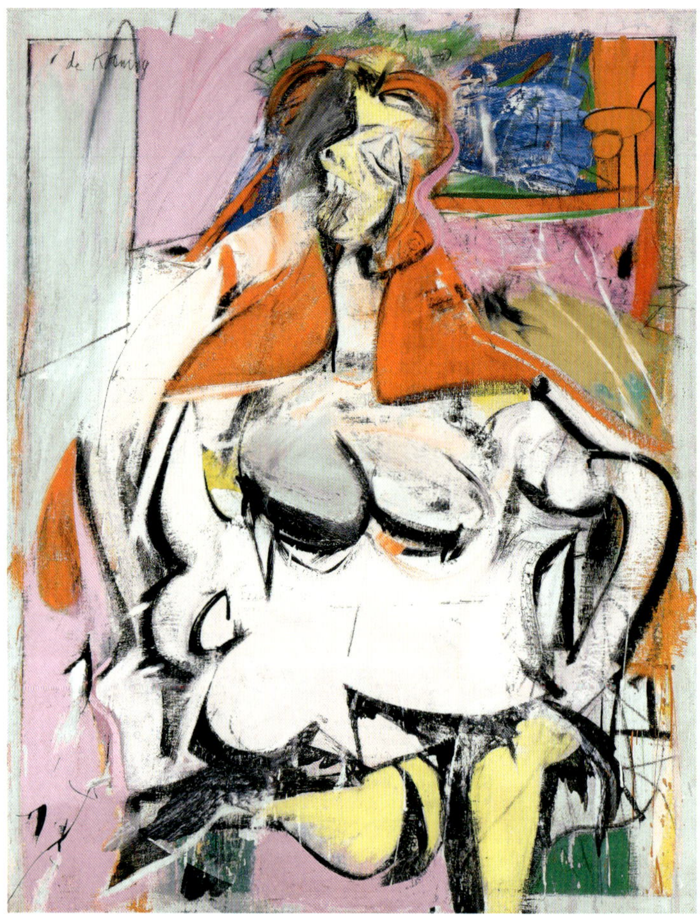

Fig. 24 Willem de Kooning, *Woman*, 1949, oil, enamel, and charcoal on canvas, 60 × 47⅞ in. (152.4 × 121.6 cm). Private Collection.

'abstract' painter," his putting the adjective in quotation marks concedes that a canvas like this can only be called abstract because it cannot be said to be representational.[4] Neither one nor the other but both, it is better described as a hybrid composition; and what follows will be concerned with the place of *Town Square* among de Kooning's hybrid canvases of 1948–49.

The hybridity and modest size of these works recall those painted by Pablo Picasso and Georges Braque in their four-year transformation of Cubism from the rudimentary abstraction of 1908 to its high Analytical style of 1911–12, before inventing collage. Moreover, some of the methods and some details of the appearance of de Kooning's paintings bear comparison with Analytical Cubist canvases of the latter half of that time span, sharing with them qualities of investigative care and patient thoughtfulness in the shaping, placing, and spacing of forms, guided by the articulation of their drawing.

De Kooning's lengthy negotiation with Cubism is a larger subject than can be explored here in the depth it requires. For present purposes, though, we do need to know that in the 1930s he had followed the lead of his elders in adopting a flat, simplified, abstract style ultimately grounded in Cubist collage and based on Picasso's then-recent work; and he clung to vestiges of that style into the first half of the following decade even while enriching it in a painterly, expressive manner. While critics have mainly, and correctly, seen an indebtedness to Picasso in de Kooning's more expressive, figurative works, he himself stressed the importance of a very different quality: in 1951, he would say, "Of all movements I like Cubism most. It had that wonderful unsure atmosphere of reflection—

a poetic frame where something could be possible, where an artist could practice his intuition."[5] Integral to what de Kooning achieved in the half decade preceding that statement is that he returned the methods of collage to their origins in Analytical Cubism and found new direction there. And it can hardly be coincidental that in the autumn of 1946, the Museum of Modern Art published Alfred H. Barr Jr.'s *Picasso: Fifty Years of His Art*, with its compelling set of illustrations of Analytical Cubist paintings—in black and white, of course.[6]

To look at *Town Square* and particularly at the *background* of a Picasso of 1910 (fig. 25), while ignoring the very different vocabulary of the drawn elements (itself, soon to be influential upon de Kooning's canvases), is to see in both paintings a wonderful, unsure atmosphere of reflection: compositions of more or less independent planes, depicting parts of not easily identified objects, set flatly in parallel to the picture plane; shading relegated to the boundaries of these planes; and a minimal amount of an illusion of space separating their own flatness from the literal flatness of the surface itself.[7] Whereas the planes in the Cubist paintings resemble the facing surfaces of solid, boxlike volumes, many folded flat, those in de Kooning's are decal-thin and layered. In either case, though, how the illusion of space is calibrated depends upon how firmly or not the artist drew the edges of the planes, edges that separate one plane from another adjacent to or overlapping it, or from an adjacent area of space; and on the number and density of planes in a composition—interrelated factors, as we shall see.

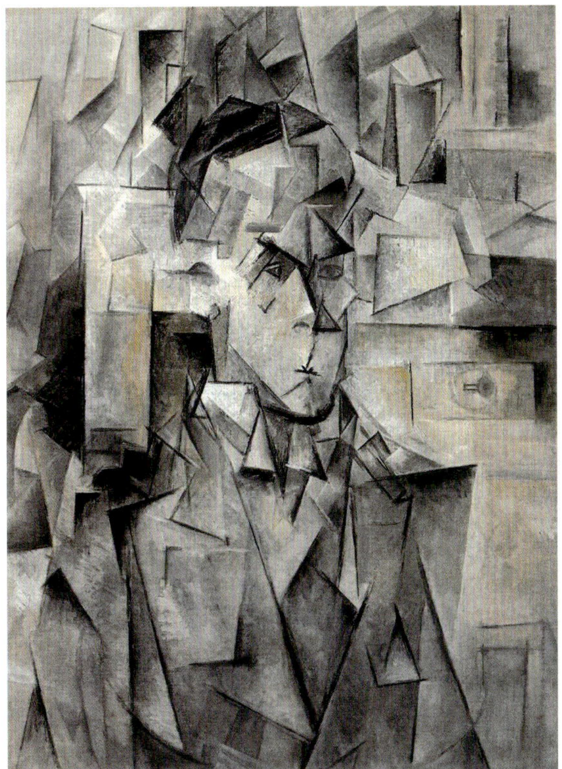

Fig. 25 Pablo Picasso, *Portrait of Wilhelm Uhde*, 1910, oil on canvas, 31⅞ × 23⅝ in. (81 × 60 cm). Private Collection.

When de Kooning went to teach at Black Mountain College in North Carolina in June 1948 after the opening of his first solo exhibition, at the Charles Egan Gallery, New York, "he spent the entire summer on one small painting," Elaine de Kooning remembered.[8] However, that is only part of the story because, she acknowledged, "he began to fill [his North Carolina studio] with pastels, working feverishly on one after the other for a couple of weeks until the walls were covered with them."[9] That was how he worked in his New York studio as well. It is not to be doubted that *Town Square* itself was the result of a similar process of feverish experimentation and gradual honing of options to produce the completed work.

As de Kooning's friend the critic Thomas B. Hess explained: "He will do drawings on transparent tracing paper, scatter them one on top of the other, study the composite drawing that appears on top, make a drawing from this, reverse it, tear it in half, and put it on top of still another drawing."[10] Describing a similar canvas to *Town Square*, one of de Kooning's former Black Mountain students observed, "He made a drawing of it, to work on parts where he felt there was a problem. He worked on that picture carefully. 'Maybe I could throw a line here,' he would say. He would erase parts, redraw it. In other words, he *did* it like Ingres. It was not throwing his guts on the wall."[11] In other words, de Kooning's methods could not be further from what the critic Harold Rosenberg called "action painting,"[12] and very precise drawing was critical to how he made these works. In fact, how he made drawing an agent of design and composition as much as of depiction is perhaps the most useful way of understanding their development in this great period.

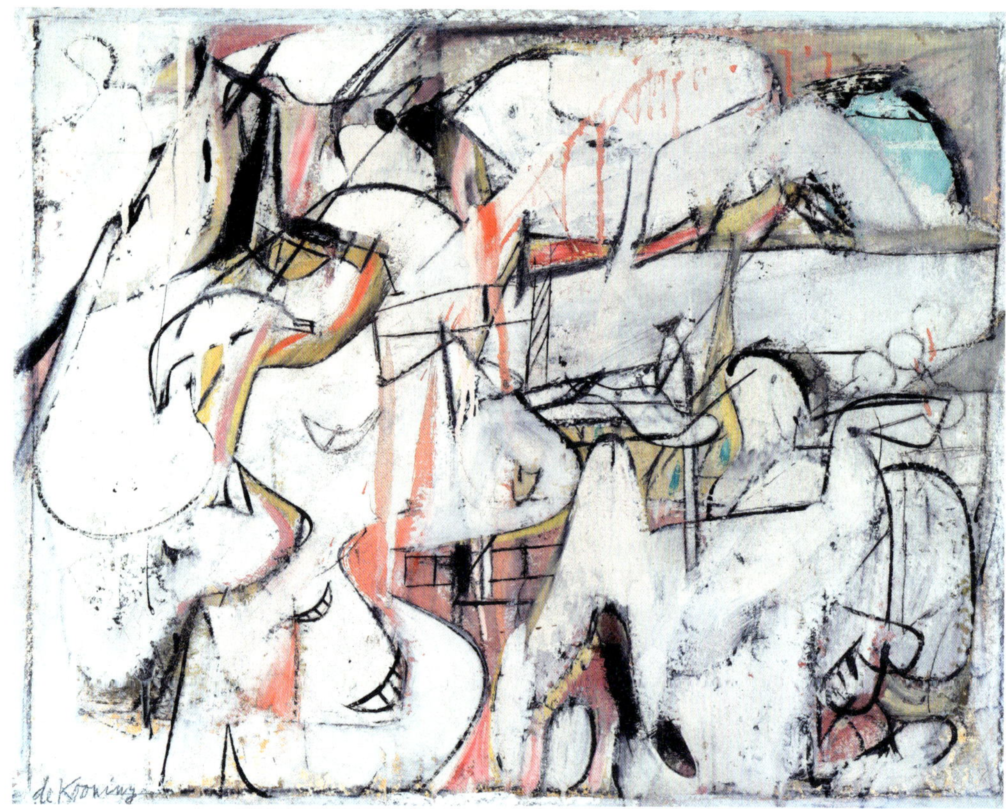

Fig. 26 Willem de Kooning, *Mailbox*, 1948, oil, enamel, and charcoal on paper on composition board, 23⅛ × 30 in. (58.7 × 76.2 cm). Private Collection.

We have in-process photographs of early stages of a small number of de Kooning's 1949 canvases—unfortunately, not of *Town Square*—showing instances where he developed a composition with detailed, methodical drawing, then buried it beneath the surface while recapitulating it there in a revised form to complete the painting.[13] If there is drawing of this sort beneath the surface of *Town Square* and similar canvases, its recapitulation upon the surface is much freer, more obviously improvised.[14] That is to say, while such canvases are far too carefully composed to be thought examples of "action painting," they are patently *performed*. As de Kooning said of Cubist canvases, they are places "where an artist could practice his intuition."[15]

Doing so, de Kooning found himself engaged in the art of adjustment. The means he employed in this task were, as noted earlier, how firmly he drew the edges of the planes, and the number and density of them he used in a painting. Both of these challenges, each a matter of surface composition, were affected by—and influenced—how de Kooning managed the planes so that they appeared to be layered.

Beginning in 1945, relative density of composition is perhaps the most conspicuous factor of change in de Kooning's art. By and large, he then began to move, sometimes simultaneously but more often sequentially, between disposing his planar shapes to greater and lesser degrees of density: making a group of more crowded canvases, then a group of less crowded, usually somewhat larger ones, and so on.[16] Hence, densely packed works of 1948–49 followed the more open ones of 1947–48 that composed the majority shown in de Kooning's first solo exhibition. Making one of the paintings in that exhibition, *Mailbox* (1948, fig. 26), he disposed the larger forms so that they all lie more or less in plane, forming the proximate layer of the depicted incident; have open spaces around them that reveal a more or less continuous drawn layer beneath them; and rest on a ground plane beneath that. There is some overlapping of these layers, but not sufficiently so as to negate the effect of foreground and background—and other paintings in the exhibition convey that effect more vividly.[17]

Painting by layering, which we see in Pollock's as well as de Kooning's work of these years, goes back to Paul Cézanne's interest in the appearance of strata in rock faces.[18] It survived in the layering of early Cubist collages before they became the flat, jigsaw-like unities—their space squeezed out of them—that shaped the airless abstractions de Kooning inherited in the 1930s. Since the mid-1940s, he had been prizing open the space in his paintings, and the works in his first solo exhibition were the result. That achieved, he then brought together and compressed not only the elements of composition but, in doing so, also the layers of stratified depth.

It is clear that de Kooning painted *Town Square* in layers, but he does not let the painting read as layers; the foreground-background effect of *Mailbox* has gone. He drew the black lines at varying speeds and densities to orchestrate movement within, around, and between the forms they describe. And he wiped and smeared areas of paint to break boundaries of forms, joining solid to solid, space to space, and space to solid. He will make an individual plane overlap another as often—or as well—as rest upon another, but there are so many places where it is uncertain whether a plane is a solid or a space. They so infiltrate one another, even as they jostle with and deform one another, that the only certainty is awareness of the ground layer as having been brought forward flat on the surface. There is nothing imaginable behind or around the frontal array of such a painting except its literal support.

Because de Kooning made *Town Square* on a rough and possibly roughened ground, his brush skipped in numerous places as he painted the black lines and areas of shading.[19] The effect, reminiscent of frottage, pits the surface with small fragments of broken lines and out-of-focus patches of shading that prevent the dark tones from unduly receding. And to further influence the perception of space, de Kooning calibrated the relative brightness of the cool white paint by varying the size and density of the areas it fills: smaller white areas enclosed by black, unless toned down, tend to seem brighter and nearer than larger ones. And he complicated these effects by warming the white paint in places by the presence of sudden glimpses of the orange-ochre ground, and by delicate warm tints produced by the brush pulling up paint from the ground or by whites thinned to function as glazes.[20] All of this brings the ground layer up to join in a dynamic play between the medium applied and the surface to which it is applied, and what is subsequently applied on that.[21] The result is, within a mere few hundred square inches, a master class in miniature on the practice of intuition in drawing and spreading paint.

To compare *Town Square* with the more or less contemporaneous *Night Square* (ca. 1949, fig. 27) is to see that the filigree drawing of the "black" painting is even more a performance than that of the "white" one. (That is generally true of this period's canvases, of which most of those in full color seem the least performed.) It is not the only difference: writing in 1960, Harriet Janis and Rudi Blesh distinguished these two kinds of paintings through the language of photography, calling them, respectively, "positives" and "negatives." Additionally, they observed, "To look rapidly back and forth at these two pictures creates an effect like that of a dark landscape upon which a searchlight flashed on and off."[22] This comparison nicely responds to de Kooning's often-quoted remark about his painting what he called a

Fig. 27 Willem de Kooning, *Night Square*, ca. 1949, enamel on cardboard on composition board, 29¾ × 39¾ in. (75.6 × 101 cm). Private Collection of David Geffen, Los Angeles.

"slipping glimpse" or "frozen glimpse."[23] And this pair of paintings well illustrates his most often-quoted description of such works: "It's like crossing the street. You want to cross the street fast—so you run across"; "I have a little glimpse of something. I want to give somebody else something of that glimpse"; "Content is a glimpse of something, an encounter like a flash."[24]

The upper-left corner of *Night Square* depicts what appears to be the edge of a square with a doorway in an adjacent line of buildings. *Town Square* does not offer anything similar, although the piled-up rectangular forms down the left margin may be thought to be architectural, implying a down-view on an urban square. However, we do know that de Kooning frequently rotated his canvases as he worked. This is evidenced by various technical devices he employed—for example, using the direction of drips of paint as lines of drawing, and creating interactions between areas of fresh, fluid paint moved onto dry or drying paint to produce seemingly transient effects; and these may be seen in *Town Square*.[25]

Additionally, though, we may intuit that canvases have been rotated in order to unsettle compositions that were becoming too stable: slipping glimpses occur when you are taken off guard; equilibrium is not desirable. Seen upside down, in the direction at which it may well have been begun, the incident in *Town Square* slides in diagonally beside a windowed building at the left, as it does in *Night Square*, and is disposed across a register line just short of what becomes the bottom of the canvas, on which stand one and probably more prominent figures, with more behind, some with strips of shadow giving them depth. Seen in its completed orientation, these dark zones disengage and flatten to the surface, serving no longer illusion but the interplay of lights and darks within a composition that is now at once suspended from that register line and thrusts diagonally up and across from the bottom-left corner. The activity is arrested by details that demand identification—eyes and orifices; the window or door shapes; perhaps a ladder now at the left; the puzzling, shield-like element beside it—but identification is as often thwarted as satisfied. "Even abstract shapes must have a likeness," de Kooning insisted.[26] A work like *Town Square* encourages curiosity about what its shapes seem to be as a means of addressing and engaging us—not to make us zealots of explanation, but in order to encourage our enjoyment of uncertainty.

NOTES

1 The account of de Kooning's 1948–49 development that follows is indebted to that in John Elderfield, ed., *De Kooning: A Retrospective* (New York: Museum of Modern Art, 2011), specifically to parts of my introduction (9–46); my chapter on the years 1946–48 (120–87), Lauren Mahony's on 1948–50 (188–237), and, within these two chapters, the chronologies by Delphine Huisinga and "Methods and Materials" analyses by Susan F. Lake and Jim Coddington. Works by de Kooning discussed but not reproduced in the present text may be found illustrated there, where events mentioned here in passing are more fully described. Further citations of this volume give only the name of the appropriate author. I am, as always on this subject, indebted to Amy Schichtel, executive director of the Willem de Kooning Foundation, and her colleagues for access to the foundation's archives and for their advice. And for her editorial review, I am grateful to Jeanne Collins.

2 *Town Square* is one of the three smallest works from these years, almost identical in size to the related "white" pictures, *Zot* and *Attic Study*. Leaving aside de Kooning's three large *Woman* paintings made in 1948–50, there are five or six with the larger dimension of about four feet or a little more (three of them in de Kooning's first solo exhibition, in 1948, perhaps because he felt the need to include some larger works) and another four with the larger dimension of three feet or more; in contrast, fourteen works measure less than twenty-four by thirty-six inches. As noted below, these are very much the typical sizes of Analytical Cubist canvases. Their varying sizes broadly correspond to the relative density of these works, a subject also discussed below.

3 *Woman* (1948) was initially conceived as a black-and-white abstraction to which anatomical elements were subsequently added. See Lake, in Elderfield, *De Kooning: A Retrospective*, 205; the three large and one smaller *Woman* paintings of 1948–50 are discussed by Mahony, in Elderfield, *De Kooning: A Retrospective*, 197–204.

4 See Elderfield, *De Kooning: A Retrospective*, 167.

5 Willem de Kooning, "What Abstract Art Means to Me," *Bulletin of the Museum of Modern Art* 18, no. 3 (Spring 1951): 7; reprinted in Thomas B. Hess, *Willem de Kooning* (New York: Museum of Modern Art, 1968), and elsewhere. The most extended discussion of de Kooning's (and Pollock's) indebtedness to Picasso appears in Michael

Fitzgerald, *Picasso and American Art* (New York: Whitney Museum of American Art, 2006), 169–237, a fine account although, concentrating on expressive works, it does not address Analytical Cubism.

6 Details of the few such works by Picasso that de Kooning could actually have seen may be found in Julia May Boddewyn's remarkable chronology in Fitzgerald, *Picasso and American Art*, 328–83.

7 The classic account of this means of composition is that in Clement Greenberg, "Collage," *Art and Culture* (Boston: Beacon Press, 1961), 71–72.

8 Elaine de Kooning, Oral history interview by Phyllis Tuchman, August 27, 1981, Archives of American Art, Smithsonian Institution, Washington, DC. See Mahony, in Elderfield, *De Kooning: A Retrospective*, 195.

9 Elaine de Kooning, "De Kooning Memories," *Vogue*, December 1983, 394, as quoted by Mahony, in Elderfield, *De Kooning: A Retrospective*, 195.

10 Hess, *Willem de Kooning*, 47. See Mahony, in Elderfield, *De Kooning: A Retrospective*, 195.

11 Gus Falk, quoted in Mark Stevens and Annalyn Swan, *De Kooning: An American Master* (New York: Knopf, 2004), 294. See Mahony, in Elderfield, *De Kooning: A Retrospective*, 211.

12 Harold Rosenberg, "The American Action Painters," *Art News* 51, no. 8 (December 1952): 22, 49.

13 See the examples illustrated by Mahony, in Elderfield, *De Kooning: A Retrospective*, 211, 214, which show the artist adjusting the drawing at different stages of a work's completion and making clear that de Kooning used drawings of individual motifs on more than a single canvas; on which see also note 25, below.

14 In later paintings, of 1949–50, notably *Attic* and the appropriately titled *Excavation*, it is as if de Kooning entirely excavated the underdrawing, their surfaces becoming detailed and methodical, the planes cut into numerous smaller, now more geometric segments, compacted in crystalline effects. De Kooning's fluid drawing-in-paint of *Town Square* and similar works was probably made with a liner brush, on which see Paul Cummings as quoted by Mahony, in Elderfield, *De Kooning: A Retrospective*, 232–34.

15 For de Kooning's idea of himself as a "performer," not an "action painter," see Elderfield, *De Kooning: A Retrospective*, 18.

16 Space prohibits elaborating these sequences here, but they become evident by simply following the illustrations in *De Kooning: A Retrospective*, 120–237.

17 This exhibition contained paintings of varying density, size, and coloration. See Elderfield, *De Kooning: A Retrospective*, 163–74.

18 I discuss this subject in "Excavations," in my *Cézanne: The Rock and Quarry Paintings* (Princeton, NJ: Princeton University Art Museum, 2020), 1–39; and its implications for Pollock (and continuing in the work of Brice Marden) in my "Marden in Three Parts," in *Brice Marden: It reminds me of something, and I don't know what it is* (New York: Gagosian, 2020), 15–35, which informed the discussion here on layering in Pollock and de Kooning.

19 On de Kooning's additions of sand, powdered glass, charcoal, and significant quantities of plaster of Paris into the off-white paint of *Woman* (1948), see Lake, in Elderfield, *De Kooning: A Retrospective*, 205–7. Owing to the coronavirus lockdown, it was not possible to examine *Town Square* to determine whether de Kooning mixed additives to its paint or whether its coarse surface is solely the result of the rough paper on which he painted it. However, Nicholas Dorman, Jane Lang Davis Chief Conservator of Paintings at the Seattle Art Museum, did determine that the broken lines were the result of the skipping of the brush over the rough texture of the support and that, while there may be some charcoal drawing in the work, it was not a primary means of creating the lines, as it was in *Woman* and, particularly, in the 1946 hybrid compositions *Fire Island* and *Special Delivery* (see Elderfield, *De Kooning: A Retrospective*, 138). The staccato black paint lines in *Town Square* resemble the beading of lines produced when de Kooning used slick black enamel on drier white paint, or vice versa, as in *Painting* (1948). See Coddington, in Elderfield, *De Kooning: A Retrospective*, 175–77). It is clear that de Kooning experimented widely to produce such effects.

20 The commentaries by both Coddington and Lake cited in the preceding note refer to de Kooning adding warmer colors to his white paint.

21 I paraphrase here a 1989 statement by Brice Marden on Pollock's layering. See Elderfield, "Marden in Three Parts," 22.

22 Harriet Janis and Rudi Blesh, *De Kooning* (New York: Grove Press, 1960), 27, 29–30, comparing *Town Square* with *Painting* (1948), which, in fact, seems more a still life than a townscape. Quoted by Mahony, in Elderfield, *De Kooning: A Retrospective*, 209.

23 While these terms do seem very appropriate to the works under discussion here, de Kooning appears to have first used them in the 1959–63 period. The examples given here are recorded in Elderfield, *De Kooning: A Retrospective*, 20, 157, 183.

24 "Content is a Glimpse," *Location 1*, no. 1 (Spring 1963): 47. Originally an interview with David Sylvester, March 1960.

25 De Kooning's most striking contemporaneous example of direction reversal was *Secretary* and *Night* (both 1948), the composition of one traced onto the other, reversed, and painted very differently. See Elderfield, *De Kooning: A Retrospective*, 157–62.

26 Quoted by Hess, *Willem de Kooning*, 47.

CLYFFORD STILL
PH-338
1949

DAVID ANFAM

Still makes the rest of us look academic.
—Jackson Pollock

The opening of Clyfford Still's namesake museum in November 2011 in Denver meant that the reclusive figure—whom a prescient modern art historian had described at the turn of the millennium as "the great unseen"—swung into view as never before.[1] Hitherto, approximately ninety-five percent of Still's corpus had lingered more or less out of sight and unknown. What had remained accessible in public collections and was at least known in private ones now turned into magnificent pendants, especially the grand donations Still granted three US museums,[2] to a larger whole. In short, an epic legacy risen from the past, redivivus, for posterity. Its long-term impact looms large enough for Abstract Expressionism's conventional histories to need revising. Having retained almost everything he made during a sixty-year career, Still thus returned to the limelight in the twenty-first century's second decade as if from beyond the grave.

The artist's work in the Lang Collection, PH-338 (1949, plate 3), sports an outstanding pedigree: it was the sole Still owned by Ben Heller. From the early 1950s onward, Heller amassed probably "the best private collection of Abstract Expressionist painting that ever existed."[3] The provenance also numbers the doyenne of Abstract Expressionism's dealers, Betty Parsons. The painting went on display at Parsons's New York gallery in the artist's penultimate solo show there in the spring of 1950, from which it traveled directly to another at San Francisco's Metart Galleries, arranged by students in honor of Still's resignation from the California School of Fine Arts. Lastly, PH-338 was among the four Stills in the Museum of Modern Art's landmark exhibition *The New American Painting*, which toured to eight European countries in 1958–59.[4] From start to finish, everything about PH-338 is top drawer—even its date, which found Still at the fecund peak of his powers while living and teaching in San Francisco from 1946 to 1950. Indeed, his activities there played a major role in establishing a "San Francisco School of Abstract Expressionism."[5] A short summary about Still's titles completes the basic facts concerning PH-338.

In general, Still placed scant importance on nomenclature, preferring instead to let the art stand by itself.

Plate 3 Clyfford Still, PH-338 [previously known as *1949-No. 2*], 1949, oil on canvas, 91½ × 68¾ in. (232.5 × 174.5 cm). Seattle Art Museum, Gift of the Friday Foundation in honor of Richard E. Lang and Jane Lang Davis, 2020.14.17.

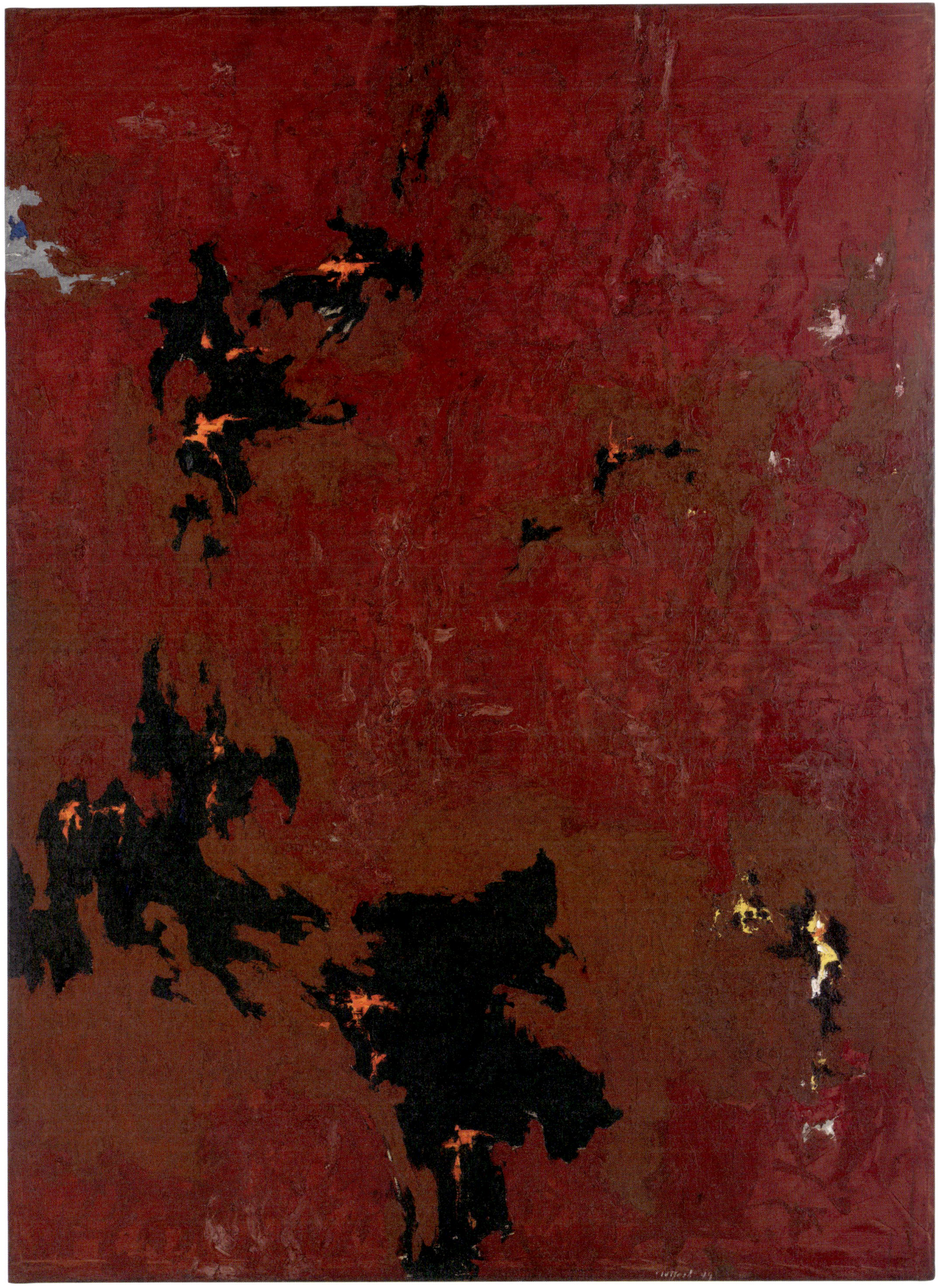

Fig. 28 Clyfford Still, PH-385, 1949, oil on canvas, 105½ × 81 in. (268 × 205.7 cm). Clyfford Still Museum, Denver, Colorado, 1.2011.682.

Nevertheless, some early canvases bore sparse titles for public identification (for example, the now-lost *A Funeral, North Dakota*, 1934)[6] and the fourteen listed in the brochure accompanying his New York solo debut at Peggy Guggenheim's Art of This Century gallery in 1946. They almost surely secreted an esoteric symbolism relating to ancient Greek myths about cyclical fate and renewal.[7] By the following March, though, the situation became unequivocal. In advance of his initial show with Parsons, Still wrote to her that "the pictures will be without titles—only identified by numbers."[8] Subsequently, he kept these numerical designations after a fashion: PH-338 was once known as *1949-No. 2*. Later, the alphanumeric system ceased when Still, aided by his family, began compiling "documentation books" for his oeuvre. Therein, each entry was assigned a "PH-" or similar label followed by a number (though the sequencing follows no particular total order), said abbreviations simply standing for "ph[otographic]" record, for example.[9] The painting now known as PH-338 has always spoken louder than whatever titular mantle it has carried anyway. Only the former "No. 2" tag has a special import insofar as it connotes the existence of a "replica," now held at the Clyfford Still Museum: PH-385, the erstwhile "1949-No. 1" (fig. 28).[10] These replicas or multiple versions point, perhaps unexpectedly, to the heart of Still's practice.

At face value, replicas suggest inauthenticity, reproduction by rote à la Andy Warhol. Yet for Still they had the opposite meaning. He explained:

> Making additional versions is an act I consider necessary when I believe the importance of the idea or breakthrough merits survival on more than one stretch of canvas. . . . Although the few replicas I make are usually close to or extensions to the original, each has its special and particular life and is not intended to be just a copy. The present work . . . was closer to my original concept than the first painting, which bore the ambivalences of struggle.[11]

Although the piece in question was not PH-338, Still's thinking applies to it and the prior replica, PH-385. True, PH-385 is slightly larger (105½ × 81 in.). Nevertheless, both possess their own strengths and differences, two firsts among equals. If anything, the Lang canvas may have a tighter "grip" about it because the various elements look a tad more compacted, while the pervasive tonality is subliminally darker. Setting aside comparisons, a key point lurks in Still's mentioning "concept." Why? The answer involves a trail leading deep into PH-338's background, the historical sources and sentiments whence it ultimately sprung.[12]

Versed in ancient Greek philosophy since his youthful days studying for a master's degree and teaching at Washington State College, Pullman, during the second half of the 1930s, Still knew his Plato (among many another scholarly forebear, from Aristotle to John Ruskin to Friedrich Nietzsche). No specialist knowledge is required to grasp that for Plato, the higher realm of ideas supported phenomenal reality itself. In fact, the material world incarnated the Platonic Idea—the physical replica to the imagination's metaphysical vistas.[13] Paralleling this logic, Still saw his individual works as the "image of an idea."[14] Here, some commentary helps.

Ideas are limitless and therefore able to generate multiple physical manifestations. A diametric opposite to mere "copies," Still's replicas exploit the mind's inherent dynamism, its ability to roam unhindered through time and space. His working process mirrored this freedom. Rather than follow a linear trajectory, Still roved back and forth across his own output, taking earlier imagery to develop its potential into new territory.[15] Consequently, PH-338 echoes numerous traits and forms from years beforehand, but recast to the stage where they no longer know themselves. Before enumerating them, it is worthwhile noting that Still couched this dialectical progress in allegory and metaphor:

> It was as a journey that one must make, walking straight and alone. . . . Until one had crossed the darkened and wasted valleys and come at last into clear air and could stand on a high and limitless plain. Imagination, no longer fettered by the laws of fear, became as one with Vision. And the Act, intrinsic and absolute, was its meaning, and the bearer of its passion.[16]

First, Still's "journey" translates his modus operandi into similes—note the initial "as . . ." signaling the narrative to be an analogy, not a literal description.[17] This puts a brake on the pedestrian misreading of Still's pictorial mechanics as nothing but landscape in disguise—Grand

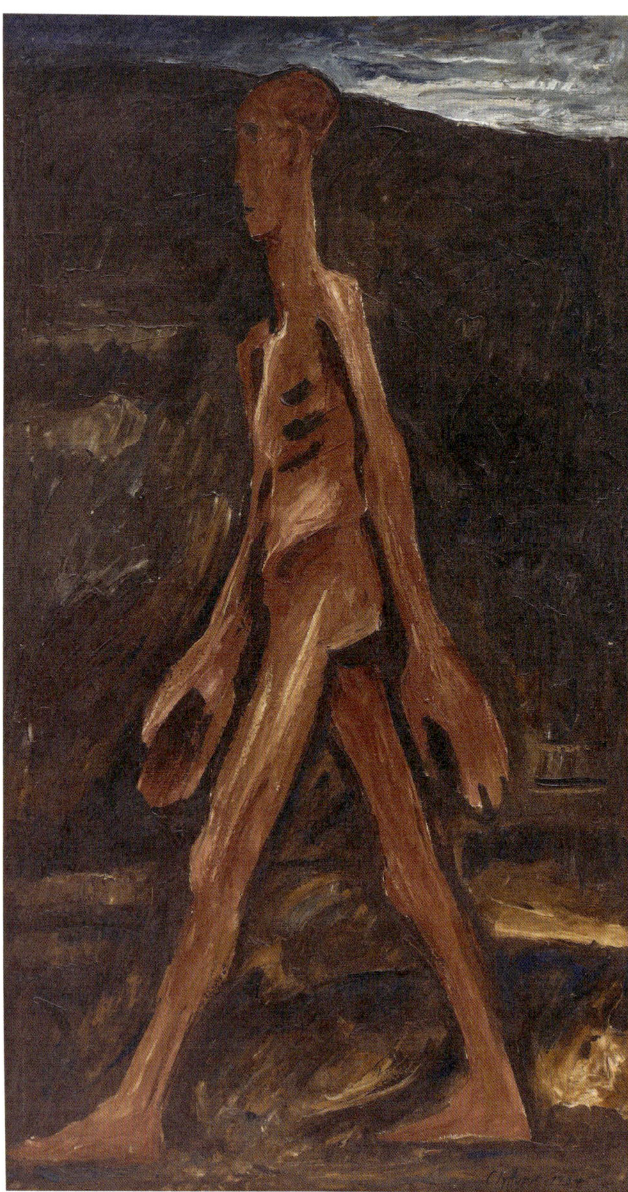

Fig. 29 Clyfford Still, PH-323, 1934, oil on canvas, 58⅞ × 32¾ in. (149.54 × 83.19 cm). San Francisco Museum of Modern Art, Gift of the artist, 75.14.

Canyons seen, as it were, through reductive lenses, so that they become non-objective schemata.[18] On the contrary, Still's pictorial heights and depths, the rugged surfaces and sudden luminous outbursts, offer vistas of the imaginative eye rather than an observational gaze (keenly recorded though his initial realist scenes were). Second, the literary critic Dennis Donoghue praises metaphor's transformative powers on the grounds that it permits the greatest freedom in the use of rhetoric because it exempts language from the local duties of reference and denotation.[19] Shift "language" from text to visuality, and this displacement neatly describes how Still's morphologies function—besides serving to rationalize his recurrent stress on "freedom." And if Still's aforementioned quest has more than a hint of the Puritan John Bunyan's allegory *The Pilgrim's Progress* (1678), then it fits his insistence that art's deepest purpose is ethical.[20] As he famously warned, "Let no man under-value the implications of this work or its power for life;—or for death, if it is misused."[21] Hyperbole? Yes and no. Yes, if taken literally. No, if understood metaphorically—for art can liberate the mind from things temporal and thus raise it above intellectual soul murder.[22] So what unites everything in Still's scheme? Ideas. (Notice his capitalization of "Imagination," "Vision" and "Act," thereby rendering these abstract generalities into full-fledged nouns native to the psyche.[23]) In turn, his aim to make ideas concrete in PH-338 bears witness to an old adage stated by the novelist Victor Hugo: "Stronger than all the armies is an idea whose time has come."[24] Finally, PH-338 marks the climax of a biographical and imaginative voyage reaching back some three decades. Encapsulating it sheds fresh light on this painting.

Still first turned to art around 1919–20. His youthful experiences in Canada farming Alberta's high prairies prompted a perpetual love-hate relationship to nature. On the one hand, the stone-strewn unbroken soil, from which a living had to be "ripped," was "meager," the labor involved in cultivating it harsh in the extreme (he remembered times when his arms were "bloody to the elbow shocking wheat") and the climate, with its summertime droughts and frigid winters, equally daunting.[25] On the other hand, he never forgot nature's sublimity, "the awful bigness, the drama of the land, the men and the machines."[26] Above all, the encompassing horizontality caused the vertical to reign

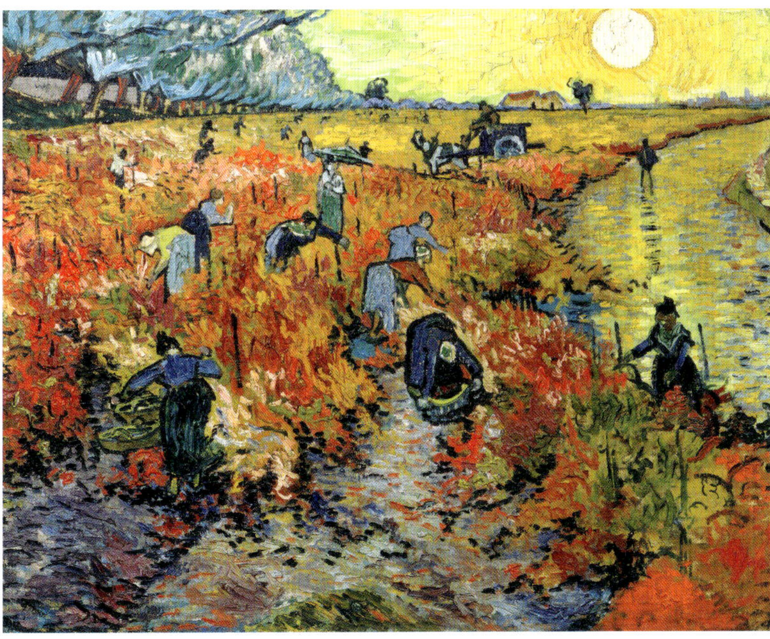

Fig. 30 Vincent van Gogh, *Red Vineyard at Arles (Montmajour)*, November 1888, oil on canvas, 28¾ × 35¹³⁄₁₆ in. (73 × 91 cm). The Pushkin State Museum of Fine Arts.

as a supreme signifier of vitality for Still. He ruminated on this formative period: "Mostly the paintings were records of air and light. Yet always and inevitably with the rising forms of the vertical necessity of life dominating the horizon. For in such a land a man must stand upright, if he would live."[27]

An oil on canvas from 1934 neatly combines most of the themes discussed so far: PH-323 (fig. 29) depicts a striding figure in a darkened valley sparked with a distant glint of light on high.[28] The wayfarer's perpendicular represents a lifeline pitted against the tenebrous expanse surrounding it. His nakedness has an Adamic cast,[29] while the setting hints at the biblical "valley of the shadow of death."[30] Already Still has visualized the journey that he would later narrate in 1959—instancing a canny ability to second-guess himself. Still's ensuing artistic drive was relentless and rapid. Other features in PH-323 that anticipate it include the earth-toned palette ranging from a bright orange-tan (the hellfire at lower right) to deepest umber shadows, relieved by the lone uppermost sky blue, as well as the palette knife's rough impasto. These structural and chromatic factors endured, except that they grew concentrated to the utmost.

Between 1934 and 1949, Still methodically stripped his verticals and their ambient pictorial masses so that, in his estimate, "by 1941, space and the figure in my canvases had been resolved into a total psychic entity."[31] He also reduced depictive volume to planar silhouettes before simultaneously jamming these shards together and cutting them short at the pictures' edges. Landscape was never the innermost preoccupation. Instead, it was an existential impulse—no matter how pared to the slightest traces—to survive against hostile forces. As Mark Rothko quoted Still in 1946, the paintings were "of the Earth, the Damned, and of the Recreated."[32] Of course, this was their spirit, not their actual semblance. At stake is a surrogate theology reminiscent of Vincent van Gogh's aesthetic credo, which pitted earthly misery against redemption through art. Likewise, the Dutch painter's coruscating radiance and aggressive tactility also surely set an example to be fiercely rewrought (fig. 30).[33] By the decade's end, Still attained the energy labyrinth that is both PH-338 and uniquely his invention.

PH-338's encrusted surface, its reflectivity ranging from a charred matte finish to a visceral gloss, justifies Still's claim the following year to have reached "new hypotheses in experience or sensibility . . . explosive forces."[34] The vertical has been laid waste by the planar masses to the degree that figure/ground demarcations no longer occur. Space seems at once imploded and projected beyond the composition's bounds. Tiny yet intense rifts suggest light trapped within the engulfing, ruddy maelstrom. Excess is everywhere, a violent romantic dramaturgy pushed to a modern point of no return such that the pigment appears to be realizing itself. No wonder Still described these effects as "swords slipped through the belly . . . life and death merging in fearful union."[35] The painting's presence confronts us as much as we behold its uncanny otherness. Rather than scan, let alone dismantle, this smoldering incandescence—which has few Abstract Expressionist equals, as attested by even Jackson Pollock in the epigraph above—the eye grapples with its dense terribilita. In the last analysis, PH-338 embodies the image of an exceedingly powerful idea-complex.

NOTES

Epigraph Jackson Pollock, quoted in Sam Hunter, *Masters of the Fifties: American Abstract Painting from Pollock to Stella* (New York: Marisa del Re Gallery, 1985), n.p.

1 John Golding, *Paths to the Absolute: Mondrian, Malevich, Kandinsky, Pollock, Newman, Rothko and Still* (London: Thames and Hudson, 2000), 232. Golding, my postgraduate mentor, ranked among Still's foremost admirers outside the United States.

2 The Albright-Knox Art Gallery, Buffalo; the San Francisco Museum of Modern Art; and the Metropolitan Museum of Art, New York.

3 Roberta Smith, "Ben Heller, 93, Collector and Dealer Who Embraced Abstract Art Early, Dies," *New York Times*, May 6, 2019. Ironically, Still despised Heller, likely because he would have regarded the collector's ambitions a threat to the priority of the art itself.

4 At the time, Still himself disapproved of his work being shown in the public domain and remained even less favorably disposed toward the Museum of Modern Art.

5 Susan Landauer, *The San Francisco School of Abstract Expressionism* (Berkeley: University of California Press, 1996).

6 The title proffers two interesting technical clues, since it presumably references Gustave Courbet's *A Burial at Ornans* (1849–50, Musée d'Orsay). First, the nod suggests that Still would have known Courbet's use of the palette knife, an implement that Still, too, almost always used. Second, the canvas was six feet high and approximately eight feet wide, indicating that Still was already adopting quite large dimensions, in the spirit of Courbet's monumentality.

7 David Anfam, "'Of the Earth, the Damned, and of the Recreated': Aspects of Clyfford Still's Earlier Work," *Burlington Magazine* 135 (April 1993): 260–69. A title in this show, *Siamese Cat and Daughters*—hitherto unattached to any known painting—may now be recognized as applicable to PH-355 (1945, Clyfford Still Museum, Denver). My thanks to Chiara Ianeselli for this suggestion. Still asserted that the titles derived from the gallery's staff.

8 Clyfford Still (March 3, 1947), quoted in David Anfam, "Clyfford Still" (PhD diss., vol. 1, Courtauld Institute of Art, 1984), 121.

9 Canvases and oils on paper were given "PH" numbers, pastels "PP" numbers, lithographs "PL," etc. The Still family's preference is not to italicize these assignations, further preventing their being read as quasi-titles.

10 The word "held" is employed advisedly, since the collection belongs to the City of Denver, not the artist's museum per se.

11 Clyfford Still (July 30, 1972), statement to the Hirshhorn Museum and Sculpture Garden, Washington, DC. Unless otherwise indicated, all further documents by Still are held at the Clyfford Still Museum Archives (henceforth CSMA).

12 Still considered his entire oeuvre a totality. Hence, he moved to keep as much of it intact as possible by forming a *Gesamtkunstwerk* for the future.

13 These and various relevant tenets feature in Murray W. Bundy, *The Theory of Imagination in Classical and Medieval Thought* (Urbana: University of Illinois, 1927). Bundy was Still's tutor at Washington State College. Forty years on, Still remained mindful enough to invite him to the opening of his retrospective at the Metropolitan Museum of Art, New York, in 1979. In correspondence with the author in 1978, Bundy had clear memories of his onetime student—so the long-standing recognition was mutual.

14 Clyfford Still to Gordon Smith, January 1, 1959, in *Paintings by Clyfford Still* (Buffalo: Buffalo Fine Arts Academy, Albright Art Gallery, 1959), n.p.; cf. Bundy, *Theory of Imagination*, 53, discussing "the image of an idea."

15 This method may account for certain detractors' skepticism about the chronology.
16 Still to Smith (1959).
17 Still to Smith (1959): "Although the reference is in a different context and for another purpose, a *metaphor* is pertinent" (italics mine).
18 The most persuasive statement of this approach remains Robert Rosenblum, *Modern Painting and the Northern Romantic Tradition: Friedrich to Rothko* (New York: Harper and Row, 1975). Rosenblum compared a 1957 Still to the British Romantic painter James Ward's *Gordale Scar* (ca. 1812–14, Tate).
19 See Dennis Donoghue, *Metaphor* (Cambridge, MA: Harvard University Press, 2014). At Washington State College, Still also studied literary criticism.
20 Bunyan's tale is, of course, pure ethics figured as allegory. By no coincidence, Still also confessed to having "Puritan reflexes." Beware, though, of considering Still a Christian in any conventional sense. "Nietzschean" is a more accurate description of his mindset (and Nietzsche tellingly wagered that there was only one Christian—and He died on the cross).
21 Still to Smith (1959).
22 The contemporary associations of the term "soul murder" should not be confused with my sense of it, which refers to the Norwegian playwright Henrik Ibsen. In Ibsen's *John Gabriel Borkman* (1896), "soul murder" means destruction of the love of life.
23 The capitalizations also accord with Still's wider taste for old-fashioned literary diction (which he probably deemed more authentic than modern vulgarity).
24 A common translated paraphrase of a line from Hugo's essay *The History of a Crime: The Testimony of an Eye-Witness* (1877).
25 Clyfford Still, in conversation with Henry Hopkins, notes in Library files, San Francisco Museum of Modern Art, quoted in Dore Ashton, *The Life and Times of the New York School: A Cultural Awakening* (New York: Viking Press, 1973), 34.
26 Clyfford Still, in Thomas Albright, "Clyfford Still: 'Seeking the Vastness and Depth of a Beethoven Sonata or a Sophocles Drama,'" *Art News* 79 (September 1980): 159.
27 Still, statement (1972), CSMA.
28 The direction in which the man heads evokes both the arduousness involved (Christian cultures habitually read from left to right, whereas the traveler is taking a sinister—that is, leftward—path) and the American West (which stands, map-wise, to any reader's left).
29 On the typology of the American "new man"—very much a theme in Still's writings—see R. W. B. Lewis, *The American Adam: Innocence, Tragedy, and Tradition in the Nineteenth Century* (Chicago: University of Chicago Press, 1955).
30 Psalm 23:4.
31 Clyfford Still, quoted in Ti-Grace Sharpless, *Clyfford Still* (Philadelphia: Institute of Contemporary Art, University of Philadelphia, 1963), n.p.
32 Mark Rothko, *Clyfford Still: First Exhibition, Paintings* (New York: Art of This Century, 1946), n.p.
33 Still's familiarity with Van Gogh is beyond doubt. See David Anfam, "Still's Journey," in *Clyfford Still: The Artist's Museum*, by David Anfam and Dean Sobel (New York: Skira-Rizzoli, 2012), 92.
34 Clyfford Still to Betty Parsons, July 9, 1950, CSMA.
35 Clyfford Still, unpublished typescript associated with the 1950 Betty Parsons show, n.d., CSMA.

AD REINHARDT
PAINTING, 1950
1950

NORMAN L. KLEEBLATT

If a title doesn't mean anything and creates a misunderstanding, why put a title on a painting?
—Ad Reinhardt

From the mid-1950s until his untimely death in 1967, Ad Reinhardt focused on his legendary black paintings. A decidedly radical approach in his relentless pursuit of purifying art, they epitomized a so-called desire to move toward the "ultimate" or "end" of painting. Enigmatic and inscrutable, seemingly deadpan yet highly complex, the black pictures have come to define his oeuvre. In their optical, spatial, perceptual, and conceptual density, these are the works most closely associated with Reinhardt's historic achievement. On the one hand, they are iconic paintings of the postwar New York School. On the other, they stand apart visually and formally from the work of many of the best-known Abstract Expressionist painters. The black paintings are ultimately the culmination of Reinhardt's earlier geometric and organic abstraction, which were pivotal to the development of his thinking and theorizing. As with the evolution of the work of the non-objective artist Piet Mondrian—and to some extent like that of the Abstract Expressionist coterie of painters with whom Reinhardt associated—the development and distillation of Reinhardt's style mainly undergoes a progressive, high-modernist trajectory.

Reinhardt's *Painting, 1950* (1950, plate 4) is a clear and important conduit en route to the climactic black pictures. As discussed later in this essay, it is also one of the few among the artist's predominantly untitled canvases (sometimes also called "abstract paintings") that bear an alternate moniker—in this case, "Brown Windows," which unexpectedly for Reinhardt links to the material world.[1] His lush Morse code of inky brown and gray/brown horizontal and vertical marks seems to intrude and begins to obliterate—some might say intensify—his luminescent, subtly graded salmon-red background. In the center of the painting's lower quarter are two sharp, brighter crimson lines that glow as they extend horizontally, like the filaments of an incandescent bulb. At the same time, they form the source for the pigmentation of the picture's background hues. In describing the evolution of Reinhardt's work from the late 1940s until 1955, the art historian Lucy Lippard, curator of Reinhardt's first major museum retrospective, in 1966,

Plate 4 Ad Reinhardt, *Painting, 1950*, 1950, oil on canvas, 60 × 36 in. (152.5 × 91.5 cm). Seattle Art Museum, Gift of the Friday Foundation in honor of Richard E. Lang and Jane Lang Davis, 2020.14.14.

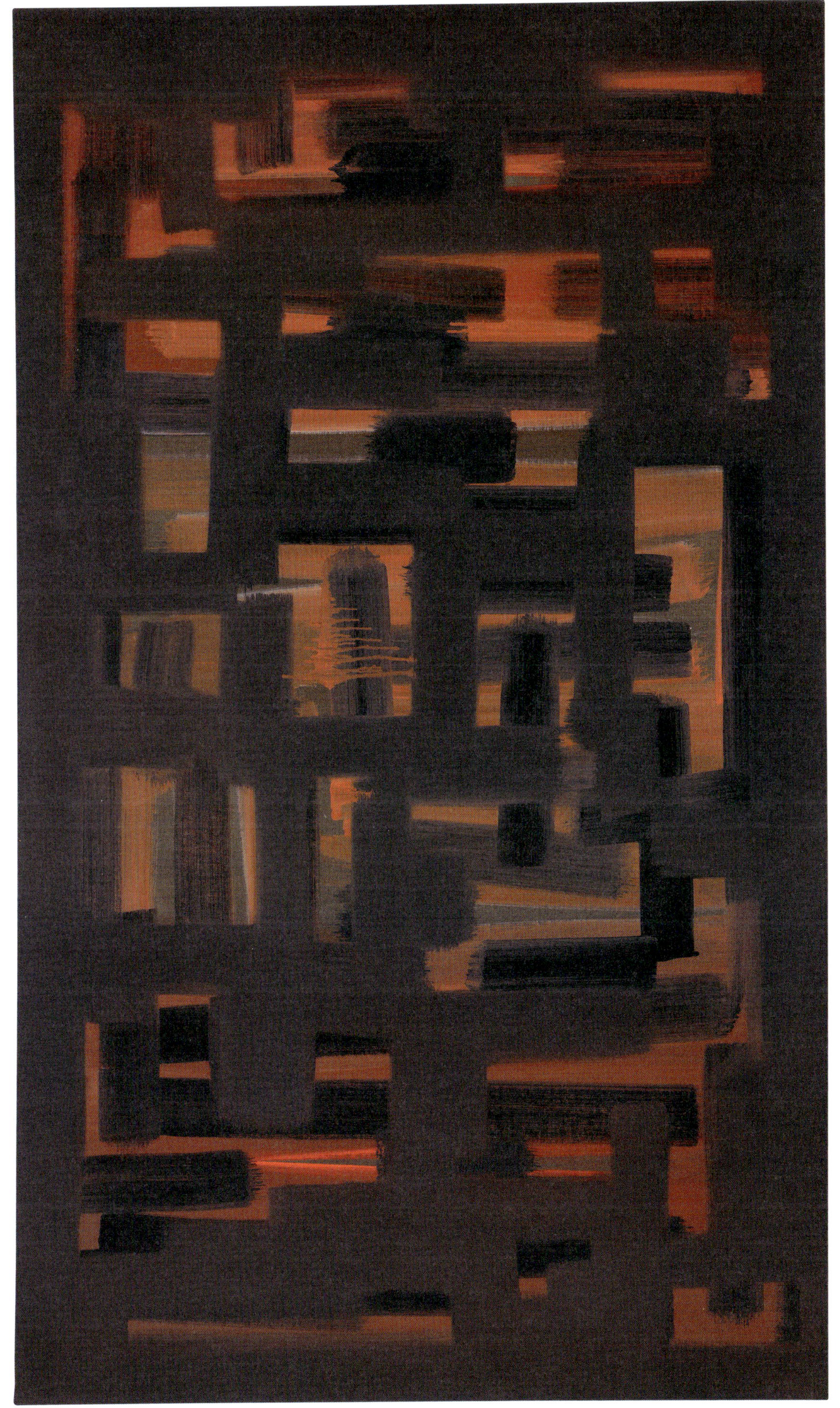

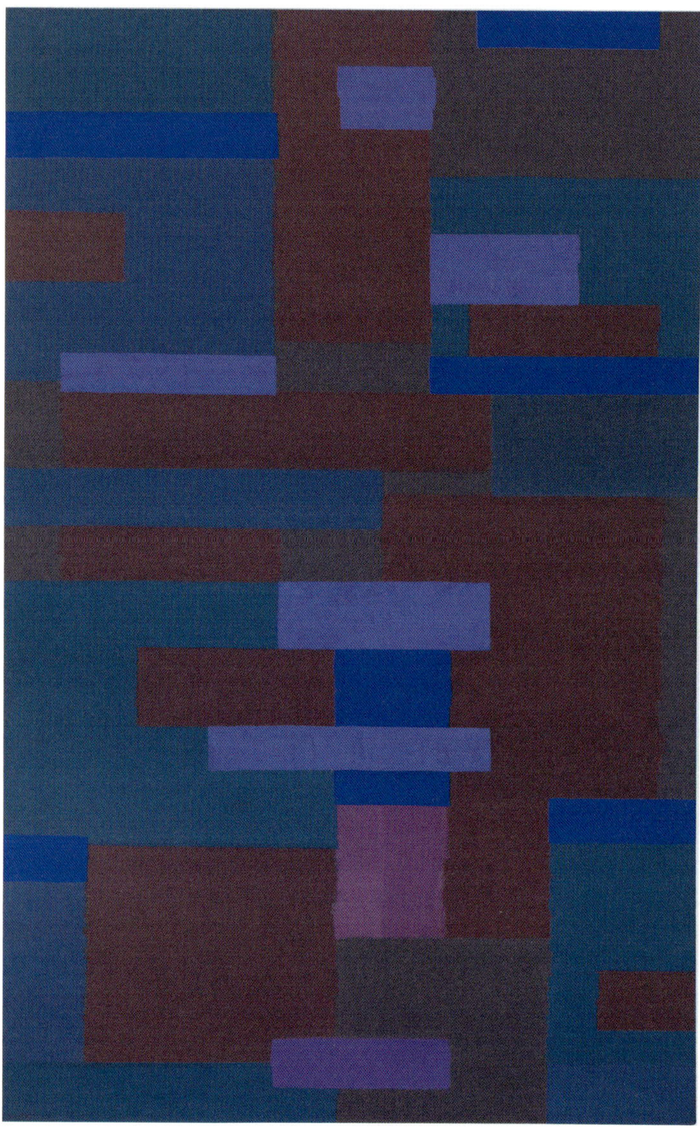

Fig. 31 Ad Reinhardt, *Abstract Painting*, 1950, oil and acrylic on canvas, 78¼ × 24 in. (198.8 × 61 cm). Courtesy of David Zwirner Gallery.

proffered a teleology for his compositions. They had evolved, she said, "from rectilinear all-color bricks to asymmetrical bars on solid grounds of neo-plastic origin, to symmetry, to fewer and fewer elements, to the single tri-section or cross."[2] The latter refers to the black paintings.

Though Reinhardt had already moved on from creating the multicolored organic/geometric abstractions of his earlier work, by the end of the forties and first years of the fifties he continued to streamline his forms and either restrain his chroma or focus on primary or secondary colors. His goal: to reduce painting to its essence. On a formal, calculated level, *Painting, 1950* might easily be considered a precursor of these tighter, generally brighter, more geometric "brick" paintings. Yet Lippard reminds us, if somewhat contradictorily, that the period from 1949 to 1952 is not as predetermined as it might seem. Rather, it generated compositions that are "chronologically confusing, for Reinhardt was working in several transitional manners" at the same time, simultaneously extracting elements of what was known as Abstract Impressionism and post-Cubism.[3] Because of this less stylistically linear, back-and-forth formal juggling in the period under discussion, it is likely that in collaborating with Lippard on his first retrospective, Reinhardt intentionally excluded some of the transitional and more eclectic works of these years. According to the art historian Yve-Alain Bois, the 1966 exhibition asserted a forward stylistic progression in his aesthetic vocabularies leading up to the black pictures. Bois thus claimed that, at Reinhardt's insistence, the retrospective glossed over the more heterogeneous, one might say experimental, period of 1949–52 about which Lippard cautioned.[4] Indeed *Painting, 1950* and other works out of clear stylistic sequence did not appear in the retrospective. Yet they are crucial to our understanding of the evolution of Reinhardt's practice.

This period was precisely when the artist became involved with Chinese, Japanese, and Islamic art, as well as with Eastern thought.[5] One can readily imagine the Lang canvas's connection with Chinese calligraphic painting and with the contemplative and meditative nature of East Asian philosophy.[6] Here, though, the application of paint in horizontal and vertical brushstrokes is more gestural, more animated, and feels a bit baroque, even expressionistic—especially given the work's graded, salmon-red background color, which Reinhardt tentatively obliterated with dryly applied, sometimes feather-edged slabs of brown and gray-brown paint. As opposed to the flatly applied background, almost an opaque stain or a traditional primer coat, the tentative gestural nature of some of these upper-layer brushstrokes in *Painting, 1950* differs considerably from the ordered, rectilinear blocks that Reinhardt called "bricks," as in *Abstract Painting* (1950, fig. 31). The latter compares with his more precise, often more colorful, geometrically controlled pictures of the same year. In fact, Reinhardt labeled a similar approach to paint application, used beginning in the late 1940s, with the paradoxically apt characterization "constructivist-calligraphic."[7]

Luminosity is critical to understanding both this painting and Reinhardt's artistic development. The often-noted association of his work with night is, according to Lippard, from this period forward certainly palpable, visually and even metaphorically. This is especially true of the artist's later "pure black" paintings, which demand that viewers slow down—virtually stop—allowing their eyes to gradually adjust to the darkness of the canvas in order to detect the varied colors (and light) emerging from seemingly empty, nearly monochromatic canvases. One might well consider the Lang Reinhardt, too, a night picture, with its gray/brown, loosely formed blocks gradually covering, and paradoxically emphasizing, the opaque washes of the crimson-based background, creating the effect of light emanating from within. The tradition of such nocturnal effects goes back to Renaissance and Baroque painters—among them the sixteenth-century Venetian Jacopo Bassano, who often used a red (or dark) primer on his canvas in an application not dissimilar to Reinhardt's flat, opaque background tones, as well as a wash of darker burnt umber directly underneath the reddish salmon layer.[8] Bois noted that writers on Reinhardt frequently described his evocation of darkness and night as both luminous and hypnotic; Bois even refers to a passage in Baudelaire's poem "Fleurs du mal" as a verbal analogy for such nocturnal light effects.[9] The painter and critic Sidney Tillim observed as early as 1959 that "darkness in Reinhardt's paintings is a form of light," and, in fact, a complex formal element of Reinhardt's pictures.[10] Yet such manifestations of light, especially as it emanates from darkness, are relatively rare among the work of Abstract Expressionists.

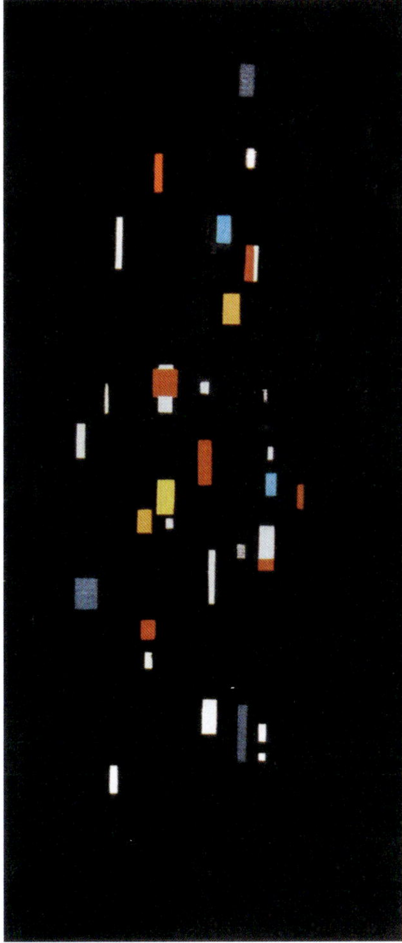

Fig. 32 Norman Lewis, *The Tenement*, 1948, oil on canvas, 40 × 18 in. (101.6 × 45.7 cm). Private Collection.

Some critics associate this elemental, formal aspect of Reinhardt's work with that of only two of his contemporaries: Mark Rothko and Clyfford Still.[11]

However, the flickering effect of *Painting, 1950*'s luminous salmon background peeking out from the gray and brown/black brushwork is also comparable to that in the pictures of Reinhardt's close friend and colleague Norman Lewis.[12] Lewis was well known for working at night, observing and abstracting urban illumination in a crepuscular evening or pitch-black nighttime. He is also credited with an important group of paintings that have themselves been called and exhibited as "black paintings."[13] One of Lewis's black paintings is the 1948 canvas *The Tenement* (fig. 32). With its polychrome abstracted windows

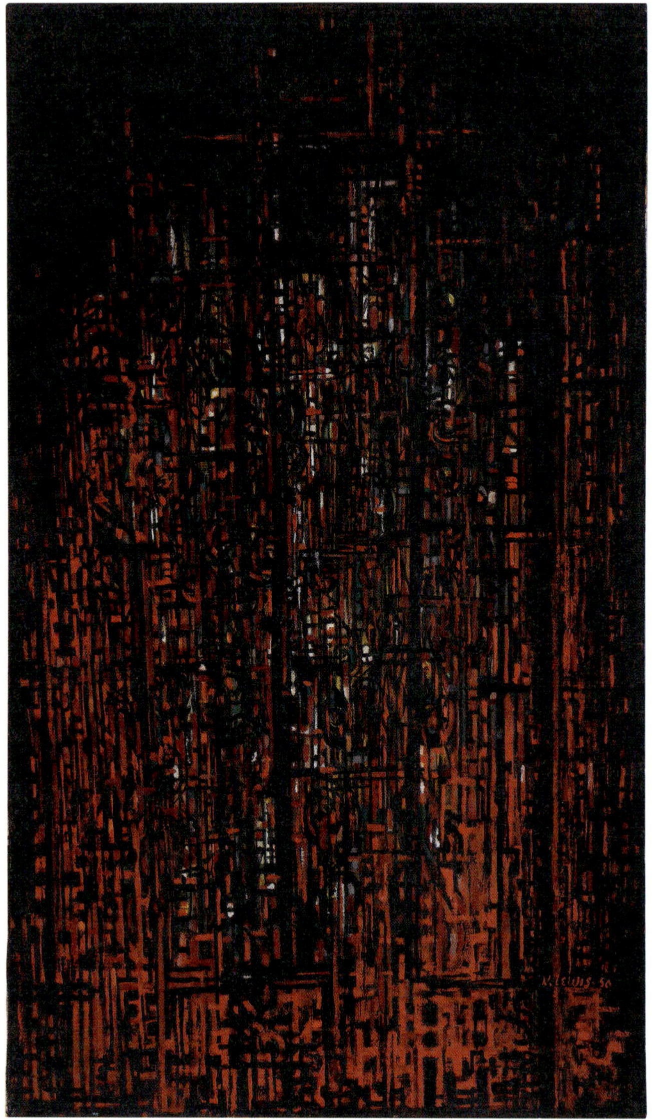

Fig. 33 Norman Lewis, *Cathedral*, 1950, oil on linen canvas, 42 × 25 in. (116.8 × 63.5 cm). Tate Modern, London, Presented by the Tate Americas Foundation 2019, T15286.

as the painting's sole light source, this work is perhaps the most Constructivist and geometrically reduced painting in Lewis's entire oeuvre. Reinhardt's *Abstract Painting* (1951–52, Tate Collection) employs similar spatial and visual organization, though Reinhardt emphasizes horizontal elements, whereas Lewis focuses on verticals. Yet the conceptual intent of Lewis's *Tenement* and Reinhardt's *Abstract Painting* differs radically. Reinhardt knew Lewis from various art-world connections in the 1930s and certainly from 1946, when they both taught at (and were both ultimately fired from) the Jefferson School in New York. They became close friends; in fact, Lewis introduced Reinhardt to his future wife, Rita Solomon Ziprowski.[14] Moreover, Reinhardt was one of the earliest peers to recognize and admire non-objective elements in Lewis's paintings of the 1940s. Lewis's historically important *Cathedral*

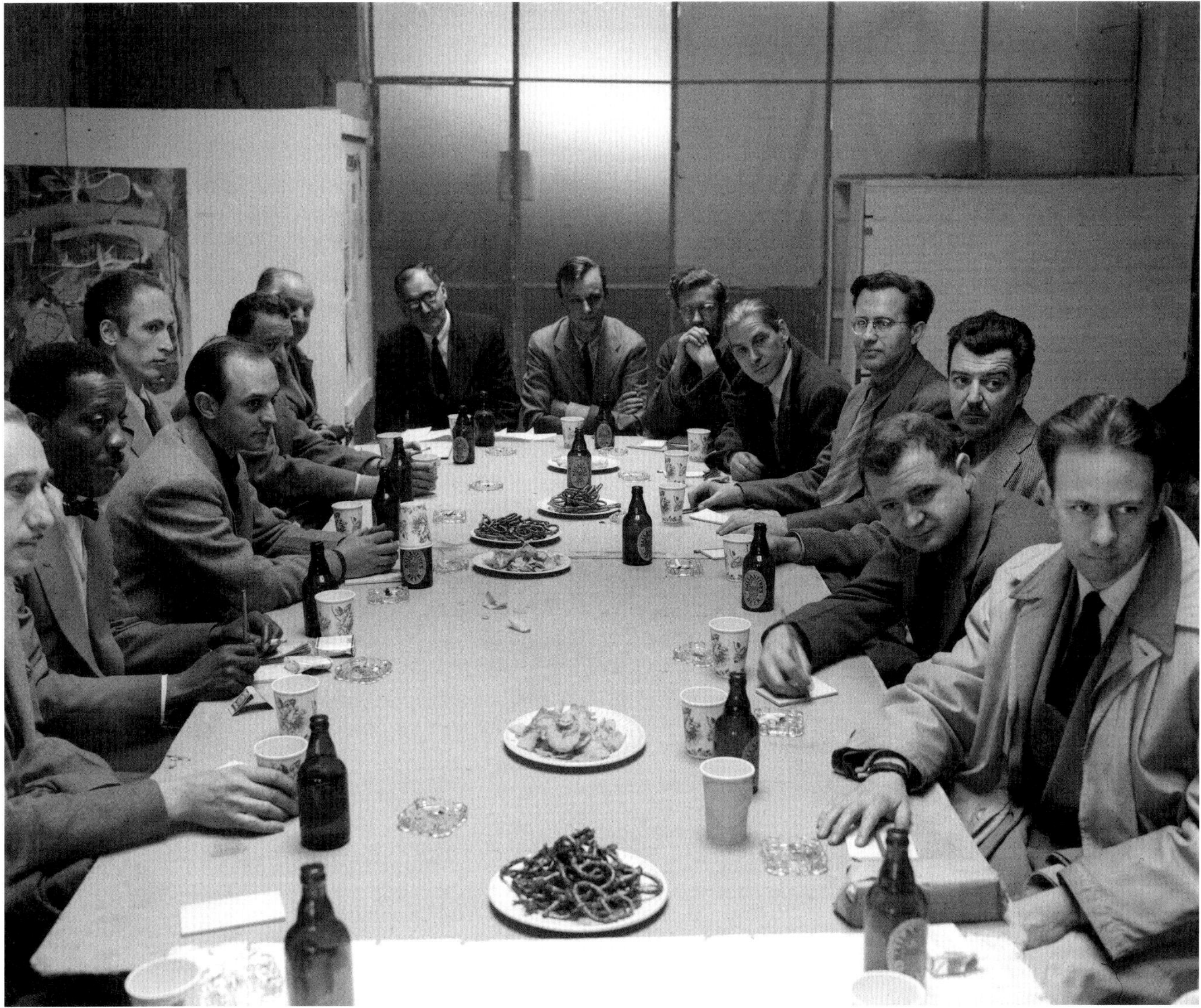

Fig. 34 Artists' Sessions 35, April 1950, (L–R) Seymour Lipton, Norman Lewis, Jimmy Ernst, Peter Grippe, Adolph Gottlieb, Hans Hofmann, Alfred Barr Jr., Robert Motherwell, Richard Lippold, Willem de Kooning, Ibram Lassaw, James Brooks, Ad Reinhardt, and Richard Poussette-Dart. Courtesy of the Ad Reinhardt Foundation.

(1950, fig. 33), a work of the same year as Reinhardt's *Painting, 1950,* suggests a similar interest in fenestration as sources of light effects emerging from a dark canvas. The painting, considered "at the pinnacle of Norman Lewis's first abstract period," was shown in the Venice Biennale in 1956 and has recently been acquired by Tate Modern in London.[15] Although Lewis's painting seems to recede, Reinhardt's pushes forward. Coincidentally, 1950 was the year of the important convening of Artists' Sessions 35, organized in part by the Museum of Modern Art's celebrated curator Alfred H. Barr Jr. At that event, Reinhardt sat across from Lewis (fig. 34). In fact, it is likely that Reinhardt brought Lewis as his guest, for Lewis's name does not appear on an extant invitation list.[16] Lewis, who was Black, was the sole person of color at the proceeding.

Reinhardt's onetime titling of *Brown Windows* remains perplexing, especially considering Reinhardt's general resistance to titles and his insistence on the self-referentiality of the work of art. How and when did Reinhardt decide to scribe (in his inimitable script) "Brown Windows" on the board covering the back of this otherwise untitled canvas? The practice of assigning titles to artworks, much debated among Abstract Expressionist painters and sculptors, was a theme under consideration at Artists' Sessions 35. Reinhardt suggested that doing so might be meaningless or even create confusion (see this essay's epigraph).[17] Nonetheless, he did title a very small cadre of pictures, such as his *Tri Landscape* (1948, private collection) and *Pictograph* (1949, private collection), which refer either to nature or to a Jungian mode of pictorial expression.[18] More typical of Reinhardt's titles, when they are not simply labeled "abstract," "untitled," or "painting," are ones that refer specifically to formal elements of the work, as in *Blue-Green Painting* (1948, Private Collection) or *Dark Painting* (1953, Private Collection). Memorable, if unusual, is the title *Ultimate Painting #39* (1960, Kröller-Müller Museum, Otterlo, the Netherlands). Here, the designation is no longer blandly descriptive but purely intellectual and conceptual, connoting the artist's purist, reductive goals and his quest to move toward the "last painting" in Western art. Yet why the more descriptive, reference "Brown Windows"?

In the catalogue to the artist's first retrospective, Lippard specifically points out the "window-like forms" in Reinhardt's output between 1949 and 1952.[19] Tantalizingly, and perhaps not coincidentally, Solomon Ziprkowski, whom he married in 1953, had studied at the Jefferson School in New York with Norman Lewis in 1946 when Reinhardt was also teaching there—and subsequently bought Lewis's *Window* (1949, Smart Art Museum) from the Willard Gallery. It is possible—in fact, probable—that Reinhardt knew this particular image. Lewis's abstracted paintings of windows and his focus on nocturnal fenestration in those years may thus offer evidence—albeit partial and circumstantial—for what prompted Reinhardt to add an alternate title on the reverse of *Painting, 1950*, an act that may have postdated its creation.[20] This unusually lush, luminescent work, with its intimations of gestural brushwork, is perhaps one of Reinhardt's most characteristically Abstract Expressionist. By contrast, the classic, highly reductive black pictures that followed, often challenging to classify under the rubric of Abstract Expressionism, made him an avatar for many in the subsequent generation of Minimal and conceptual artists.

NOTES

Epigraph Ad Reinhardt (1950), quoted in Robert Goodnough, ed., *Artists' Sessions at Studio 35 (1950)*, rev. ed. (Chicago: Soberscove/Wittenborn, 2011), 24.

1 The backing board of the painting bears the inscription "Brown Windows" in the artist's distinctive handwriting, and the bill of sale for *Painting, 1950* from Marlborough Gallery, made out to Richard Lang and dated 1974, lists *Brown Windows* as a previous title. In 1951, in the exhibition *Ad Reinhardt: Recent Oil Paintings* at Betty Parsons Gallery, New York, the work was installed opposite its current orientation (see p. 50 of this volume). By 1960, in the catalogue for *Ad Reinhardt: Twenty-Five Years of Abstract Painting* at Parsons, where it was simply titled *Painting*, the artist had decided to rotate the canvas 180 degrees. Inscriptions on the back of the painting confirm this new orientation.

2 Lucy Lippard, *Ad Reinhardt* (New York: Jewish Museum, 1966), 18.

3 Lippard, *Ad Reinhardt*, 17. Lippard also makes the case for a "decade of logical stylistic evolution" from 1950 to 1960 that culminated with the black paintings. The term Abstract Impressionism was in use during the late 1940s and early 1950s and refers, in part, to the New York School's appreciation of late works by Claude Monet. The 2018 exhibition *The Water Lilies: American Abstract Painting and the Last Monet* (Musée de l'Orangerie, Paris) explored this connection between the taste for late Monet and American midcentury abstraction. See also Norman L. Kleeblatt, exhibition review, *Brooklyn Rail*, September 2018, http://brooklynrail.org/2018/09/artseen/The-Water-Lilies-American-Abstract-Painting-and-the-Last-Monet.

4 Yve-Alain Bois, "The Limit of the Almost," in *Ad Reinhardt* (New York: Rizzoli in association with the Museum of Modern Art, New York, and Museum of Contemporary Art, Los Angeles, 1991), 30. In fact, according to the "Catalogue of the Exhibition" in Lippard, *Ad Reinhardt*, 70–73, the 1966 Jewish Museum exhibition included ten works from 1950, four from 1951, and twelve from 1952. The works were evidently selected to make the case for a teleological stylistic and formal advance.

5 Barbara Rose, ed., *Art as Art: The Selected Writings of Ad Reinhardt* (Los Angeles: University of California Press, 1991), 3.

6 Rose, "Editor's Note," in Rose, *Art as Art*, 81–82.

7 Reinhardt, "[Five Stages of Reinhardt's Timeless Stylistic Art-Historical Cycle]," in Rose, *Art as Art*, 10.

8 Refer to email of examination report by Nicholas Dorman, Jane Lang Davis Chief Conservator of Paintings, Seattle Art Museum, to Catharina Manchanda of October 28, 2020, and the attendant email sent to Norman Kleeblatt by Manchanda of the same date.

9 Bois, "Limit of the Almost," 33n93.

10 Sidney Tillim, "What Happened to Geometry?," *Arts*, June 1959, 43.

11 Lippard, *Ad Reinhardt*, 22. In her essay, Lippard notes Sidney Tillim's observations on light as a formal element in Reinhardt's paintings from the late 1940s to the 1960s. See also Tillim, "What Happened to Geometry?," 54.

12 The closeness of their friendship is supported by the little-discussed fact that Reinhardt made Lewis godfather to his daughter, Anna Reinhardt. This information was supplied to the author in an email from Tarin M. Fuller, Norman Lewis's stepdaughter and director of his estate, January 29, 2021.

13 Ann Eden Gibson, "Black Is a Color: Norman Lewis and Modernism in New York," in *Norman Lewis: Black Paintings 1946–1977* (New York: Studio Museum in Harlem, 1999), 11–29.

14 Anna Reinhardt, quoted in email correspondence with the author from J. R. Valenzuela and Lisa Cherkerzian, Reinhardt Foundation, March 8, 2021: "Norman Lewis was not an 'official' documented godfather to me as I was not baptized, but in a more informal way my parents and I certainly considered him to be my godfather. He introduced my parents and was a supportive and loving adult in my childhood memories." Max Rosenberg at the David Zwirner Gallery helped facilitate this communication.

15 Swann Auction Galleries, *Ascension: A Century of African-American Art*, auction catalogue, sale 2378, lot 46.

16 Goodnough, *Artists' Sessions*, 24. Lewis's name did not appear on the list of artists who were sent letters of invitation. I thank Lucy Partman, PhD candidate in art history at Princeton University, for this observation. See Lucy Partman, "Norman Lewis: A Complex Conversation," *Nka Journal of Contemporary African Art* 20, no. 47 (2020): 57–58.

17 Such discussion is included in William C. Seitz's *Abstract Expressionist Painting in America* (Cambridge, MA: Harvard University Press, 1983). Though published posthumously, it was the first commercial appearance of his PhD dissertation of the same title, submitted to Princeton University in 1955.

18 Although many Abstract Expressionist artists occasionally deployed pictographic devices in their works (for example, Mark Rothko from the early to mid-1940s), the painter Adolph Gottlieb sustained an interest in this format from 1941 to 1953. See Sanford Hirsch, ed., *The Pictographs of Adolph Gottlieb* (New York: Hudson Hills, 1995); and Hirsch's essay in this volume, "Adolph Gottlieb, *Crimson Spinning #2*, 1959," p. 112.

19 Lippard, *Ad Reinhardt*, 17.

20 Ruth Fine, "The Spiritual in the Material," in *Procession: The Art of Norman Lewis*, ed. Ruth Fine (Los Angeles: Pennsylvania Academy of Fine Arts in association with University of California Press, 2015), 60, 102. I thank Ruth Fine for clarifying the sequence of surnames that Rita Reinhardt went through prior to her marriage to Ad Reinhardt in 1953.

FRANZ KLINE
PAINTING NO. 11
1951

DAVID ANFAM

The only works of art America has given are her plumbing and her bridges.
—Marcel Duchamp

One horizontal and three verticals, all black, stand amid an off-white field. These elements span dimensions—slightly more than five feet tall by nearly seven feet wide—neither diminutive nor epic. Rather, they combine a certain tactile intimacy with a monumental aura. The oil pigment layers range from a thinness exposing the underlayer (notice where the rightward vertical terminates near the canvas's lower edge) to sufficiently thick to record the strokes with a housepainter's brush. In various passages, the medium self-destructs, as it were, into splatters, streaks, scrapes and scumbles. Overall, the image has a quick, head-on impact—as any apparent gestalt should. However, an alert gaze may query whether the general configuration could be the skeletal semblance of a table or some similar quotidian, household object. Still, everything thus described requires immediate qualification, as though what looks obvious is not.

For a start, the "horizontal" splinters into two or three segments. The leftward rises slightly and the rightward tilts a bit downward (each direction depending on whether one reads from above to below or vice versa), while the central section is almost level. Consequently, this rule is, more accurately, a slight diagonal. How many parts has it? Two for sure, given the rupture at right. Ambiguously, three, because to the left of center the line crumbles into a trace resembling a faint afterimage compared to the much denser black parallel band above. Likewise, the verticals are less than foursquare,[1] not to mention that each stops or fades as it nears the composition's edges. Neither is "black and white" quite the correct label. All the white is palely mottled—grayed by its opposite color, while it makes inroads upon this selfsame black. "Grisaille" sounds more apt, though even then there lurks a second hue, an almost subliminal creamy tone. Pentimenti and blurs, inimical to a true gestalt, also prevail. Nor is this really any old table unless, perhaps, conjured by imagination—the composition teases us, so to speak, to identify it. At the end of the proverbial day, Franz Kline's *Painting No. 11* (1951, plate 5), despite seeming forthright, baffles the viewer.

Plate 5 Franz Kline, *Painting No. 11*, 1951, oil on canvas, 61 × 82¼ in. (155 × 208.9 cm). Seattle Art Museum, Gift of the Friday Foundation in honor of Richard E. Lang and Jane Lang Davis, 2020.14.12.

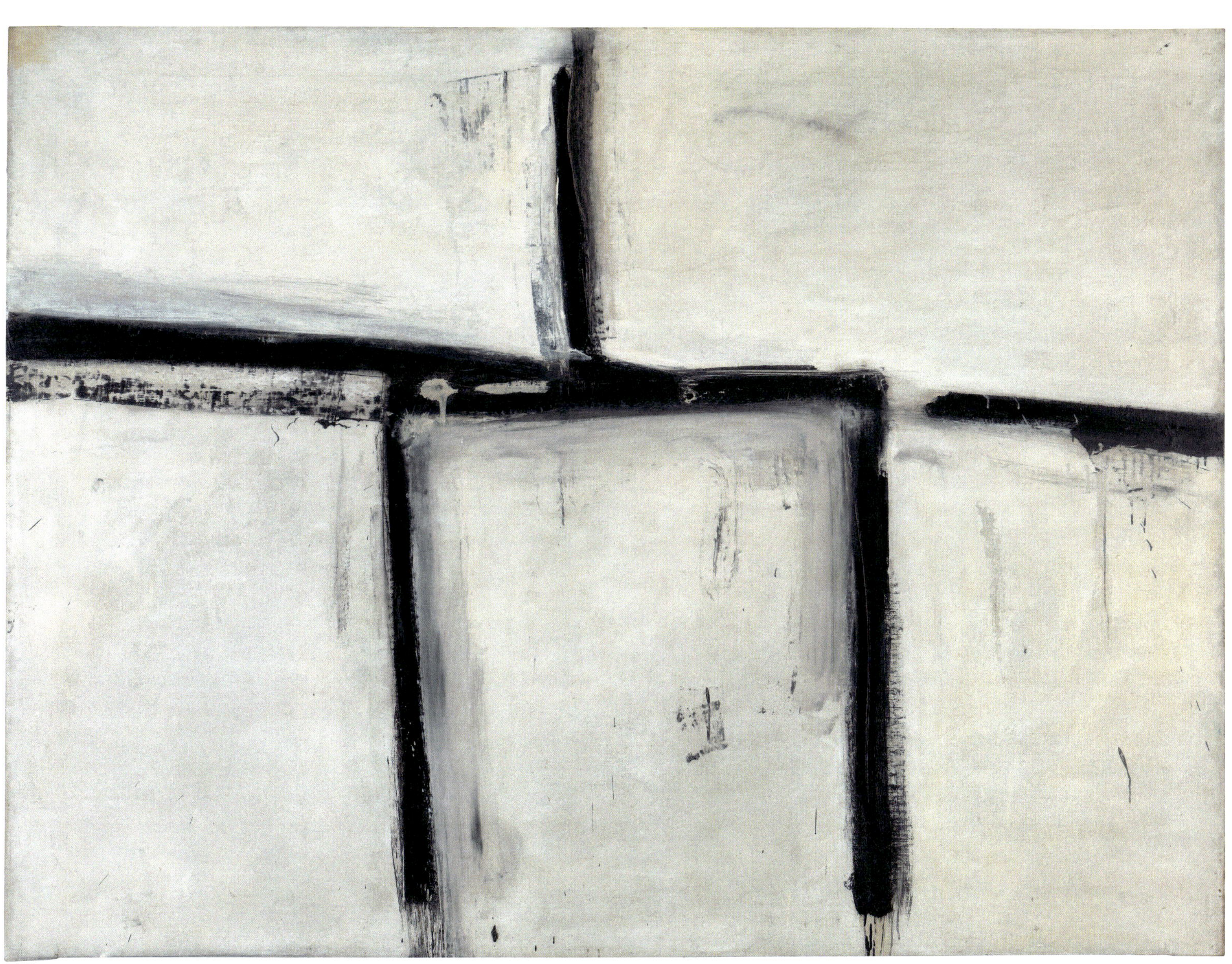

Puzzlement is one explanation for why *Painting No. 11* demands such detailed description. Puzzles also have another knack: to solve them (successfully or not) sharpens the faculties. They make us look or think again—which is what Kline's mature art does. Certainly, his pictorial strategies are not "about" the phenomenology of perception (to recall Maurice Merleau-Ponty's famous 1945 account of seeing, knowing and feeling).[2] Nevertheless, they grab our attention in a phenomenological way, a mode entailing a level of scrutiny that alters mere looking into apperception. As the French philosopher explained, the task is "to reawaken perception and foil its trick of allowing us to forget it as a fact and as perception in the interest of the object which it presents to us."[3] Simply stated, what a sentient spectator gets in front of a quintessential Kline such as *Painting No. 11* involves not just "understanding" (mind) or even "seeing" (vision) per se. Instead, it evokes more an encounter where the two blend into a single experience that feels as vivid as it proves hard to verbalize. The art historian Irving Sandler had this kind of awakening when he happened upon Kline's *Chief* (1950, fig. 35) at the Museum of Modern Art in 1952. Probably it applies to many of those who admire Kline too.

Sandler's recollection simplifies matters that phenomenology can render unduly difficult to comprehend and therefore merits quoting in full. Pondering on what it was about the picture that astonished and moved him, Sandler wrote:

> The painting did not provide any particular pleasure or delight. Nor did I "understand" it. I responded in another way—with my "gut," as it were. The painting had a sense of urgency and authenticity that gripped me. . . . It was at once surprising, familiar, and imposing. . . . *Chief* revealed to me the power of the visual in my being. It was like releasing the flood gates of seeing.[4]

Even to my own eyes—long jaded by studying Abstract Expressionist artworks over and again—*Painting No. 11* still possesses, seven decades after its execution, a comparable tug. In short, an everyday epiphany. Its oddity lies in an inexplicable power, like coming across some well-worn sentimental object that abruptly sparks diverse memories and associations exceeding or at variance with the sum of its particulars.[5] When the curator William C. Seitz passed his doctoral verdict on Kline in 1955, he observed that the artist "staked everything on single units of black-and-white calligraphy."[6] Seitz got Kline's means right without mentioning their ends.

Until now I have deliberately focused on *Painting No. 11* in isolation for good reasons. The main justification is that Kline's biography, its effect on his work and status as an Abstract Expressionist, has been discussed so often that it has become almost common knowledge—a lore involving facts, factoids, clichés and interpretations well known enough to need only the most summary retelling here. Indeed *Painting No. 11*'s singularity is fresher and outpaces the timeworn art historical narratives surrounding Kline.[7]

Suffice it to say that as a person, Kline was dynamic (an ace at football in high school),[8] witty (his cartoons are deft),[9] bohemian (after settling in Greenwich Village he was, of course, a hard-drinking habitué at the Abstract Expressionists' favored watering hole, the Cedar Tavern) and gendered in a well-established America-at-midcentury man's-man kind of mold.[10] Late in life, he drove a black Thunderbird and a silver-gray Ferrari. Questioned in 1961 as to whether he regarded himself as an American painter, Kline responded, "Yes, I think so. I can't imagine myself working very long in Europe or, for that matter, anywhere but New York. I find Chicago terrific but I've been living in New York now for twenty-odd years and it seems to be where I belong."[11] Likewise, Kline maintained a lengthy love affair with his native eastern Pennsylvania: *Lehigh V Span* (1959–60, San Francisco Museum of Modern Art) typifies the numerous titular allusions to roots (he attended Lehighton High School).[12] Now prime Rust Belt, in Kline's youth this hilly region spelled raw power: coal, trains, industry, effort and energy.[13] Early landscapes such as *Palmerton, PA* (1941, Smithsonian American Art Museum) literally depict said scenery. In this lively panorama with a chugging locomotive at its center, the overriding impression is also unkempt. To invoke an American paradigm, the machine disrupts the garden.[14]

In turn, the literature always discerns the foregoing biographical cues transformed into style and metaphor throughout Kline's subsequent oeuvre. A typical historical reading compared his *Mahoning* (1956, Whitney Museum of American Art) with Pierre Soulages's *23 March '55* (1955,

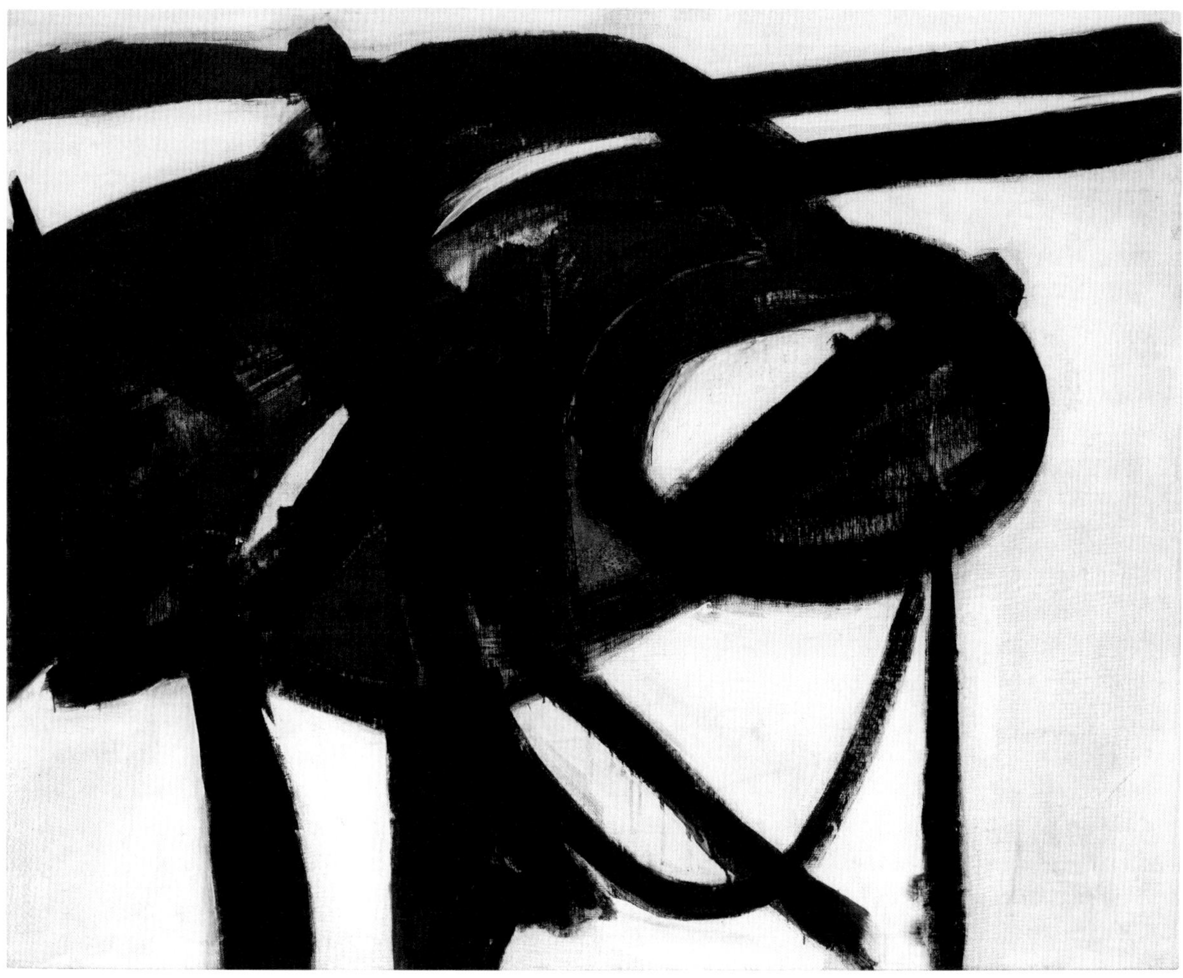

Fig. 35 Franz Kline, *Chief*, 1950, oil on canvas, 58⅜ × 73½ in. (148.3 × 186.7 cm). The Museum of Modern Art, New York, Gift of Mr. and Mrs. David M. Solinger, 2.1952.

Private Collection). According to the author John McCoubrey, the French painter's canvas came across as structured, precise, restful and well crafted. By comparison, he described *Mahoning* as raw, violent, impulsive and restless.[15] Stereotypes? Yes. Wrong? No. On the contrary, stereotyping may bespeak truth. Furthermore, Kline's transition from representational to abstract was fairly late and brisk. He considered *The Dancer* (1946, Private Collection), very influenced by Cubism, his first abstraction.[16] Two or three years later, a friend, none other than Willem de Kooning, encouraged Kline to project his drawings onto the studio wall with a Bell-Opticon.[17] Whatever was once decipherable became estranged, an optical mind game. The little grew large. By no coincidence, scale is inherently a somatic sensation. Kline acknowledged that some forms, no matter how effaced, felt figurative to him. Nor is gesturalism or Action Painting conceivable without the body's agency, which leaves its indexical marks in pigment.[18]

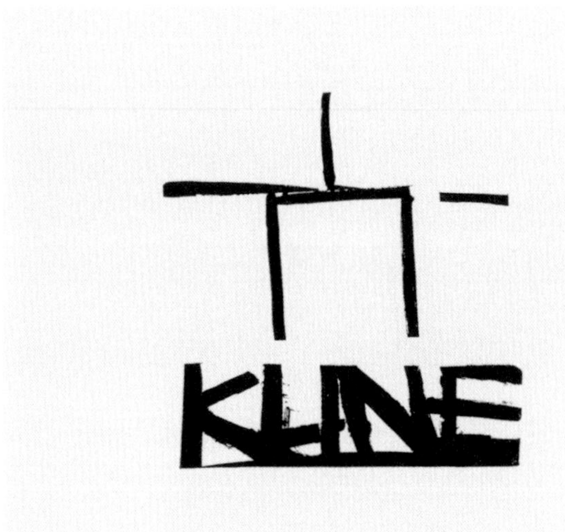

Fig. 36 Invitation to *Franz Kline* exhibition opening, Egan Gallery, 1951.

By 1950, Kline had found himself. In October, his first solo show opened at the Charles Egan Gallery in Manhattan. The selection had some of his most iconic achievements, including the ultra-stark *Wotan* (Museum of Fine Arts Houston), *Hoboken* (Private Collection) with its circular motif, and the more linear *Giselle* (Private Collection), all from 1950. Worth noting in the present context is that the output from 1950 and the next four or five years exudes a grainy frankness—*Painting No. 11* has it in spades—that later tended to diminish when Kline's manner became more rehearsed and, at its least persuasive, a tad slick. That *Painting No. 11* also featured as the poster and on the invitation for his second solo show at Egan in 1951 reflects its primacy (fig. 36). Frequently, the shock of the new outdid its sometimes formulaic replay.

As for the key themes underlying Kline's iconography, they are those historically equated with American power and facticity. To wit, engineering feats such as the Brooklyn Bridge (often Kline's structures foster a sense of suspension or torque),[19] skyscrapers (New York was Franz's kind of town), speed as symbolized by railroad engines (*Cardinal* [1950, Private Collection] and *Chief* both refer to locomotives)[20] and motion itself. In fact, Kline's shapes are always vectors insofar as they either seem forever in flux and/or suggest impending collapse—*Painting No. 11*'s shaky armature conveys precarious imbalance.[21] And if imbalance sounds antithetical to "power," think again. Remember how powerful is the often-shown documentary footage of the Tacoma Narrows Bridge's juddering collapse in 1940,[22] not to mention the explosions that have energized a zillion Hollywood movies from at least the huge gas tank's immolation at the apocalyptic end of *White Heat* (1949; dir. Raoul Walsh) to today's "exploding helicopter" melodramas. In a nutshell, then, Kline redid what had already been the idealized subject of an earlier American movement, Precisionism, in the process ravaging it. Charles Sheeler's *Water* (1945, fig. 37) exemplifies the massiveness, concentrated energies, hard angles and cool architectonics that compose this "technological sublime."[23]

Motion has been an American idée fixe ranging from the quest that led to Plymouth Rock, via Walt Whitman's "Song of the Open Road" (1855), to Jack Kerouac's seminal *On the Road* (1957) and its innumerable cinematic progeny.[24] The diagonal in *Painting No. 11* breaks, yet it also continues apace beyond the frame. Lastly, the impersonal, sparse aura of such works links them to the birth of the "cool" in postwar America.[25] On the one hand, Kline could wax emotive with his jagged dramas. On the other hand, he was savvy enough to make feelings into things, material and matter-of-factual. At their leanest, we encounter pictorial holophrases. In a sense, his colliding visual syntax is a "list" of quiddity—encompassing black and white, rectangles, circles, wedges, intersections and so forth. Nothing is more homespun America than the propensity to make lists.[26] The overabundant attributes that Herman Melville listed to evoke the whiteness of the whale in *Moby Dick* (1851) remain a locus classicus for such paeans to quiddity. But a rupture with tradition and easy categories looms. Speaking of which, what happened to the would-be table in *Painting No. 11*?

According to the gallerist Allan Stone,

> I raised this question of origins with Charles Egan, Kline's first dealer, good friend and a pioneer in championing the Abstract Expressionist movement. "Tables and chairs," was Egan's answer. "Charles, what are you talking about? You're joking!" "Not at all," Charles replied and pulled out a small abstraction, which upon close inspection turned

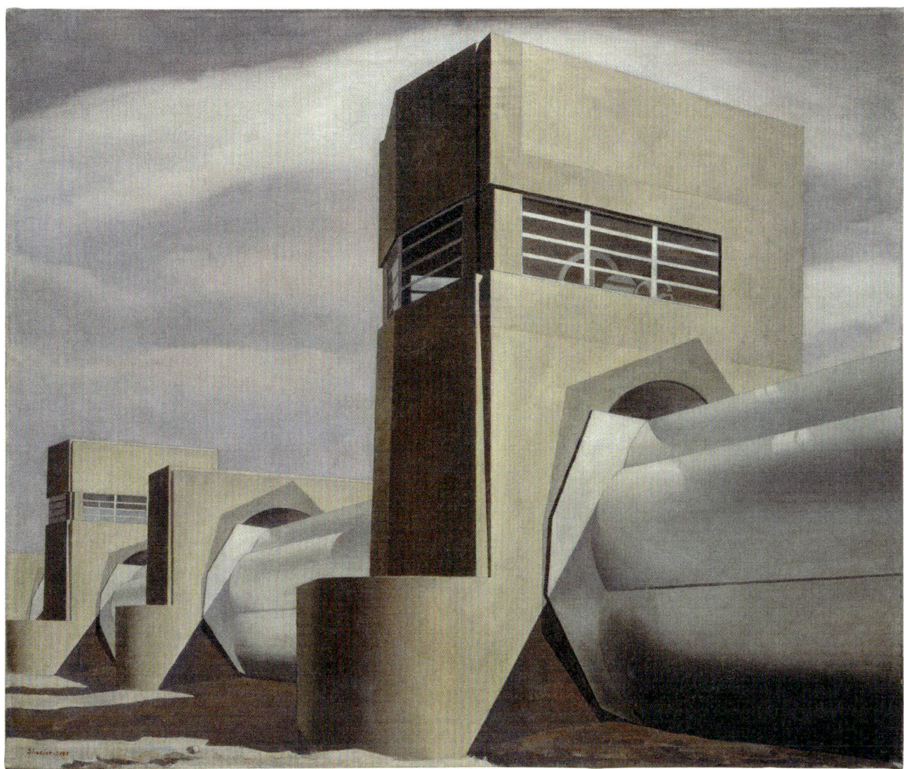

Fig. 37 Charles Sheeler, *Water*, 1945, oil on canvas, 24 × 29¼ in. (61 × 74.3 cm). The Metropolitan Museum of Art, New York, Arthur Hoppock Hearn Fund, 1949, 49.128.

> out to be a rocking chair. . . . Similarly, Egan maintained that the very spare early abstract paintings like *Wotan* (1950) were inspired by the reduction of tables.[27]

This erstwhile homely plot thickens further. Kline's dynamism hid skeletons in the closet. His father died in mysterious circumstances that may have been suicide. In 1947, Kline portrayed himself as a *Red Clown* whose masklike face approaches a pale death's head.[28] The following year or thereabouts witnessed a variant, *Large Clown (Nijinsky as Petrouchka)* (1948, Wadsworth Atheneum Museum of Art), representing the Russian ballet dancer gone insane. Finally, Kline's path away from realism pivoted around multiple studies of his wife, Elizabeth (who had been a ballerina), seated in a rocking chair. In May 1948, Elizabeth went off her rocker (as they say) and was institutionalized.[29] To conclude: the tough, ebullient all-American boy persona hid a darker side to Kline's psyche. We are nearer film noir territory than the gung-ho arena of Action Painting.[30]

What happened to the tables and chairs is that they became revenants, signs that emit mixed emotions, at once sturdy emblematic icons and sites laden with an uncanny instability.[31] There is no dialectic because Kline, unlike Piet Mondrian, suspends dualities. Grids are shaken, certainties blurred (blurs stand midway between directed gestures and the formless).[32] Figures and furniture disappeared into force fields. *Painting No. 11* epitomizes this conflict, its riddles embedded within spartan simplicity—as well as an ultimate retort to Marcel Duchamp's put-down regarding American industrialism (see this essay's epigraph). In *Painting No. 11* and its kin, Kline achieved what some modern thinkers believe is a central purpose in art: that is, to defamiliarize humdrum reality so that we perceive it anew, strange and starkly indelible.[33]

NOTES

Epigraph Marcel Duchamp, "The Richard Mutt Case," *The Blind Man* 2 (May 1917): 5.

1 The perhaps ironic or punning title of a canvas that is neither foursquare nor contains four squares: Franz Kline, *Four Square*, 1956, oil on canvas, 78⅜ × 50¾ in. (199 × 128.9 cm), National Gallery of Art, Washington, DC.

2 Maurice Merleau-Ponty, *Phenomenology of Perception*, trans. Colin Smith and Forrest Williams (London: Routledge Classics, [1945], 2002). To (over-)simplify an often-difficult text, Merleau-Ponty's aim was to reassert the ascendancy of embodied perception above traditional, Cartesian mind-body dualities.

3 Merleau-Ponty, *Phenomenology of Perception*, 66.

4 Irving Sandler, *A Sweeper-Up after Artists* (New York: Thames and Hudson, 2004), 10.

5 A process tantamount to an uncanny reversal of Freudian overdetermination.

6 William C. Seitz, *Abstract Expressionist Painting in America* (Cambridge, MA: Harvard University Press, [1955], 1983), 165. *Pace* the fact that Kline himself was not keen on the "calligraphy" idea.

7 The main studies include Harry F. Gaugh, *The Vital Gesture: Franz Kline* (Cincinnati: Cincinnati Art Museum and Abbeville Press, 1986); David Anfam, *Franz Kline: Black and White, 1950–1961* (Houston: Menil Collection, 1994); Carolyn Christov-Bakargiev, ed., *Franz Kline 1910–1962* (Rivoli-Turin: Castello di Rivoli Museo d'Arte Contemporanea, 2004); and Robert S. Mattison, *Franz Kline: Coal and Steel* (Allentown, PA: Allentown Art Museum of the Lehigh Valley, 2012).

8 *Vawdavitch* (1955, Museum of Contemporary Art, Chicago) references an American football star.

9 Cartoons perforce involve reducing things to (mostly linear) essentials, a process of obvious relevance to Abstract Expressionism.

10 The mid-1940s photograph of Kline in Gaugh, *Vital Gesture*, 52, shows a brooding figure in a cutoff check shirt that would still be trendy today and conforms to the "rebel without a cause" persona later established by Marlon Brando, James Dean and their kind.

11 Franz Kline (1961), quoted in Katharine Kuh, *The Artist's Voice: Talks with Seventeen Modern Artists* (New York: Harper and Row, 1962), 153.

12 Absence may also have made Kline's heart grow fonder for his early days.

13 The railroad in country music echoes in microcosm the mingled pathos and appeal of the railroad writ large. See Norman Cohen, *Long Steel Rail: The Railroad in American Folksong*, 2nd ed. (Urbana: University of Illinois Press, 2000). Kline's imagination accommodated this folksy aspect, immortalized in *The General* (1926; dir. Clyde Bruckman and Buster Keaton).

14 Leo Marx, *The Machine in the Garden: Technology and the Pastoral Ideal in America* (Oxford: Oxford University Press, 1964).

15 John McCoubrey, *American Tradition in Painting* (Philadelphia: University of Pennsylvania Press, [1963], 2000), 4.

16 Gaugh, *Vital Gesture*, 79–80.

17 Kline's predilection for monochrome owes a lot, among sundry other sources, to de Kooning.

18 Following the art historian Richard Shiff, himself subscribing to the American philosopher C. S. Pierce's theories, indexicality implies a direct physical contact between an image and its source (for example, a handprint), whereas iconicity instead indicates a visual resemblance between the former and the latter (as in conventional mimesis); Richard Shiff, "Performing an Appearance on the Surface of Abstract Expressionism," in Michael Auping, *Abstract Expressionism: The Critical Developments* (Buffalo: Albright-Knox Art Gallery and Harry N. Abrams, 1987), 94–123.

19 Typified by the levitated square and horizontal in *Suspended* (1953, Private Collection).

20 "Power and freedom" were associated with the railroad at its first appearance in the landscape; Susan Danly and Leo Marx, *The Railroad in American Art: Representations of Technological Change* (Cambridge, MA: MIT Press, 1998), 46.

21 See Franz Kline, quoted in Selden Rodman, *Conversations with Artists* (New York: Devin-Adair, 1957), 109: "To think of ways of disorganizing form can be a form of organization, you know."

22 Kline's *The Bridge* (ca. 1955, Munson-Williams-Proctor Arts Institute) presents a tangled upheaval.

23 See David E. Nye, *American Technological Sublime* (Cambridge, MA: MIT Press, 1994). Irving Sandler's essay title tweaks this phrase to "The Industrial Sublime," in Mattison, *Franz Kline*, 108; I prefer "industrial primitivism."

24 On speed, motion and their relationship to the American 1950s, see Anfam, *Franz Kline*.

25 The literature is extensive. Worthwhile starting points are Lewis MacAdams, *The Birth of Cool* (New York: Free Press, 2001); and Joel Dinerstein, *The Origins of Cool in Postwar America* (Chicago: University of Chicago Press, 2017).

26 Robert E. Belknap, *The List: The Uses and Pleasures of Cataloguing* (New Haven, CT: Yale University Press, 2004).

27 Allan Stone, *Franz Kline: Architecture and Atmosphere* (New York: Allan Stone Gallery, 1997), n.p.

28 The "clown" typology goes back to Walt Kuhn and forward to Wayne Thiebaud and Bruce Nauman. It may denote painting's intrinsic artifice in an "on with the motley" spirit—performativity gone, by turns, sad or wild.

29 Rocking chairs are the corniest of stage props in countless horror movies, perhaps the foremost being *Psycho* (1960, dir. Alfred Hitchcock).

30 An obvious though overlooked comparison is with Frank Sinatra. His jazzy ebullience could segue to the moodiness of his *Only the Lonely* album (1958). Tellingly, the record's sleeve depicts Sinatra as a Pagliaci-type clown.

31 A remarkably similar process occurs in the Ulsterman William Scott's art.

32 No mention of the grid is complete without acknowledgment of Rosalind E. Krauss, "Grids" (1978), in *The Originality of the Avant-Garde and Other Modernist Myths* (Cambridge, MA: MIT Press, 1985), 8–22. Krauss posits the grid as the foundational modernist pictorial bedrock. To estrange the grid therefore entails a radical volte-face.

33 The Russian Formalist Viktor Shklovsky coined the concept "defamiliarization" in his essay "Art as Device" (1917). "The purpose of art is to impart the sensation of things as they are perceived and not as they are known. The technique of art is to make objects 'unfamiliar,' to make forms difficult to increase the difficulty and length of perception because the process of perception is an aesthetic end in itself and must be prolonged"; Shklovsky, quoted in *Viktor Shklovsky: A Reader*, ed. and trans. Alexandra Berlina (London: Bloomsbury, 2017), 80.

JACKSON POLLOCK
UNTITLED
1951

CARTER E. FOSTER

Jackson Pollock's place in art history owes much to the celebrated images of him engrossed in making his work caught on film and in photographs—almost as much as it does to the actual paintings and drawings that represent his paradigm-shifting artistic output.[1] The curator Kirk Varnedoe described Pollock as a "huge permission giver,"[2] and critics and other artists recognized how his technique, especially as recorded on film by Hans Namuth, pointed toward new categories of art that would develop and flourish in subsequent decades. Aspects of performance and installation art link back to Pollock's small, humble, shack-like studio on Long Island where he created his most celebrated paintings, the large-scale canvases on which he famously poured, dripped, flung, and pooled commercial enamel paints to create his profoundly original formal vocabulary. Weaving in and out of a large, ground-laid canvas in Namuth's famous film,[3] Pollock seems the very embodiment of the critic Harold Rosenberg's phrase about Abstract Expressionist painting being "an arena in which to act."[4] Rosenberg's other famous descriptor, "action painting," would seem to put Pollock at odds with the traditional notion of drawing, generally a quieter, more intimate medium not associated with large-scale, broad, gestural application. Yet in many ways, drawing and painting merge in Pollock's work, especially when one considers the foregrounding of line that was inherent to the artist's pour technique.

Pollock called his drawing ability as a high school student in Los Angeles "rotten," and his brother Sande seemed to concur, stating that the young Jack could not render form mimetically in convincing fashion.[5] By the time he moved to New York in 1930 and began to study under Thomas Hart Benton at the Art Students League, Pollock's fellow students apparently recognized his ability to create powerful images on paper, even if his teacher felt he lacked an understanding of drawing's fundamentals.[6] Susan Davidson's overview of Pollock's works on paper notes that his drawing style follows the same general arc as his painting.[7] By the late 1930s, he had begun using colored pencils and produced an extraordinary group of sheets, some of which show his interpretations of European Renaissance and Baroque painters; others he used in therapy sessions with a Jungian analyst. The most impressive of these powerful formal explorations that toggle between figuration and abstraction and reflect the influence of Surrealism, the Mexican muralists, and Pablo Picasso

Plate 6 Jackson Pollock, *Untitled*, 1951, black and colored ink on mulberry paper, 24¾ × 39¼ in. (63 × 99.7 cm), irregular. Seattle Art Museum, Gift of the Friday Foundation in honor of Richard E. Lang and Jane Lang Davis, 2020.14.13.

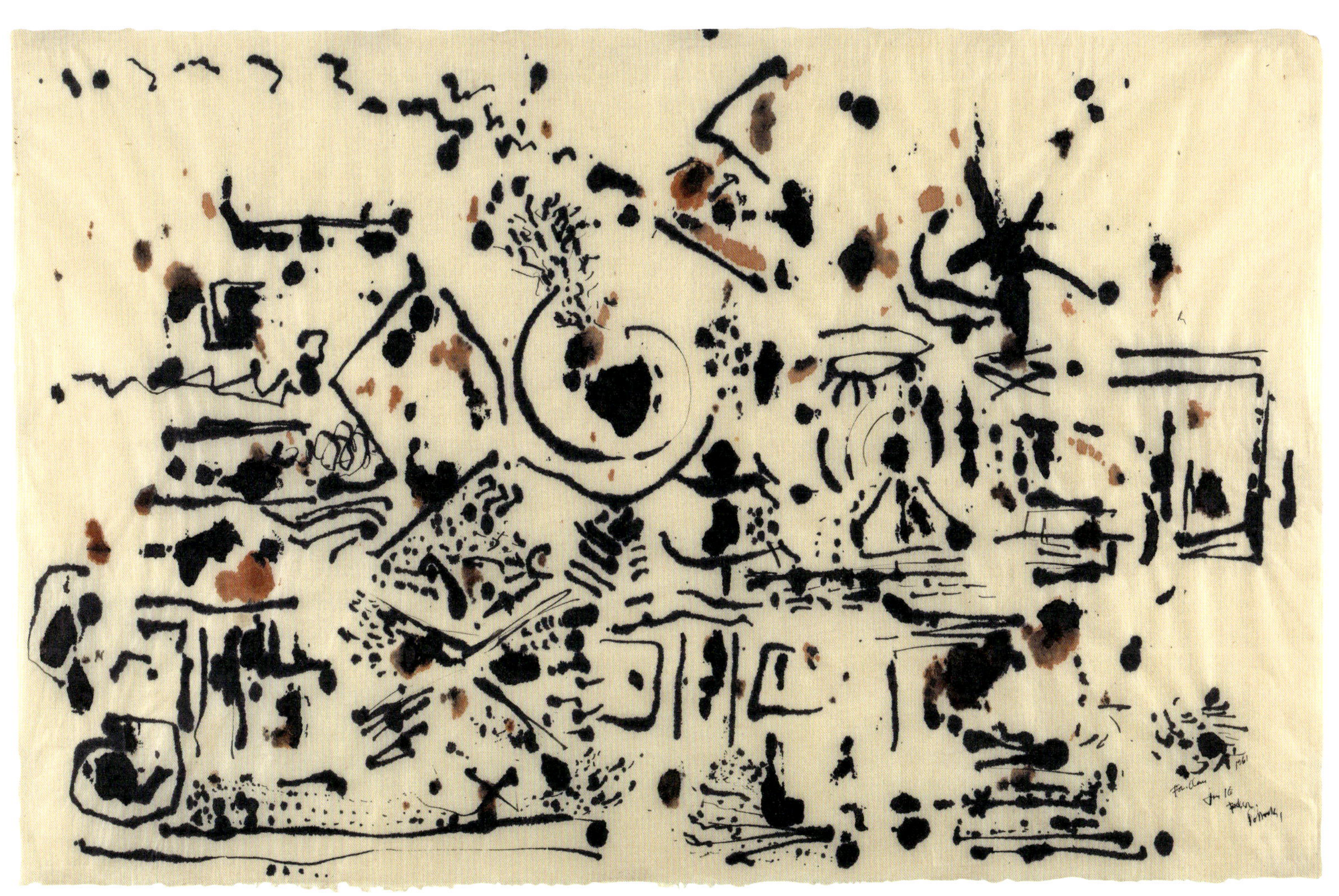

show an artist able to coax subtle tonalities and wildly inventive shapes from his medium.

This group helps establish that drawing is, in fact, a distinct category in Pollock's oeuvre, separate from painting, regardless of the strong connection between painting and drawing discussed below. I would argue that his mature pour works on paper are a subcategory of his painting, smaller in scale but similar in technique, style, and aesthetic effect to his classic, much-celebrated large-scale drip paintings of 1947–50. Pollock's drawings, on the other hand, might be defined as works in which the paper support asserts itself and influenced the types of marks the artist made. The categories can be blurry, especially when the artist used gouache and watercolor, but a number of sheets from the mid-1940s use media and instruments traditionally associated with drawing—pen and ink, pencil, pastel, crayon—with Pollock exploring graphic, linear vocabularies in which one feels the motion of the hand rather than the arm, the forms appropriate to drawing's smaller and more intimate scale. This is especially true of some of his pen-and-ink drawings featuring tangles of jagged lines that positively brim with energy, such as the Art Institute of Chicago's 1944 untitled sheet.[8]

Many writers on Pollock, and the artist himself, have described how drawing and painting are essentially the same thing in his work: that the poured lines he created with his celebrated drip technique are the essence of drawing precisely because they emphasize linearity. In 1965, Michael Fried described the artist's innovation as a freeing of line "from the job of describing contours and bounding shapes. It has been purged of its figurative character. . . . Pollock's line bounds and delimits nothing—except, in a sense, eyesight."[9] Fried's emphasis on what he called "opticality" in Pollock's work became a touchstone for many of the formalist interpretations of Pollock that had begun with Clement Greenberg in the 1940s. Later, the first in-depth study of Pollock's drawings, by Bernice Rose, was titled *Drawing into Painting* to emphasize their interconnection in his practice,[10] a title very much aligned with statements by the artist himself, such as, "I approach painting in the same sense as one approaches drawing; that is, it's direct."[11]

The year Pollock made the Lang Collection sheet (plate 6), 1951, he had begun a new series—now known as the black pour paintings—that he described as "drawing on canvas in black," and which marked a significant stylistic shift.[12] This drawing belongs to a group executed on an absorbent Japanese paper given to him by a friend, the artist Tony Smith. He referenced working on them in a letter to his patron Alfonso Ossorio in January, which suggests he made them in New York, where he was staying at the time, before he returned home to East Hampton in May and began a new group of paintings.[13] Crucially, the porosity and absorbency of this particular paper determined the types of marks Pollock could make and his manner of working, for as he started on the top sheet, capillary action carried some of his marks through to sheets below. In a perceptive essay about these late drawings, Stephanie Straine notes that the "structural and conceptual implications of the 'stack' is that it moves yet further away from optical flatness. . . . It becomes sculptural in its multi-sidedness. There is a play of call and response across the sheets of mulberry paper."[14] Pollock responded in various ways to the paper's quality and the staining process, sometimes flipping a sheet and reworking a mirror image on the verso, sometimes elaborating on the stains created from previous sheets. There was, in other words, a temporal and spatial connection across a number of the drawings united by this paper type. And although the layering of Pollock's marks is not as dense and subtle as some of his earlier poured paintings on paper, due to the way in which the mulberry fibers absorbed the ink, some works in this group do share the "overall" quality of compositional density that is such a hallmark of his most celebrated work.

However, this drawing and its companion sheet—the one that was underneath it and thus absorbed Pollock's marks through capillary action as he was working—are relatively spare for his work, quite a bit less dense than several of the others in the series (fig. 38). They make a fascinating pair because their marks correspond fairly closely, and the only reworking the artist seems to have done on the lower sheet was to add some drippings of white gouache. The second sheet is also a kind of monotype, the first thus both an independent drawing and the matrix used to create its companion. Printmaking was not a significant practice for the artist, so it is interesting to find him working in a "printerly" manner here, whether or not he was aware of it and doing so intentionally.[15] Their

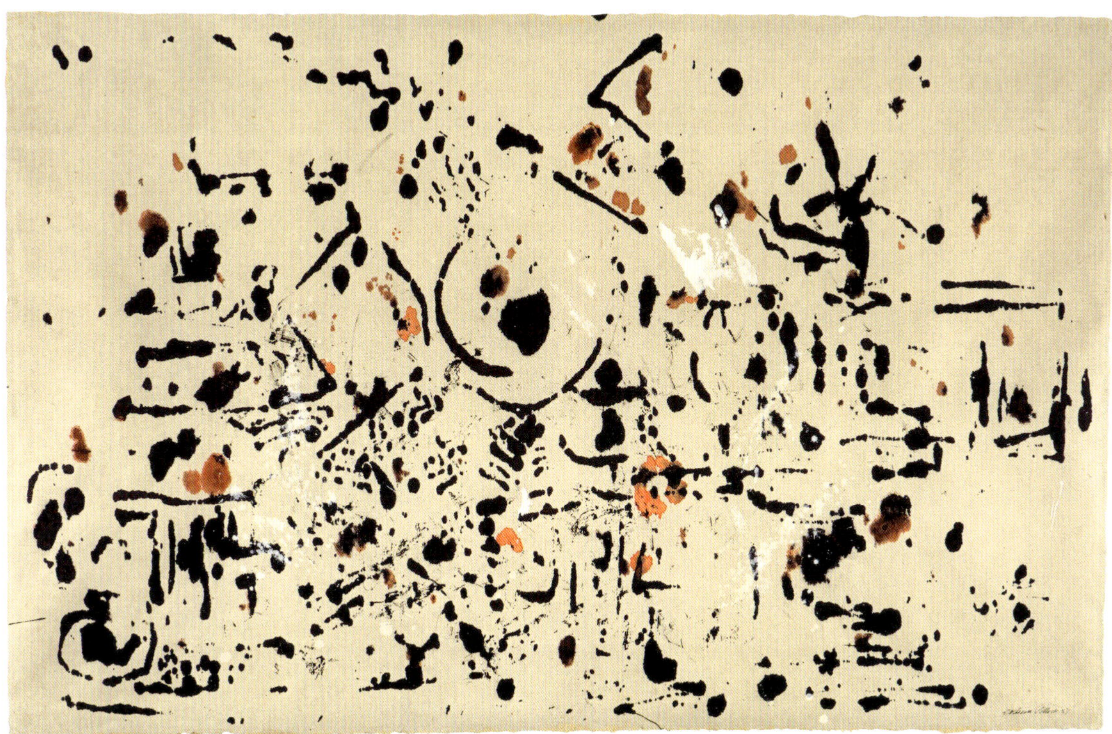

Fig. 38 Jackson Pollock, *Untitled*, 1951, colored inks and gouache on Japanese paper, 24¾ × 39 in. (62.9 × 99.1 cm). The National Galleries of Scotland, GMA 849.

spareness also allows one to focus more easily on the individual marks and their formal character, as there is abundant negative space without many overlapping elements. It seems likely Pollock was here taking advantage of a new type of drawing instrument, the felt-tipped pen, which was also marketed as a "fountain-brush" or "brush-pen." Margaret Holben Ellis, who researched the drawing tools Pollock used, quotes an advertisement explaining how "different textural effects can be obtained with a single stroke."[16] By varying the speed and pressure of his strokes, the artist could get thin and thick marks in the same motion, or he could hold the instrument to let the ink seep and penetrate the paper more thoroughly. The Lang sheet is virtually a catalogue of such effects.

It also has—unusually for a nonfigurative Pollock—a focal point: the large blobby stain close to the composition's center, whose form the artist expanded by looping a circular swirl of ink around it. The shape evokes an eye, underscoring how the haptic and the visual merge beautifully here. The artist repeated the motif several times, twice in the lower left and again in the center right half (directly below another form that looks much like a closed eyelid with eyelashes), so it clearly interested him. Pollock's use of such forms involving combinations of angled, straight, and curved lines with soaked-in blobs of ink recalls the hieroglyph-like marks his wife, Lee Krasner, had used in her series of *Little Images* paintings, works she executed, as one normally would a drawing, on a flat tablet and in a smaller scale (fig. 39). Although her series dates to the late forties, thus a few years before her husband made this sheet, Krasner's approach intersects here in interesting ways with Pollock's drawing, whether the influence was

Fig. 39 Lee Krasner, *White Squares*, ca. 1948, enamel and oil on canvas, 24⅟₁₆ × 30⅟₁₈ in. (61.1 × 76.5 cm). Whitney Museum of American Art, Gift of Mr. and Mrs. B. H. Friedman, 75.1.

direct or not. One could even assert that just a few other works by Pollock share the hieroglyphic nature of this drawing and its companion—that they are in some ways outliers in his oeuvre. On the other hand, they still embody the controlled chance that is the hallmark of his drip technique, albeit in another manner. Here, the capillary action in the paper fibers created chance conditions, ones the artist could affect but not completely control by pressure and time as he applied his instrument to paper. An artist whose works are celebrated for speed and energy has slowed down quite a bit here.

NOTES

1 Pepe Karmel, "Pollock at Work: The Films and Photographs of Hans Namuth," in *Jackson Pollock: New Approaches*, ed. Kirk Varnedoe and Pepe Karmel (New York: Museum of Modern Art, 1998), 86–137.

2 Kirk Varnedoe, interview with Charlie Rose, "Great Masters with Charlie Rose," PBS, January 18, 1999, YouTube, accessed October 30, 2020, http://www.youtube.com/watch?v=_t3Smr1WKQo, quote at 15:54.

3 Hans Namuth, *Jackson Pollock 51* (1951), 10:13, http://www.youtube.com/watch?v=6cgBvpjwOGo&feature=player_embedded.

4 Harold Rosenberg, "The American Action Painters," in *Reading Abstract Expressionism: Context and Critique*, ed. Ellen G. Landau (New Haven, CT: Yale University Press, 2005), 190.

5 Susan Davidson, "The Gesture of Intimate Scale: Jackson Pollock Paintings on Paper," in *No Limits, Just Edges: Jackson Pollock Paintings on Paper*, ed. David Anfam and Susan Davidson (New York: Solomon R. Guggenheim Foundation, 2005), 10.

6 Davidson, "Gesture of Intimate Scale," 11.

7 Davidson, "Gesture of Intimate Scale," 11.

8 Jackson Pollock, *Untitled*, 1944, pen and brush and black and colored inks on ivory wove paper, 18⅞ × 24⅞ in. (48 × 63.2 cm). Art Institute of Chicago, 1966.250.

9 Michael Fried, *Three American Painters: Kenneth Noland, Jules Olitski, Frank Stella* (Cambridge, MA: Fogg Art Museum, Harvard University, 1965), 14.

10 Bernice Rose, *Jackson Pollock: Drawing into Painting* (New York: Museum of Modern Art, 1980).

11 Jackson Pollock, quoted in Pepe Karmel, ed., *Jackson Pollock: Interviews, Articles, Reviews* (New York: Museum of Modern Art, 1999), 22.

12 Jackson Pollock, quoted in Varnedoe and Karmel, *Jackson Pollock*, 326.

13 Stephanie Straine, "Beyond Work: Pollock Drawing," in *Jackson Pollock: Blind Spots*, ed. Gavin Delahunty (London: Tate Publishing, 2015), 104.

14 Straine, "Beyond Work," 107.

15 Straine, "Beyond Work," 107, makes the connection to the monotype process. I borrow the term "printerly" from Jennifer Roberts, "The Printerly Art of Jasper Johns," in *Jasper Johns / In Press: The Crosshatch Works and the Logic of Print* (Cambridge, MA: Harvard Art Museum, 2012), 10–42. Charles F. Stuckey has also noted Pollock's interest in mirroring and the conceptual and structural connection between two sides of the same artwork. See Charles F. Stuckey, "Another Side of Jackson Pollock," in Karmel, *Jackson Pollock: Interviews*, 183.

16 Margaret Holben Ellis, "Materials, Tool, and 'Technics': Works on Paper by Jackson Pollock," in Anfam and Davidson, *No Limits, Just Edges*, 130.

PHILIP GUSTON
TO B.W.T.
1952

ROBERT STORR

Born in Montreal, Canada, in 1913 to Ukrainian immigrant parents who settled in Southern California, Philip Guston knew poverty and social strife from an early age. His first artistic love was the comic strips that he copied from the Sunday newspapers in the solitude of a closet. His next aesthetically formative discovery was the Italian Renaissance, to which a high school teacher introduced him. Nevertheless, despite the revelation the old masters and his mentor provided, Guston dropped out before graduation, never to return, enrolling instead in classes at art schools in Los Angeles. Hardworking and prodigiously gifted, he excelled at emulating neoclassical figuration with a high level of finish. When still in his twenties, he made a reputation for himself in Mexico and across the United States as a painter of heroic-scale murals and complex allegorical canvases. Then, at the age of 36, he unexpectedly turned his back on a promising career in the various representational idioms he had mastered and began, tabula rasa, to improvise abstract compositions out of dense accumulations of simple vertical and horizontal marks, in the process taking his place in the forefront of postwar American modernism alongside Mark Rothko, Willem de Kooning, and his erstwhile high school classmate Jackson Pollock.

The most elegiac of these early abstractions, *To B.W.T.* (1952, plate 7), is dedicated to the most refined and lyrical member of the artist's New York cohort. Among the bold, gestural painters of first-generation Abstract Expressionism, Bradley Walker Tomlin was a deft calligrapher. With strokes on some occasions leisurely and nearly meandering, while on others short, crisp, and cryptic, he deployed brushes of varying widths like italic pens trailing bands of tone and color (fig. 40). The contrast between a Tomlin line and one by Pollock, for example, is between quivering ribbons and a snapping whiplash. That distinction put Tomlin at roughly an equivalent aesthetic distance from the downtown Manhattan school of muscular angst and from the Northwest Coast master Mark Tobey's work. With this difference: whereas Tobey seldom mingled socially with his East Coast contemporaries (and not all that frequently on gallery walls), Tomlin lived among his New York School peers and exhibited alongside them like an elder brother or youthful uncle.

Of that legendary group, Tomlin—an archetypal "painter's painter" whose work was owned by no less discriminating a talent than the proto-Minimalist Robert Ryman—had perhaps the closest painterly affinity with

Plate 7 Philip Guston, *To B.W.T.*, 1952, oil on canvas, 48 × 51 in. (122 × 129.2 cm). Seattle Art Museum, Gift of the Friday Foundation in honor of Richard E. Lang and Jane Lang Davis, 2020.14.10.

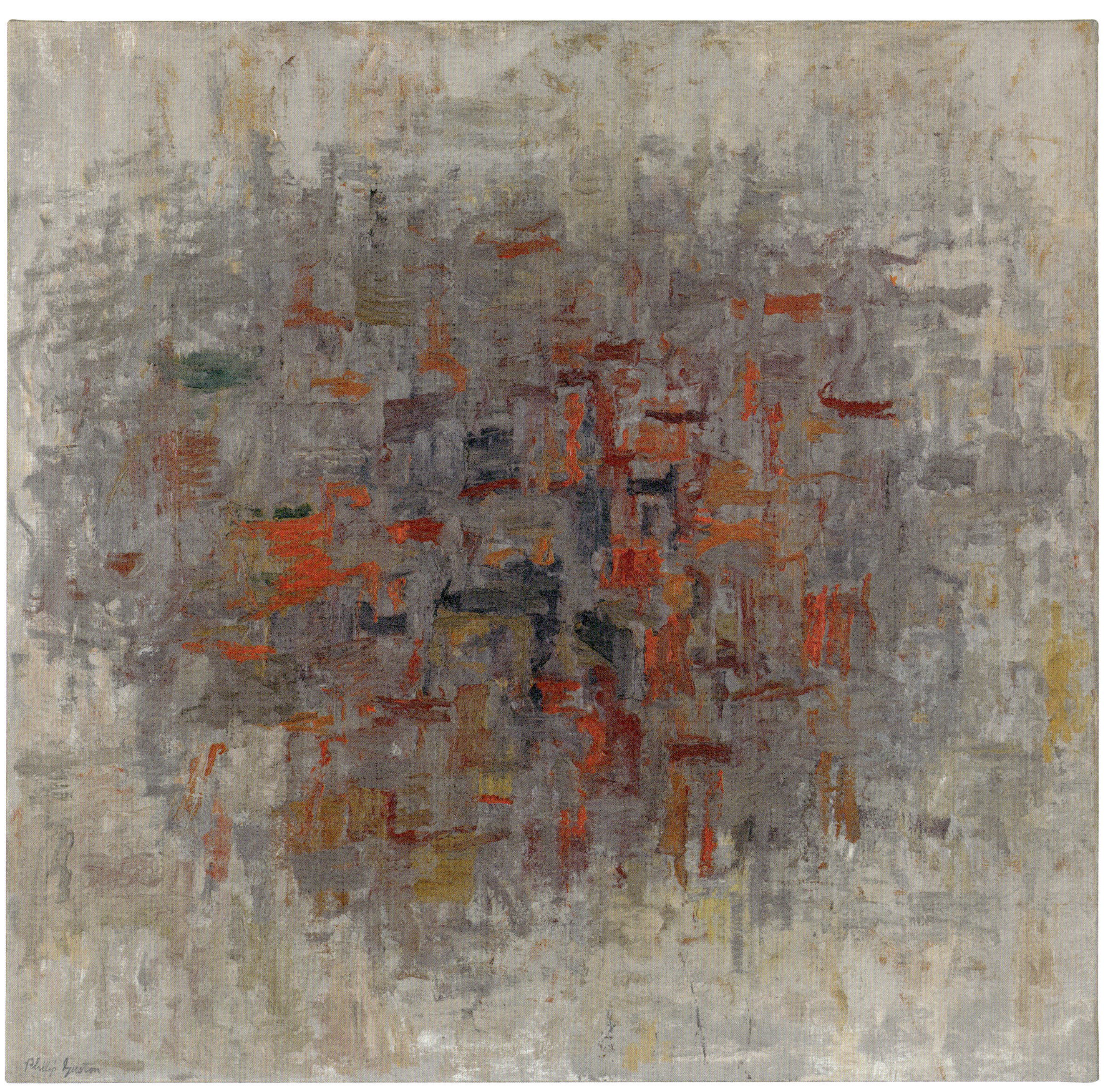

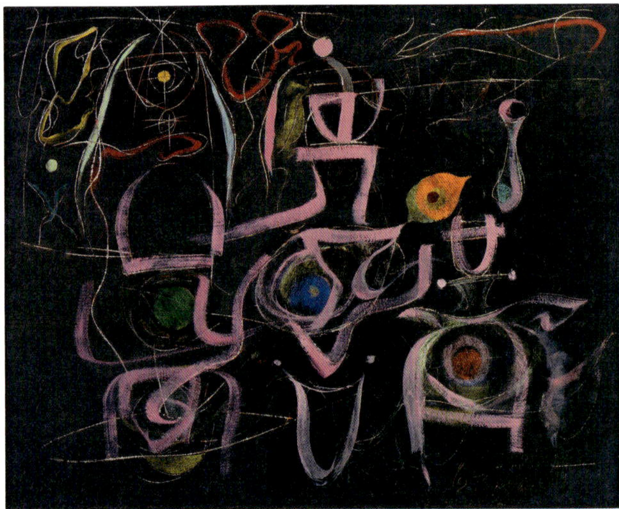

Fig. 40 Bradley Walker Tomlin, *Number 3*, 1948, oil on canvas, 40 × 50⅛ in. (101.3 × 127.2 cm). The Museum of Modern Art, New York, Gift of John E. Hutchins in memory of Frances E. Marder Hutchins, 423.1960.

Guston, Pollock's coeval, approximately a dozen years Tomlin's junior. Graceful tracery and formal embroidery, rather than propulsive drawing or dramatic mark making, were Tomlin's forte. Possessed of a fluent command of academic contouring and shading equaled only by Willem de Kooning, Guston harnessed those capacities to the task of delineating intricate scenarios that by the end of the Depression won him precocious fame and numerous prizes and public commissions, including one for the facade of the Works Progress Administration Pavilion at the New York World's Fair in 1939.

However, by the late 1940s, Guston grew impatient with his acquired facility and the figurative conventions that had paved his way to wide national recognition, and he went back to basics—which for him meant simple structural annotations and tonal as well as chromatic harmonies. The use of musical metaphor is not incidental. Guston's acquaintance with the avant-garde composer John Cage—who became aware of Tobey while teaching in Seattle at the Cornish College of the Arts—was essential in clearing a path through the thicket of ideas and imagery that had accumulated during the artist's long apprenticeship to old masters such as Piero della Francesca and modern ones like Giorgio de Chirico and Pablo Picasso, thereby freeing Guston to disregard the picture-laden past and lose himself in the non-objective present.

Thus, starting in 1949–50, for the first time in his life, Guston embarked on paintings without a carefully worked-out conception of what the final result would look like—that is to say, without detailing what the subject matter or ultimate formal design of his canvases would be. And, inasmuch as Cage provided him the artistic permission to enter into and reconnoiter the "nothingness" of pure abstraction as an alternative to the fully understood but increasingly daunting "too muchness" of his previous figurative work, the Dutch modernist Piet Mondrian gave him the means for doing so.

In the early teens of the twentieth century, Mondrian had arrived at a reductive method for charting pictorial space based on fracturing the traditional grid that had underpinned Western perspective since the Renaissance. He then moved the fragments around within the standard rectangle of the pictorial field he had emptied out (and sometimes within ovals inscribed upon such fields, as had been done by the Cubists slightly before him, as well as by portraitists and landscape painters going back centuries). In short, Mondrian delineated the armatures upon which representational art had been hung, leaving out the depiction of natural or human-made forms altogether. Or, at most, hinting at them with details—a curve for a tree branch, a vertical rectangle for a church window—for which no one but the artist could specify the referent with much assurance. These drawings and paintings by Mondrian became known as his Plus/Minus works (fig. 41), because all that remained for viewers to get their bearings were the intersections of vertical and horizontal lines that had once articulated the structural matrix of the image. Instead, that broken matrix *was* the image in and of itself.

Picking up where Mondrian had left off, Guston, in effect, dispensed with the intermediate stage of disassembling the archetypal grid and mapped out the vacuum of the spatial construct of the canvas with increments of painterly substance. That is to say, he filled the void with solid patches of pigment applied intuitively rather than in accordance with any a priori idea of what the result would or should be, patterning the surface with improvised rhythms and intervals much as a composer like Cage would fill silence with random sounds.

In these transitional works, Guston achieved a degree of ambiguity and suspended animation that suggests the gradual coalescence or dissolution of something evolving or devolving that transformed the painting as a whole into a drama of accretion or, conversely, one of disintegration. Viewed another way, Guston created paintings that served as existential clocks that told the time of becoming and of decay.

To B.W.T. is a prime example of this chapter in the story of Guston's unceasing metamorphosis as an artist. Indeed, metamorphosis is the leitmotif of his art, both abstract and figurative, from the early 1950s through to the end of his life thirty years later. In this instance, the shreds or fibrous facets of forms float in a shallow pool of mottled grays, massing toward the center of the horizontal canvas in something resembling an oval that recalls Mondrian's paradigm, but devoid of rigid angles. The net effect of this loose, trial-and-error approach to composition is the exact opposite of the hard-and-fast quality of so much Cubist and Cubist-derived painting. Rather, it is an emblem of perpetual flux, of the shift and shimmer of scintillating natural forms in a tide pool.

The analogies used here, or similar ones, frequently occur to viewers anxious to translate paintings that are neither more nor less than that—paintings. Yet the work is not, as some critics of the 1950s were quick to infer, an incidence of Abstract Impressionism; any claim to the overt emotions associated with the rubric of Abstract Expressionism would be similarly hard to justify. Palpable emotion is certainly present in each brush mark Guston made, but that feeling is anything but demonstrative. Rather, it is doubt laden and nervously probing, though never tentative, like a stick poking a banked fire or the still-glowing embers in the ashes of one that has all but burned out. In short, characteristics that lend the image its tenuous intensity, its elegiac aura, its look of a once-blazing hearth that has almost consumed its fuel.

Its special muted radiance is owed to the subtle contrasts between dispersed patches of golden yellows, blood reds, and dense orange, dull greens and a full spectrum of quiet grays whose chromatic neutrality and faint unnamable tinting assume the glow of hues complementary to the colors to which they are juxtaposed. The amalgam they constitute is held together in space by the vibrant optical tensions Guston is able to orchestrate in the dim ambience of his painterly field.

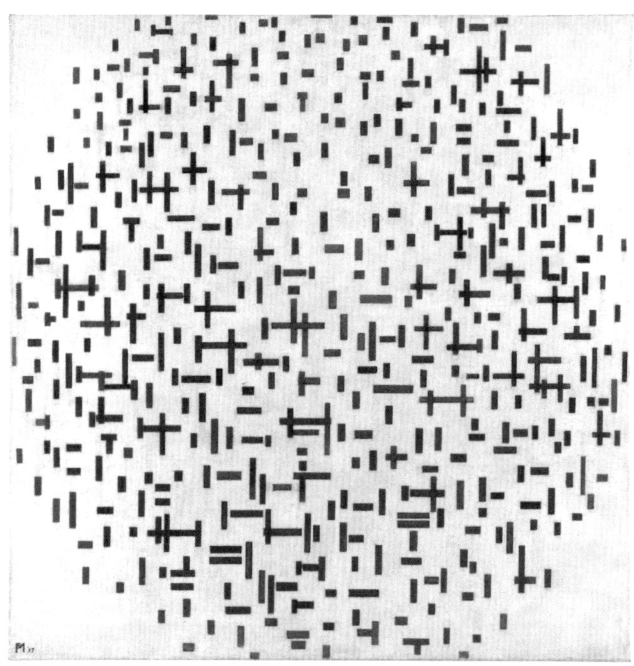

Fig. 41 Piet Mondrian, *Composition in Line, Second State*, 1916–17, oil on canvas, 42½ × 42½ in. (108 × 108 cm). Kröller-Müller Museum, Otterlo, the Netherlands, KM 106.482.

Comparing the evanescent quietude of *To B.W.T.* to Guston's figurative work of the 1940s, one finds the same moody, elegant inwardness in a radically different stylistic idiom; in short, one meets the same man. Compared to the grand manner of his murals, these canvases almost appear to be the work of a different artist altogether. However, this discrepancy reminds us that the two approaches are all of a piece, since the drama of Guston's art is precisely that of a sensibility that is not so much at odds with itself as one that refuses to look away from its multifaceted dualities. During the last ten years of Guston's career, they fused in tragicomic figurative works of astonishing poetic scope, emotional complexity and force, and unprecedented graphic invention, works that made Guston the touchstone for the Neo-Expressionists and New Image artists who emerged in the decade following his death in 1980. The later, 1970s paintings (see plate 19) resonate as wholly contemporary even today because of their prescient articulation of America's abiding malaise and bad conscience.

JOAN MITCHELL
THE SINK
1956

AMY RAHN

A true and accurate painting condenses and concentrates aspects of things . . . without coordinating them, without storytelling. It tells of their accretion, their accumulation.

—Yves Michaud

Joan Mitchell's 1956 painting *The Sink* (plate 8),[1] a gestural abstract painting more than nine feet across, rotates around a turbulent center in currents of ivory-gray-white amid a hail of precisely tuned yellow, pale green, and aqua flashes. Painted in a time of heady artistic success and personal transition for Mitchell, *The Sink* "condenses and concentrates" these turnings, to borrow Yves Michaud's phrase, delivering the gyre of Mitchell's mid-1950s, still roiling, into our present.

Mitchell, an American painter born and raised in Chicago, spent her formative years as an artist among the New York School of the 1950s. She painted consistently—and often monumentally—from the late 1940s until her death, a lifetime of sustained painterly achievement that is both characteristic of her generation of New York School painters and singular in its power, scale, ambition, and continuity. Arriving in New York in 1950 after a year in France on a painting fellowship, she admired the works of Willem de Kooning and Franz Kline and sought them out in their studios. Within the then-small world of downtown New York, she quickly became an integral participant in the intense culture of making paintings, talking about painting, and socializing around painting in studios, panel discussions, art galleries, and bars (fig. 42). Later in the decade, Mitchell's relationships in these social circles became fraught, and she removed herself to Paris for the summer—a decision that would shape the rest of her life. As Mitchell explained to an interviewer, she went to Paris in 1955 to "get away from . . . personal things," but then, "of course ran into other personal things."[2]

Establishing a new life in Paris meant acclimating to and rediscovering the city; it also meant searching for studio space in which to work. Mitchell maintained her painterly momentum while moving between five different studios between May and October 1955. By the following summer, she had secured the American painter Paul Jenkins's studio on the rue Decrès while he borrowed hers on St. Mark's Place in New York; the early fall found her

Plate 8 Joan Mitchell, *The Sink*, 1956, oil on canvas, 54⅝ × 111¾ in. (138.7 × 283.9 cm). Seattle Art Museum, Gift of the Friday Foundation in honor of Richard E. Lang and Jane Lang Davis, 2020.14.15.

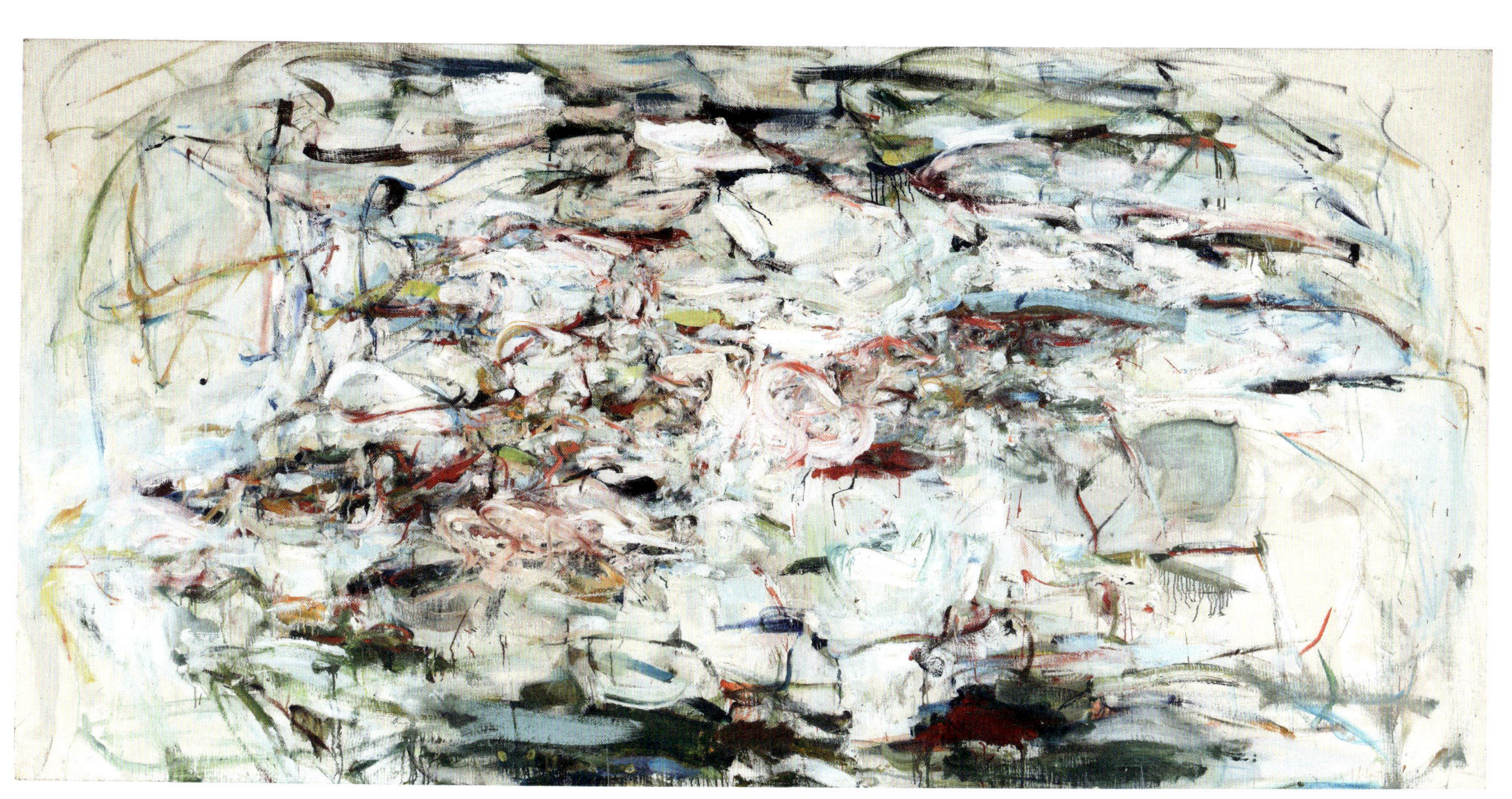

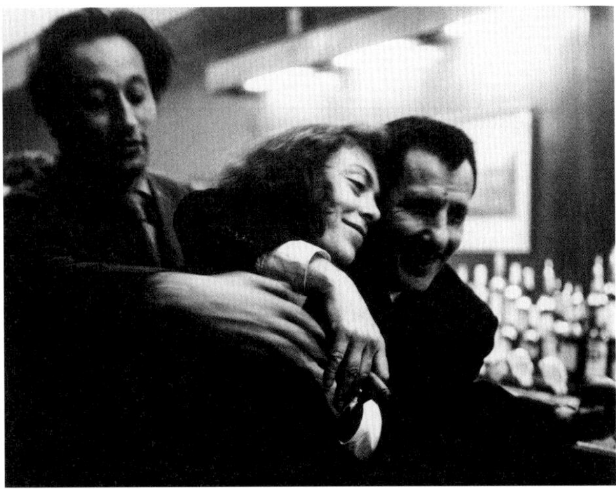

Fig. 42 Arthur Swoger, *Norman Bluhm, Joan Mitchell, and Franz Kline*, 1957, gelatin silver print, 10½ x 13¾ in. (26.7 × 34.9 cm). RISD Museum, Museum Acquisition Fund, 2003.12.1.

working in a studio on the rue Daguerre (fig. 43) before returning to painting in New York in the late fall and winter of 1956–57. Engaged in an affair with the artist Jean-Paul Riopelle and integrated with an artistic community that included Shirley Jaffe, Sam Francis, and Alberto Giacometti, Mitchell painted intensively in two places and in two social and artistic circles for four years before moving to Paris permanently in 1959. *The Sink* emerged from this transitional and transnational period.

Near *The Sink*'s center, viscous white reaches vertically to the top and bottom edges of the painting like an axis; beside it, a mass of shorter strokes of vibrant red, spring green, white, and pink simultaneously build to a point and shatter laterally, pushing into the more broadly painted white areas near the canvas's center and right. Intense bursts of color and expanses of white press and balance against one another, making the whole seem to rotate, a slow hurricane with a red-white curlicue near the painting's center as its eye (fig. 44). This inner knot spins the composition toward the painting's upper surface and the canvas taut below it, even as it pivots laterally around its core. In other words, the painting rotates within itself in two directions, swirling around its center while cycling toward and away from the viewer. *The Sink*'s interconnected turns, built of thousands of painterly decisions in color and stroke that seem to move at different speeds, form a visual choreography over which the painting's title hangs like a question.

"The Sink" *could* reference a less-charged rotation than Mitchell's passages from Paris to New York and back—namely, the everyday whorl of an ordinary studio sink. The painting's rushing quality and rotational composition might even invite such an interpretation. Yet even the title of this dynamic work refuses to stay still: the painting has been referred to as both *Sink* and *The Sink*, refusing to resolve into the grammatical clarity of a verb or a noun.[3] Indeed, Mitchell's titles can be an unreliable guide to any imagined imagery they might contain, and even a misdirection. For example, an art dealer once claimed *The Sink* referred to "a low depression of land filled with water," supposedly located near a studio of Mitchell's near Chicago's Lincoln Park.[4] Since Mitchell did not have a studio in Chicago after moving to New York in the late 1940s, that referent seems unlikely at best.

The desire to map Mitchell's abstraction back onto nameable referents, though, is understandable; a viewer would certainly not be alone in looking for *something* in her paintings, whether a studio fixture or topographical feature. Mitchell worked from memory and feeling, and feelings about memory, and surely those memories and feelings were suffused with the forms and figures of the world. Still, Mitchell's titles do not so much correspond to their subject matter as ride over the surface of her works, adding a linguistic experience likely associated with a private memory of Mitchell's to a fusion of inner- and outer-world fragments, transformed into paint. When, for example, the critic Irving Sandler narrated the painting of two of Mitchell's canvases for his watershed 1957 *Art News* article "Joan Mitchell Paints a Picture," he figured her process of painting as discovering and losing a memory-image in the work. He wrote of Mitchell's *George Went Swimming at Barnes Hole, but It Got Too Cold* that the painting began with a memory of her poodle Georges du Soleil swimming, but the painting eventually got too white, too bleak, "too cold."[5] Sandler quoted Mitchell, "If a painting comes from [my personal meanings/references] then they don't matter. Other people don't have to see what I do in my work."[6] Concluding with Mitchell seeing her paintings *as* paintings, as new works transformed from personal recollections, Sandler wrote: "the vital matter is transferred to works in progress."[7]

The artist's titles might have also served a practical purpose. Before 1955, Mitchell often titled major paintings

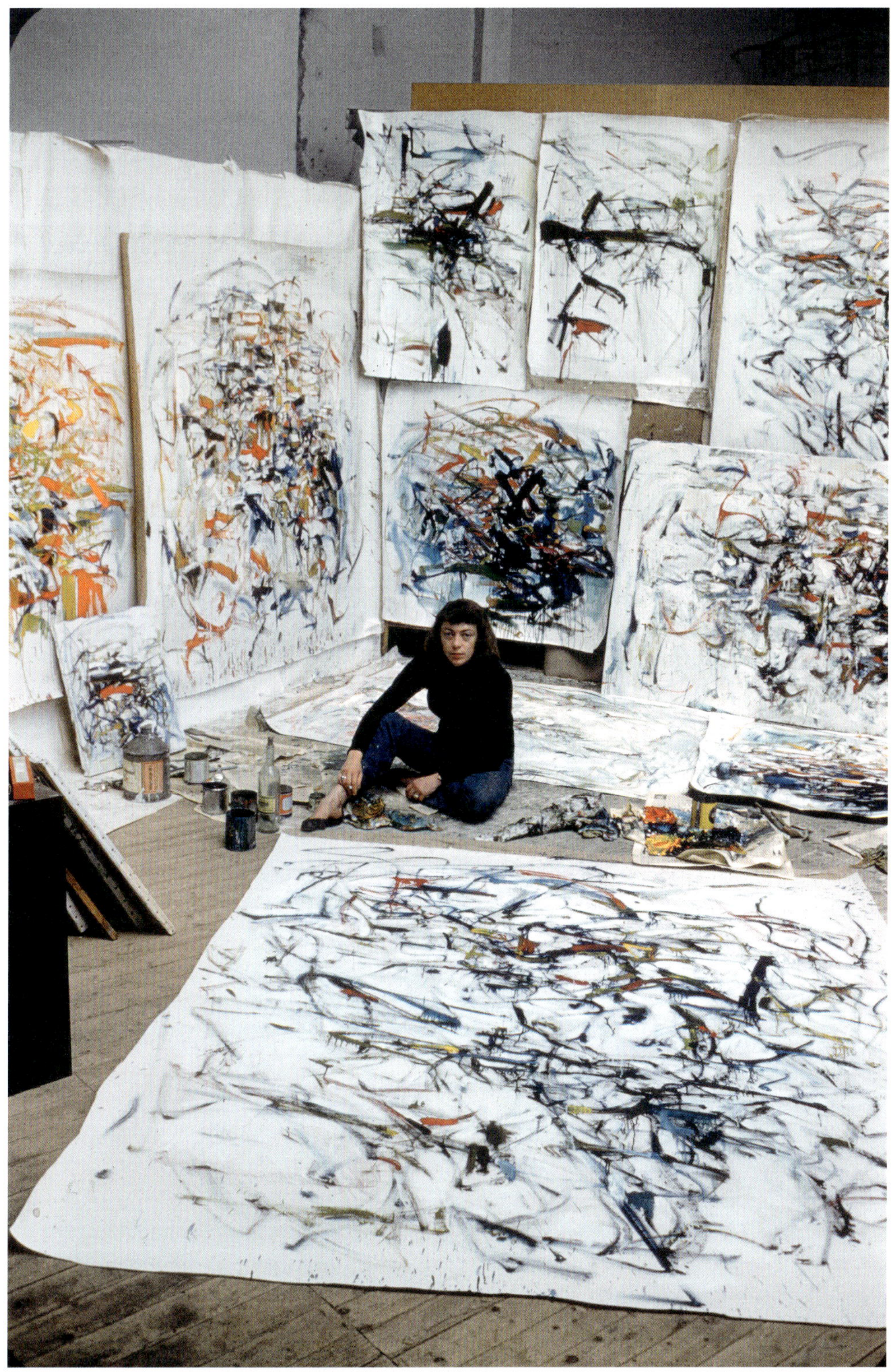

Fig. 43 Joan Mitchell in her studio at 77 rue Daguerre, Paris, 1956. Photograph by Loomis Dean. The LIFE Picture Collection via Getty Images.

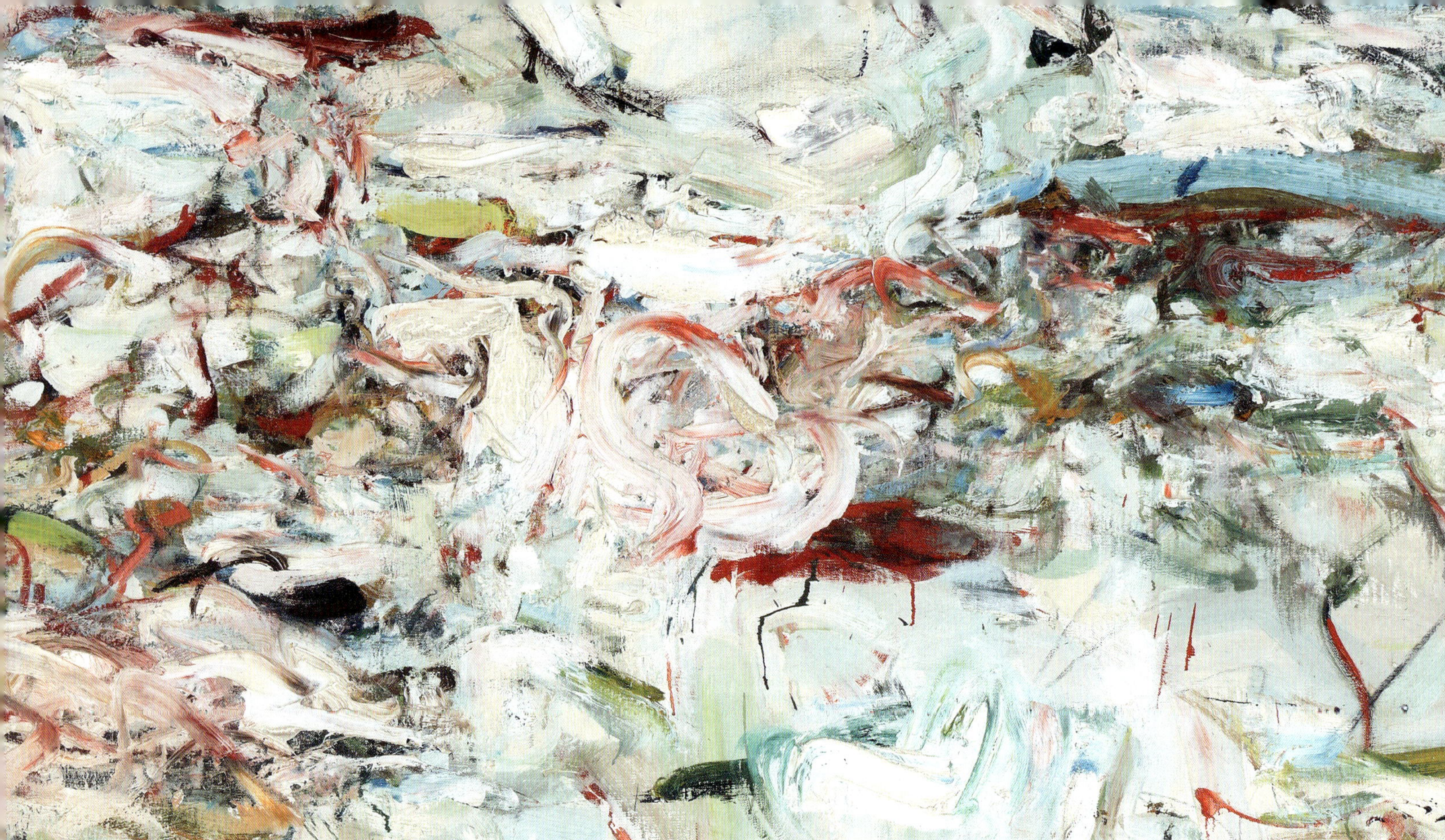

Fig. 44 Joan Mitchell, *The Sink*, 1956 (detail, plate 8).

Untitled. From the mid-1950s onward, she titled her works more lucidly, assigning titles like *The Sink*. Since, at this point, she was sending her paintings from Paris to New York and tracking payments and ownership for her works sold through the Stable Gallery, Mitchell might have changed her titling practices to ease the logistical headaches of her transatlantic career. "The Sink" might thus summon an external referent, an impression consonant with the work's final form, a name cast over the painting to track its passage between places, or all three. Reading titles as a potential sign of Mitchell's acuity in the management of her career resonates with *The Sink*'s originary moment in the mid-1950s—a moment of transition for Mitchell as her professional acclaim mounted. As she and her works flew between continents, her career accelerated.

These were years of critical celebration and institutional sanction. Mitchell's March 1955 exhibition was named one of the year's best by *Art News*, alongside those by Mark Rothko and Ad Reinhardt, making her the youngest artist so honored that year.[8] Mitchell had four solo exhibitions at the Stable Gallery between 1953 and 1958 while also showing her work nationally and internationally, often in exhibitions designed to demonstrate what was most "current" in American art. Her inclusion in a 1957 exhibition at the Jewish Museum, *Artists of the New York School: Second Generation*, marked the esteem of insider critics and other artists,[9] and the Whitney Museum of American Art acquired her painting *Hemlock* in 1958. That same year, her *City Landscape* appeared in the Society for Contemporary American Art annual exhibition at the Art Institute of Chicago, which subsequently purchased the work for its collection. Mitchell was also selected for the Venice Biennale in 1958, and in 1959 her work appeared in the Corcoran and São Paulo Biennials as well as the landmark exhibition *documenta II*.[10] If Mitchell had begun the 1950s as a young artist seeking out the lions of the downtown painting scene, she closed the decade as an established artist with her own national and international reputation as an exemplar of the New York School.

Critics saw Mitchell's works as capturing the energy of their moment. In his 1957 review of Mitchell's Stable Gallery exhibition, which included *The Sink*, Irving Sandler wrote, "The love for painting which pulses through these canvases engulfs the viewer. This show should be seen in the morning, for it can animate the entire day."[11] Mitchell's paintings radiated the energy of their making, "animating" the viewer's lived experience. The French critic Pierre Schneider used the metaphor of natural and electric light to allude to Mitchell's work across geographic contexts as a source of strength. In remarks made during the 1961 *Salon de mai*, Schneider transposed this inner/outer question of representation to the light itself, describing Mitchell's 1960 painting *Whaler* as hybridizing the "electric" light of (German-then-American) Expressionist painting with the "natural" light of (French) Impressionist painting, concluding evocatively: "A painting by Joan Mitchell seems to me in a strangely hybrid zone—one has the impression of an electric bulb in broad daylight."[12] Schneider conceived the conditions of plein-air and studio painting as echoing outer and inner worlds. Electric in daylight, American in France, Mitchell's paintings transformed her in-between position into a strength.

The Sink, a "condensed" and "concentrated" accumulation of time and experience in marks made during a pivotal moment in the artist's life, knots her past and our present moment of emergence and possibility in its tense coiling. Painted during Mitchell's own productive period of restless transition in the mid-1950s, the slippery riddle of *The Sink* draws us into its dislocations and revelations, a whorl that resonates with its time in Mitchell's life and with our own complex moment, refusing to resolve into a single decodable meaning. The painting's interior turns amid a rushing torrent in which we might experience the tension and possibility of the threshold, the incandescent in-between. Here it is, vital, burning in daylight.

NOTES

Epigraph: Yves Michaud, "Chords," in *Joan Mitchell: Peintures 1986 et 1987, RIVER, LILLE, CHORD* (Paris: Galerie Jean Fournier Éditions, 1987), 61.

1. This painting has alternately been titled both *Sink* and *The Sink*.

2. Joan Mitchell, Oral history interview with Dorothy Gees Seckler, May 21, 1965, Dorothy Gees Seckler Collection of Sound Recordings Relating to Art and Artists, 1962–1976, Archives of American Art, Smithsonian Institution, Washington, DC. Author's transcription.

3. In the Stable Gallery records, for example, the painting is frequently titled "Sink" in inventories of Mitchell's works—as it is, notably, in a September 9, 1960, letter from Walter Hopps of the Ferus Gallery to Eleanor Ward of the Stable Gallery with news of the painting's sale. Stable Gallery Records, Archives of American Art, Smithsonian Institution. By the time the Langs purchased the painting in 1977, it had become "The Sink." See Adler Gallery correspondence, September 2 and 12, 1977.

4. Abe Adler to Richard Lang, September 2, 1977, Friday Foundation archives.

5. Irving Sandler, "Joan Mitchell Paints a Picture," *Art News* 56, no. 6 (October 1957): 70.

6. Sandler, "Joan Mitchell Paints a Picture," 70.

7. Sandler, "Joan Mitchell Paints a Picture," 70.

8. Alfred Frankfurter, "The Year's Best: 1955," *Art News* 54, no. 9 (January 1956): 10.

9. This exhibition was selected, in part, by Meyer Schapiro at the Jewish Museum in 1957, and its catalogue includes an essay by Leo Steinberg.

10. *documenta II* (1959) was the second installment of an international art exhibition first held in Kassel, Germany, in 1955, as an effort to reconnect Germany with the wider world of the arts after World War II. *documenta II*, in which Mitchell participated, proposed abstract art as a language that could unite Europe. This explicitly internationalist (though primarily European and American) exhibition included 336 artists, among them first-generation Abstract Expressionist artists like Willem de Kooning and Jackson Pollock and second-generation Abstract Expressionists such as Helen Frankenthaler and Grace Hartigan. Held every five years for one hundred days, *documenta* continues to be a highly anticipated event. See "Retrospective: *documenta* 2, July 11–October 11, 1959, Art after 1945; International Exhibition," *documenta*: retrospective website, accessed November 2, 2020, http://www.documenta.de/en/retrospective/ii_documenta#.

11. Irving Sandler, "Young Moderns and Modern Masters: Joan Mitchell (Stable)," *Art News* 56, no. 1 (March 1957): 64.

12. Pierre Schneider, in Jacques Putman, Jean-François Revel, Pierre Schneider, and Albert Schultze-Vellinghausen, "Au Salon de mai," *L'Oeil*, June 1961, 53. Translation by the author.

ALBERTO GIACOMETTI
FEMME DE VENISE II
1956

CATHERINE GRENIER

The Swiss-born sculptor Alberto Giacometti was just 21 years old in January 1922 when he arrived in Paris to study under Antoine Bourdelle at the Académie de la Grande Chaumière. Subsequently, though he regularly returned to Switzerland to visit his family, it was in France, in Paris, that he made his career. Throughout the 1920s, Giacometti explored and experimented with numerous styles, from archaism and primitivism to post-Cubism, without ever fully abandoning figuration. In 1929, his planar sculptures, which verged on abstraction, began to attract attention, notably from the Surrealist circle around André Breton, which Giacometti joined in 1930. But this foray into Surrealism was brief, and beginning in 1935 Giacometti distanced himself from the movement and returned to modeling his works from life. Representing the human figure as he saw it became his main concern. Between 1935 and 1947, Giacometti struggled with self-doubt, destroyed much of his work, and rarely exhibited. During this period, his sculptures progressively diminished in scale until some stood just a few centimeters tall; only after World War II did his works grow taller again. This elongation, along with the lumpy surfaces of his sculptures, became one of the principal characteristics of the artist's mature style, as exemplified in the Lang Collection's *Femme de Venise II* (plate 9). Works in this new style contributed to Giacometti's steadily growing fame throughout the 1950s.

In December 1955, Giacometti was invited to represent France at the next Venice Biennale—as a sculptor. The request came at a difficult moment: frustrated by his sculptural practice, he was instead more focused on painting. Nevertheless, gratified by the honor of the invitation, he accepted and quickly set to work, as the biennale would open the following year.

The artist was accustomed to periods of discouragement and doubt in his creative work—grappling with challenges in both his sculpture and his painting. That feeling of incapacity had weighed heavily on him throughout World War II, most of which he spent in Switzerland, but he had experienced a respite after the war. His return to Paris after several years in Geneva, his reunion with his studio and friends, and also the fresh perspective of an exhibition at the Pierre Matisse Gallery in New York had all fostered renewed productivity and the creation of numerous works in a new style. Yet, following a reassuring few years in which each work seemed to advance from the preceding ones, and despite the success he was enjoying,

Plate 9 Alberto Giacometti, *Femme de Venise II*, 1956 (side view), bronze, overall: 47⅜ × 5¾ × 12⅞ in. (120.2 × 14.8 × 32.7 cm). Seattle Art Museum, Gift of the Friday Foundation in honor of Richard E. Lang and Jane Lang Davis, 2020.14.8.

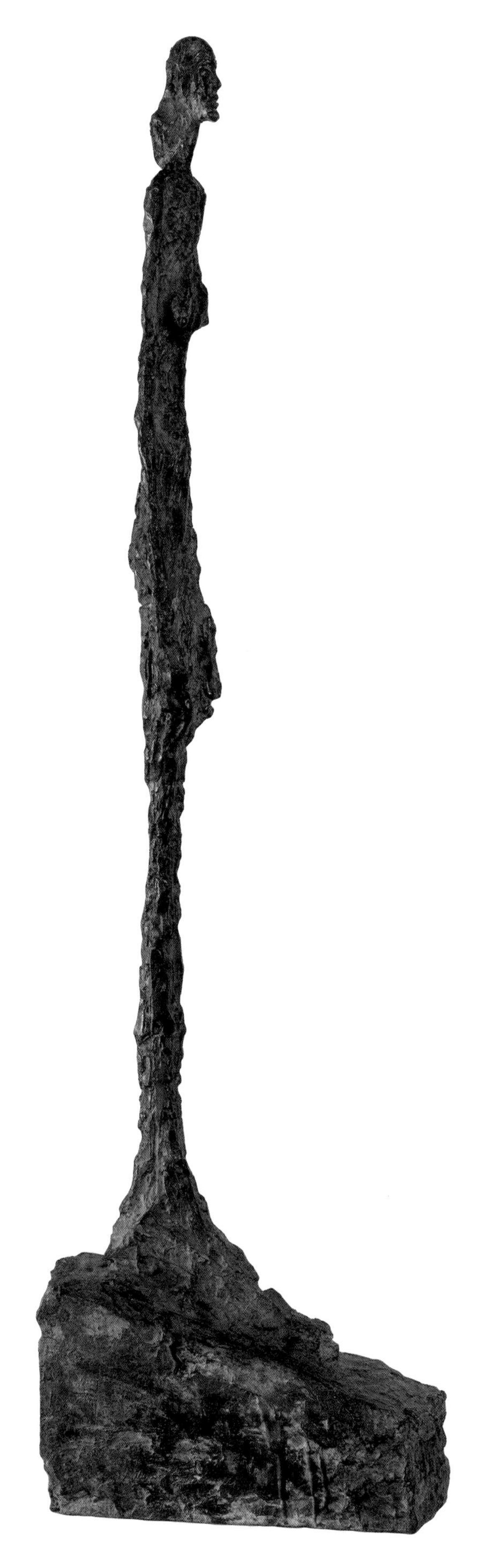

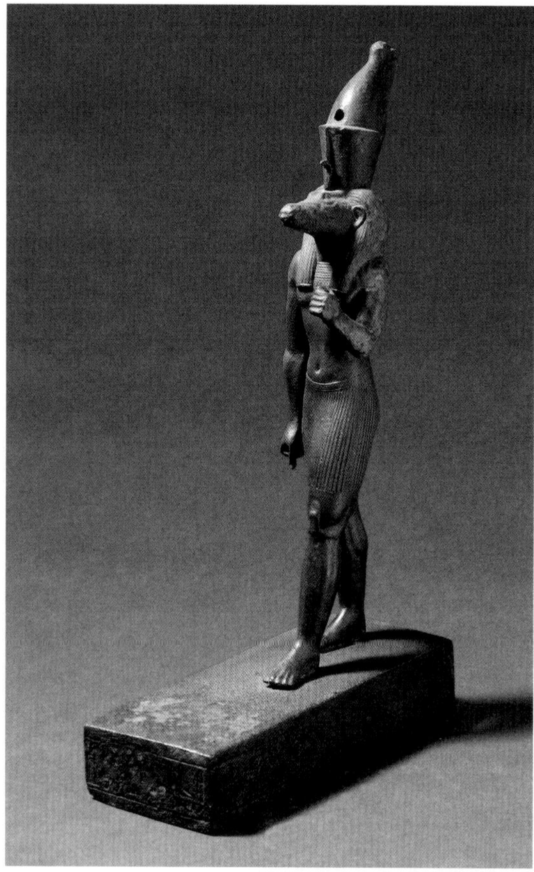

Fig. 45 Sebek statuette with crocodile head, Egypt, Late Period, 664–332 BCE, bronze, 29.8 × 18 cm. Musée du Louvre.

in 1952 the artist was again undermined by uncertainty. He began endlessly reworking his pieces. "Actually," he explained to Pierre Matisse, "it's not so much about exhibiting anymore for me, but rather seeing if I can still make a sculpture and painting stand. I'm terribly stuck; I've done everything to get to this point but now I need to get out; I've called into question every grain of plaster, I've hit bottom, that's at least one thing that I've accomplished!!!" he lamented.[1] The year 1953 brought a period of transition in which Giacometti vacillated between highs and lows. That spring, he turned back to sculpture and focused on realizing female nudes and busts. His brother Diego, who served as Giacometti's studio assistant and collaborator, casting his plaster models in bronze, was at his side. "Alberto, I hope you're continuing with your sculpture; whatever you do, don't demolish them,"[2] he wrote, worried that Giacometti would destroy his work while making it, as he had too often done in the past.

His small studio, where he labored fiercely, was filled at the time with sculptures in progress, along with some abandoned works. The philosopher Isaku Yanaihara, whom Giacometti met in November 1955 and who would become his model, described this "prodigious accumulation." When he first visited the artist, on November 17, he was astounded by the condition and mess of the "very poorly lit studio with its windows too small. . . . Near the entrance, there was a large table against the wall with an entire collection of dusty bottles and old brushes thrown into a pile." Yet, Yanaihara continued, amid the chaos he discovered "what one can only describe as the final residue of human existence once stripped of anything superfluous; like phantoms and yet incredibly fraternal, audacious and with unending humility, a row of plaster figurines that seemed to be frozen in place."[3] Characterized by their spindly appearance, the nude female figures Yanaihara saw evoke Egyptian funerary sculpture, especially in the massive bases anchoring each one (fig. 45). Their extreme proportions, stretched almost to abstraction, enact a kind of violence that can also be felt in the rendering of the surface, vividly cut with the sculpting knife. "It's in sculpture that I feel something like a contained violence that touches me," the artist explained.[4] Moreover, his interest in archaeological objects from ancient Egypt and Greece, deformed and reshaped over time, drove him to retain in his own sculptures the accidental traces left by the modeling and plaster casting processes.

It was a month after meeting Yanaihara when Giacometti agreed to represent France at the Venice Biennale as a sculptor, with Jacques Villon representing French painting. A few weeks later, Giacometti had to refuse a request to represent his native Switzerland at the same biennial. These twin honors followed a series of recent international achievements, including a one-man show at the Santa Barbara Museum of Art in 1953, his first at an American museum, and two important retrospectives that opened in 1955 at the Solomon R. Guggenheim Museum in New York and then at the Arts Council Collection in London. During that same period, a third exhibition had traveled to three German museums. Despite the fact that Giacometti had been working in Paris for thirty years, recognition came first from abroad—in particular from the United States, where his most important collectors were. The French invitation in late 1955 was therefore all the more welcome. In lieu of representing Switzerland at the biennale, Giacometti was asked to present a retrospective at the Museum of Fine Arts in Bern, which would fully establish his reputation as a leading European artist of his generation.

Giacometti prepared for the two exhibitions simultaneously and began a series of female figures. These departed from the recent nudes realized in sessions with his wife, Annette, as model, in which he had turned away from the hieratic, or highly stylized, stances reminiscent of Egyptian priestly gestures that he had sculpted from memory after the war. Those earlier, elongated figures were especially distinctive for the diminutive scale of the heads in sharp contrast with the proportions of the bodies. He now embarked on a series of medium-size, attenuated female figures, each unique despite their similarities to one another. The choice of scale reflected his desire to eschew heroic qualities in his sculpture and to play with the viewer's sense of simultaneous proximity and distance—a sense reinforced by the disproportion between the figures and their tall, Egyptian-style pedestals. Even if the artist was spurred by the pressure of looming exhibition deadlines, the resulting series is in no way simplistic. Yanaihara, who sat as a model for Giacometti a few months later, vividly attested to his turbulent creative process. When confronting the material, the artist swore, destroyed, and began again, every day drawn back to the studio by the failure of the stint before: "He clenched his teeth while forcing himself to paint and from his mouth surged the darkest phrases, cries of despair and curses."[5] According to Yanaihara, Giacometti was stimulated by the failure he strove to combat. Yet the expressions of despair—"Catastrophe!" "That's no good!" "Shit!"—alternated with signs of renewal—"There's a start!"[6]

Nearly a decade earlier, in 1947, Giacometti had been seized by a kind of frenzy that pushed him to create nearly identical sculptures one after another. "Recently, I've been making a life-size human figure every night,"[7] he wrote his mother at the time. Each had the same attitude: immobile and straight, the arms extended along the body. Those shadowlike, slender figures were stripped down to the essential, their irregular surfaces capturing the light in bursts. He drew on that model in executing the works for the biennale, which he would title *Femmes de Venise*. Despite difficulties and discouraged outbursts, he completed the 1956 series in time. "I made thirteen medium figures rendered a bit like the ones from 47 that I sent you," he explained to Pierre Matisse. "That was very useful: I think there was a progression from one to the other, right up to the last one, which Diego is casting now."[8]

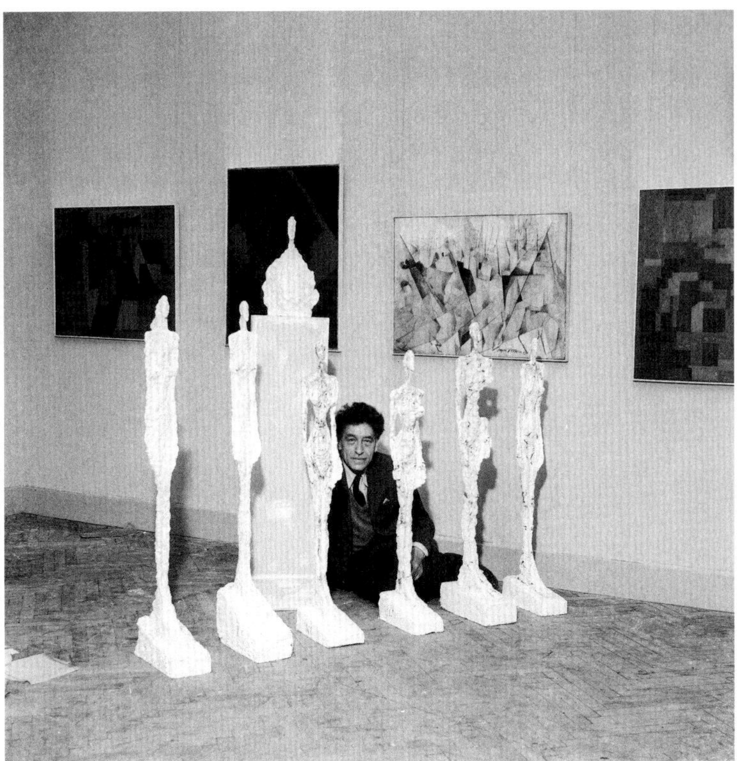

Fig. 46 Alberto Giacometti with his sculptures at the 28th Venice Biennale, June 1956. *Femme de Venise II* is second from left.

Ten were presented at the biennale, in plaster cast versions with the surface painted or incised (fig. 46). Hieratic, with arms hanging alongside the body, these female figures were a kind of synthesis between the 1947 series made from memory and inspired by antiquity, and the nudes that Giacometti made from life when Annette began posing for him.[9] Thus, they brought together the timelessness and generalization of Egyptian figures and Greek korai (figs. 47 and 48) with the sense of embodiment that belongs to portraiture. Like the earlier group, the biennale figures seem very similar when seen from afar, but differences emerge upon closer examination. Of the thirteen models initially created, only ten would survive, nine of which would later be cast in bronze.

The writer Jean Genet, who at the time that the *Femmes de Venise* were being executed came to sit as a model for the artist, described them in this way:

> Aside from his walking men, all of Giacometti's statues have feet that seem bound to a single, angled block, very thick, more like a pedestal. The body stems from there and supports—far away, very high—a miniscule head. That enormous mass of plaster or bronze—proportionally to the head—might lead one to believe that its feet are loaded with all the materiality the head has gotten rid of. . . . Not at all; between these massive feet and head, an uninterrupted exchange occurs. These ladies are not dragging through heavy mud: at dusk, they will glide down a slope drenched in shadows.[10]

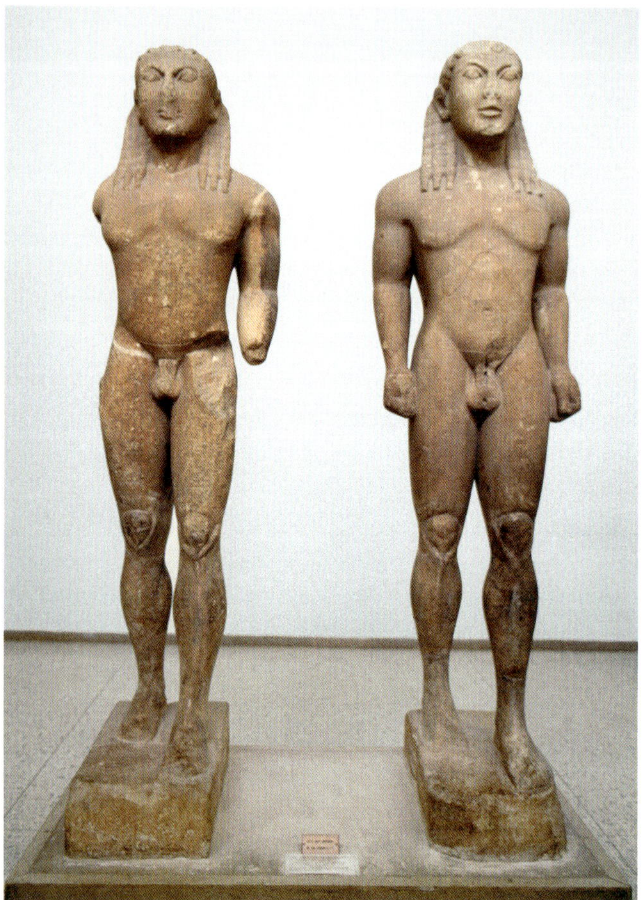

Fig. 47 Statues of Kleobis and Biton dedicated to Delphi by the city of Argos, signed by [Poly?]medes of Argos, marble, ca. 580 BCE, height: 77½ in. (1.97 m), after restoration. Archaeological Museum of Delphi, no. 467, 1524.

Among this series of female nudes, which the artist showed individually immediately after the biennale, *Femme de Venise II* goes the farthest in sculptural simplification. The utter rejection of anecdotal detail, the arms conjoined along the length of the body, and the simple suggestion of hair confer a radical essence. Feigning nothing, this reduction of the means of representation, as Genet articulates so well, authentically conveys the feeling of a glorious humanity. In that paradox, one finds the very quality that so struck young Giacometti upon discovering Egyptian sculpture: "These past few days, I've gone several times to the museum of Egyptian art. Now that is real sculpture. They kept only what was necessary for the entire figure, there isn't even a hole for a hand to fit in, and yet one has the impression of movement and form that is extraordinary in its manner," he wrote his parents in 1920.[11] Genet, whose book *L'Atelier d'Alberto Giacometti* is one of the finest literary texts on an artist's studio, poetically describes this turning back in time toward the essence of humanity by the sculptor: "Every work of art, if it wants to achieve the grandest proportions, must, with patience, with infinite diligence from the time of its development, descend into millennia past, reunite if it may with the immemorial night inhabited by the dead who will see themselves in the piece."[12] In his dialogue with the past, Giacometti creates figures that are profoundly material, as evidenced in his highly worked and rough surfaces. At the same time, the artist arrived at silhouettes that are so starkly reduced that they border on abstractions.

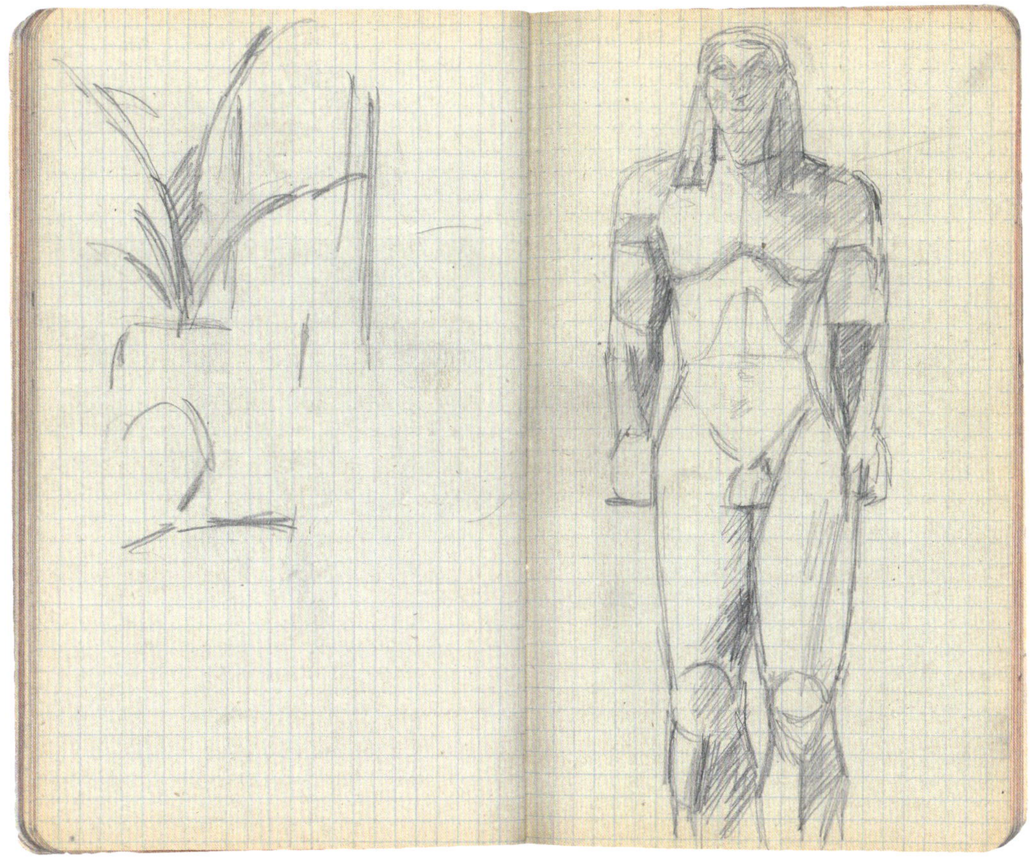

Fig. 48 Alberto Giacometti, copy after the statue of Biton at Delphi, 1923, pencil on notebook paper, 7¾ × 9¾ in. (19.7 × 24.8 cm). Giacometti Foundation.

NOTES

Translated from French by Molly Yakusan Stevens.

1 Alberto Giacometti to Pierre Matisse, late April 1952, Pierre Matisse Gallery Archives, Morgan Library, New York.

2 Diego Giacometti to Alberto and Annette Giacometti, April 11, 1953, Giacometti Foundation Archives, Paris.

3 Isaku Yanaihara, *Dialogues avec Giacometti* (Paris: Allia, 2015), 25.

4 Alberto Giacometti, "Entretien avec Georges Charbonnier," radio interview, Radio France, 1954.

5 Yanaihara continued, "And sometimes even, on top of it all, he hurled an aaah! as loudly as possible. The little Rue Hippolyte-Maindron where his studio was located was most often deserted, but anyone who by chance passed by on a night in November 1956 would have certainly been frightened by the strange vociferations coming through the walls of that shaky shack. It sounded like the delirium of a senseless madman." Yanaihara, *Dialogues avec Giacometti*, 141.

6 Yanaihara, *Dialogues avec Giacometti*, 141.

7 Alberto Giacometti to Annetta Giacometti, fall 1957, Alberto Giacometti-Stiftung, Zurich.

8 Alberto Giacometti to Pierre Matisse, June 1956, Pierre Matisse Gallery Archives, Morgan Library, New York.

9 Giacometti worked with certain models for long periods of time. His wife, Annette, and brother Diego were frequent models.

10 Jean Genet, *L'Atelier d'Alberto Giacometti* (Paris: L'Arbalète, 1963), n.p.

11 Alberto Giacometti to Giovanni and Annetta Giacometti, December 8, 1920, Alberto Giacometti-Stiftung, Zurich.

12 Genet, *L'Atelier d'Alberto Giacometti*, n.p.

ADOLPH GOTTLIEB
CRIMSON SPINNING #2
1959

SANFORD HIRSCH

There are disparate feelings in both my painting and my concept of life: love-hate, freedom-restraint, openness-closedness. I recognize these and other feelings in my paintings after I have finished them. Opposites are my view of life.

—Adolph Gottlieb

Crimson Spinning #2 (plate 10), painted by Adolph Gottlieb in 1959, is considered one of the artist's Burst paintings. These works are identified by two spherical forms, one defined and one expanding, positioned just above and below the horizontal center of Gottlieb's vertical canvases. Burst paintings are quite simple in appearance; that is the artist's plan. But their apparent simplicity is a device Gottlieb uses to convey complex emotional and formal subject matter. He was in his fifties when he began this phase of his art, and he was building on over thirty years of study, practice, and innovation.

Gottlieb's career began in the early 1920s. As his work progressed, he became increasingly focused on the role of abstraction and meaning in visual art. His first major breakthrough occurred in 1941, when he began the group of paintings he labeled Pictographs. Pictographs were a unique concept that rejected the role of narrative or representation in painting. Rather than tell stories, Gottlieb wanted to connect with viewers on a subconscious level where meaning derived from an individual viewer's emotional responses to a given work. To reach that goal, he created paintings that a viewer can take in in one glance. In his Pictographs, Gottlieb achieved these ends by structuring the image via a loosely drawn grid in order to eliminate illusionistic space and substitute simultaneity for narrative, and by the intuitive placement of spontaneous images within sections of the grid.

Toward the end of the 1940s, the all-over method of painting that was analogous to his use of the grid became a common device among several colleagues. From that time, Gottlieb began to explore how he could achieve his goals for abstract painting while moving away from the dense, crowded compositions of painters like Jackson Pollock or Willem de Kooning. Gottlieb labeled his paintings of the early to mid-1950s as Labyrinths, Imaginary Landscapes, or Unstill Lifes. In each of these types of

Plate 10 Adolph Gottlieb, *Crimson Spinning #2*, 1959, oil on canvas, 90 × 72 in. (228.7 × 182.9 cm). Seattle Art Museum, Gift of the Friday Foundation in honor of Richard E. Lang and Jane Lang Davis, 2020.14.9.

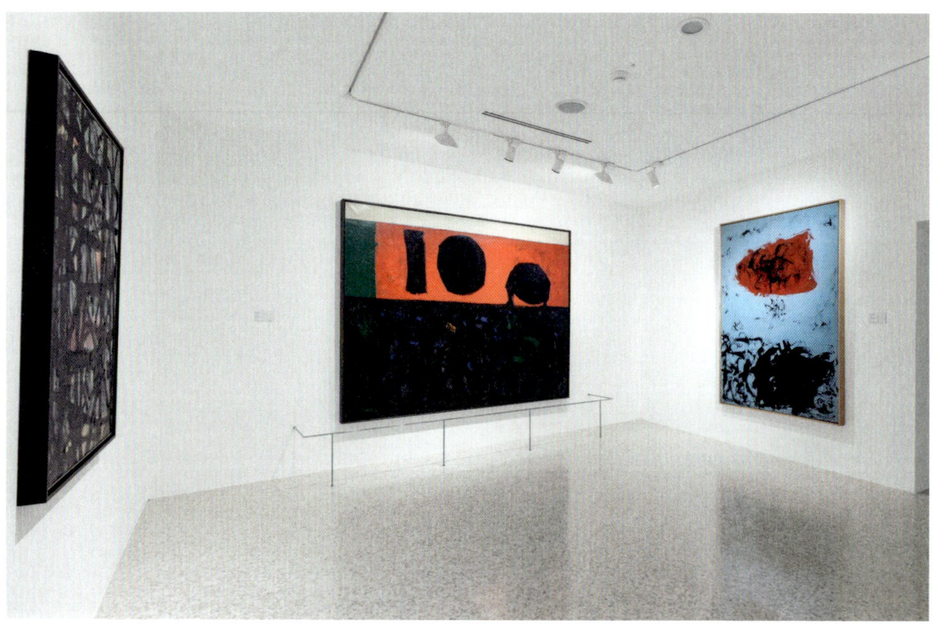

Fig. 49 Installation view, *Adolph Gottlieb: A Retrospective*, Peggy Guggenheim Collection, Venice, 2010. Paintings, left to right: *The Cage*, 1954; *Red at Night*, 1956; *Black, Blue, Red*, 1956.

painting, he utilized elements of the Pictographs to achieve the emotional and conceptual meaning he valued through consciously limited means. As he remarked to the curator Martin Friedman: "Since I eliminated almost everything from my painting except a few colors and perhaps two or three shapes, I feel a necessity for making the particular colors that I use, or the particular shapes, carry the burden of everything that I want to express."[1]

Gottlieb's Burst image developed organically from his Imaginary Landscape paintings (such as *Red at Night*, fig. 49, center). These earlier works consist of two horizontal registers placed on a horizontally oriented canvas with a few ovoid shapes suspended in the upper register. The lower register is usually densely packed with staccato brushstrokes and/or bits of imagery in near-chaotic action. In a 1956 painting titled *Black, Blue, Red* (fig. 49, right), Gottlieb oriented his canvas vertically, and the horizon line disappeared. The upper and lower registers were still in dynamic opposition, but imagery was concentrated in the interplay of two large, massed shapes. Gottlieb refined that image into his Burst paintings.

Burst paintings occupied Gottlieb almost exclusively from mid-1957 into 1960. *Crimson Spinning #2* is part of that first intense exploration of the artist's new direction. As was his usual practice, Gottlieb needed to work his ideas out on canvas, and he would explore each idea until he felt he had exhausted it. He explained to interviewer Gladys Kashdin in 1965:

> What I'm looking for when I'm doing the painting—those things which I don't know. In other words, I'm feeling my way and then I find something—and there to my surprise is something that wasn't in the world before, and this can become more and more refined and subtle. . . . [I]f I start out with something which is absolutely new to me, I've never done anything like it before—this is a kind of a breakthrough. Then I develop it. I finally reach the point where it is no longer a breakthrough it is something that I already know. I've done this over many times. But then I begin to get nuances—then I'm interested in finding out how far I can go with this without exhausting it. What are the possibilities of exploring in this territory?[2]

The vertical orientation of the image is one of the important changes Gottlieb made in the Burst paintings. The majority of them are between 7 and 9 feet high and about 5 and 7½ feet wide, placing them in direct relation to the proportions of an individual viewer. The critic and curator Lawrence Alloway observed that Gottlieb's Bursts are "a subtle and sustained contribution to the investigation of the visual-physical relationships of image and spectator that is central to the Abstract Expressionists' big pictures."[3] The historian Pepe Karmel likewise noted the importance of the physical aspect of these relationships, stating, "Gottlieb used the language of painting to evoke these qualities of the physical environment, determining the conditions of our existence as human beings."[4]

Alloway also spoke of what he called the "dyadic" nature of these works.[5] Gottlieb's paintings are complete statements within which the two main forms relate to each other and, as a pair, to the entire painting—including the exact physical dimensions of the canvas. The broader surface areas of his paintings, which are usually referred to as fields, are as carefully painted as the paired forms that occupy them, and with which they contrast. Gottlieb created images in which each element is part of a subtle and tenuous balance. That aspect of Gottlieb's work is another part of meaning, since balance is a momentary state that is bound to change. The image thus parallels the experience of emotional states: both are transitory, precariously balanced, the result of and subject to opposing urges and tendencies; both develop over time and include a history of that development. In contrast to the "action painting" of the period, usually defined as a record of the unstructured flow of the artist's hand and body in creating a painting, Gottlieb paints the act of being in a moment.

In *Crimson Spinning #2*, the two large forms interact with each other in various ways. The upper form has more regular contours and is encircled by a halo of color that might imply either stasis or movement, while the lower form is unencumbered and expands toward the outer edges of the canvas. To exaggerate both the difference and the connection between these forms, the upper field is painted a warmer shade, while the lower field is overpainted in a cold white and has no clearly defined edge. Instead, the lower field alternately blends with and encroaches onto the upper, forming an irregular curve that extends across the width of the canvas. Gottlieb's theme here is the constancy of change.

To realize this abstract thought as a painting, the artist created each form with different paints, using different tools. The final layer of the upper form is painted with thick artist's oil paint applied with a brush and palette knife, while the lower form consists of a commercial paint applied using a squeegee with enough speed and force to produce the drips and splashes that vector out from its edges (fig. 50). The juxtaposition of the contained and open spheres marks one statement of a whole carefully built of opposing pairs. Despite the ultimate appearance of balance, by locating those forms off-center (actually, off-two-centers), Gottlieb underscored the transitory nature of that balance. Either form has the capacity to subsume, exchange with, or replace the other. What we are shown in the painting is a moment in which all elements are in balance, but it is an active moment that is open to infinite variation.

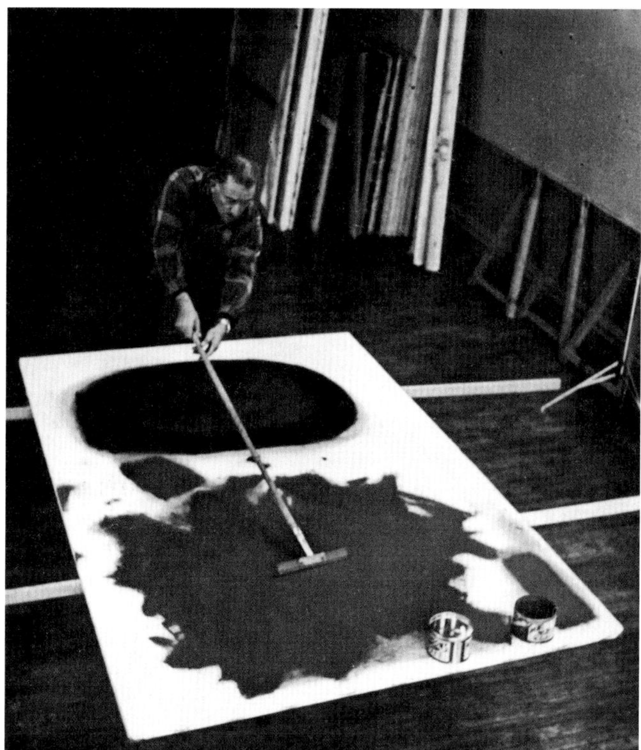

Fig. 50 Adolph Gottlieb working on *Ascent*, 1958.

In articulating the large forms in the painting, Gottlieb emphasized the interrelatedness of these different, but mutually supportive, bodies. The shapes convey similarity, despite the two forms' opposite contours. The flat surface of the lower form directs the eye to scan toward the expanding contours, while the dense and varied surface of the upper form draws vision inward, reinforced by the brushwork and knife work and the more regular curve of

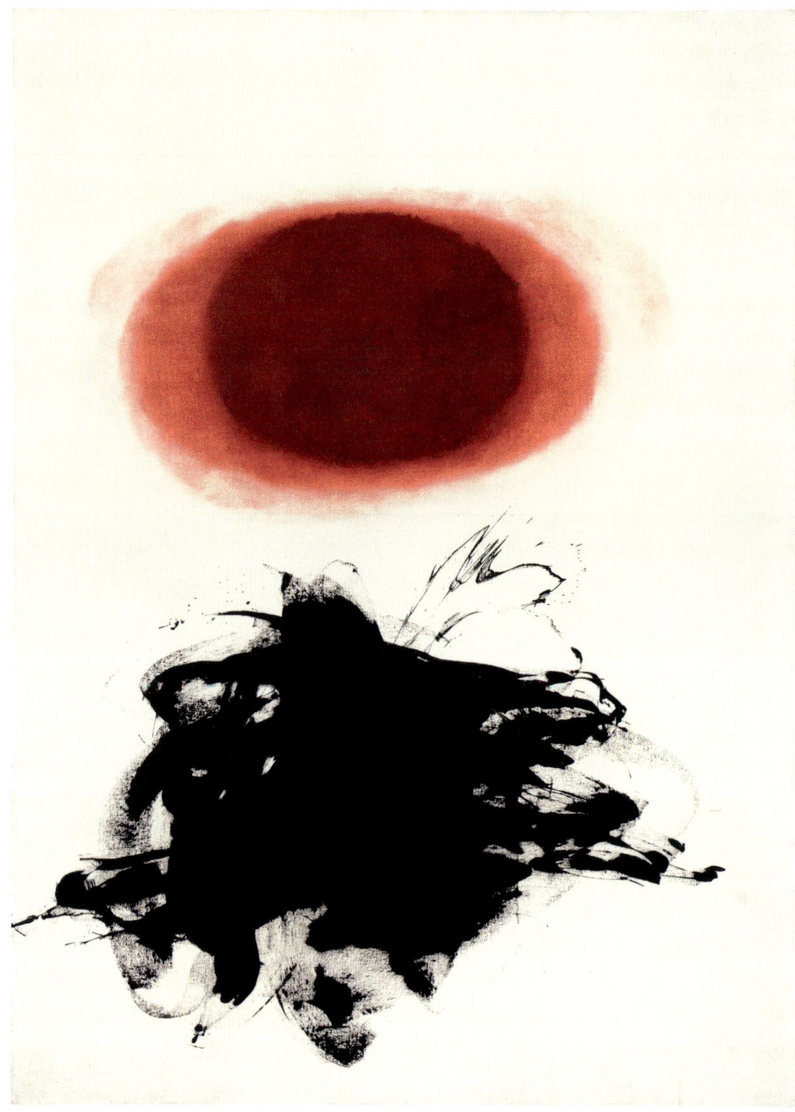

Fig. 51 Adolph Gottlieb, *Crimson Spinning*, 1959, oil on canvas, 92 × 68 in. (233.68 × 172.72 cm). San Francisco Museum of Modern Art, Donald and Doris Fisher Collection.

the red underpainting. The relationships between the field and the large forms draw on similar contrasts of methods and materials. The apparent simplicity of the image at first glance belies its complex construction.

The title *Crimson Spinning #2* makes clear that this is the second painting of the same name. *Crimson Spinning* (fig. 51), also painted in 1959, while compositionally similar, is substantively different. Gottlieb titled his paintings after they were completed, based on his own reactions to each canvas. Most of the titles of his later works are somewhat neutral, like *Crimson Spinning*,[6] as the artist did not want to impose or imply a specific meaning for any work. He insisted that a painting has broader meanings than even the artist might be aware of, and he did not want to limit any viewer's ability to relate to his paintings. Nonetheless, that humanist impulse also drove his determination to title his paintings—as opposed to the practice of several colleagues who used numbers instead of titles. Gottlieb reacted strongly when asked why he gave his paintings descriptive titles, rather than numbering them. His answer: "Prisoners have numbers."[7]

The philosopher Finley Eversole wrote a lengthy essay about another Burst painting, titled *Blast I* (1958, Museum of Modern Art, New York). Among his observations are the following thoughts that apply to all of Gottlieb's Burst paintings: "Much of the poetic power of *Blast I* comes from its simplicity as an abstract image, purified of all specific historical and cultural content. Its truth is existential, not cultural. . . . Behind it stands the archetypal war of opposites—Freud's eros and thanatos—and a thousand myths of battle between sun-god-heroes and the dragons of the deep."[8] This fundamental opposition—the dependence of one pole on its opposite—was key to the artist, who called himself a "conceptual painter."[9] It can, and does, contain all aspects of perception, bringing us closer to what Gottlieb termed his "view of life" in the epigraph to this essay. The word "perception" in the English language has several definitions. According to Merriam-Webster's dictionary, these include: "a result of perceiving (observation), a mental image (concept), awareness of the elements of environment through physical sensation (color perception), and a capacity for comprehension."[10] Gottlieb believed that his role as an artist was to create images that embody all of these possible interpretations, simultaneously. In making his paintings, he used his knowledge and skills as a painter to encompass the complexity that Eversole described, and more. Gottlieb both agreed with Eversole's interpretation and believed that it was only one aspect of the kinds of experiences his manipulation of these images could express. "I don't identify my paintings when I work with any philosophy of any sort. And I don't think that my painting is the direct expression of a certain philosophy—there are too many other elements in it which have to do with a sensuous reaction and with a physical effect on the eyes and traditions of painting and so on."[11]

The complexity of Gottlieb's art is often overlooked. Through carefully constructed pairs of opposites, both visual and actual, he was committed to presenting the abstraction and imperfections that he observed as constants: "We have aspirations and we have defeats, and in the life process we have all the experiences which make us feel anxiety or terror or joy and so on. I think all of this is legitimate material, which enters into a painting, but these are abstractions."[12] Another important pairing, when considering Gottlieb's work, is of the particular painting with the individual viewer. His is an art that communicates one to one rather than attempting to reach a mass audience. It avoids concepts like the "sublime," which was the goal of some of his friends, like Barnett Newman and Mark Rothko. Gottlieb doesn't believe in absolutes; he accepts limitations and doubt as experience. In his view, art and language are themselves abstractions that, in their distinctive ways, reflect and allow individuals to consider and review the imperfect realities they must manage. *Crimson Spinning #2*, like Gottlieb's other late paintings, defines limits and potential in the same moment.

NOTES

Epigraph Adolph Gottlieb, quoted in Stephen Polcari, "Gottlieb on Gottlieb," *Nightsounds*, March 1969, 11.

1 Adolph Gottlieb, interviewed by Martin Friedman, August 1962, tape 2A, transcript, p. 6, Adolph and Esther Gottlieb Foundation, New York.

2 Gladys Kashdin, "Conversation with Adolph Gottlieb," New York, April 28, 1965, typescript of tape recording, p. 13, Adolph and Esther Gottlieb Foundation, New York.

3 Lawrence Alloway, "Adolph Gottlieb and Abstract Painting," in *Adolph Gottlieb: A Retrospective* (New York: Art Publisher, 1981), 57.

4 Pepe Karmel, "Artist and Cosmos," in *Adolph Gottlieb: Gravity, Suspension, Motion: Paintings, 1954–1972* (New York: Pace Gallery, 2012).

5 Alloway, "Adolph Gottlieb and Abstract Painting," 57.

6 For example, he titled some other paintings from 1959 *Aureole*, *Black and Black*, *Levitation*, and *Cadmium Red above Black*.

7 Friedman interview, 51.

8 Finley Eversole, "*Blast I*: Image of Renewal," *Art Directions*, no. 4 (Summer 1967): 7.

9 Friedman interview, 40.

10 *Merriam Webster*, s.v. "Perception," accessed December 22, 2020, http://www.merriam-webster.com/dictionary/perception.

11 Kashdin, "Conversation with Adolph Gottlieb," 15.

12 "A Discussion between Sister Corita, I.H.M. and Adolph Gottlieb," December 1964, unedited typescript, p. 7, Adolph and Esther Gottlieb Foundation, New York.

LEE KRASNER
NIGHT WATCH
1960

ELEANOR NAIRNE

In December 1978, the poet and critic Richard Howard interviewed the artist Lee Krasner (fig. 52).[1] She had just turned 70 and was a notoriously prickly character; "Oh yes, yes, I was irascible," she had confessed to Barbara Rose a few years earlier.[2] Her spikes were surely necessary, given the machismo of the postwar American art world, in which she and so many others were lumbered with the loathed qualifier of *woman* artist.[3] But Howard was a dear friend who had summered with Krasner in Long Island, so their tone was warm, intimate. The Pace Gallery in Manhattan had organized the conversation to coincide with an exhibition of work that she had made some twenty years earlier. Back then, she had been suffering from terrible insomnia—or so the story goes.[4] Working almost exclusively at night (and believing it sacrilegious to use color under artificial light), she had restricted her palette to earthy tones: raw umber, burnt sienna, ash gray, and creamy white. Which is why these formidable paintings came to be known, somewhat unfortunately, as the *Umber Series*. The Pace Gallery elided the problem with the restrained, if equally drab, exhibition title *Paintings, 1959–1962*. Howard liked to call them her "Night Journeys," as I do too.[5]

How could their exchange begin anywhere but the dramatic circumstances of the paintings' making? These were the early years after the fateful summer of 1956, when Krasner had been in Paris, on her first foray to Europe, and the critic Clement Greenberg had telephoned with grave news. Krasner's husband, Jackson Pollock, had crashed his Oldsmobile convertible, killing himself and Edith Metzger, a friend of his lover, Ruth Kligman, who had been injured but survived.[6] On August 12, the front cover of the *New York Times* reported: "8 Killed in 2 L.I. Auto Crashes; Jackson Pollock among Victims."[7] Krasner flew home immediately to make arrangements for the funeral. "Did the paintings represent for you not only a descent into a new crucible of emotions," Howard ventured, "but also a specific registration of grief? Were these not mourning paintings?"[8] Sometime in 1957, Krasner decided to make Pollock's much-mythologized barn into a studio space of her own. Then loss compounded loss: her mother died in 1959, and a furious row with Greenberg led to the canceling of her exhibition at French & Company after he expressed disdain at the direction of her new work. The muted colors and sheer violence of the mark making in the Night Journeys seem to roil directly from the tumult of this time.

Plate 11 Lee Krasner, *Night Watch*, 1960, oil on canvas, 70 × 99¼ in. (177.8 × 252.1 cm). Seattle Art Museum, Gift of the Friday Foundation in honor of Richard E. Lang and Jane Lang Davis, 2020.14.4.

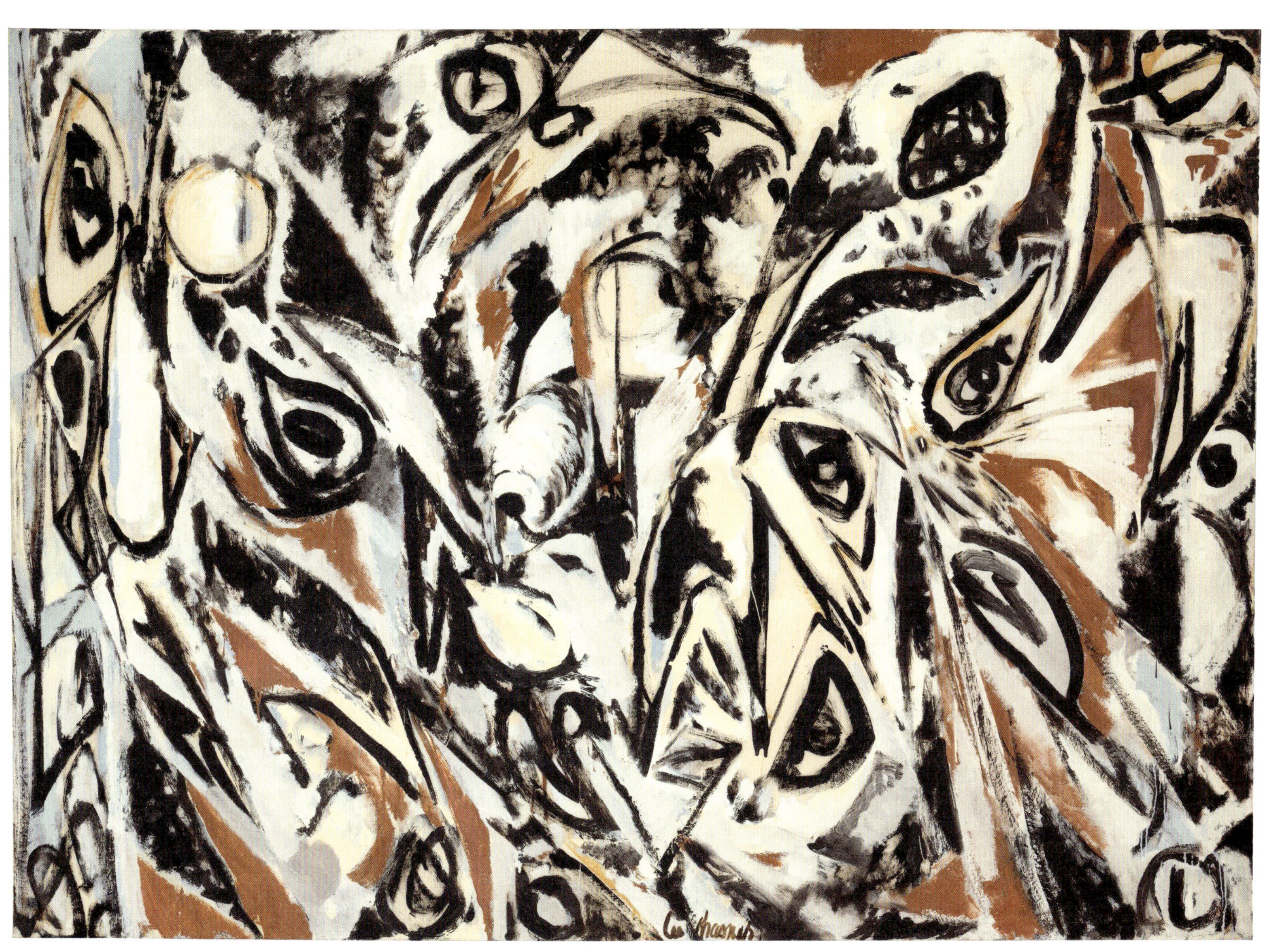

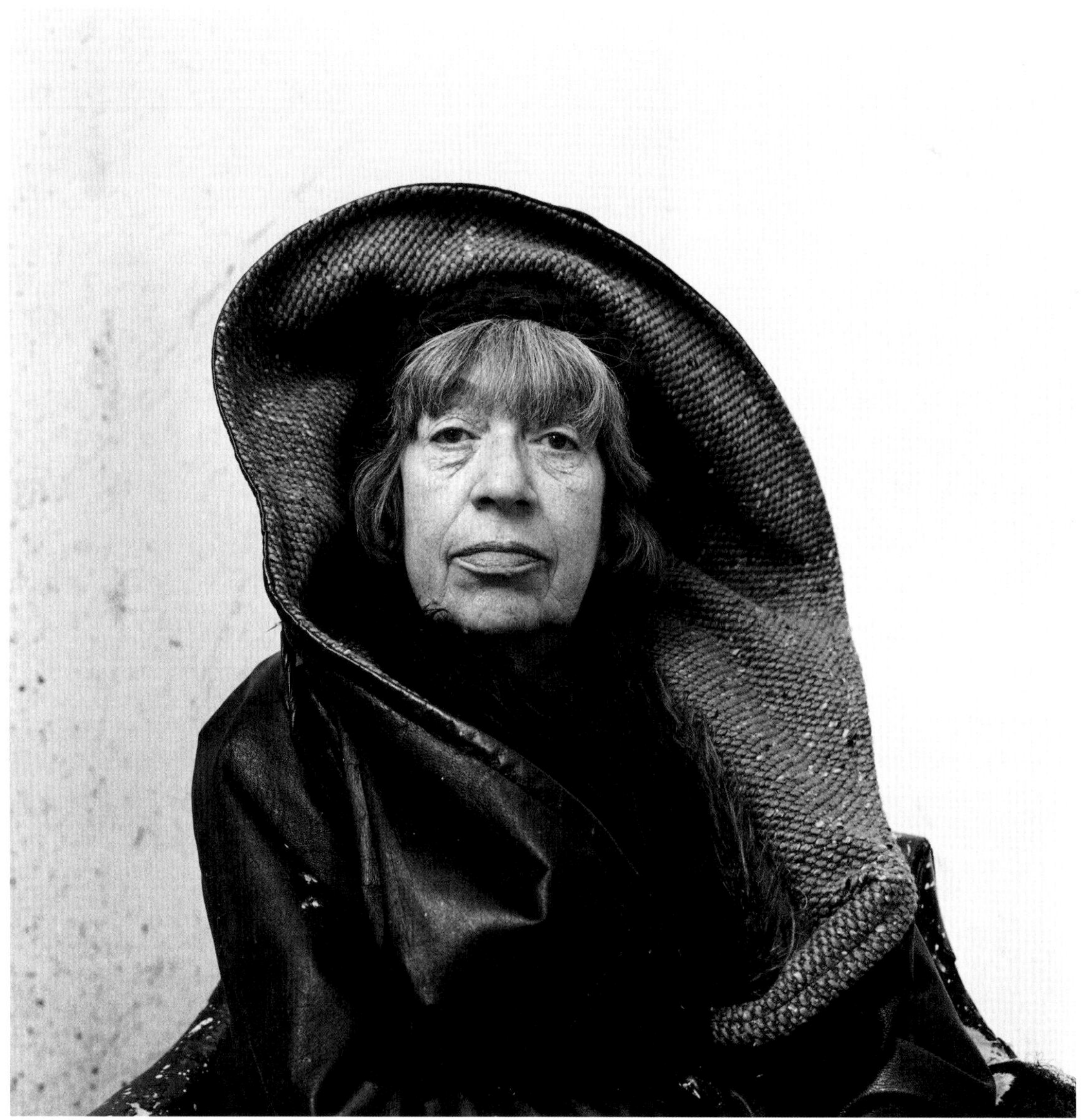

Fig. 52 Lee Krasner in Springs, New York, 1972. Photograph by Irving Penn.

Krasner answered Howard cautiously: "It's hard for me to put my finger on it in those terms."[9] Although she worked in cycles, she had always been a committed colorphile. Henri Matisse was an artistic hero precisely for the sorcery that he could enact with hot oranges and lush greens, with their fragrance of North Africa and the Pacific Islands. Although she had periods of abstinence, such as the dreaded "gray slabs" of the early 1940s, she was known and admired as a colorist. Howard called her work "chromatic fantasies"; look at the scintillating flecks of cobalt in a Little Image painting like *Shellflower* (1947, fig. 53) or the dense flanks of crimson in a Collage Painting like *Desert Moon* (1955) and you soon see why.[10] The Night Journeys denied their viewer any such sensuous pleasure. As a critic at the time quipped about *Night Watch* (1960, plate 11): "Let's face it, brown and cream don't make a

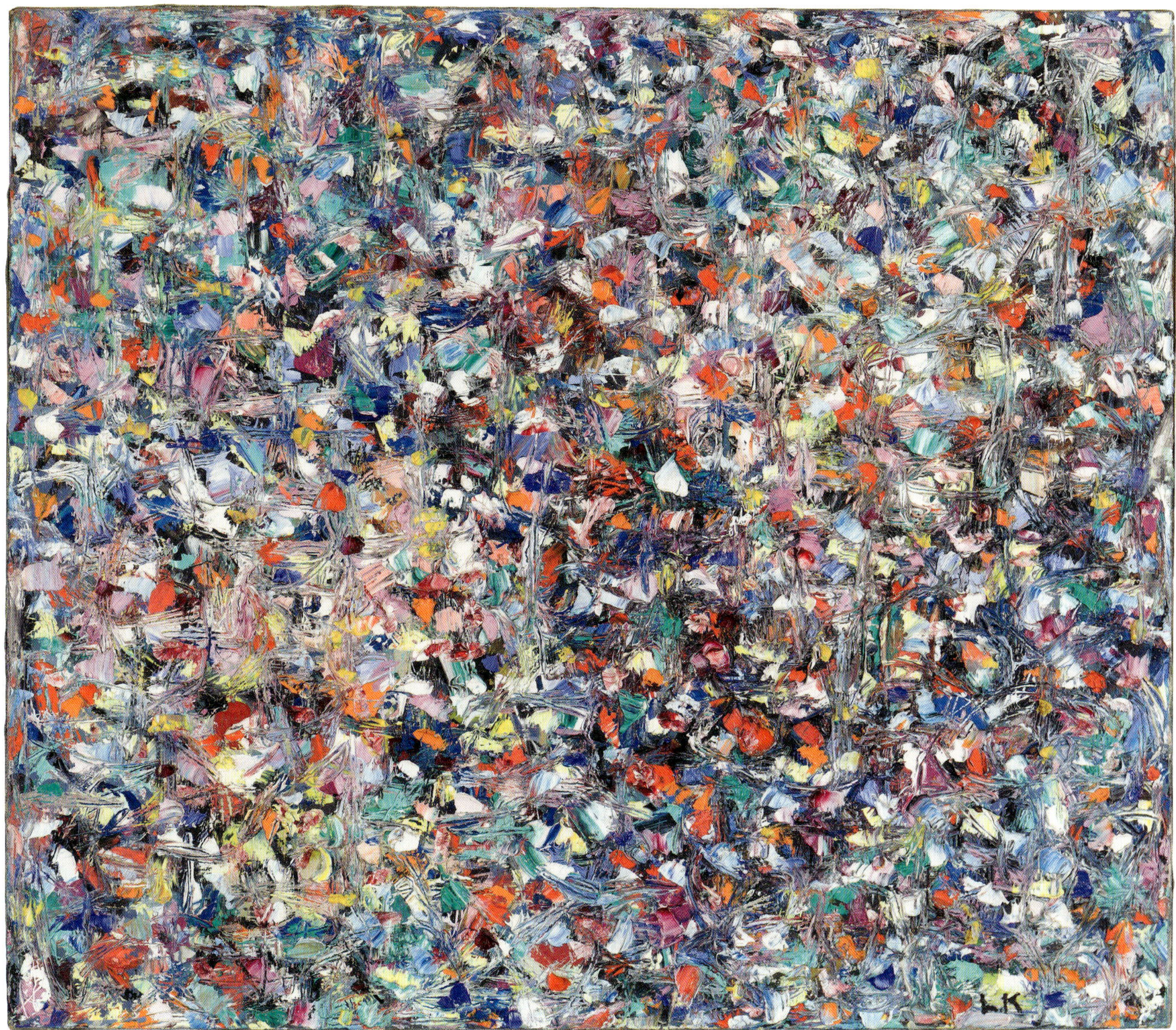

Fig. 53 Lee Krasner, *Shellflower*, 1947, oil on canvas, 24 × 28 in. (61 × 71.1 cm). Private Collection.

giddy color combination."[11] It is said that depression can deplete a person's capacity to register color; as if a tint of rose could simply drain from one's lenses. Krasner articulated her withdrawal matter-of-factly: "I realized that if I was going to work at night I would have to knock out color altogether, because I couldn't deal with color except in daylight."[12] Which could be seen as another way of saying the same thing.

Not being able to cope with color was certainly new: the *Earth Green* paintings shown at Martha Jackson Gallery in February–March 1958 were some of Krasner's brightest and most lyrical to date.[13] But then, appearances can be deceiving: "I can remember that when I was painting *Listen* which is so highly keyed in color . . . I almost didn't see it, because tears were literally pouring down" (fig. 54).[14] This wateriness is in the work too, as Krasner

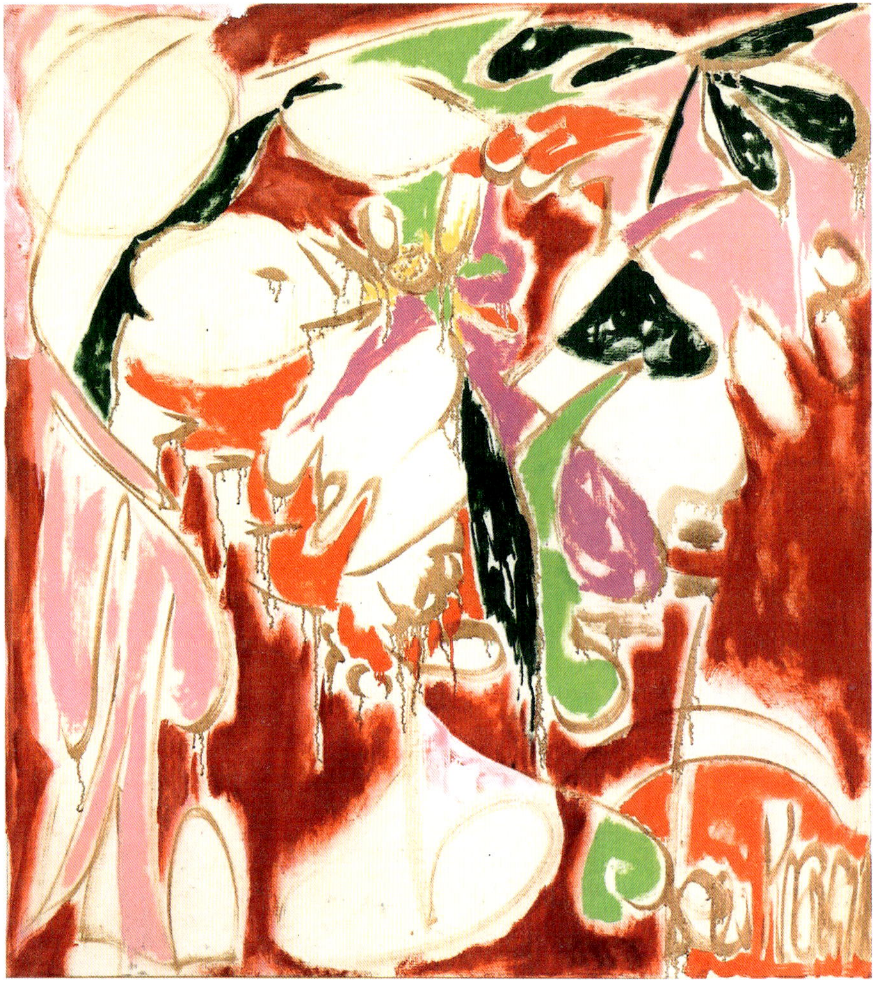

Fig. 54 Lee Krasner, *Listen*, 1957, oil on cotton duck, 63¼ × 58½ in. (160.7 × 148.6 cm). Private Collection.

stained the canvas with thinned-down paint, creating a sense of tributaries overflowing with feeling. Afterward, she thought *Listen* looked peculiarly like "such a happy painting," a disparity that she explained as a kind of emotional jet lag: "The time sequence between what one feels and what is happening is not simultaneous."[15] In the popular modeling of grief by Elisabeth Kübler-Ross (first published in 1969 in *On Death and Dying*), denial comes first—accompanied by feelings of shock, confusion, and elation—before anger, depression, and bargaining bring a person into a state of acceptance.[16] In this light, the vividness of the *Earth Green* works might be seen to reflect ecstatic denial. Or, indeed, release; Krasner spoke of life with Pollock as like catching "a comet by the tail,"[17] and there must have been some relief (albeit conflicted) in letting go of a flying celestial object.

The Night Journeys that followed were seen by Krasner to be a path leading beneath, rather than beyond, where she had been: "Let me say that when I painted a good part of these things, I was going down deep into something which wasn't easy or pleasant," she told Howard.[18] In this respect, her subdued palette might be read as relating to the subtle tones of the geological strata of rock or the organic pigments of prehistoric cave paintings—both frequent metaphors for the layers of the psyche. When Krasner spoke to Howard of "descending once more, bringing forth from the unconscious," her phrasing suggests the influence of Carl Jung and his "collective unconscious"—the theory that certain primordial or archetypal images swim in an inherited part of the brain common to all of humankind.[19] She had read Jung's *Integration of Personality* in the summer of 1940 and found it "marvelous, you know, that he speaks in my language," and her home library in Springs, New York, also contained a copy of *Essays on a Science of Mythology* (1949), coauthored by Jung with Carl Kerenyi.[20] From 1939 to 1940, Pollock had been a patient of the Jungian Joseph Henderson, and Krasner was in therapy for much of the 1950s with a controversial Sullivanian, Leonard Siegel, whom she described as working in "the direction of Freud."[21]

Of all the Night Journeys, *Night Watch* feels perhaps the most loaded with psychic content. The painting borrows its title from the popular name for Rembrandt's *Militia Company of District II under the Command of Captain Frans Banning Cocq* (1642, Rijksmuseum)—a work famed for its epic pageantry and dramatic use of light and dark. The title brings to mind the apprehension induced by the very need for nocturnal policing: act 1, scene 1 of *Hamlet*, for instance, in which the guards anxiously "watch the minutes of this night" in haunted Elsinore.[22] The canvas is covered in a whorl of thick arcs of somber paint, from which a number of eyes seem to peer out menacingly. In dropping the definite article from Rembrandt's title, Krasner unleashes the question of who is watching whom. Oracular imagery also features in other works in the series, such as *The Eye Is the First Circle* (1960, Glenstone Museum), named after the first line of the 1841 essay "Circles" by Ralph Waldo Emerson, and *Vigil* (1960, Private Collection), which Krasner described to Howard as having "to do with being on guard at every moment while one is descending."[23] To where, you might ask? The homonym of "eye" and "I" suggests a journey *within* subjectivity and could be a direct allusion to Jung, whose statements on this link include: "My consciousness is like an eye that penetrates to the most distant spaces."[24]

At the time, many artists and writers working internationally wanted to plumb the depths of interior life. During the war, André Breton and fellow Surrealists seeking refuge in New York had brought with them techniques like automatism as a pathway to the unconscious, as well as a predilection for mythic origin stories and a revival of primitivism. In 1937, the writer and artist John Graham published "Primitive Art and Picasso," an article that Krasner likely read, given that she much admired Graham's *System and Dialectics of Art*, published the same year.[25] In 1943, fellow Abstract Expressionists Mark Rothko and Adolph Gottlieb wrote a letter to Edward Alden Jewel, art critic of the *New York Times*, explaining that "to us art is an adventure into an unknown world, which can be explored only by those willing to take the risks. . . . That is why we profess spiritual kinship with primitive and archaic art."[26] There would be countless other statements of this kind by those who gathered at the Cedar Tavern, which might be best summarized by Pollock's infamous declaration that he did not need to rework images of nature, since "I am nature"—itself a brilliant reworking of Paul Cézanne's earlier statement that "nature is on the inside."[27]

For Michael Leja, these are prime examples of what he describes as "Modern Man discourse," which was very much in the air in postwar New York.[28] In 1959, the year that Krasner embarked on her Night Journeys, Miles Davis released *Kind of Blue*, his pioneering experiment in improvisatory modal jazz, and the Solomon R. Guggenheim Museum opened to the public, designed by Frank Lloyd Wright as a conscious inversion of the stepped pyramids of Mesopotamia and invoking the biomorphic forms marveled at by Darcy Wentworth Thompson in his influential study *On Growth and Form* (1917). This was also the year that Peter Selz curated *New Images of Man* at the Museum of Modern Art, featuring the work of twenty-two men, including Francis Bacon, Willem de Kooning, Jean Dubuffet, Alberto Giacometti, Leon Golub, and Pollock, alongside that of one woman—Germaine Richier (fig. 55). In the introduction to the catalogue (a copy of which is also in the library in Springs), Selz writes:

> The imagery of man which has evolved from [mid-twentieth-century life] reveals sometimes a new dignity, sometimes despair, but always the uniqueness of man as he confronts his fate. Like Kierkegaard, Heidegger, Camus, these artists are aware of anguish and dread, of life in which man—precarious and vulnerable—confronts the precipice, is aware of dying as well as living.[29]

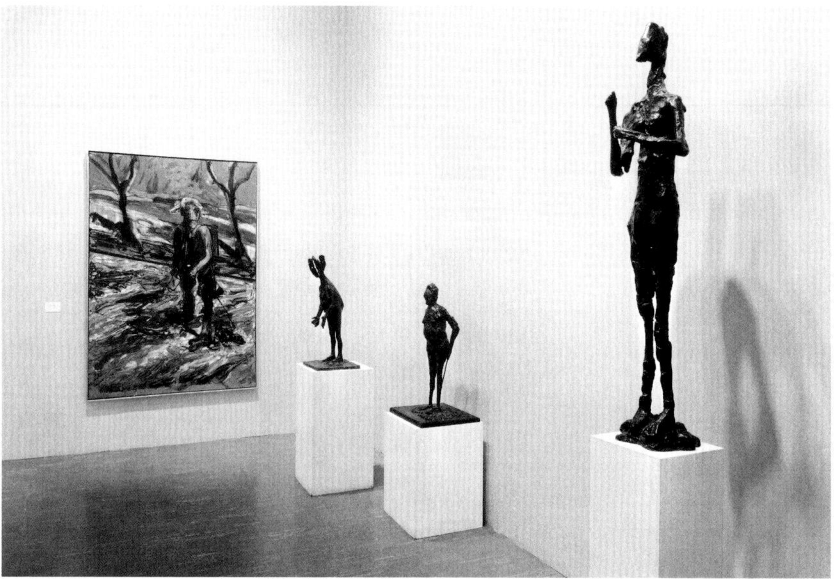

Fig. 55 Installation view of the exhibition *New Images of Man*, the Museum of Modern Art, New York, September 30–November 29, 1959, with (L–R) Germaine Richier's *Hydra*, *Ogre*, and *The Grain*. The Museum of Modern Art Archives, New York, IN651.8.

Being a woman made Krasner no less susceptible to the dominance of Modern Man ideology, which is powerfully at play in her Night Journeys—paintings wrought of an awareness of an existential precipice. The critics of the day on both sides of the Atlantic appraised her work within this framework too. In an article for *Arts Review* coinciding with her exhibition at the Whitechapel Gallery in 1965, Kenneth Coutts-Smith wrote that her "images are not so much created but released from the very deep levels of the imagination."[30] When we look at them today, we might be struck by the confluence of these different forces: the dramatic impact of personal grief and the need to be pragmatic through a period of desperate sleeplessness; the artistic impulse to break into a new cycle of imagery; the working through of collective trauma, including the Second World War and the intensification of Cold War politics; and the urgency felt transnationally to drill down into what had made humankind capable of such atrocities. As the painter Amy Sillman recently articulated: "That psychic landscape of trying to produce new knowledge, new subjectivity, new insight, new form—that's the mandate of that kind of painter. And that is such a burden."[31] Yet with the Night Journeys, Krasner found a way to whip that weight into a state of electric grace, watched over by eyes looking within and without the edges of the canvas—into its maker and onto its viewer, with alarming perspicacity.

NOTES

1 Richard Howard, "A Conversation with Lee Krasner," 1978, in *Lee Krasner: Paintings 1959–1962* (New York: Pace Gallery, 1979), n.p.

2 Lee Krasner, interview by Barbara Rose, ca. 1975, box 10, C77, Barbara Rose Papers, 930100, Getty Research Institute.

3 Krasner had many artist contemporaries who were women, including Mary Abbott, Perle Fine, Louise Nevelson, Anne Ryan, Janet Sobel, and Hedda Sterne, as well as the famous four covered in Mary Gabriel's gripping *Ninth Street Women: Lee Krasner, Elaine de Kooning, Grace Hartigan, Joan Mitchell, and Helen Frankenthaler—Five Painters and the Movement that Changed Modern Art* (Boston: Little, Brown, 2018).

4 We must, of course, treat artists' stories with a degree of caution; Krasner, for instance, liked to tell and retell the same anecdotes until they were as ossified as stone. What is useful here is to consider how it served her to tell the story in this way.

5 In his conversation with Krasner, Howard said that "there is a category of experience that in Hebrew mythology is in fact called a night journey, a descent down into the darkness—and it seems to me that you . . . are working in this mode here." Howard, "Conversation," n.p. Krasner was raised in an Orthodox Jewish Russian émigré home in Brooklyn, which may have strengthened the connection to Hebrew myth for Howard.

6 For more on this period, see Gail Levin, *Lee Krasner: A Biography* (London: Thames and Hudson, 2020), 350–60.

7 Cover, *New York Times*, August 12, 1956.

8 Howard, "Conversation," n.p.

9 Krasner, in Howard, "Conversation," n.p.

10 Howard, "Conversation," n.p.

11 Vivien Raynor, "Lee Krasner" [Wise Gallery], *Arts Magazine* 35 (January 1961): 54.

12 Krasner, in Howard, "Conversation," n.p.

13 *Lee Krasner: Recent Paintings*, Martha Jackson Gallery, New York, February–March 1958, featured seventeen works, including *Listen*, *Earth Green*, *Spring Beat*, *Upstream*, and *The Seasons*.

14 Krasner, in Howard, "Conversation," n.p.

15 Krasner, in Howard, "Conversation," n.p.

16 Elisabeth Kübler-Ross, *On Death and Dying* (New York: Macmillan, 1969).

17 Lee Krasner, quoted in Geoff Dyer, ed., *John Berger: Selected Essays* (London: Bloomsbury, 2001), n.p.

18 Krasner, in Howard, "Conversation," n.p.

19 Carl Jung, "The Concept of the Collective Unconscious," accessed July 13, 2020, http://www.bahaistudies.net/asma/The-Concept-of-the-Collective-Unconscious.pdf.

20 Levin, *Lee Krasner*, 147. My thanks to Helen Harrison of the Pollock-Krasner House and Study Center for allowing me to visit the house and explore the library—as well as the record collection.

21 Levin, *Lee Krasner*, 297.

22 William Shakespeare, *Hamlet*, 1599–1601, ed. Harold Jenkins (London: Arden, 1982), 1.1.30.

23 Krasner, in Howard, "Conversation," n.p.

24 Herbert Read, Michael Fordham, and Gerhard Adler, eds., *C. G. Jung: The Collected Works* (London: Routledge, 1973), 1,482.

25 John Graham, "Primitive Art and Picasso," *Magazine of Art* 30, no. 4 (April 1937): 236–39; and John Graham, *System and Dialectics of Art* (New York: Delphic Studios, 1937).

26 Mark Rothko and Adolph Gottlieb, "Rothko and Gottlieb's Letter to the Editor, 1943," in *Writings on Art: Mark Rothko*, ed. Miguel López-Remiro (New Haven, CT: Yale University Press, 2006), 36.

27 Jackson Pollock made this remark in 1942 after being introduced by Krasner to her teacher Hans Hofmann, who warned of the risks of repeating yourself if you did not work from nature. See Paul Crowther and Isabel Wünsche, eds., *Meanings of Abstract Art: Between Nature and Theory* (New York: Routledge, 2012). For more on Cézanne's relationship to nature, see Joyce Medina, *Cézanne and Modernism: The Poetics of Painting* (New York: State University of New York Press, 1995), 97.

28 Michael Leja, *Reframing Abstract Expressionism: Subjectivity and Painting in the 1940s* (New Haven, CT: Yale University Press, 1993).

29 Peter Selz, *New Images of Man* (New York: Museum of Modern Art, 1959), 11.

30 Kenneth Coutts-Smith, "An Interview with Lee Krasner," *Arts Review*, October 2, 1965, republished August 20, 2019, http://artreview.com/archive-2-october-1962-feature-lee-krasner/.

31 Amy Sillman, in conversation with Helen Molesworth, on "Lee Krasner: Deal with It," *Recording Artists: A Podcast from the Getty*, Season 1: Radical Women, accessed 8 July 2020, http://www.getty.edu/recordingartists/season-1/krasner/.

FRANCIS BACON
PORTRAIT OF MAN WITH GLASSES I
1963

MARTIN HARRISON

The two paintings by Francis Bacon in the Lang Collection, *Portrait of Man with Glasses I* (1963, plate 12) and *Study for a Portrait* (1967, plate 17), were painted four years apart and at very different scales. At first sight, they are connected only by the fact that both ultimately entered the same collection, in 1974 and 1976, respectively. However, I shall propose that they have some salient aspects in common, and that they inform each other in significant ways.

In 1957, Allen Ginsberg was staying in Tangier, Morocco, and "spending lots of time with Paul Bowles & an excellent English painter, Francis Bacon."[1] Ginsberg wrote his father that in the Museum of Modern Art, New York, there was "a big picture" by Bacon "of a gorilla in a tuxedo under a deathly black umbrella."[2] He was referring to *Painting* (1946, fig. 56), which had been acquired at the instigation of Alfred Barr Jr. in 1948 and was the first of Bacon's paintings to be purchased by a museum. I was intrigued by Ginsberg's description of the umbrella as "deathly," and by his suggestion that the figure it obscured was a gorilla. I had always read it as a man. Did Ginsberg somehow intuit an alternative identification? For although it is unlikely that he knew it, a contemporaneous, and in many respects similar, Bacon painting, *Study for Man with Microphones*, was exhibited (before Bacon destroyed it) as *Gorilla with Microphones*.

Even if we decide, ultimately, that the figure in *Painting* is a man, we should remember that for Bacon, human/simian boundaries were fluid. But Ginsberg's observation underlines that interpreting Bacon's paintings is not a straightforward matter, and their ambiguities continue to frustrate those of us who seek to decode their nominal subjects. After his death in 1992, Bacon, who had said he didn't know what most of his paintings meant, was no longer able to influence the way they were read; in his lifetime, he could control interviews and refuse reproduction rights for paintings that would have appeared in situations of which he disapproved. Now, as a consequence of the turn to art theory, he has become the protean Bacon, the site of contested meanings. He is a phenomenon to be deconstructed through the contexts of various ideologies or philosophical frameworks. Simultaneously, the study of iconography has become unfashionable, and consequently there are fewer incentives to address the problematic content of Bacon's paintings.

Bacon liked to think of himself as a reporter, as a painter of the real, or, as he put it, the "factual."[3] These

Plate 12 Francis Bacon, *Portrait of Man with Glasses I*, 1963, oil on canvas, 14$\frac{1}{16}$ × 12$\frac{1}{16}$ in. (35.7 × 30.6 cm). Seattle Art Museum, Gift of the Friday Foundation in honor of Richard E. Lang and Jane Lang Davis, 2020.14.6.

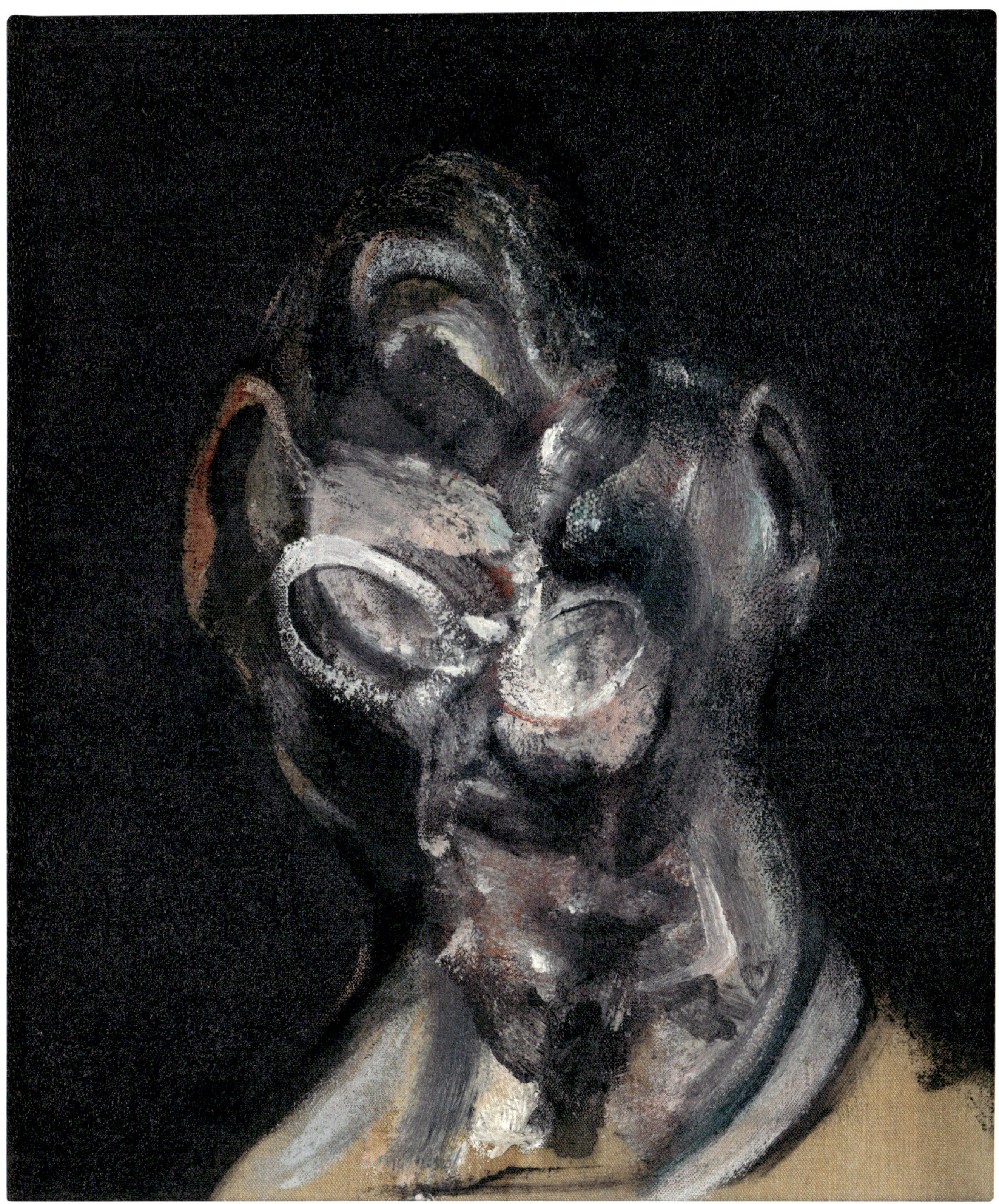

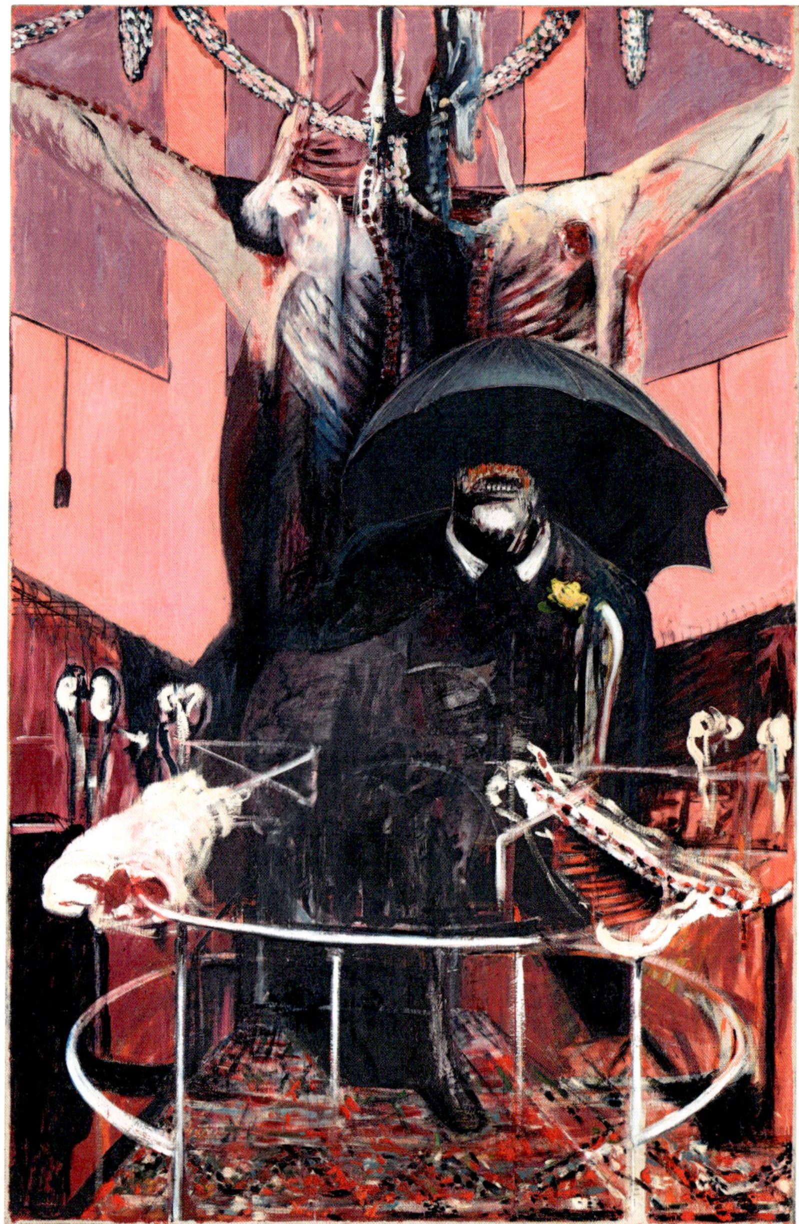

Fig. 56 Francis Bacon, *Painting*, 1946, oil and pastel on linen, 77⅞ × 52 in. (197.8 × 132.1 cm). The Museum of Modern Art, New York, Purchase, 229.1948.

self-characterizations need not be taken too literally. Apart from *Three Studies for Figures at the Base of a Crucifixion* (1944, Tate, London), which has been interpreted as his response to the horrors of the Second World War, it is difficult to align his paintings with the tumultuous events that befell the world after 1945, notwithstanding his declared aim to paint the history of Europe in his lifetime. Yet to argue, instead, that he painted the human condition, we must ask, Which humans did he have in mind? Surely his motivations to paint were technical, formal, and, most significantly, personal; they stemmed from a conviction that raw flesh equated with beauty (or sex), and life and death with violence. Rather than representing something external, he was enacting his feelings in paint on canvas through a system of personal metaphors. Significantly, he described one of his most overtly violent subjects, *Three Studies for a Crucifixion* (1962, Solomon R. Guggenheim Museum), as "almost nearer to a self-portrait."[4] Following the implications of Bacon's remark involves straying toward intentionality or etiological theorizing, hence the attraction in academe of Gilles Deleuze's antibiographical/antipsychological/antinarrative stance that Bacon was a painter of abstract sensation. Love and death are, of course, abstract nouns, but Bacon expressed his feelings in images. We need to ask why Bacon painted the images he did, to interpret the marks on the canvas; the partial interpretations essayed here try to do this, while making no rash claims to resolution.

When Bacon was still in his teens, it was Picasso's example that had inspired him to try to become a painter; in a sense, Bacon remained in a dialogue with him throughout his life. Picasso's influence, which was overt in the period up to 1945, resurfaced in 1962, when, in the first of a celebrated series of interviews, Bacon suggested to David Sylvester that potential stimuli in Picasso's Surrealist Cannes/Dinard period paintings had remained "unexplored"; he believed there were new possibilities in their "organic form that relates to the human image but is a complete distortion of it."[5] Thus, Bacon reopened the dialogue, extending it in both *Portrait of Man with Glasses I* the following year and *Study for a Portrait* four years later.

As a figurative modernist, Bacon had few peers, although, intriguingly, the Lang Collection includes three of the most important among them—Willem de Kooning, Alberto Giacometti, and Philip Guston. Despite some of Bacon's greatest paintings being held in American museums and private collections, his reputation in the United States has always been mixed, with critics from Clement Greenberg to Rosalind Krauss among the prominent detractors. For his part, Bacon has been portrayed as rigidly antipathetic to Abstract Expressionism. This is comprehensible, based as it is on repetitions of his inebriated rhetoric—a widely circulated remark being his characterization of Jackson Pollock as "the old lace-maker."[6] Yet a sober Bacon, interviewed by two Tate Gallery curators in 1983, discussed Pollock with sympathy and intelligence. He could seldom date his own paintings accurately, but he was aware that Pollock's *Blue Poles* was made in 1952 and went on to demonstrate a keen interest in the artist's partial return to figuration in 1953. Bacon increasingly simplified the grounds in his own later paintings, and the flat planes of color he employed indicate his awareness of, say, Mark Rothko and Barnett Newman, irrespective of his dismissive public statements about them: his supposed contempt for them is, therefore, a misperception based on casually uttered remarks and gossip.

That Bacon described his paintings as essentially self-portraits, as noted above, is plausible given that he almost invariably painted his psyche. Nonetheless, a minority of his paintings are not readily classifiable as self-portraits, among them the four versions of *Portrait of Man with Glasses* he painted around July 1963. They were originally titled simply *Head 1* through *Head 4*; the change to more descriptive titles, which was uncharacteristic, may embody a clue to his intention with the paintings. Unfortunately, Bacon remained resolutely silent about the man's identity, but it nonetheless seems likely that he intended these works as portraits of a quite separate individual. A strong contender is Patrick Trevor-Roper, a leading London eye surgeon. Although Bacon disliked being seen in public wearing glasses, he had worn them when he was alone in the studio since the 1930s. Trevor-Roper treated Bacon's horizontal astigmatism, and he and Bacon saw a lot of each other at the time these paintings were made as they socialized in London's still semi-covert gay scene. If a specific individual was intended, alternative identifications include Mahatma Gandhi and James Joyce (Bacon had photographs of both in his studio).

In Bacon's oeuvre, there was a precedent for the *Portrait of Man with Glasses* series in the four similarly sized *Head* paintings made in 1961. Three of the slightly earlier suite depict Bacon's partner, Peter Lacy, and the fourth is possibly a self-portrait. The portraits of Lacy are, by Bacon's standards, relatively undistorted, while the deformations are far more conspicuous in the *Portrait of Man with Glasses* paintings. David Sylvester's observation

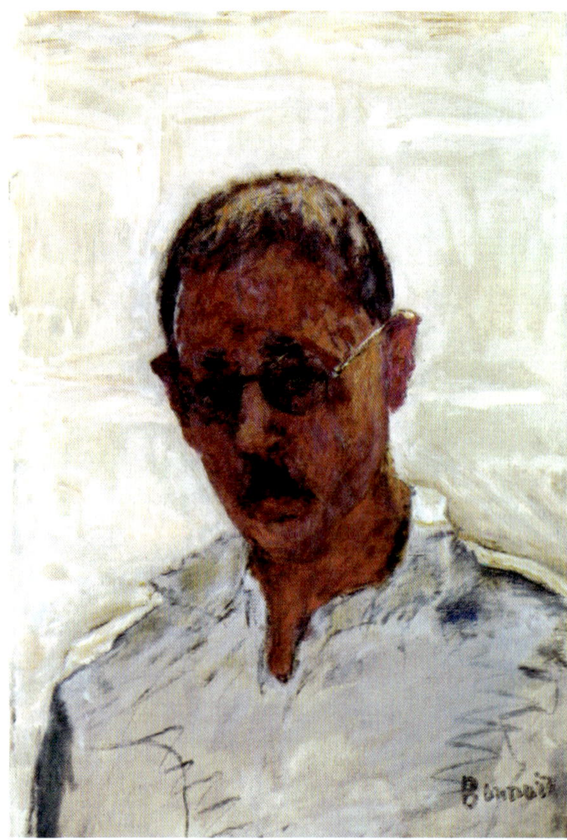

Fig. 57 Pierre Bonnard, *Self-Portrait on White Ground with an Open Collar*, 1933, oil on canvas, 20⅞ × 14¼ in. (53 × 36.2 cm). Fondation Bemberg, Toulouse, France.

that Bacon's depictions were informed by Picasso's *Portrait of Jaime Sabartés with Ruff and Cap* (1939, Museu Picasso, Barcelona) is most convincing in relation to numbers III and IV in the series, in which the glasses are more exaggeratedly lopsided. Often, when Bacon painted in series, he would seek variation by making small adjustments such as these; he may also have been familiar with Picasso's pre-Cubist renditions of Sabartés, which established a less deformed representational basis.

It should also be noted that Bacon had painted figures wearing glasses long before this, most conspicuously in *Head III* (1949, Private Collection). The history of art is replete with other potential exemplars, for example, Jean-Baptiste-Siméon Chardin's *Self-Portrait with Spectacles* (1771, Musée du Louvre), which was the model for Bacon's *Study of Reinhard Hassert* (1979, Private Collection). But arguably the most compelling comparators are the late self-portraits of Pierre Bonnard. Bacon does not directly quote any of Bonnard's self-portraits, but his paintings share the brooding intensity of gaze that is not a characteristic normally associated with Bonnard (fig. 57). It was again David Sylvester who noted that Bacon used to praise

Bonnard so highly "that I had the impression there was no twentieth century painter he preferred,"[7] and the art critic Giles Auty recalled a visit to Bacon's studio in St. Ives in late 1959 and talking with him, during a long, sunlit afternoon, mainly about Bonnard. Bacon had famously been reimagining Diego Velázquez since 1949 and Vincent van Gogh in 1957; the revisiting of Bonnard may be seen as a similar co-opting of art historical precedent as both a departure point for visual extemporizations and a vehicle for exploring his own feelings and sensations.

The numbering of the series does not constitute proof that Bacon painted them in the order he indicated; however, that the sequence commenced with *Portrait of Man with Glasses I* is the most logical inference. In the Lang Collection work, the painterly onslaught is at its most intense. The head is deformed, crumpled, violated. It resembles the raw flesh of the hanging carcasses that had fascinated Bacon since childhood. Unusually, the mouth—a crucial expressive site for Bacon—is almost obliterated. His color-mixing skills are employed to suggest blood or bruising, and his pressing of fabrics into the wet paint emphasizes the nonrepresentational nature of the painting—its semiabstract range of textures. The necessarily short, sweeping, and arching brushstrokes define the visceral ferocity of the assault, as though Bacon fashioned a kind of golem in two dimensions, from thick paint rather than from clay. Features are erased in dissolving, flickering paint, the structure of the head folds in under Bacon's entropic attack. Close looking at the head, at its physical, material presence in the middle of the canvas, is essential—and richly rewarded. The area of canvas at the bottom of the frame is left raw, unpainted; this is common to all four works in the series, as is the texture of the black ground, its bituminous density, achieved by thickening with linseed oil, coagulating into a void. While the glasses in this version are fairly perfunctory—they resemble the white ellipses Bacon would add, almost arbitrarily, to heads long afterward—they were more identifiable as spectacles with frames in the second, third, and fourth portraits; only in *Portrait of Man with Glasses III* does Bacon show us the man's angrily bared and skewed teeth. *Portrait of Man with Glasses I* has not been analyzed in any detail before, and this first essay leaves many of its mysteries intact: hopefully, the renewed attention to this compelling painting will open it up to fresh interpretations.

NOTES

1 Allen Ginsberg, quoted in Michael Schumacher, ed., *Family Business* (London: Bloomsbury, 2001), 60.

2 Schumacher, *Family Business*, 60.

3 See, for example, David Sylvester, *The Brutality of Fact: Interviews with Francis Bacon* (London: Thames and Hudson, 1997), 56.

4 Francis Bacon, quoted in Sylvester, *Brutality of Fact*, 48.

5 Bacon, quoted in Sylvester, *Brutality of Fact*, 8.

6 Bacon, quoted in David Sylvester, *Looking Back at Francis Bacon* (London: Thames and Hudson, 2000), 246.

7 Sylvester, *Looking Back*, 87.

MARK ROTHKO
UNTITLED
1963

JEFFREY WEISS

Our first impression of the Lang Collection's 1963 painting by Mark Rothko (plate 13) is apt to be one of value and scale. A white bar emblazoned in the work's upper reaches intensifies its dark palette. Below, three elongated, narrowly separated forms spread across a horizontal field that they redouble and almost fill—the composition is at once expansive and constrained. Yet, moving close to the painting, we see an unexpected detail: flecks of white so small and scattered they can only be detected from within several feet of the canvas. Paint flecks of this kind occur throughout Rothko's work of the 1950s and early 1960s; they are generally accidental, the residue of process (rather than having been produced by deliberate, well-aimed flicks of the brush). Rothko used thinned paint, drops of which can fly off the bristles when, on being dipped, the brush is waved in front of the painting before landing to make a mark. The dimensions of the canvases were such that he worked as much from the shoulder as from the elbow and wrist. Elsewhere in Rothko's works on canvas we also often detect running rivulets or drips.

The process of the work is thus exposed.[1] It is important to acknowledge that the artist's painterly finesse does not represent a polished refinement—the kind of fastidiousness that might be attributed to the work were we to know it only through reproductions in books. Rothko did not speak much of process in this way, but the signs of it are clear, and they ask to be accounted for. A sensation of breadth is partly attained through the layered application of thin veils of paint that lightly hold the feathered gestures of the brush. A certain loose immediacy obtains. As the paintings are sized but not primed, paint both saturates the canvas and sits on its surface. In the course of making the work, other things happen—the flecks, the drips—that, although unplanned, are accepted by the artist as wholly in keeping with the material character of the painting overall.

As David Anfam, author of the catalogue raisonné of Rothko's paintings, has fully discussed, the period of roughly 1958 to 1966 in Rothko's work was dominated by mural commissions: the Seagram murals (1958–62), the Harvard murals (1962–64), and his works for the Rothko Chapel in Houston (1965–66). Anfam identifies paintings produced independently of these projects as having been closely related in palette and, in some cases, structure to the murals, which were the object of intensive campaigns of work. Accordingly, the Lang Collection painting falls

Plate 13 Mark Rothko, *Untitled*, 1963, oil on canvas, 69 × 90 in. (152.4 × 228.6 cm). Seattle Art Museum, Gift of the Friday Foundation in honor of Richard E. Lang and Jane Lang Davis, 2020.14.16.

within what Anfam refers to as the period of the Harvard murals and related works.[2] Paintings for the Harvard mural project were distinguished by a palette of dark reds and plummy browns as well as deep blues and reddish, greenish, and bluish grays, a narrow range of hue and value that matches that of the Lang Collection painting. That said, Rothko introduced that palette during the late fifties, around the time of his work on the Seagram commission (fig. 58).

Moreover, like a number of other works of 1963 and 1964, the Lang Collection painting closely anticipates the even darker cast of the Houston murals, with their repertoire of near-black colors that have long been said to defy the specificity of a conventional name. In sum, the last ten or twelve years of Rothko's production, within which the Lang painting falls, demonstrate various kinds of darkness that came increasingly to prevail.

In form, the Lang Collection painting bears no resemblance to the Harvard mural paintings, which were constructed as a friezelike arrangement of notched frames that expand and contract from one image to the next, a device that Rothko extrapolated from his work on the Seagram commission. Yet, while its "stacked" arrangement of forms follows the by-then classic configuration of Rothko's work since 1950, the large horizontal format of the Lang Collection painting—which he had employed only around a half-dozen times prior to embarking on the Seagram commission—might be said to respond directly to the wide-format nature of the murals. As Dore Ashton first observed, the very idea of mural painting supports Rothko's ambition for his work in general: to produce a kind of painting that rewards the close proximity of the beholder with a visual immersion. For this reason, Rothko preferred not to exhibit in the company of others, and was given to installing his paintings close together.[3] The artist said that crowding in this way subordinates the wall to the surface of the paintings.[4] The large horizontal-format painting is related to this idea: "The best way I can involve the viewer," Rothko said to the curator Katherine Kuh, "is to make the painting so big that he can't absorb it in one easy glance. He has to be enveloped by the painting. He has to be able to see it by turning in space."[5]

Yet we should not forget that while Rothko's nonmural paintings are autonomous works, they often also share features with other paintings, as if they loosely belong to sets, sequences, or groups. While not systematic, such resemblances allow us to observe the artist investigating variants of specific combinations of color and form. For

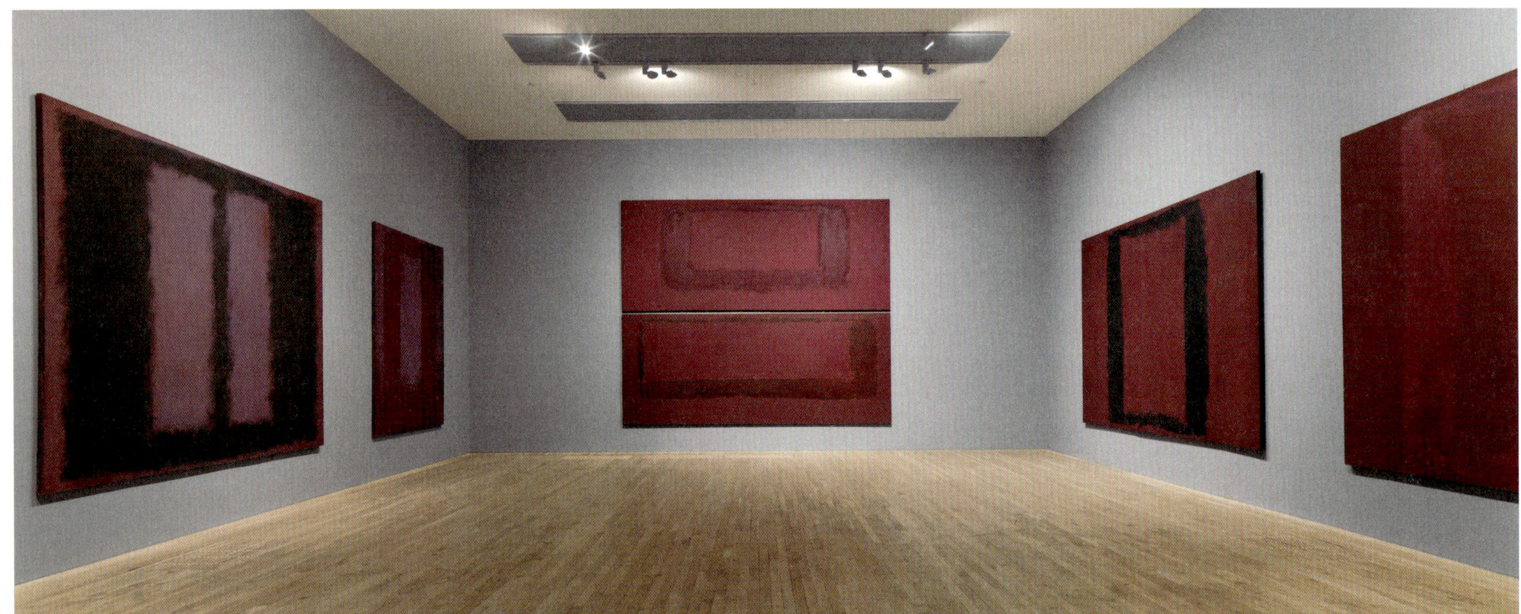

Fig. 58 Installation view of Mark Rothko's *Seagram Murals* at Tate Modern, 2008.

Fig. 59 Mark Rothko, *Untitled (Black, White, Grays on Maroon)*, 1963, oil on canvas, 89⅜ × 68⅞ in. (227 × 175 cm). Kunsthaus Zürich, 1971, 1971/0005.

example, we note that the distribution of dark colors with a single white form in the Lang Collection painting closely corresponds to various works of this period in which the white area changes position—top, middle, bottom—within a field that is otherwise dark. One such painting, the much larger, horizontal-format *No. 9 (White and Black on Wine)* of 1958 (Glenstone), may have been painted as a possible Seagram mural panel (before Rothko developed a new image for the commission). Another work, *Untitled (Black, White, Grays on Maroon)* (1963, fig. 59), is vertical in format but identical in size to the Lang painting. Here, the matching dimensions—as if the same canvas had been rotated a single turn—expose a pictorial thought process that is, at least in part, analytical. In other words, while we often speak of Rothko in affective, metaphysical, and symbolic terms, we are reminded in a case like this that his studio practice was grounded in material and formal considerations.

What, then, of those other terms? The literature on Rothko's work is filled with names from the history of culture called upon as sources and models to help us account for meaning: Plato, Aeschylus, Michelangelo Buonarroti, Rembrandt van Rijn, William Shakespeare, Søren Kierkegaard, J. M. W. Turner, Friedrich Nietzsche, Stéphane Mallarmé, T. S. Eliot, Jean-Paul Sartre, and beyond—it is a long and distinguished list, including artists, writers, and composers (leaving aside anonymous sources and the Old and New Testaments). Indeed, such references were common among Rothko and his contemporaries of the New York School. During the late 1950s, Rothko claimed that his works engage grand themes—tragedy, ecstasy, and doom among them. His remark was intended to keep the paintings from being taken as strictly abstract exercises in color and form, implying instead that his works function in metaphorical and/or symbolic ways. In his account of the history of the interpretation of Rothko's work, the art historian Glenn Phillips addresses the different forms of experience or states of mind that have been invoked by Rothko's observers, according to whom the works have been variously characterized as "transcendental, tragic, mystical, violent or serene; as representative of the void; as opening onto the experience of the sublime; as exhilaratingly intellectual; or as profoundly spiritual—to mention just a few examples." These things conflict, yet, as Phillips observes, each draws from the conviction that the work's chief function is to intensify the process of seeing.[6] It seems clear that Rothko meant to address large themes through subjective experience. In this regard, he said that the large size of his canvases instigates a direct, "intimate" physical relation of the painting to the observer.[7] In turn, heightened seeing—or beholding—belongs to the realm of consciousness, and this is where form and process open other doors of apprehension.

Seeing in Rothko's work is often described as a slowed process. Writing of the dark paintings, which arguably push this quality to an extreme, the art historian Briony Fer observes a "withholding of affect" that "entails a deferral in time."[8] (Similarly, Barbara Novak and Brian O'Doherty identify "two conflicting modes of Rothko's practice" that come to late fruition in the dark paintings for the Houston chapel commission: "disclosure and withdrawal, the dialectic of his construction of mystery through equivocation."[9]) A work like the Lang Collection painting can, of course, be perceived at a glance, but everything about it opposes an all-at-once apprehension. The thinness of the paint layer and the breadth of forms instigate a gradual perceptual commingling of figure and ground in shallow space. In this way, the painting is, at once, both empty and full, conjuring a condition of immanence. Speaking of the theorization of painting as a window, the art historian David Summers credits the Renaissance architect Leon Battista Alberti with an "extraordinary and original transformation of painting into a metaphor for our subjective experience of the world taken altogether."[10] Having abandoned Alberti's window, a work of Rothko's might be said to qualify as a site that now activates the subjective experience of *painting* taken altogether. With his work, Rothko devised a new way to activate color, value, surface, scale, and pictorial space as elements that now serve a direct encounter. In turn, these elements instigate a play of analogy that signifies deeper reserves.

Form, color, and value in Rothko's work possess connotations of both weight and luminosity. In the Lang Collection painting, dark forms dwell in liminal obscurity. Set off by the work's white form, a softly brushed nimbus-like slab with intimations of light and lightness, they exercise an almost gravitational pull. The size and format of the painting are enveloping, but the work's physical limits are also clear. Displayed without a frame (which Rothko abandoned after the late forties), the painting wants to exceed itself and thereby belong to the actual space of the room, even as what occurs within it happens before us, not around us. The qualities I have enlisted—fullness, emptiness, suspension, extension, containment, weight—are both actual and metaphorical. The painting's pictorial means can be described using these terms, yet those elements also figure ideas and sensations that charge the work's potential for allegory. It must be said that vision already possesses such a charge, and that a Rothko painting allegorizes itself in this regard. It is a key achievement of Rothko's work, perhaps culminating with the period of the Lang Collection painting, that an historical thematics of seeing—surface and depth, vision and touch, absence and presence, blindness and insight, desire and loss—can itself be said to hold the full range of connotations we associate with the work's metaphysical depths.

NOTES

1 There are various places to turn for a close material analysis of Rothko's process, a large topic. Here, I will simply follow Briony Fer, who observed that Rothko distinguished his work from that of Ad Reinhardt, his contemporary, by referring to the exposed signs of touch on the surface of his works. "The difference between me and Reinhardt is that he is a mystic. By that I mean that his paintings are immaterial. Mine are *here*, materially. The surfaces, the work of the brush and so on. His are untouchable." Quoted in Briony Fer, "Rothko and Repetition," in *Seeing Rothko*, ed. Glenn Phillips and Thomas Crow (Los Angeles: Getty Research Institute, 2005), 170. The distinction between a primarily optical form of painting and a more openly or engagingly material one is useful. For an important descriptive account of Rothko's paint surfaces, see David Anfam, *Mark Rothko: The Works on Canvas* (Washington, DC: National Gallery of Art, 1998), 84–86; and for a close analysis of materials and techniques that contribute to Rothko's complex paint surfaces, see Carol Mancusi-Ungaro, "Material and Immaterial Surface: The Paintings of Rothko," in *Mark Rothko*, ed. Jeffrey Weiss (New Haven, CT: Yale University Press, 1998), 282–301.

2 Anfam, *Mark Rothko*, 88–97.

3 Dore Ashton, *About Rothko* (New York: Da Capo, 1983), 130.

4 Mark Rothko, "Statement on His Attitude in Painting," *Tiger's Eye*, no. 9 (October 1949): 114.

5 Mark Rothko, Oral history interview with Katherine Kuh, 1983–84, Archives of American Art, Smithsonian Institution, Washington, DC.

6 Glenn Phillips, "Introduction: Irreconcilable Rothko," in Phillips and Crow, *Seeing Rothko*, 1–9.

7 Mark Rothko, "A Symposium on How to Combine Architecture, Painting and Sculpture," *Interiors* 110 (May 1951): 104.

8 Fer, "Rothko and Repetition," 41.

9 Barbara Novak and Brian O'Doherty, "Rothko's Dark Paintings: Tragedy and Void," in Weiss, *Mark Rothko*, 274.

10 David Summer, *Vision, Reflection, and Desire in Western Painting* (Chapel Hill: University of North Carolina Press, 2007), 13.

ROBERT MOTHERWELL
IRISH ELEGY
1965

JACK FLAM

Robert Motherwell's *Irish Elegy* (plate 14), which was painted in early 1965, is a monumental and austere painting, straightforward in structure but charged with complex associations and overtones.[1] It is one of the artist's most pared-down Elegy paintings: the basic composition contains a single black oval set against two dark vertical forms, rather than the multiple ovals and vertical bars that are typical of the series. The color is also unique among the Elegies, most of which are painted in starkly contrasting areas of black and white, which the artist associated with the duality between life and death.[2] In *Irish Elegy*, the black oval is set against a gray ground, and the black verticals that press against it are enwreathed by sinuous areas of green. A bold-blue rectangle is painted over the right-hand vertical form, adding a dissonant geometric element to the supple forms in the rest of the composition. The only white passage in this picture is a thin, unevenly painted line that descends from the top left of the painting like a bolt of electric current, creating an unexpected laceration in the large black form it traverses.

This painting, perhaps more than any of the other large Elegies, is intensely intimate and somber. Composed in a close range of tonal values rather than what Motherwell called the "éclat" of bright whites set against blacks, it radiates the kind of pensive melancholy that is inherent in minor-key music. The sense of intimacy, solemnity, and self-containment is enhanced by the directional thrust of the two oblong vertical forms from right to left—rather than left to right, as in almost all the other Elegy paintings, which lends them an air of lightness and movement. Since our Western way of reading a picture is, like reading text, from left to right, the directional thrusts of the vertical forms in this painting instead create a certain amount of resistance to the eye, adding to the somber, bounded feel of the composition as a whole. Although Motherwell has stated that his Elegy paintings were "for the most part, public statements,"[3] this painting is an exceptionally private and personal one.

Irish Elegy is unique in another way: it is the only painting in Motherwell's celebrated Elegy series that refers to a place outside of Spain.[4] And yet the impulses behind this painting are very similar to those that were at the root of the artist's *Elegies to the Spanish Republic*: a complex amalgam of literature, politics, and a deep sense of tragedy.

Motherwell created the very first Elegy-like composition during the summer of 1948 in a brush-and-ink drawing

Plate 14 Robert Motherwell, *Irish Elegy*, 1965, acrylic on canvas, 69½ × 83¾ in. (176.5 × 212.8 cm). Seattle Art Museum, Gift of the Friday Foundation in honor of Richard E. Lang and Jane Lang Davis, 2020.14.1.

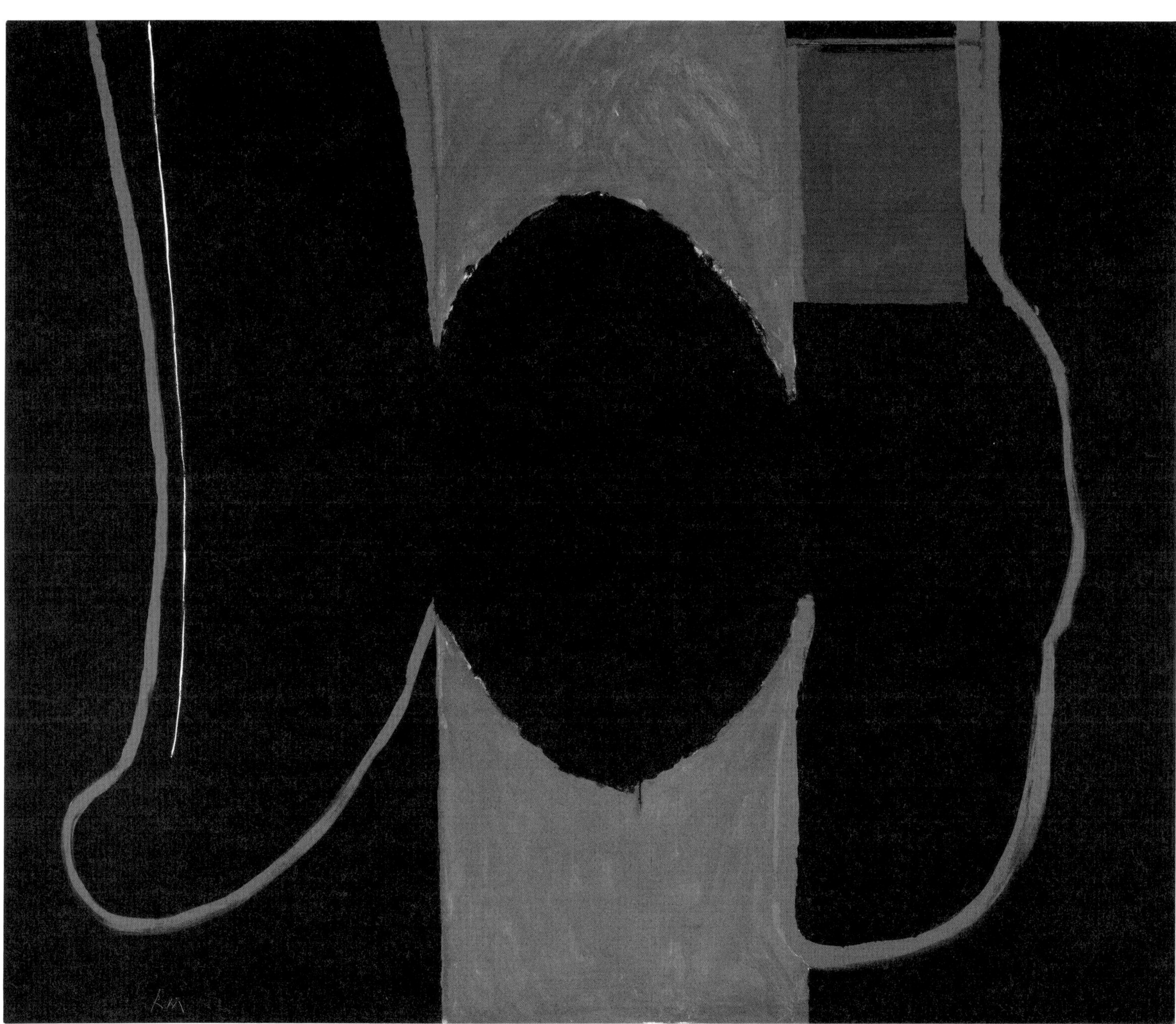

Fig. 60 Robert Motherwell, *At Five in the Afternoon*, 1948–49, casein and graphite on paperboard, 15 × 20 in. (38.1 × 50.8 cm). Collection of the Estate of Helen Frankenthaler.

made to illuminate the concluding lines of a poem by Harold Rosenberg called "A Bird for Every Bird." Text and image were supposed to appear in the never-published second issue of the art and literature revue *possibilities*, which Motherwell was coediting with Rosenberg. In the fall, Motherwell was inspired to return to the imagery of that drawing and use its compositional format of ovals set against vertical bars as the point of departure for his first painting of the Elegy motif, *At Five in the Afternoon* (1948–49, fig. 60). That painting takes its title from the refrain of Federico García Lorca's poem "Llanto por Ignacio Sánchez Mejías," which is an elegy for a great matador (himself also a poet) who was fatally gored in the bullring "at exactly five in the afternoon."

Between 1949 and the beginning of 1965, Motherwell created over one hundred paintings in the series *Elegies to the Spanish Republic*, meant to commemorate the overthrow of the Spanish Republican government by fascists, which Motherwell considered one of the great political tragedies of his time. But the paintings were also meant to transcend any specific political situation and convey a general sense of tragedy, what Motherwell described in 1950 as "funeral pictures, laments, dirges, elegies—barbaric and austere."[5] Although almost all the Elegy paintings were rendered primarily in black and white, some contained blocks of color, often used in an overtly symbolic way. The bright colors on the left side of *Elegy to the Spanish Republic XXXIV* (1953–54, fig. 61), for example, recall those of the flag of the Second Spanish Republic (1931–39).

The colors in *Irish Elegy* are also symbolically related to its nominal subject. Green is, of course, closely associated with Ireland, and Motherwell surely meant for this association to be clear. When the painting was shown at his 1965 retrospective exhibition at the Museum of Modern Art, *Time* magazine reported that it "was so titled, says Robert Motherwell, whose ancestors hailed from Ireland, because the winding green lines convey a feeling of the old sod."[6] Moreover, green and blue are the colors of the flag of the City of Dublin (fig. 62), to which the blue rectangle in *Irish Elegy* appears to allude. Such indirect but firmly imbedded symbolic associations are typical of Motherwell's works, which eschew direct or literal narrative but embrace the idea of expressing various aspects of their subject matter through complex and resonant networks of associations.

These associations, and the explicit title of *Irish Elegy*, lead one to ask: Why did Motherwell paint an Irish-themed Elegy at this particular time, in 1965?

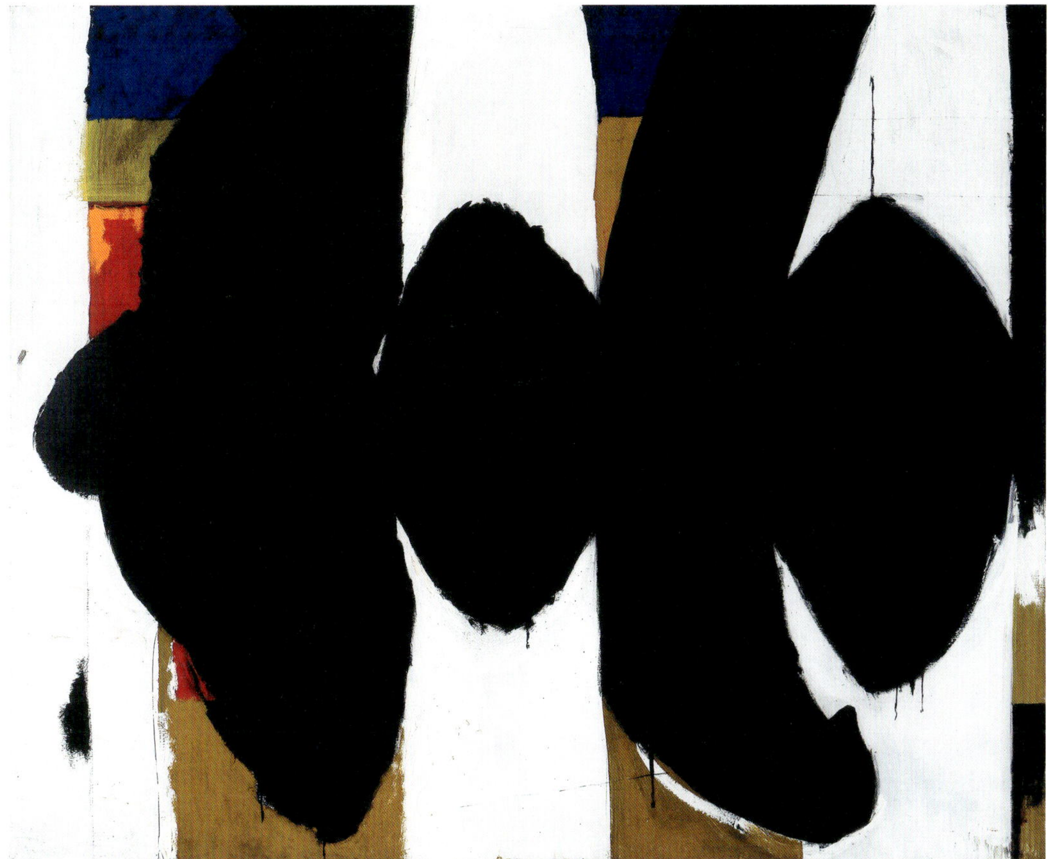

Fig. 61 Robert Motherwell, *Elegy to the Spanish Republic XXXIV*, 1953–54, oil on canvas, 80 × 100 in. (203.2 × 254 cm). Albright-Knox Art Gallery, Buffalo, New York, Gift of Seymour H. Knox Jr., 1957.K1957:6.

Here, it is worth noting that Motherwell, who proudly referred to himself as "a Celt,"[7] was a passionate admirer of the works of William Butler Yeats, whose centenary was celebrated in 1965, and especially of James Joyce, who inspired several of Motherwell's works. Moreover, two of Motherwell's closest friends in 1965 were of Irish descent—the sculptor David Smith and the poet Frank O'Hara—though neither of them appears to have been especially interested in Irish politics.

Irish politics, however, were very much in the air at the time. Although "the Troubles" in Northern Ireland between the Catholic Nationalists and Protestant Unionists are usually said to have started in 1968, the term was being used at least as early as 1964, a year when intense violence in Northern Ireland was reported by the US press.[8] Motherwell's interest in the Irish situation was given tangible expression in April 1964, when he finished his large painting *Dublin 1916, with Black and Tan* (Empire State Plaza Art Collection), which alluded directly to the Irish Republican rebellion during Easter week 1916, as well as to Yeats's celebrated poem "Easter 1916," and to the "Black and Tan" British troops who fought against the Republicans during the subsequent Irish War of Independence.

But another, very specific event seems to have served as a major inspiration for *Irish Elegy*: the death of President John F. Kennedy. This is something that Motherwell alluded to in a conversation with Walter Barker, who reviewed his 1965 retrospective at the Museum of Modern Art. Barker

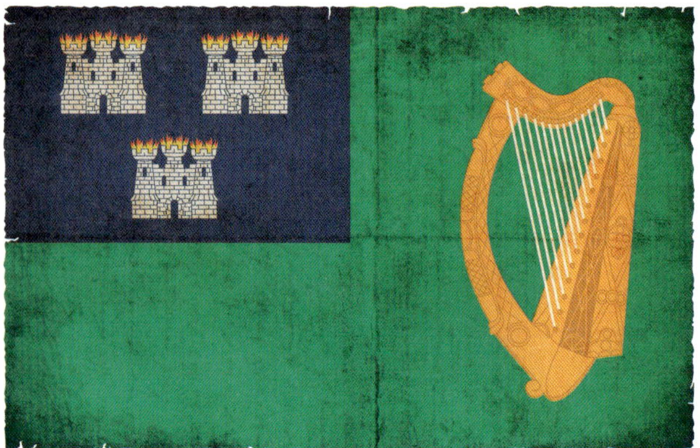

Fig. 62 Flag of the City of Dublin.

wrote that when asked about the titles of his paintings, "Motherwell explained that they exist on a number of associative levels. 'Irish Elegy,' for example, relates to his maternal ancestors, the Irish famine, Yeats, Joyce, whose work he loves, and the Kennedy family whom he admires."[9] It is not surprising that Motherwell felt a particular affinity with John F. Kennedy, who was only two years his junior, shared similar political views, and had brought a vigorous feeling for high culture to the White House.

Motherwell painted *Irish Elegy* only fifteen months after Kennedy was assassinated, and at a time when Kennedy's legacy was receiving a good deal of media attention. Toward the end of May 1964, organizers announced that a John F. Kennedy memorial garden would be created near the "Kennedy ancestral home" in Ireland, "financed by Irish-American societies."[10] On May 29, which would have been Kennedy's 47th birthday, Irish president Eamon de Valera laid a wreath on Kennedy's grave and attended a "solemn pontifical requiem mass" for him at the Shrine of the Immaculate Conception in Washington, DC. Both were widely covered in the press.[11] These tributes to Kennedy coincided with a number of events related to James Joyce. In February 1964, the visit to New York by Joyce's sister May (Mary Kathleen) Joyce Monaghan received a good deal of attention.[12] And only a few months later, in May 1964, the James Joyce Society was formed, with the initial aim of placing a plaque at Joyce's birthplace.[13]

Kennedy and Ireland were also on Motherwell's mind at the beginning of 1965 for another reason. In December 1963, just a week after Kennedy was assassinated, the US General Services Administration had announced that the federal office building that was to be built in Boston would be named after the late president. The architects for the building, who had been appointed in January 1961, were Walter Gropius and his firm, the Architects Collaborative, working with the assistance of the Boston architect Samuel Glaser. Motherwell had worked with Gropius and the Architects Collaborative as far back as 1950, when he had been commissioned to paint a mural for a Gropius-designed junior high school in Attleboro, Massachusetts, and the two men had a cordial relationship. Gropius had planned to commission art for the Boston building since the beginning of the project, and he and Motherwell appear to have discussed the possibility of his painting a large mural for the main lobby of the building sometime in late 1964 or early 1965.

Thus, at the time he painted *Irish Elegy*, Motherwell was thinking about a mural commission for the lobby of the John F. Kennedy Federal Building; and only a few months after he finished *Irish Elegy*, he began to work on the large mural painting that would come to be known as the *New England Elegy*—although the liquid forms in that painting look nothing like the established Elegy format of ovals played against oblong verticals. Significantly, Motherwell had originally intended to call the mural painting for the Kennedy building *Tragic Elegy*—a title that would have carried a great emotional charge, but which was apparently deemed inappropriate for a federal office building.[14]

Motherwell's deep feeling for his *Irish Elegy* is reflected in its exhibition history. It was shown for the first time at an exhibition called *Critics' Choice: Art since World War II*, which opened on March 31, 1965, at the Providence Art Club, in Rhode Island, and was curated by three of the leading critics of the time, Thomas B. Hess, Hilton Kramer, and Harold Rosenberg.[15] The three prominent critics had been asked to vote on whom to include as "Artists of Outstanding Significance after World War II," with each to be represented by a single work. Motherwell's recently painted *Irish Elegy* proudly represented him alongside works by colleagues such as Franz Kline, Willem de Kooning, Barnett Newman, Jackson Pollock, Mark Rothko, and David Smith, as well as older European artists including Balthus, Jean Dubuffet, Alberto Giacometti, and Henry Moore. *Irish Elegy* was also included in Motherwell's retrospective at the Museum of Modern Art in the fall of 1965, and in his 1983 retrospective at the Albright-Knox Art Gallery; both were exhibitions for which Motherwell himself chose most of the works.

If *Irish Elegy* was, in effect, an elegy to John F. Kennedy, one might ask why Motherwell gave the painting such a general title. This goes to the heart of Motherwell's aesthetic philosophy. Throughout his career, Motherwell avoided literal narrative and followed the principle of painting not the subject but his feelings for the subject. And in this instance, he must have felt that naming the painting for Kennedy would have been unseemly and would have undercut the resonance of what he hoped would be a universal image. Instead, by investing the work with multilayered Irish references, he was able to open it up to a deeper and broader range of feelings and meanings, very much in accordance with his belief that works of art accumulate meaning through networks of associations.

"I take an elegy to be a funeral lamentation or funeral song for something one cared about," Motherwell stated in the catalogue for his 1963 exhibition at Smith College.[16] And, life being what it is, an Elegy for one person who was "cared about" can eventually come to serve as an Elegy for others. Indeed, only a few months after Motherwell painted *Irish Elegy*, David Smith was killed in a car crash, and just a year after that, Frank O'Hara also died in an accident. The broad title of *Irish Elegy* enabled the painting to pay tribute to those the artist cared about, not only in the past but in the future, just as the intensity of its imagery encompassed generations of tragedies from the Great Famine to the Troubles.

NOTES

1 *Irish Elegy* was probably painted in late February, as suggested by entries in the artist's 1965 datebook, now in the Dedalus Foundation Archives, where he notes receiving a shipment of canvas on February 11 and records all-day painting sessions on February 21, 22, and 27; the painting was included in a show at the Providence Art Club that opened on March 31.

2 "My Spanish Elegies are also free-association," Motherwell stated in 1962. "Black is death, anxiety; white is life, éclat." See Charles Chetham, "Robert Motherwell: A Conversation at Lunch," in *An Exhibition of the Work of Robert Motherwell* (Northampton, MA: Smith College Museum of Art, 1963), n.p.

3 See Jack D. Flam, "With Robert Motherwell," in *Robert Motherwell*, Jack D. Flam and Dore Ashton (Buffalo, NY: Albright-Knox Art Gallery; New York: Abbeville Press, 1983), 22.

4 *Havana*, 1951, has an Elegy-like composition but is not called an Elegy; *New England Elegy*, discussed below, does not follow at all the visual format of the Elegy series.

5 Robert Motherwell, quoted in Kootz Gallery, *Motherwell: First Exhibition of Paintings in Three Years* (New York: Samuel M. Kootz Gallery, 1950), n.p.

6 "Painting: Lochinvar's Return," *Time*, October 8, 1965, 85. Motherwell's father was from a Scottish Protestant family; his mother's background was Irish Catholic.

7 See Stephanie Terenzio, ed., *The Collected Writings of Robert Motherwell* (New York: Oxford University Press, 1991), 196, 203. Motherwell referred to himself as such many times in conversation with me.

8 See, for example, "Violence Erupts in Belfast over Removal of Irish Flag," *New York Times*, October 2, 1964. Horace Reynolds, "Growing Up in Ireland," published in the October 11, 1964, issue of the *New York Times*, speaks of "Ireland with its political and religious excesses, its Troubles and its Puritanism." See also Tyrone Guthrie, "Close-Up of Ireland's Basic Problem," *New York Times*, January 19, 1962.

9 Walter Barker, "Painter of the Indomitable Gesture: Robert Motherwell Retrospective at the Modern," *St. Louis Post-Dispatch*, November 21, 1965.

10 "Ireland Will Get a Kennedy Garden," *New York Times*, May 26, 1964.

11 "De Valera Lays Wreath on Kennedy's Grave," *New York Times*, May 30, 1964.

12 See Brian O'Doherty, "A Sister Recalls Joyce in Dublin: Mrs. Monaghan Is Here for Writer's 82nd Anniversary," *New York Times*, February 3, 1964.

13 The society was founded by Frederic H. Young, a professor at Montclair State College in New Jersey, who on his first trip to Ireland had been surprised to find that there was no plaque there. See *New York Times*, May 10, 1964.

14 In an April 20, 1966, letter to Gropius, Motherwell wrote, "I call the mural 'Tragic Elegy,'" but acknowledged that the mural would be considered "far out" in relation to public taste (Walter Gropius Papers, Archives of American Art, Smithsonian Institution). For details about the *New England Elegy*, see Jack Flam, Katy Rogers, and Tim Clifford, *Robert Motherwell Paintings and Collages: A Catalogue Raisonné, 1941–1991*, 3 vols. (New Haven, CT: Yale University Press, 2012), 1:107–9, 2:205–7.

15 The rationale behind the exhibition, which was mounted in honor of the bicentennial of Brown University and ran from March 31 to April 24, 1965, is discussed in the catalogue, *Critics' Choice: Art since World War II. Artists Selected by Thomas B. Hess, Hilton Kramer and Harold Rosenberg* (Providence, RI: Providence Art Club, 1965).

16 Robert Motherwell, in Chetham, "Robert Motherwell," n.p., caption to plate 16.

DAVID SMITH
CUBI XXV
1965

MICHAEL BRENSON

David Smith finished his first *Cubi* in March 1961 and his twenty-eighth and last *Cubi* on May 5, 1965, less than three weeks before his death in a road accident near Bennington, Vermont. He made them while the *Zigs*, *Voltris*, *Voltri-Boltons*, *Circles*, and *Wagons*, other prominent series, came and went. He made them during the first years of a tumultuous decade in which Pop Art, Minimalism, and Earth Art seized the spotlight from Abstract Expressionism, the movement to which he most belonged. Smith had long pursued many artistic directions at once—his fall 1964 show at New York's Marlborough-Gerson Gallery "contains works in no less than five styles," *New Yorker* critic Robert M. Coates wrote[1]—but during what turned out to be the last months of his life, the *Cubis* were his primary focus. In a slide talk at Bennington College on May 12, 1965, he revealed his continuing captivation by stainless steel. From Stonehenge through ancient Greece, Michelangelo to Bernini, Medardo Rosso to Constantin Brancusi and Alberto Giacometti, sculptors had found revelatory ways of animating matter with light. With stainless steel, Smith did too. On his hillside in Bolton Landing, in New York's Adirondack Mountains, the sun, moon, and clouds seemed to play and even dance over and into the *Cubis*' burnished surfaces, in effect painting on them or making them seem like photographic plates, or like membranes or skins. In his iconic photographs of his sculptures set against the hills and sky, Smith had revealed his desire for the landscape to be in his sculpture. In the *Cubis*, it did participate in the sculpture, and the participation seemed reciprocal. Smith told his Bennington audience that this series, already more numerous than any of his others, was not done with him. "Every time I do four or five I think I've exhausted my thinking in that way, but then I buy more stainless steel and make more sculptures. But I hope it finishes off pretty soon."[2]

Like Smith's other sixteen series, the *Cubis* are distinct in materials and process.[3] They are his only series made entirely of stainless steel. While he was known for hands-on involvement in every stage of his work, all the *Cubi* parts may have been fabricated by Ryerson Steel, and Smith asked Leon Pratt, his assistant, to wield the revolving carborundum disc with which he made the scribbles that turned the surfaces into magnets for light.[4] Ryerson tack welded the stainless steel boxes it shipped to Smith, but it was Pratt who sealed their welding, Pratt who welded the parts into place after he and Smith had hoisted the tack-welded constructions so that Smith could adjust them

Plate 15 David Smith, *Cubi XXV*, 1965, stainless steel, 119¼ × 120¾ × 31¼ in. (302.9 × 306.7 × 79.4 cm). Seattle Art Museum, Gift of the Friday Foundation in honor of Richard E. Lang and Jane Lang Davis, 2021.1.2.

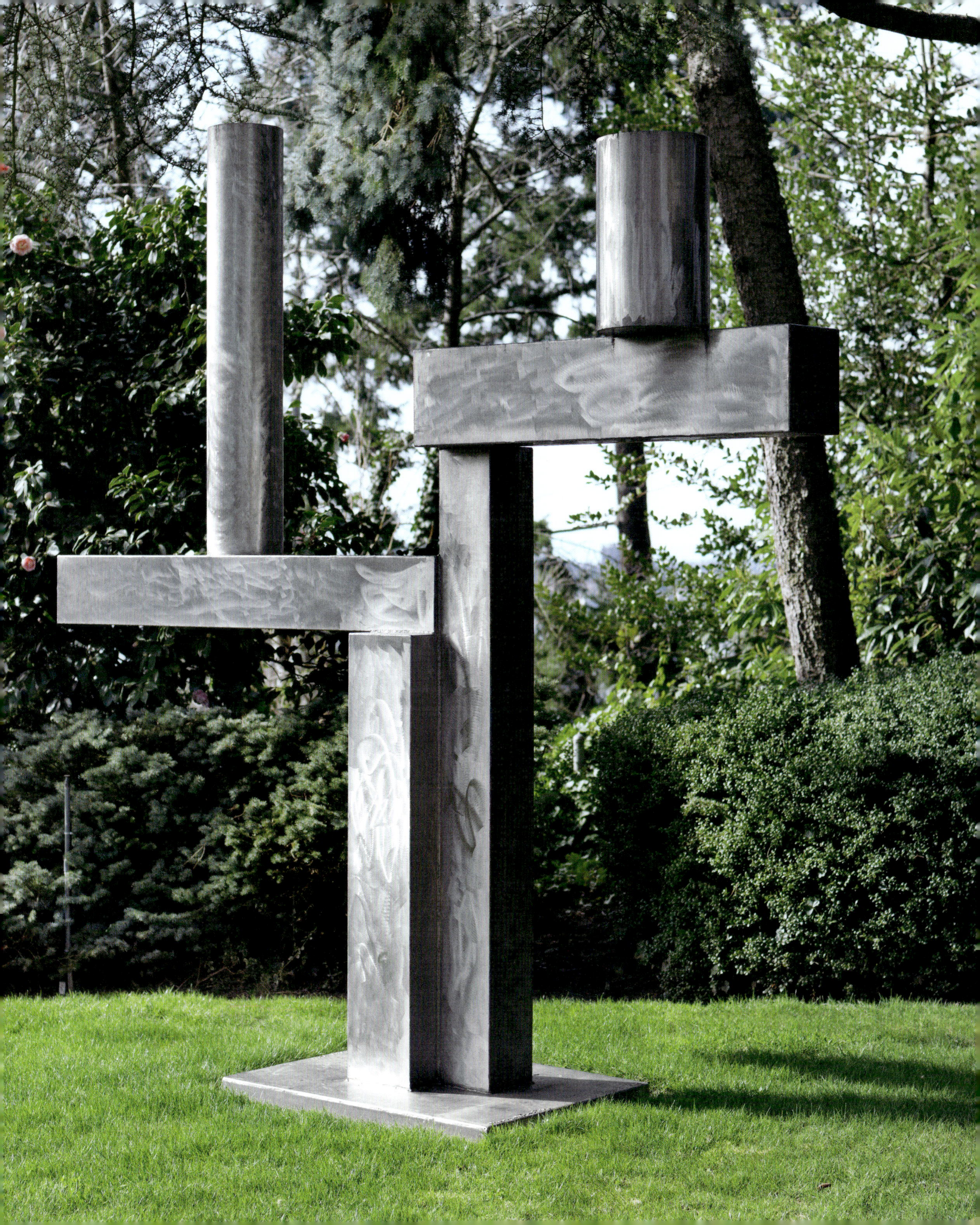

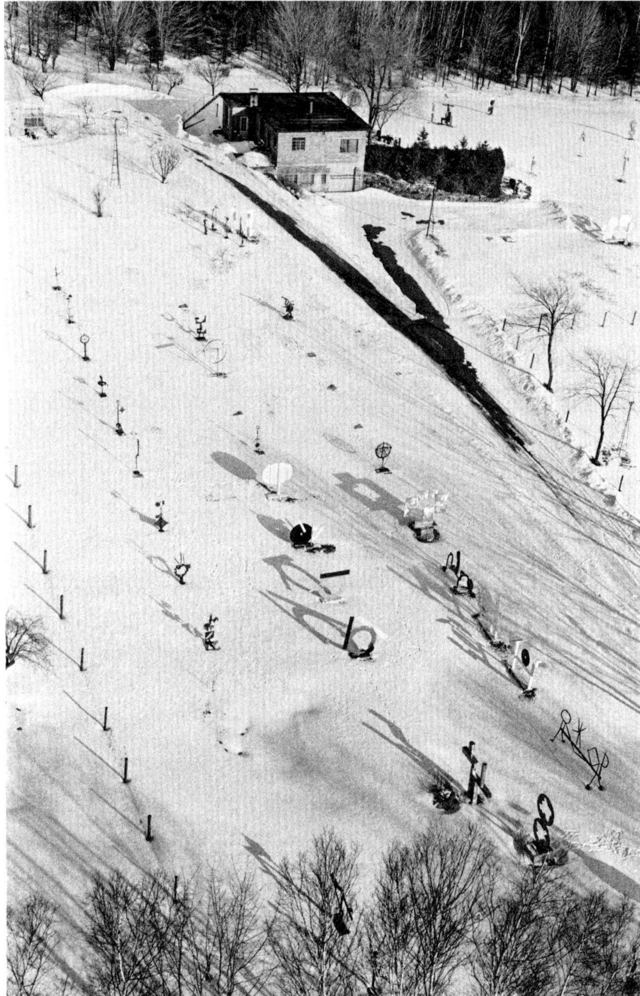

Fig. 63 Aerial view of David Smith's upper field, Bolton Landing, New York, ca. 1967. *Cubi XXV* is visible at lower right.

after they had arisen. The *Cubis* can seem more impersonal than other Smith sculptures; fantasy is less apparent in them than in the twenty-seven *Voltris*, for example, which Smith made in an abandoned Italian steel factory in spring 1962, assisted by seven workmen whose knowledge and companionship he treasured, in an astonishing burst of creativity.[5] But in the *Cubis*, Smith adds fire and ice to his already mysterious mix of personal and impersonal, subjective and objective, and these combinatory geometries are monumental. The art critic Hilton Kramer felt "an almost terrifying sense of power in them."[6]

Indoors and outdoors, the *Cubis* can seem like entirely different works. "They are designed for outdoors," Smith said of them, but he wanted his sculptures to hold their own in any setting, and in a museum the *Cubis* can be intimidating and strange.[7] There, embedded in the history of art, their distinctive and often poignant conversations with Impressionism, Brancusi, Cubism, Piet Mondrian, and Abstract Expressionism can be studied. But indoors, the *Cubis* cannot be as dynamic. On Smith's hillside, or in a garden or courtyard, their variability can be mercurial, and they can seem to invite gatherings and ritual events. To the poet and curator Frank O'Hara, Smith's sculpture had one identity outdoors and another in museums. In Bolton Landing, O'Hara wrote:

> One was struck by these brilliant and sophisticated stainless steel or painted structures, poised against the rugged hills and mountains, the lake in the distance, and the clouds, an assertion of civilized values not nearly so surprising in the confines of a gallery or museum, where, conversely, these same sculptures took on an aspect of rugged individualism and often an almost brutally forthright power.[8]

Smith began putting his sculpture outdoors in the early thirties. In the fifties, responding to the increasingly dire problem of storage space and concerned about the treatment of his work by institutions that presented it according to their interests, not his, he began installing his sculptures around his house and shop-studio. By 1960, his sculptural fields had become a work in itself, a proliferating, ever-changing sculptural community. No artist or critic who visited the fields forgot the experience of encountering row after row of sculptures, wild and almost shocking in their diversity, spread across his hillside like a troupe or troops, or like letters in a word or words in a sentence (fig. 63). By May 1965, Smith had installed around eighty sculptures in the fields; some visitors would remember the number as one hundred—or hundreds. In the denser north field, *Cubi XXV* (1965, plate 15) became one of the first sculptures visitors saw after entering the property. He installed it parallel to the long driveway, pointing toward the shop-studio and the house, a clue that his sculpture had a grammar and the fields were a script.

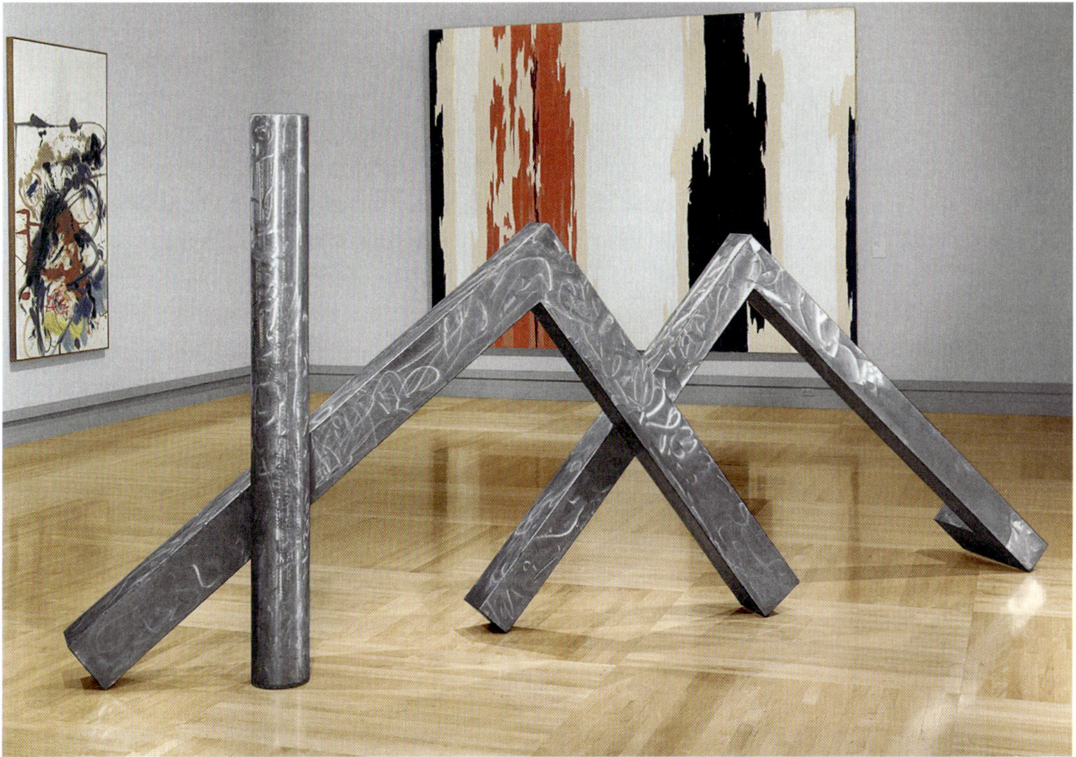

Fig. 64 David Smith, *Cubi XXIII*, November 30, 1964, stainless steel, 76¼ × 172⅞ × 35⅜ in. (193.67 × 439.1 × 89.85 cm). Los Angeles County Museum of Art, Modern and Contemporary Art Council Fund, M.67.26.

Cubi XXV is about ten feet tall, ten feet long, and two and a half feet thick. From front and back—and there is no distinction between them—the sculpture has a left and right side, each of which contains two rectangular boxes, one vertical and one horizontal, perched on top of which is a cylinder extending well over the edge of each horizontal container. The inverted L shapes are welded together along the vertical axis so as to create a sense of formidable adhesive pressure. By contrast, the horizontals and cylinders project outward, and both seem to have the capacity—or perhaps the inclination—to unload, or fire. One cylinder is squat, the other elongated. Although they are separated by only a few feet and appear to have the ability to move, capable of revolving or of sliding along the horizontals like balls on a juggler's arms, their energy seems not just effusive but also closed in, even imprisoned within their cylindrical bodies. The space between the two cylinders seems a chasm, as thick in its own way as the spaces inside the steel containers, each one like a canister holding a secret that only some future civilization could reveal. With its reflective surfaces, *Cubi XXV* is visually interactive with its environment, but it may also be physically interactive, an invitation to walk or pause under the lintels. Like an Alice-in-Wonderland road sign, the sculpture seems to say, "Go in this, no, go in that direction." Or maybe it recalls a story, one of children and parents and family drama. But any narrative thread is discontinuous, and the sculpture cannot be scripted. While it could hardly be more present, here, with us, in so many ways, at the same time it is as if we can't find it, or even see it.

Cubi XXV belongs to one of the *Cubi* clusters to which Smith referred at Bennington. In all of the *Cubis* he made in the late fall of 1964 and January 1965, he is concerned with language and image. *Cubi XXIII* (fig. 64), which he dated November 30, 1964, includes an upright cylinder that suggests an *I* and four rectangles that form two inverted

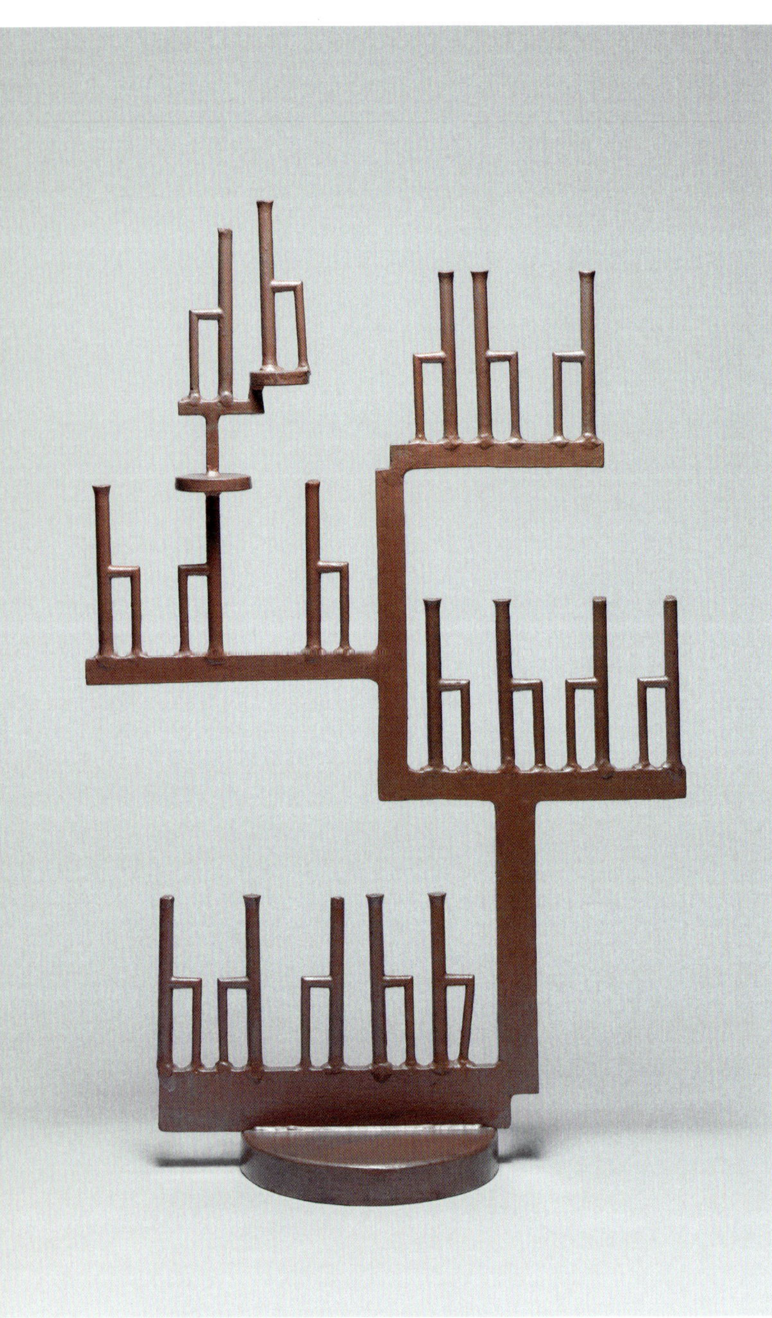

Fig. 65 David Smith, *17 h's*, 1950, steel, paint, 44½ × 28⁹⁄₁₆ × 12¼ in. (113 × 72.3 × 31.1 cm). The Estate of David Smith, New York.

V's, together suggesting an upside-down *w* or, more prominently, an *m*, as well as almost fourteen-foot-long creaturely limbs eager to stride over the earth, and five-foot-tall triangular arches that people, particularly children, can pass underneath. Smith dated *Cubi XXIV*, the first of the three *Cubi Gates*, December 8, 1964. Its open, square-like structure suggests a giant letter, an *o*, but it, too, is architectural—in this case a portal to rest on or step through. *Cubi XXVI*, dated January 12, 1965, three days after *Cubi XXV*, is more overtly alphabetic. Its multiple associations include a figure on its back with another figure standing on its belly, a cannon, and a roughly triangular arch, as well as letters that could be read as *T*, *I*, and *W*. TIW were the initials for Terminal Iron Works, Smith's name for his improbable sculpture factory in Bolton Landing. All letters in Smith's sculpture, however, drift in and out of legibility, still being discovered, in the process of becoming something else. In *Cubi XXIII*, the suggestions of *I* and *m*—"I'm"—promise a declaration of identity, but the message is forever deferred.

In *Cubi XXV*, the alphabetic memory is profound. The construction suggests a single letter but also a compound letter, or components that want to be a letter, one that would have the authority of a biblical commandment. But here, too, a letter is not just a letter, or even surely a letter. It is, first of all, image. This particular letter-image recalls ancient image-languages, perhaps including cuneiform—a form of writing that Smith came across in his grandmother's Bible in Decatur, Indiana, when already as a small boy he was convinced of the violent reductiveness of words. Historically, image preceded language. "A developed system of writing of any kind did not appear before 3,000 BC," wrote Herbert Read, a critic Smith referred to many times. "Writing, therefore, and the whole conceptual mode of reasoning which depends upon it, is of very recent origin compared with man's use of visual symbols."[9] In his 1952 essay "The Language as Image," Smith wrote, "Judging from Cuneiform, Chinese and other ancient texts, the object symbols formed identities upon which letters and words were later developed." For him, this "development" marked a decline, a loss of fullness and of what Smith called "creative extensions." The "business and exploitation use" of words, he continued, "has become dominant over their poetic-communicative use, which explains one

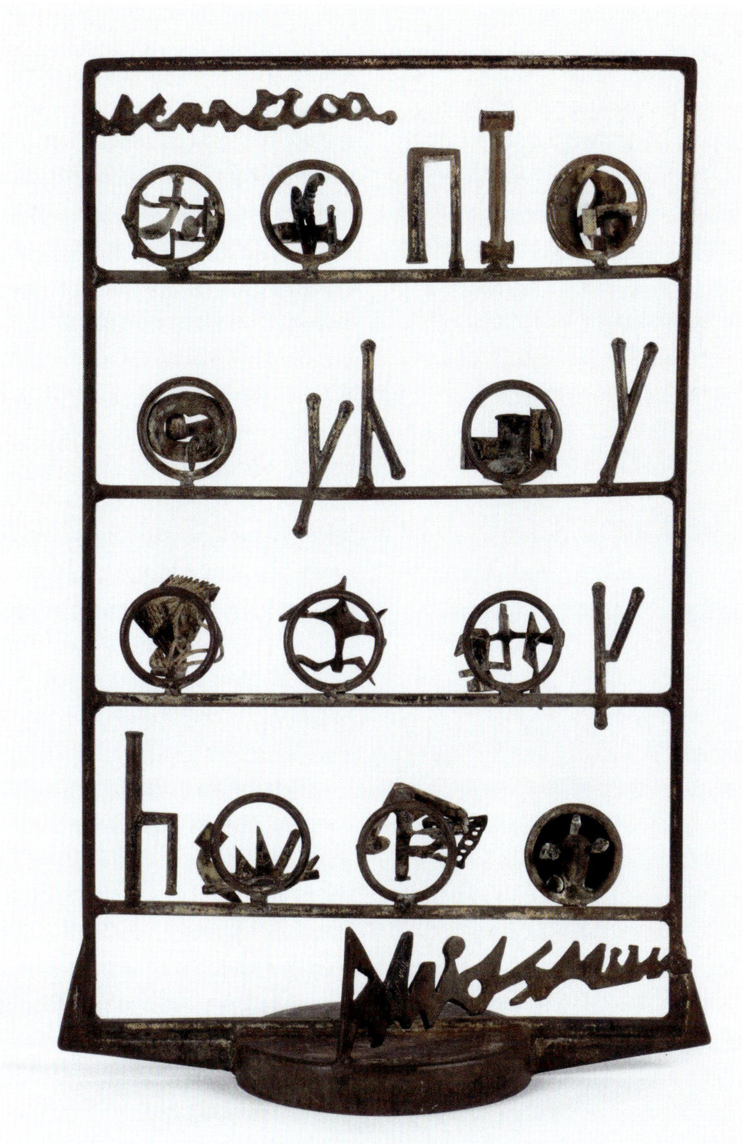

Fig. 66 David Smith, *The Letter*, 1950, welded steel, 37½ × 25 × 12 in. (95.3 × 63.5 × 30.5 cm). Munson Williams Proctor Art Institute, Museum Purchase, 51.37.

facet of their inadequateness." With exceptions, notably James Joyce, who could make words move in multiple directions at once, Smith "resented" the word "world."[10]

Smith was constantly reinscribing and rephrasing earlier ideas and images. *Cubi XXV* recalls his 1950 sculpture *17 h's* (fig. 65), in which he welded seventeen small painted-steel forms resembling frontward or backward *h*'s, to the steel ledges of a tiered three-and-half-foot-tall horizontal and vertical display structure. The stock steel forms appear as letters and as objects—as teeny chairs—and the letters can seem to face off and become musical chairs, or even a script that could turn into a musical score. *Cubis XXIII* to *XXVI* also recall another 1950 sculpture, *The Letter* (fig. 66), in which all eighteen of the steel forms are alphabetic: hints of *o*'s, *y*'s, and *h*'s, and of an *n* and an *l*. Each "letter" provides a lens onto, frames, or expands into an image that looks ancient, or even prehistoric, and not so much nonverbal as preverbal. "What do the letters say?" the art critic Emily Genauer asked Smith. He replied: "What any letter says. What Buddy Doran's letter said in [Joyce's] 'Finnegan's Wake' . . . 'You sent for me.'"[11] In "The Secret Letter," his remarkable 1964 interview with Thomas B. Hess, published in the catalogue for Smith's 1964 Marlborough-Gerson exhibition, Smith again referred to *Finnegan's Wake*; its impact on him was as indelible as it was on many Abstract Expressionist painters. "You know the Little Red Hen that scratched up a letter," Smith said to Hess. "Well I'm always scratching up letters." Smith returned to the Little Red Hen's letter later in the interview. "'You sent for me.' Something like a very simple little cryptic message," Smith said. This is "what the secret letter said. I don't think anybody knows what the secret letter said. . . . All letters say you sent for me as far as I'm concerned."[12]

"You sent for me" is a wonderful clue to Smith's mode of address. His sculpture seems to come from far back and project out, toward the viewer, toward us, with an anticipatory energy that can lead us to believe that it is we who asked for—or *sent*—for it. It is not just the animation—and mutational desire—of the lines, forms, and surfaces that make the sculpture an offering. Its associative abundance is an offering as well. The *Cubis* can suggest an array of entertainers—dancers, magicians, acrobats, tumblers, and clowns—all of whom are eager to reward an audience's desire for enchantment. With their multitude of associations, Smith's sculptures acknowledge multiple subjectivities. Smith understood perception to be an instantaneous visual response that is almost unfathomable in its undifferentiated complexity. "Perception through vision is a highly accelerated response, so fast, so complex, so free that it cannot be pinned down by the very recent science of word communication," he wrote in 1951.[13] Four years later, he said: "In one flash of time the mind can recall so much vision and action, complex and extensive, that it would take days to relate it."[14] For Smith, perception was not hierarchical, available to one person and not another. "In perceiving I believe all men are equal. . . . No man has sensed anything another has not, or lacks the components and power to assemble."[15] He wanted his sculpture both to be like a perception and to appeal to perception, to be grasped as it was seen. In that perceptual instant, the image sticks. But it is fluid. It keeps moving, and, as it does, it keeps revealing potentialities buried within it. Smith's sculpture is always prior to a coherence that it points toward but never arrives at. *Cubi XXV* is a sequence of building blocks that can be imagined and reimagined in different sequences. Smith's alphabetic signs project the immanence of a message, even as they turn from the verbal toward the image. They encourage viewers to participate in a creative process that is forever expectant, in need of fantasy and thought, and forever against completion.

Cubi XXV leads deep into Abstract Expressionist territory. Smith began his artistic career as a painter and never stopped painting. Most of his artist friends, including other Abstract Expressionists, were abstract painters. For many of them too, the making and experiencing of art had an archaeological dimension. Acutely aware that in relation to painting sculpture was considered second class, Smith set out to raise sculpture to the level of painting. Adolph Gottlieb's Pictographs can be felt in *Cubi XXV*. So can Barnett Newman's paintings and sculptures conjuring biblical utterance, and Franz Kline's gestures that could be the beginnings of architecture or language, and Mark Rothko's emanations of color in which some energy, some light, seems to be appealing to the viewer, proposing the fullness of perceptual experience. Pollock is a presence, too, if his "drips" are understood as scriptural flow, related to language but shunning and ultimately subsuming it. Smith's 1951 sculptures *Hudson River Landscape* and *Australia*, his signature "drawings in space," have a tremendous cursive potency. Like Pollock's landmark paintings, they are haunted by figuration, but they are not worried about it and they want to be experienced as written as well as drawn. "I don't differentiate between writing and drawing," Smith told Hess. "Not since I read that part of Joyce. . . . The little red hen scratched up a secret message."[16] Written as well as drawn in space, the image becomes apparitional.

Smith aspired to the eidetic image. "The eidetic image art of the cave man, 30,000 years ago, was reality," Smith said in 1951. "The directives of my work come from reality. My reality . . . is not one thing; it is a chain of interlocking visions."[17] In the cave art he revered, incised drawing activates painted stone, making its mass seem porous and spatial. Such images were performative. They oriented and presided over, and made the insides of the earth sites for ritual gathering. “Eidetic images,” the curator Kirk Varnedoe wrote,

> are forms of waking hallucination, in which normal boundaries between the productions of the mind and the evidence of the senses are broken down, and a subject sees an image of extraordinary completeness and impact, without the person or object in question actually being present to the eye. . . . The eidetic ability elevated the “mind’s eye” to co-equality with visual sensation, dissolving the boundaries between imagination and perception, myth and reality.[18]

In the eidetic image, what is seen is inseparable from what is remembered, what is remembered from what is dreamed, and what is known from what is felt. *Cubi XXV* is matter and memory, a precisely delineated constellation of block forms and an afterimage, an attack on the stopped image of the statue and prophetic statuary.

NOTES

1 Robert Coates, “The Art Galleries,” *New Yorker*, November 2, 1964, 165.

2 David Smith, “Some Late Words from David Smith,” 1965, in *David Smith: Collected Writings, Lectures, and Interviews*, ed. Susan J. Cooke (Oakland: University of California Press, 2018), 428.

3 Seventeen is the number of Smith series determined by the new David Smith catalogue raisonné of Smith’s sculpture. Christopher Lyon, ed., *David Smith Sculpture: A Catalogue Raisonné, 1932–1965* (New York: Estate of David Smith, 2021).

4 I’m grateful to Marc-Christian Roussel for sharing his knowledge of the making of the *Cubis*.

5 The workers were provided by Italsider, the Italian steel company that invited Smith and nine other sculptors to work in its factories throughout Italy and make works for *Sculpture in the City*, an outdoor exhibition at the 1962 Spoleto Festival.

6 Hilton Kramer, *David Smith (1906–1965)* (Los Angeles: Los Angeles County Museum of Art, 1965), 6.

7 David Smith, “Interview by Thomas B. Hess,” 1964, in Cooke, *David Smith*, 406.

8 Frank O’Hara, “Introduction,” *David Smith 1905–1965* (London: Arts Council of Great Britain, 1966), 9.

9 Herbert Read, “Art as a Symbolic Language,” in *The Forms of Things Unknown: Essays toward an Aesthetic Philosophy* (New York: Meridian Books, 1963), 45.

10 David Smith, “The Language as Image,” 1952, in Cooke, *David Smith*, 145.

11 Emily Genauer, “Art and the Artist,” *New York Post Magazine*, April 5, 1969, 14.

12 David Smith, “Interview by Thomas B. Hess,” 1964, in Cooke, *David Smith*, 390, 408–9.

13 David Smith, “Lecture, Williams College,” 1951, in Cooke, *David Smith*, 138.

14 David Smith, “The Artist in Society,” 1955, in Cooke, *David Smith*, 246.

15 Smith, “Lecture, Williams College,” 138.

16 Smith, “Interview by Thomas B. Hess,” 409.

17 Smith, “Lecture, Williams College,” 138.

18 Kirk Varnedoe, “Abstract Expressionism,” in *‘Primitivism’ in 20th Century Art: Affinity of the Tribal and the Modern*, vol. 2 (New York: Museum of Modern Art, 1984), 651.

HELEN FRANKENTHALER
DAWN SHAPES
1967

ELIZABETH A. T. SMITH

Not yet forty but with close to twenty years of work and significant professional recognition behind her, Helen Frankenthaler was at a mature and self-assured phase of her practice when she painted *Dawn Shapes* (1967, plate 16).[1] Her bold explorations of abstraction intensified in the 1960s as she probed the coexistence of pictorial structure and atmospheric effects. Stemming from her roots in Abstract Expressionism, these evolving investigations manifest a responsiveness to conditions of climate and place; a desire to infuse her work with a palpable, yet ambiguous, sense of mood; and a keen engagement with old master painting.

Dawn Shapes is both representative of and distinctive within Frankenthaler's work of the mid to late 1960s.[2] Unlike many of her contemporaries who were also prominent abstract painters, such as Kenneth Noland or Frank Stella, she refrained from working in series, asserting that each canvas resulted from a unique set of investigations and describing her practice as "a kind of disciplined free-wheeling."[3] Frankenthaler painted prolifically in 1967. That year, she made paintings vastly different from one another, ranging from bold, monumental works like the luminous *Flood* (Whitney Museum of American Art) and the magisterial *Guiding Red* (no longer extant) to the more somber and structured *Indian Summer* (Hirshhorn Museum and Sculpture Garden), with its vertically stacked, quasi-rectangular forms. A compelling example of her singular artistic vocabulary, *Dawn Shapes* is among the subtler, more introspective works of this period.

Exploring the dynamics of adjacency and containment in *Dawn Shapes*, Frankenthaler positioned rounded, oblong forms at the center of a zone of contrasting color that seemingly frames the shapes within, mostly surrounded on three sides by a slender band of yet another color. This structure lends a clarity and assertiveness to the composition of forms within forms, while departing from any sort of rigid geometry. Avoiding the use of hard or straight edges in favor of irregular contours, Frankenthaler achieved boundaries between the various zones of color that are simultaneously crisp and tremulous. Points where color/shape come together, abutting or overlapping, convey vibrancy and tension, creating defined but also amorphous edge conditions. Likewise, at the edges of the canvas itself, these forms function as compositional focal points.

In her use of color, Frankenthaler's approach varied notably from painting to painting. Utilizing an expansive

Plate 16 Helen Frankenthaler, *Dawn Shapes*, 1967, acrylic on canvas, 77¼ × 94½ in. (196 × 240 cm). Seattle Art Museum, Gift of the Friday Foundation in honor of Richard E. Lang and Jane Lang Davis, 2020.14.5.

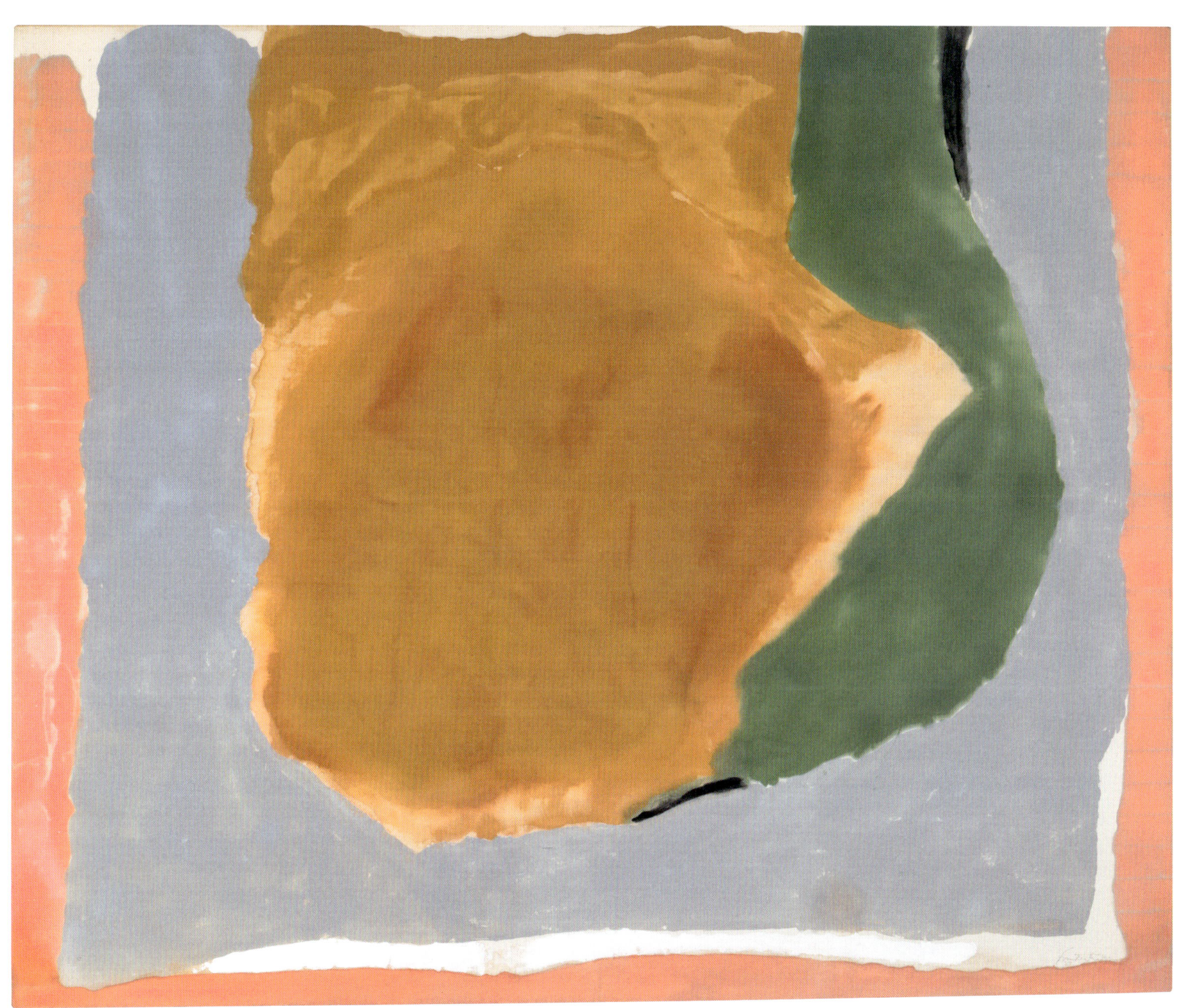

range from bright hues to deeper, darker ones to quieter, pastel tones, she often experimented with surprising juxtapositions of color and frequently modulated the thickness or thinness of the paint to emphasize spatial relationships. In *Dawn Shapes*, she opted for a palette where adjacencies of more muted colors—mustard, green, and gray tonalities—evoke the shifting, hazy shapes and ambiguity of the early morning light. She employed various additional contrasting colors strategically. Slender areas of black at the top right and lower center of the composition, along with a band of white between the wavering lines of a square of gray and a narrow U-shaped border of salmon pink, deepen and enhance the implied spatiality of the work.

Creating the suggestion of three-dimensional space on a painting's two-dimensional surface was of consummate importance to Frankenthaler, arising from her early training in Cubism and honed over decades of exploring a more ambiguous abstraction. She once said,

> I tried consciously and otherwise to provide space without line, . . . but to delineate line in other ways, meaning if you join a fat shape with a fat orange shape or a green shape or a mud shape, and it's joined to something else or not to something else or it's placed in the right spot, then that particular line or formation of color and colors *creates* a kind of line that moves in space and yet rests on the surface.[4]

In *Dawn Shapes*, Frankenthaler achieved a palpable sense of movement and space by deftly orchestrating these elements. Zones of the painting are rife with evidence of the artist's gestures and process, wherein she not only deployed the "soak-stain" technique of pouring thinned acrylic paint onto a canvas laid on the floor but also utilized a variety of tools and instruments to swiftly guide and modulate its flow.

Of foremost significance in *Dawn Shapes* is how Frankenthaler configured and manipulated the predominant area of ochre at the painting's center. Here, she achieved a nuanced range of yellow and more earthen hues—from dark mustard to dusky orange to peach—applied through a combination of pouring and brushwork to enhance the subtlety of the variations in density and tone. The resulting form, while emphatic, lacks clear definition, evoking various possible associations, from the mutable conditions of visibility at dawn to the gathering of storm clouds and the emergence of sunbeams peeking around and through them. This suggested condition of indistinctness gave rise to the title she ultimately chose for the work.

Despite the presence of allusive qualities, Frankenthaler frequently emphasized that the origins of her work were internal and formal. "I work intuitively and without objects," she said to a reviewer of a 1971 exhibition in which *Dawn Shapes* was included.[5] Acknowledging Frankenthaler's intentions to achieve an ambiguous statement with her work, the reviewer commented, "If a form appears that someone recognizes, we gather that the painter feels that the viewer himself has created it in his own imagination. Yet there is a feeling of life in all her forms, as though the very warp and weft of living has been translated visually."[6]

Dawn Shapes relates compositionally to other paintings in Frankenthaler's corpus of work. *Small's Paradise* (Smithsonian American Art Museum), *Interior Landscape* (San Francisco Museum of Modern Art), *Buddha's Court* (Private Collection), and *Tangerine* (Private Collection), all from 1964, present centrally positioned irregular forms "framed" by bands of contrasting color around the perimeter of the canvas. In the mid to late 1960s, she made various works centering on large rectangular or oblong shapes that anchor their compositions visually and spatially. The dominant forms in those paintings, however, tend to be markedly slenderer and more elongated than the eccentric, bulbous ones in *Dawn Shapes*.

This tendency aligns with an awkward formal asymmetry found in other paintings of the mid-1960s such as *Canyon* (1965, Phillips Collection) or *Coalition* (1968, fig. 67)—the former with a predominantly square shape and the latter with a largely circular shape at center, edged by borders of contrasting colors. Frankenthaler once stated, "Instead of 'mastery,' you want to be—well, two words I frequently use—*clumsy* or *puzzled*. Now clumsy or puzzled are not exactly mastery, but they often lead to the same risk or another word I use: *magic*."[7] She embraced and consciously pursued this quality of awkwardness across the decades of her practice; she well understood that this element infused her work with a sense of freshness and vitality.

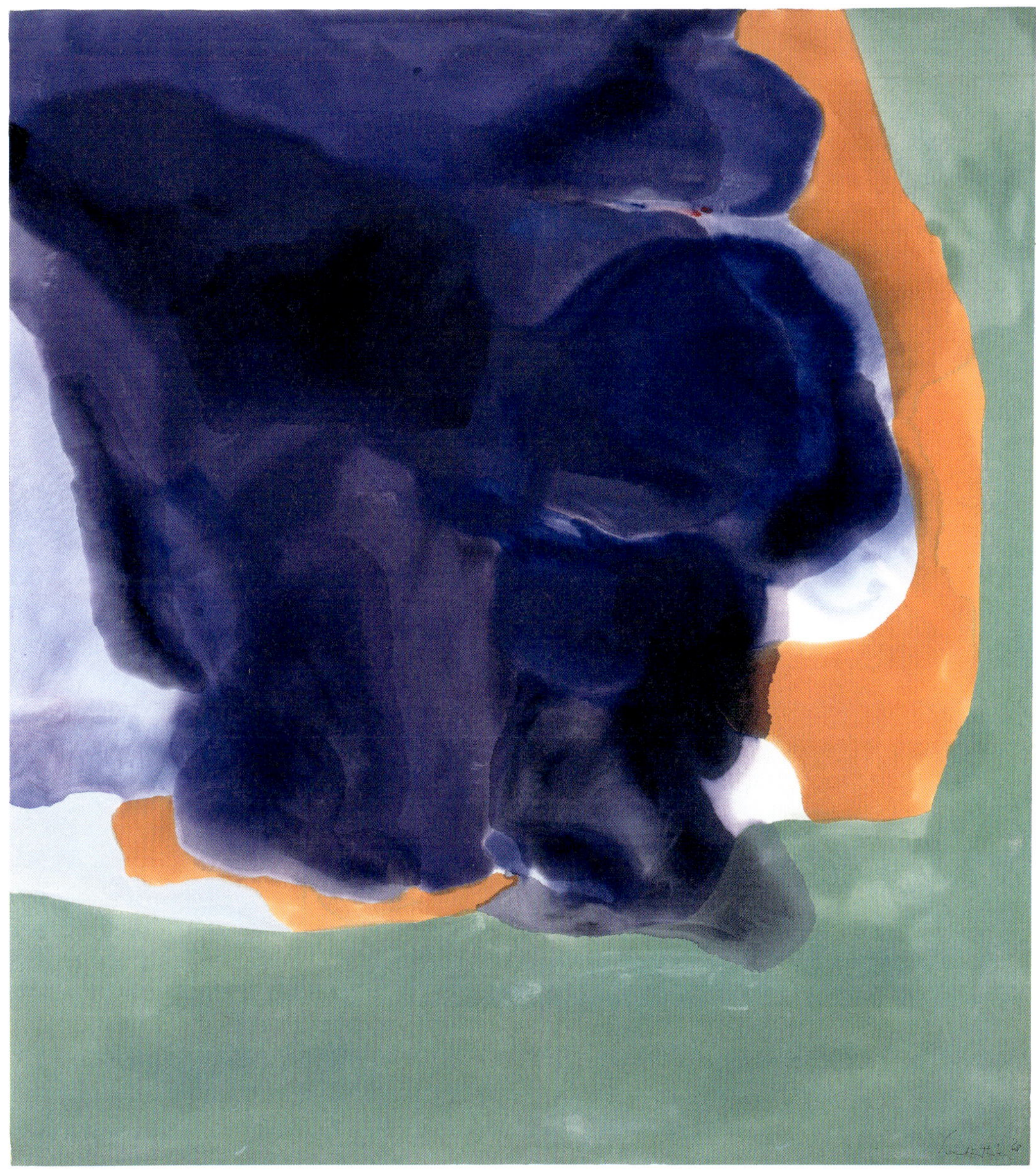

Fig. 67 Helen Frankenthaler, *Coalition*, 1968, acrylic on canvas, 83 × 75½ in. (210.8 × 191. 7 cm). Private Collection.

An additional related feature in certain of Frankenthaler's paintings of this period is the presence of bannerlike shapes that seemingly "hang" within the space of the canvas. In *Mauve District* (1966, fig. 68), for instance, a ragged-edged rectangle of mauve appears to balance off-kilter in the lower area of the composition, exerting a powerful gravity tempered by a touch of whimsy. Frankenthaler's arguably best-known work of this type is *The Human Edge* (1967, Everson Museum of Art, Syracuse University), its chosen title underscoring her preference for the impact of the imperfect, irregular gesture. The gray field in *Dawn Shapes*, functioning visually as a backdrop or surround for the ochre and green forms, reveals a kinship with the elements in these paintings.

Fig. 68 Helen Frankenthaler, *Mauve District*, 1966, acrylic on canvas, 103 × 95 in. (261.5 × 241.2 cm). The Museum of Modern Art, New York, Mrs. Donald B. Straus Fund, 2668.1967.

Yet the structure of *Dawn Shapes*, revolving around the relationship between the forms at center and along the edges, is inflected differently. Its rising, swelling central shapes, floating balloon-like in an airy arena, connect to but seem almost untethered from the top of the canvas, creating a suggestion of infinite spatial extension. The condition of ambiguity that Frankenthaler sought to achieve in her work is pronounced in *Dawn Shapes*. As the poet and critic Bill Berkson commented in 1965, "Frankenthaler leads you through a labyrinth of speculations about placement, scale and meaning and back out to the picture itself as an aesthetic statement of fact. Her more difficult works reject associations as quickly as you can make them."[8] And as the art historian Anne Wagner later astutely observed, "In Frankenthaler's hands painting moves farther toward its redefinition as a practice that is both arbitrary and intended as well as both figurative and abstract, produced of moves and gestures whose effects are as decisive as their motives are hard to specify."[9] For Frankenthaler, these characteristics resulted from the intertwining of an intuitive and highly considered approach to painting in which ambiguity and awkwardness yielded a sense of visual and interpretive boundlessness. In *Dawn Shapes*, the complexity of color, subtle implication of anthropomorphic form, and an almost disorienting atmospheric spatiality coalesce as a subdued yet compelling statement by an artist whose approaches to abstraction ranged broadly over the decades of her practice.

NOTES

1 By this time, Frankenthaler had shown extensively in national and international contexts ranging from the landmark 1951 *9th Street Exhibition of Painting and Sculpture* in New York City, where she was the youngest participant; to the Première Biennale de Paris in 1959, at which she won first prize in painting; to the 1966 Venice Biennale, where she was one of four artists representing the United States. Beginning in 1951, her painting had appeared in numerous solo exhibitions throughout the United States and Europe, and important museums had begun to acquire her works.
In 1960, the poet and art critic Frank O'Hara had surveyed her work of the previous decade at New York's Jewish Museum, and in 1969 it would be the subject of a midcareer retrospective at the Whitney Museum of American Art that then traveled to Europe.

2 Frankenthaler painted two works titled *Dawn Shapes*. The first, from 1963 (Private Collection), was painted in oil rather than acrylic and measures 67⅞ × 57½ in. (172.4 × 146 cm).

3 Helen Frankenthaler, quoted in Irene Heywood, "Twenty Years toward Instant Success," *Montreal Star*, February 28, 1971.

4 "Helen Frankenthaler Interviewed by Nancy Miller at Her East 83rd Street Studio, New York, 1977," produced by Chris Crossman, Video Vasari, April 7, 1977, U-Matic, 26:34. Courtesy of Albright-Knox Art Gallery.

5 Frankenthaler, in Heywood, "Twenty Years."

6 Heywood, "Twenty Years."

7 Helen Frankenthaler, quoted in Cindy Nemser, "Interview with Helen Frankenthaler," *Arts*, November 1971, 53.

8 Bill Berkson, "Poet of the Surface," *Arts*, May–June 1965, 45.

9 Anne Wagner, "Pollock's Nature, Frankenthaler's Culture," in *Jackson Pollock: New Approaches*, ed. Kirk Varnedoe and Pepe Karmel (New York: Museum of Modern Art, 1998), 192.

FRANCIS BACON
STUDY FOR A PORTRAIT
1967

MARTIN HARRISON

Francis Bacon painted *Study for a Portrait* (1967, plate 17) midway between two major solo exhibitions: a 1962 retrospective at the Tate Gallery, London, and a 1971 exhibition at the Grand Palais, Paris. The Tate exhibition had focused Bacon's attention on his art with a new urgency after his production in the years since 1957 had grown scattered, haphazard, and intermittent. As the exhibition deadline loomed, its importance appears to have registered with him. It became the catalyst for rethinking his artistic practice, as his Grand Palais exhibition would the following decade; moreover, the external stimuli of these prestigious retrospectives helped overcome a perpetual problem—his psychological resistance toward facing the challenge of the bare canvas on his easel. Singular in a number of ways, *Study for a Portrait* belongs to that period of renewed productivity.

One consequence of the Tate retrospective was that Bacon began to simplify the formats of his paintings. Thereafter, they conformed, almost invariably, to one of two dimensions: the small portraits on 14 × 12–inch canvases, like *Portrait of Man with Glasses I* (1963, plate 12), and the large "subject" paintings measuring 78 × 58 inches. At 61 × 55 inches, the Lang Collection *Study for a Portrait* does not, of course, fit in either category. As such, it may be regarded as a pendant to the almost identically sized painting Bacon had completed shortly before it, *Two Figures on a Couch* (1967, Private Collection); the latter was his first painting since 1954 to depict coupling males. A plausible explanation for the unusual format of the two paintings is that they were painted not in London but in the studio of his friend Denis Wirth Miller, at Wivenhoe, Essex, which Bacon used frequently at this time and in which his usual 78-inch canvases would have been cumbersomely large and an imposition on his friend's space.

The sitter in Bacon's *Study for a Portrait*, who has sometimes been identified as the artist Isabel Rawsthorne, is, in fact, Henrietta Moraes. Bacon was a close friend of both women, but he made a sharp distinction between their respective roles in his paintings. All of his paintings of female nudes after 1962 were based on photographs of Moraes, whereas Rawsthorne never appeared in nude depictions, only in portraits. In the 1950s, Moraes had worked occasionally as an artists' model, notably for Lucian Freud. Bacon commissioned John Deakin to take the nude photographs of her that provided the body positions for most of the female nudes that he painted between

Plate 17 Francis Bacon, *Study for a Portrait*, 1967, oil on canvas, 61 × 55 in. (155 × 139.8 cm). Seattle Art Museum, Gift of the Friday Foundation in honor of Richard E. Lang and Jane Lang Davis, 2020.14.7.

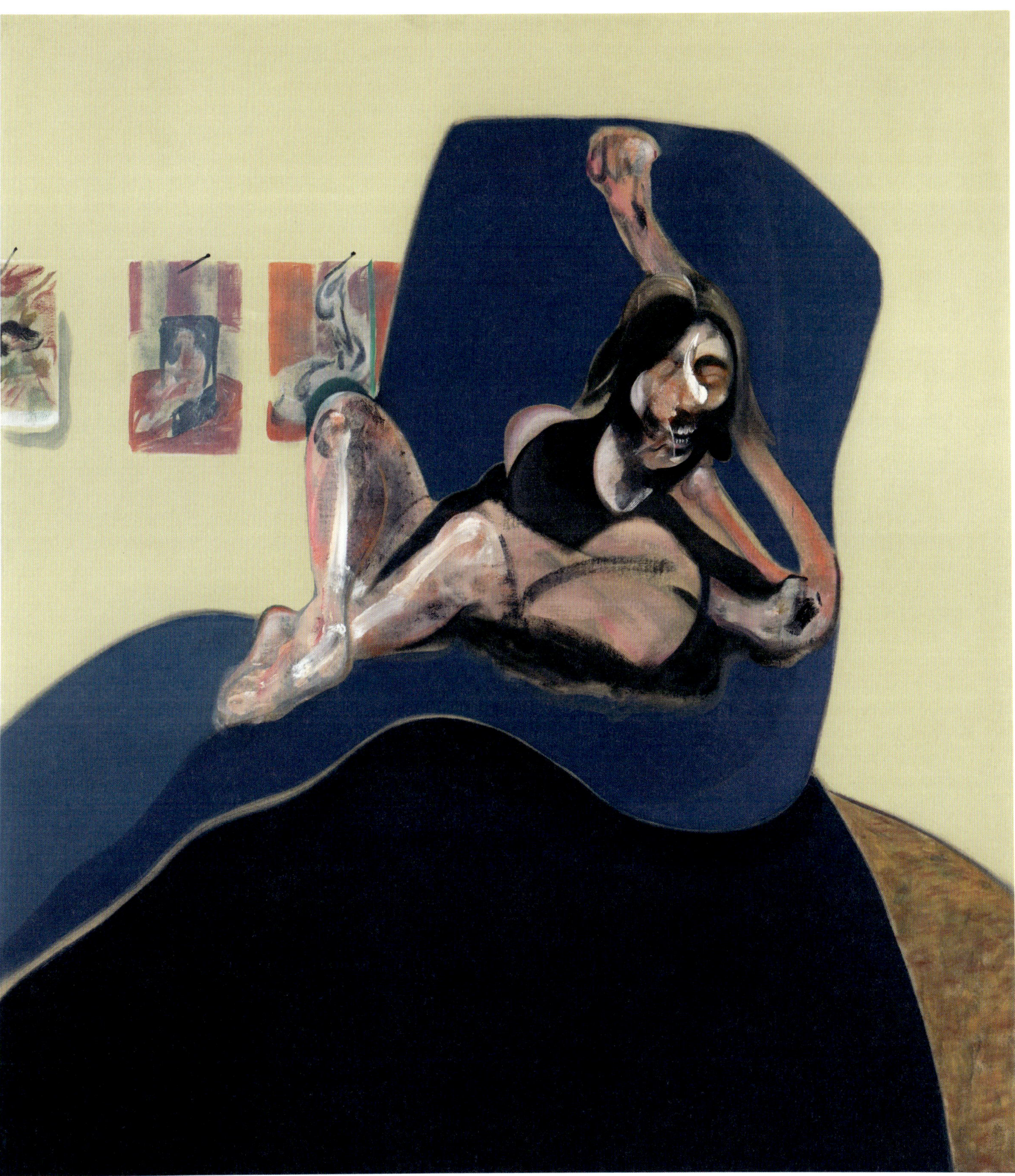

1961 and 1972. Rawsthorne had inspired Jacob Epstein, André Derain, Pablo Picasso, and Alberto Giacometti in the 1930s, which no doubt held a fascination for Bacon, but it played no part in his painting practice, and she never sat for his nude females. Irrespective of Bacon's friendship with Moraes, his most extreme depictions of women as viragos or termagants were exclusively of her or, it should be said, began with her.

Study for a Portrait is unique in Bacon's oeuvre. From 1948 onward, he tended to work sequentially and self-referentially. Consider his reworkings of themes such as the Popes, crouching figures or lying figures, which should be seen as striving for refinement—a clearer explication of his first idea—rather than mere repetition. But the configuration of *Study for a Portrait*, like that of *Landscape near Malabata, Tangier* (1963, Private Collection) and *Three Studies from the Human Body* (1967, Private Collection), was never repeated, and was perhaps considered by Bacon too completely resolved to lend itself to replication. Nonetheless, certain elements of the composition had been present in Bacon's work for several years. For example, the first nude painted from John Deakin's photographs, *Crouching Nude* (1961, Private Collection), acted as a springboard for other nudes, both female and male, including *Study for a Portrait*, in which Bacon's distortions, the "additional" or superfluous limbs, verged on the anatomically ludicrous.

When embarking on *Study for a Portrait*, Bacon must have had in mind, in addition to Robert Yerkes's chimpanzees and possibly Joan Miró's *Seated Woman* (October 1932, Private Collection), the attenuated, exaggerated limbs of Henri Matisse's sculpture *La Serpentine* (1909, fig. 69). Matisse's initial reliance on a photograph (now in the Archives Matisse, Paris) when making the bronze was a rehearsal of Bacon's practice. In addition to the extreme sinuousness of the body, there are specific correspondences in the crooked elbow on which the women in both works lean as well as the legs crossed just above the ankles. The classically posed, raised, arched arm, found in many of Matisse's odalisques, is developed into Moraes's anatomically impossible elongated limb in *Study for a Portrait*. The crouching figures that became an obsessive theme of Bacon's from 1952 were similarly indebted to the left-hand figure in Matisse's *Bathers with a Turtle* (1908, St. Louis Art Museum). Such appropriations are apparently at odds with Bacon's denials of Matisse's importance for him, his typically bipartite assessment that he lacked Picasso's "brutality of fact," but Bacon probably considered the co-opting of a body position as fundamentally different from being inspired by the core of another artist's practice.

The sofa on which Moraes reclines is virtually a sofa-bed. Bacon had been painting these enveloping couches since 1962, and in the context of his own spartan, *unheimlich* living quarters, the luxury and comfort they convey may seem paradoxical; Bacon, though, partly cancels out the comfort by perching Moraes uneasily on her support, like the Oceanid nymph Perseis about to be consumed by waves. The incorporation of a patch of Aubusson carpet at the lower right functions to indicate that the room has a curved rear wall. Bacon firmly resisted linking elements of his paintings with his autobiography, yet he proposed to interviewers that these spaces may have been spurred by memories of the curved bays in his grandmother's house in County Laois, Ireland, where he had stayed as a child. Traditional perspective was irrelevant to Bacon, and instead his figures occupy liminal zones—sometimes claustrophobic or, as in *Study for a Portrait*, thrusting the figure toward the spectator.

The device of reproducing three of his earlier paintings, pinned to the rear wall, occurs nowhere else in Bacon's oeuvre. The image on the right refers to the right panel of *Three Studies for a Crucifixion* (1962, Solomon R. Guggenheim Museum), and the central image closely resembles *Seated Figure* (1962, Private Collection); the latter painting incorporated an early version of the enveloping sofa that dominates *Study for a Portrait*. The image on the left, bisected by the picture's edge, is executed with an expressionist abandon that cannot be compared with any of Bacon's paintings, unless it refers, inexplicably, to one of his earliest works, *Composition* (1933, Henry Moore Family Collection). The incorporation of the device may have been suggested by the reproductions of his own work that Bacon habitually stuck to the walls of the kitchen/bathroom area of his living quarters at 7 Reece Mews, as well as in his studio. It was a common enough motif in the paintings of many artists Bacon admired, and he may have had in mind, for example, Édouard Manet's dramatic portraits of Berthe Morisot, *La Repose* (1870, Rhode Island

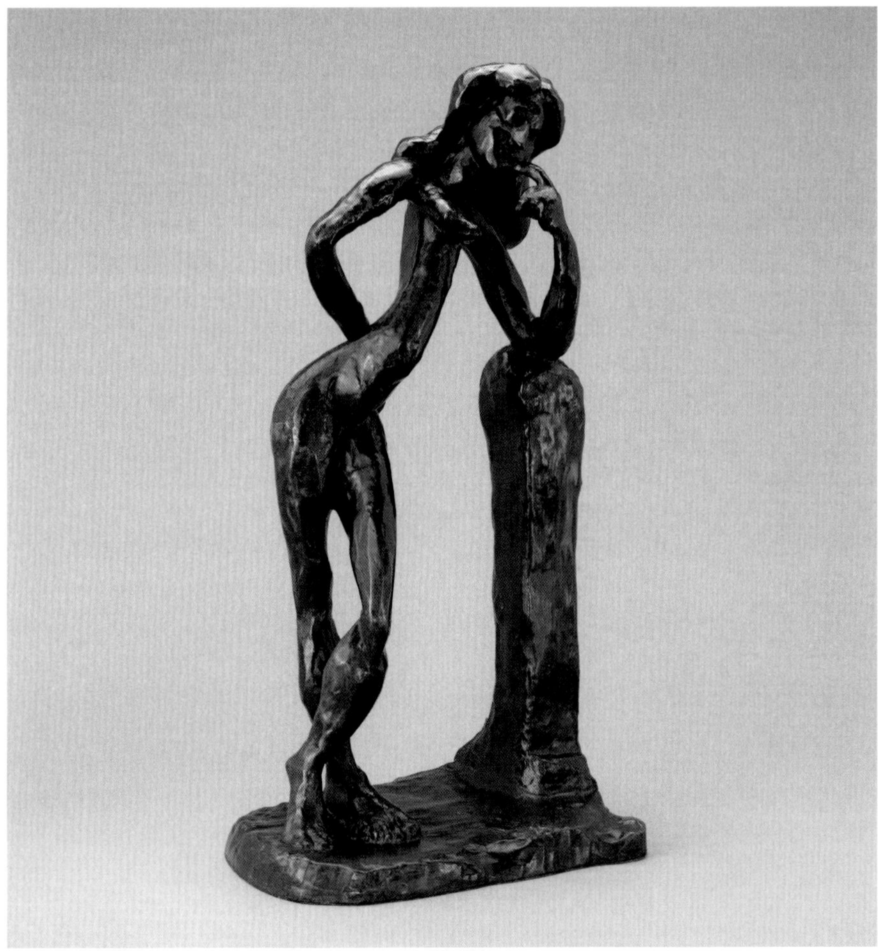

Fig. 69 Henri Matisse, *La Serpentine*, 1909, bronze, 22¼ × 11 × 7½ in. (56.5 × 28 × 19 cm). The Museum of Modern Art, New York, Gift of Abby Aldrich Rockefeller, 624.1939.

School of Design), on a sofa, and *Le Suicidé* (1877–81, Fondation E. G. Bührle), on a bed. In Manet's *Portrait of Emile Zola* (1868, Musée d'Orsay), the three prints on the rear wall include the artist's own *Olympia*, a self-referencing akin to that Bacon employed in *Study for a Portrait*.[1]

Bacon first appropriated the African mask aspect of the heads of the women in Picasso's *Les Demoiselles d'Avignon* (1907, Museum of Modern Art, New York) in his *Study for Portrait of P.L.* (1962, Private Collection). Umberto Boccioni's futurist distortions, seen in both his sculptures and paintings, such as *Dynamism of a Man's Head* (1913, Private Collection), may also have been at play with Bacon. In the present painting, Moraes's head was further modified by a still frame from Alain Resnais's film *Hiroshima mon amour* (1959). The image that resonated with Bacon, and which he conflated with Picasso's demoiselles, was from the shower scene featuring the film's costars, Eiji Okada and Emmanuelle Riva. Many illustrated books were devoted to this influential classic of French New Wave cinema, and in their reductive half-tone reproductions, Riva's teeth closely resemble those of Moraes in Bacon's painting. One of these images (now in the Hugh Lane Gallery) was found in Bacon's studio; it is paint spattered, folded, and paper-clipped onto cardboard, evidence of his repeated usage (fig. 70). Bacon turned Riva's smile into a sinister, predatory snarl, a signifier, perhaps, of his ambivalence toward female sexuality. The strands of wet hair falling over Riva's face, closely replicated in Bacon's small

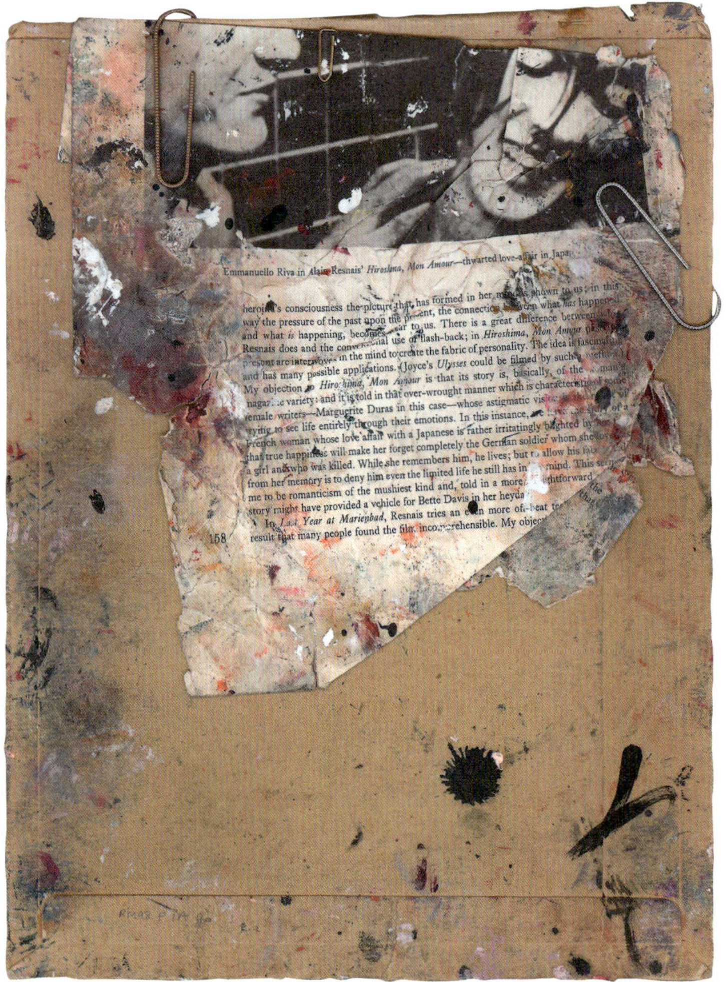

Emmanuello Riva in Alain Resnais' *Hiroshima, Mon Amour*—thwarted love-affair in Japa

heroi[illegible]'s consciousness the picture that has formed in her m[illegible] is shown to us; in this
way the pressure of the past upon the pr[illegible]ent, the connectio[illegible] [illegible]ween what *has* happen[illegible]
and what *is* happening, becomes [illegible] to us. There is a great difference between [illegible]
Resnais does and the conv[illegible]nal use of flash-back; in *Hiroshima, Mon Amour* p[illegible]
[illegible]esent are interwove[illegible] in the mind to create the fabric of personality. The idea is fascin[illegible]
and has many possible applications. (Joyce's *Ulysses* could be filmed by such [illegible]
My objection [illegible] *Hiroshima, Mon Amour* is that its story is, basically, of the [illegible]
[illegible]aga[illegible]e variety: and it is told in that over-wrought manner which is characteristic of some
[illegible]emale writers—Marguerite Duras in this case—whose astigmatic vis[illegible]
[illegible]ying to see life entirely through their emotions. In this instance, [illegible]
[illegible]rench woman whose love affair with a Japanese is rather irritatingly blighted by [illegible]
that true happi[illegible] will make her forget completely the German soldier whom she [illegible]
a girl and who was killed. While she remembers him, he lives; but [illegible] allow his [illegible]
from her memory is to deny him even the limited life he still has in [illegible] mind. This se[illegible]
me to be romanticism of the mushiest kind and, told in a more [illegible]ightforward
story might have provided a vehicle for Bette Davis in her heyda[illegible]
In *Last Year at Marienbad*, Resnais tries an even more off-beat te[illegible]
result that many people found the film incomprehensible. My objec[illegible]

158

Fig. 70 Francis Bacon, reproduction from book, Emmanuelle Riva in Alain Resnais's film *Hiroshima mon amour*, 1959, paper-clipped onto cardboard, ca. 1967, 12¾ × 9¾ in. (32.4 × 24.6 cm). Dublin City Gallery The Hugh Lane.

portrait *Study of Henrietta Moraes* (1969, Private Collection), are rendered more obliquely in *Study for a Portrait*, with what was becoming, by that time, a Bacon trope: a spurt of thick white oil paint.

What, then, are we to make of Bacon's appropriations from Matisse and Picasso? There was probably an element of high-level, art historical sanction in Bacon's modus operandi, which also permitted him to steal from any images he chose, selecting them at will as components he sought to reconfigure and transcend in the act of painting. Of the less-elevated sources that came into play, the exposed bone structure of Moraes's legs in *Study for a Portrait* depended on photographs in K. C. Clark's *Positioning in Radiography*, a book Bacon consulted frequently, attracted by its potent mix of scientific detachment and the reduction of humans to flesh, or meat. I have referred to *Study for a Portrait* as a nude depiction, but seminude is more accurate, for Moraes is wearing what may be an item of black lingerie, or a bathing top. Bacon painted four more female nudes through 1972, but ceased to do so subsequently, with the exception of the almost caricatural *Sphinx—Portrait of Muriel Belcher*, in 1979 (Museum of

Modern Art, Tokyo). The kind of V-shape formed by two thinned black strokes across Moraes's lower body was a recurrent motif in the 1960s that Bacon employed to denote, cursorily, a figure's sex, or possibly stocking-tops or suspenders, both of which he wore as sexual attractants. Thus, Bacon's dual gender identification becomes another motivational impulse for the painting.

Study for a Portrait was delivered with the paint still wet to Marlborough Gallery, London, in July 1967. There is no particular explanation for the apparent urgency, although the gallery was always anxious to get paintings out of Bacon's studio before he reconsidered and destroyed them. Bacon was adamant that his paintings should be framed under glass, not so much to protect their (stable) oil surfaces, but because he wanted the painted image to be seen in conjunction with the reflections in the glass—a simultaneous presenting and withdrawing that points to his complex psychological motives. Interestingly, his instructions on the Lang Collection canvas's stretcher confirm this insistence (fig. 71). *Study for a Portrait* was first exhibited in the sixth John Moores exhibition at the Walker Art Gallery, Liverpool, in November 1967, but as an *hors concours* work it did not have to be submitted to the selection committee. The first prize in that exhibition was awarded to David Hockney's *Peter Getting Out of Nick's Pool* (1966, Walker Art Gallery). In his breakthrough years at the Royal College of Art, Hockney had been inspired by Bacon's example, both by the male-orientated subject matter and by his brusque painting technique. After Hockney moved to Los Angeles in 1964, his paintings became more vivid in color and their compositions pared down. Bacon, too, was simplifying his pictorial formats, employing household (alkyd) paints for the flattened planes of his grounds, rather than the acrylics used by Hockney; these were almost invariably added after the figure had been laid down, and frequently modified after "completion."

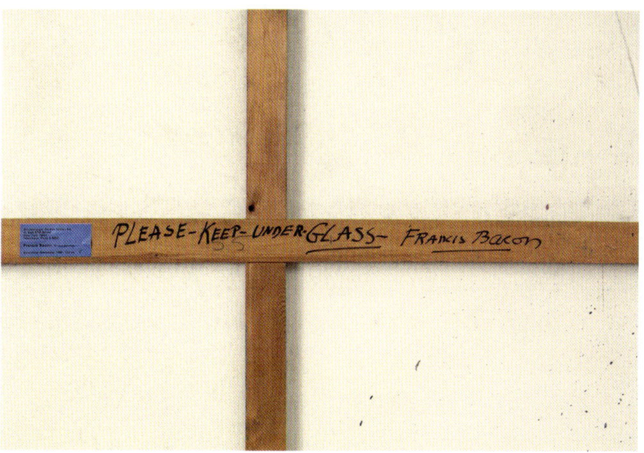

Fig. 71 Reverse of *Study for a Portrait* showing the stretcher clearly signed by Bacon, with his instructions that the painting must be placed under glass. Bacon had been painting on the unprimed side of the canvas for twenty years, but always had his canvases primed, as this image also shows.

In the *Portrait of Man with Glasses* series painted in the early 1960s, Bacon had not entirely emerged from the "black cavern" of the previous decade, whereas the brighter blue and yellow palette of *Study for a Portrait* is comparable with Hockney's swimming-pool paintings. That Bacon was paying attention to British Pop Art and American Abstract Expressionism is often overlooked, but it is a topic that warrants closer study. *Study for a Portrait* was, then, an important marker of the modernizing agenda that increasingly distinguished Bacon's paintings in the last twenty-five years of his life. With gestural, *malerisch* intensity now reserved for the essence of the image—the head, or selected parts of the body—the greater economy of his "very clear"[2] backgrounds reflects his striving for, as he put it, the immaculate.

NOTES

1 I wish to thank Catharina Manchanda for the conversation in which she raised the question of the Zola portrait, which I might otherwise have forgotten.

2 David Sylvester, *The Brutality of Fact: Interviews with Francis Bacon* (London: Thames and Hudson, 1997), 120.

ROBERT MOTHERWELL
BEFORE THE DAY
1972

JACK FLAM

Before the Day (plate 18), which was finished on August 30, 1972, is one of the more complex and haunting works from Robert Motherwell's Open series, which he began in 1967 and worked on for most of the rest of his life. The first Open (fig. 72) established the general format for the series, which consisted of variations on the motif of a rectangular U-shape drawn in charcoal on a painted field of color. During the first few years that Motherwell worked on the series, he varied the colors of the grounds and often used contrasting colors inside and outside the rectangular U-shapes; the charcoal lines in those early Opens were usually straight, as if drawn with a straightedge, and set at right angles to one another. As a result, the early Opens convey a feeling of austere tranquility.

By the summer of 1972, when he painted *Before the Day*, Motherwell had created well over a hundred paintings in the Open series, in addition to several related drawings and prints. He assigned numbers to some of the paintings in the series, but a great many were unnumbered and had other kinds of titles.

During that summer of 1972, Motherwell was especially preoccupied with exploring variations on the basic Open motif. He became increasingly interested in varying the nature of the charcoal lines, drawing them more freely and making them more irregular, which lent the paintings a fresh kind of energy. On July 10, he finished the first state of *Riverrun* (fig. 73), in which the Open form was more irregularly shaped than usual and contained three emphatic verticals. (Originally, these vertical lines were left as areas of blank canvas, on which he subsequently drew dark lines in charcoal.[1]) On August 19, he completed *In Plato's Cave No. 1* (fig. 74), widely acknowledged as one of his most passionate and moving paintings.[2] Unlike most of the earlier Opens, in which the painted grounds provided a tranquil ambience within which the charcoal lines seem to hover calmly, here the ground is rendered with unevenly applied dark washes, which appear to flow onto and bleed down from the rectangular charcoal lines, like drips of blood. The title of this painting alludes not only to Plato's Allegory of the Cave in Book 7 of *The Republic*, which deals with the nature of truth and illusion, but also to Delmore Schwartz's poem "In the Naked Bed, in Plato's Cave," a dark and anguished poem in which an exhausted insomniac ruminates on the nature of perceived reality.

Before the Day, which Motherwell worked on during the same time as *In Plato's Cave No. 1*, and which is exactly

Plate 18 Robert Motherwell, *Before the Day*, 1972, charcoal and acrylic on canvas, 72½ × 96⅝ in. (184.1 × 245.3 cm). Seattle Art Museum, Gift of the Friday Foundation in honor of Richard E. Lang and Jane Lang Davis, 2021.1.1.

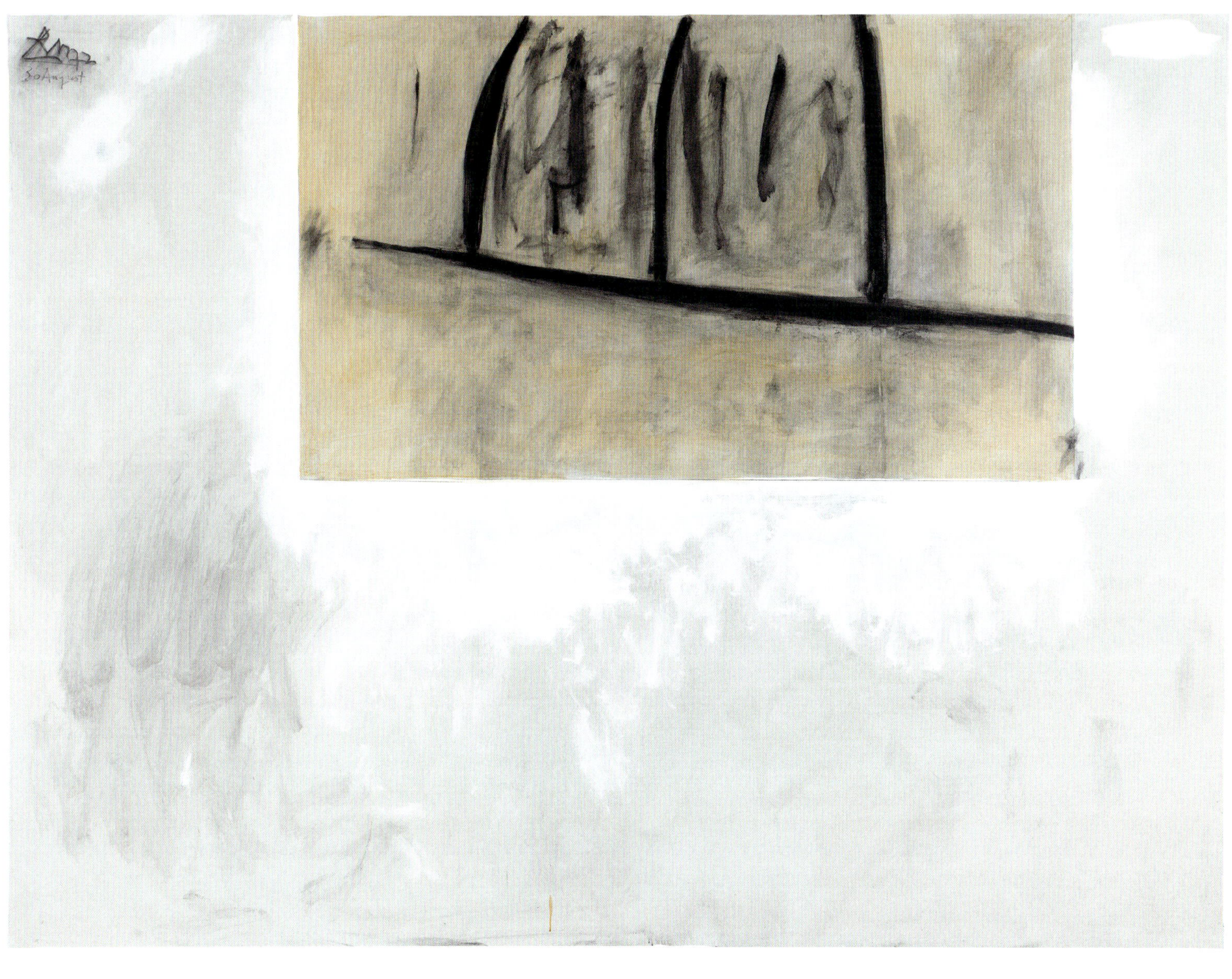

Fig. 72 Robert Motherwell, *Open No. 1: In Yellow Ochre*, 1967, acrylic on canvas, 114 × 84 in. (289.6 × 213.4 cm). Reinhard and Sonja Ernst-Stiftung.

the same size, expresses an equally strong kind of passion, but now imbedded in gradations of whiteness instead of black.[3] It seems likely that Motherwell intended these two paintings to serve as complements to each other, a kind of pair. He was deeply engaged with ideas related to the relativity of perceptions and emotions, and throughout his career he often sought different, even opposing, ways of expressing strong feelings. Four years earlier, for example, he had simultaneously created two large, same-size Opens, one in orange, the other in blue; later, he described how he had painted the orange one as a kind of "after-image" of the blue one.[4]

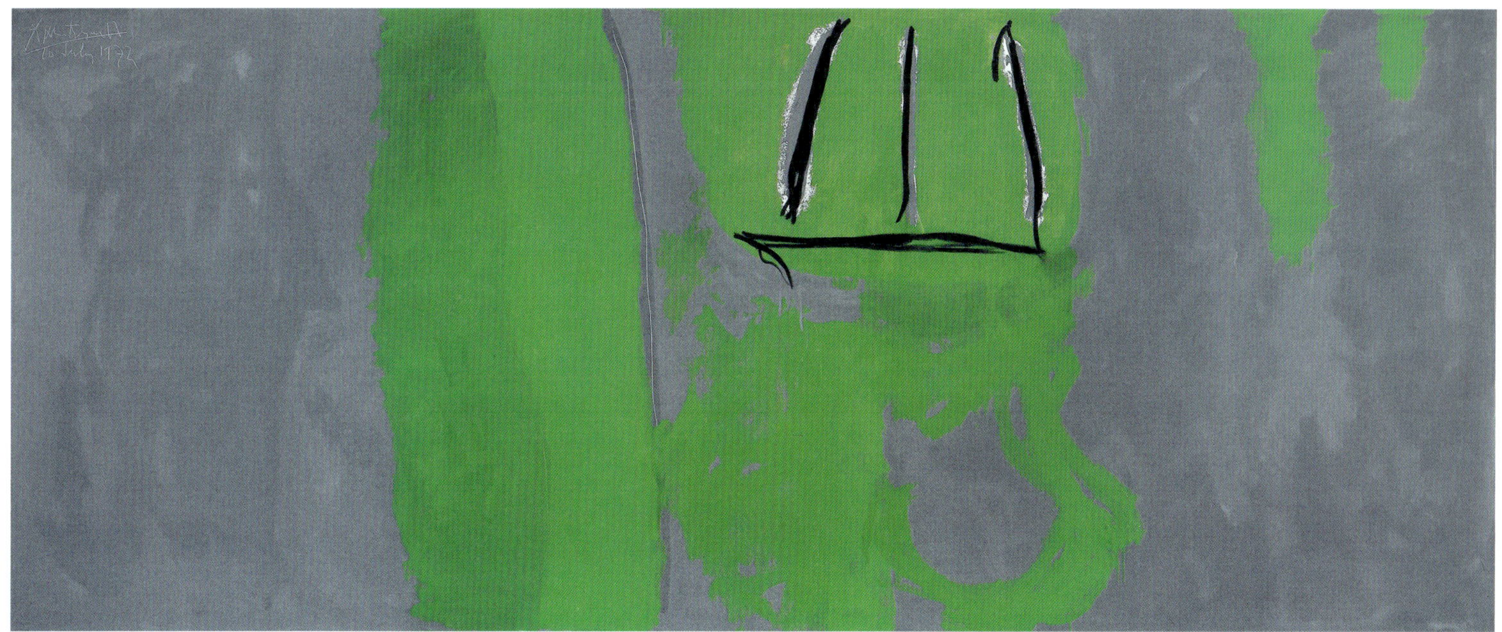

Fig. 73 Robert Motherwell, *Riverrun*, 1972, acrylic on canvas, 60 × 150 in. (152.4 × 381 cm). Private Collection, New York.

In *Before the Day*, Motherwell created the rectangular Open form not with lines drawn in charcoal but with the hard-edged white area that frames the central rectangle of the canvas, itself inscribed with freely drawn charcoal lines. Agitated brushstrokes, in which the white paint is sometimes mixed with varying amounts of charcoal powder, fill the framing area, whitest where it defines the edges of the Open rectangle. The vigorously drawn charcoal lines within the Open form function somewhat like a picture within the picture (or rather, as a drawing within the painting), while the hazes of charcoal dust that surround them (as well as the signature and date in the upper-left corner) convey a strong sense of urgency and passion. The barely visible, rubbed-out remainders of what appear to be handwritten words make the dynamism we sense in this area of the painting even more intense. These not-quite-legible words suspended beneath emphatic strokes of charcoal are a kind of palimpsest, reinforcing the sense of process and vitality felt throughout the painting. One of the most impressive aspects of this work is the way it balances passages of amorphous form with subtly stated geometry. Imbued with a sense of both great tension and ultimate harmony, *Before the Day* balances chaos and order, emptiness and creation, ethereal essence and physical presence.

The way this painting acquired its title is especially intriguing.[5] In early August 1972, Richard and Jane Lang saw the painting in progress in Motherwell's Provincetown studio and expressed their interest in acquiring it. When they asked Motherwell when he expected it to be finished, he estimated around the end of August, and they arranged a follow-up visit to see the completed work in his Greenwich, Connecticut, studio (fig. 75). Since the birthday of Jane Lang's son, Donald Hussong, was coming up on August 31, Motherwell agreed to complete the painting on that day and to title it accordingly. But as it turned out, he misremembered the date and finished it instead on August 30.[6] Interestingly, in an October 12, 1972, letter to Motherwell, Dick Lang referred to the title of the painting as "Done Yesterday."[7] But Motherwell decided instead to call it "Before the Day," as is evident in the handwritten inscription of the words "Before The Day" near the top of a carbon copy of an October 31 letter from Richard Lang's secretary, Veronica Whittaker, to Motherwell.[8]

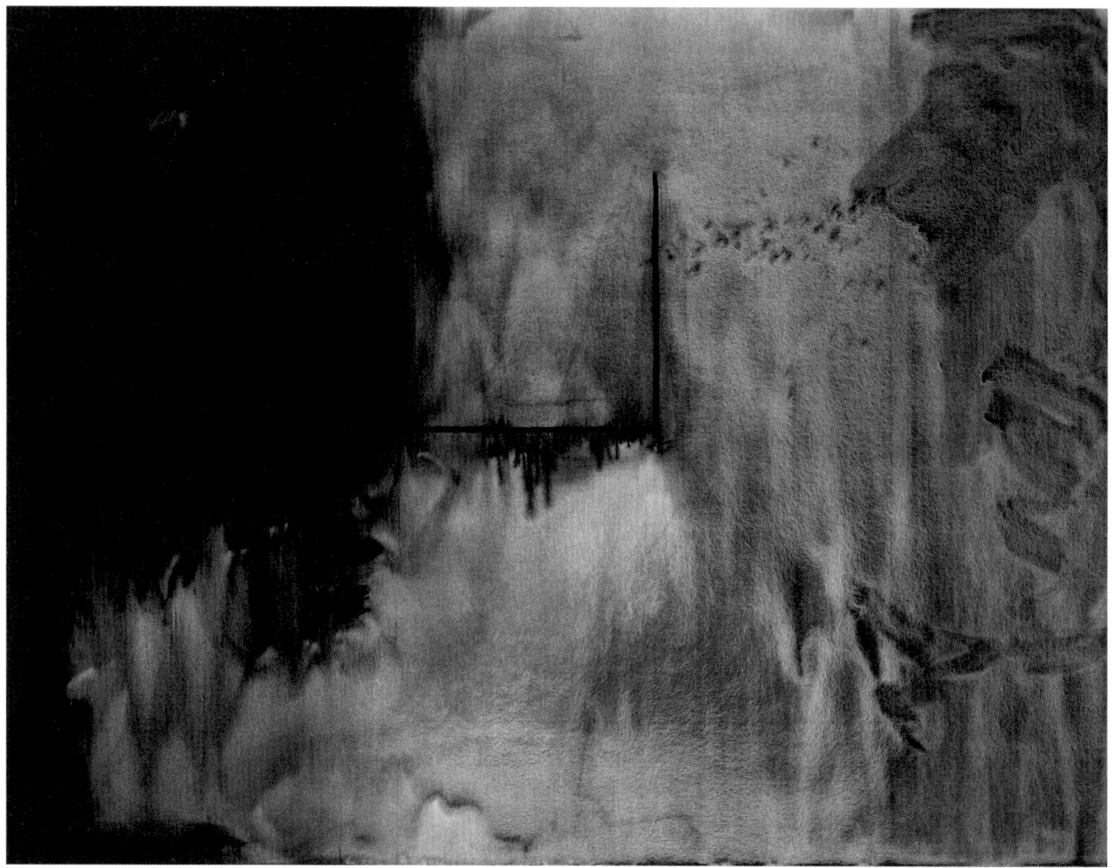

Fig. 74 Robert Motherwell, *In Plato's Cave No. 1*, 1972, acrylic on canvas, 72 × 96 in. (182.9 × 243.8 cm). National Gallery of Art, The Nancy and Perry Bass Fund, 1999.1.1.

The words "before the day" not only are more ambiguous than "done yesterday" but also evoke a sense of the first, hopeful light of day, an emergence from darkness. And, seen in retrospect, they seem to anticipate the new direction that Motherwell's Opens were about to take, as exemplified by the irregular strokes of charcoal surrounded by charcoal dust in *Before the Day*. These haloed marks anticipate a similar use of dynamic line drawing and charcoal dust in many of his subsequent Opens, such as the *Shem the Penman* series later in 1972 and the *In Beige with Charcoal* paintings and drawings of 1973, which *Before the Day* seems to have inspired.[9]

NOTES

1 See Jack Flam, Katy Rogers, and Tim Clifford, *Robert Motherwell Paintings and Collages: A Catalogue Raisonné, 1941–1991*, 3 vols. (New Haven, CT: Yale University Press, 2012), 2:336.

2 See Flam, Rogers, and Clifford, *Robert Motherwell*, 2:342–45.

3 Motherwell had already begun painting *Before the Day* when Richard and Jane Lang visited him in early August, and he finished *In Plato's Cave No. 1* on August 19.

4 See Flam, Rogers, and Clifford, *Robert Motherwell*, 2:235. The paintings are *Open No. 24: In Variations of Orange* (Museum of Modern Art, New York) and *Open No. 23: In Blue with Variations of Ultramarine* (Private Collection), both from 1968.

5 One cannot help but wonder what title Motherwell might have given to *Before the Day* if external circumstances had not determined the way he decided to title it. Since he originally gave *In Plato's Cave No. 1* the title *Dark Elegy*, and even showed it

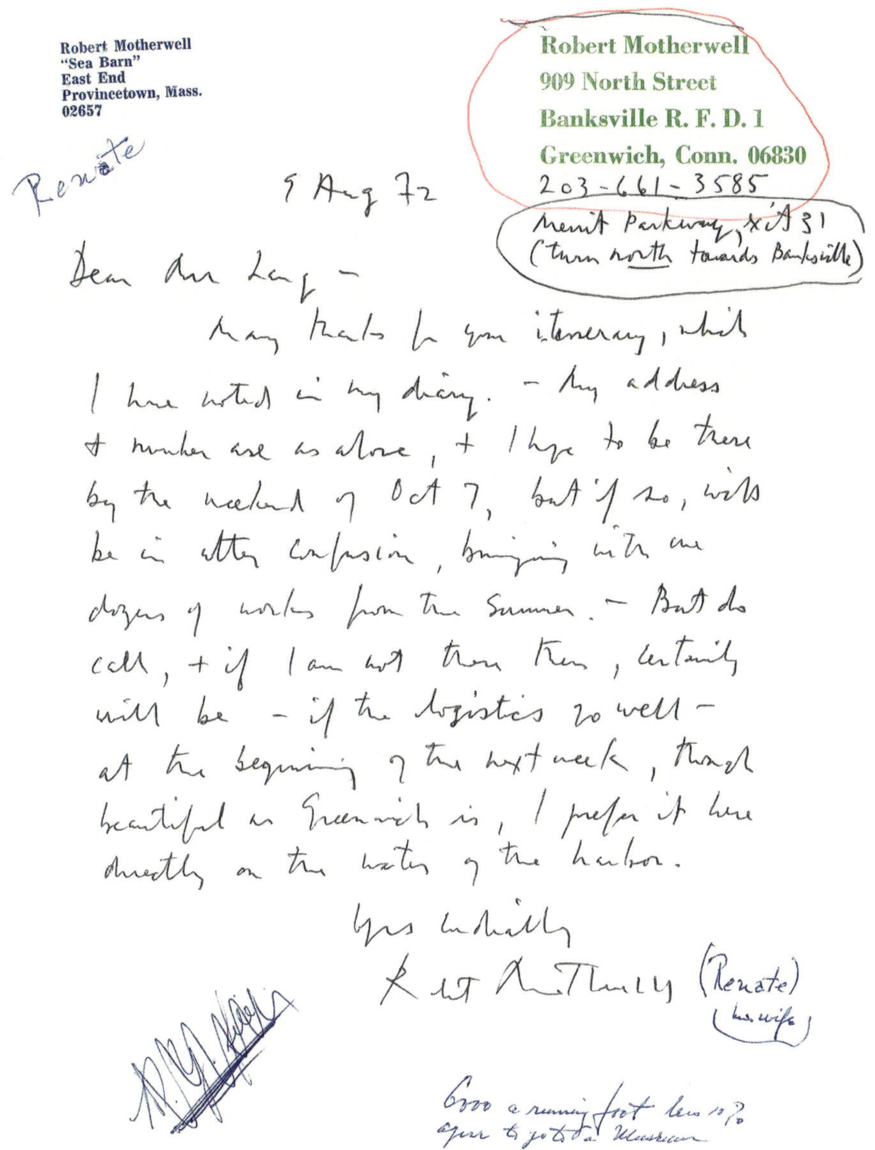

Robert Motherwell
"Sea Barn"
East End
Provincetown, Mass.
02657

Robert Motherwell
909 North Street
Banksville R. F. D. 1
Greenwich, Conn. 06830
203-661-3585
Merritt Parkway, exit 31
(turn north towards Banksville)

Renate

9 Aug 72

Dear Mrs Lang —

Many thanks for your itinerary, which I have noted in my diary. — My address & number are as above, & I hope to be there by the weekend of Oct 7, but if so, will be in utter confusion, bringing with me dozens of works from the summer. — But do call, & if I am not there then, certainly will be — if the logistics go well — at the beginning of the next week, though beautiful as Greenwich is, I prefer it here directly on the water of the harbor.

Yrs cordially

Robert Motherwell (Renate) (his wife)

Fig. 75 Letter from Robert Motherwell to Jane Lang arranging for a visit to his Greenwich, Connecticut, studio, August 9, 1972.

under that title in the fall of 1972, might he have given *Before the Day* a similarly descriptive title?

6 Lyn Grinstein, telephone conversation with the author, January 8, 2021.

7 Richard Lang to Robert Motherwell, October 12, 1972, carbon copy, Friday Foundation archives.

8 Veronica Whittaker to Robert Motherwell, October 31, 1972, carbon copy, Friday Foundation archives.

9 *Before the Day* was shown at Motherwell's 1977 retrospective at the Musée d'Art Moderne de la Ville de Paris, where Stephanie Terenzio remarked on its strong connection with Motherwell's later Opens, noting, "One of the finest moments in this exhibition is seeing *Before the Day* and the three related drawings *In Beige with Charcoal*." Stephanie Terenzio, *Robert Motherwell & Black* (Storrs, CT: William Benton Museum of Art, 1979), 3.

PHILIP GUSTON
THE PAINTER
1976

ROBERT STORR

Although he lacked the reputation for stall-kicking brashness that Pollock earned early on, and despite the fact that he had a command of traditional skills that Pollock for the most part lacked, Philip Guston was among the great risk takers of his generation of American artists. Contrary to the logic that living free is easy if you've got nothing left to lose, by 1950, when Guston had just reached his early forties and put everything on the line to explore a radical abstraction, he had a great deal to lose. By 1966, when he again bet the farm on what seemed an abrupt about-face, he had still more at risk.

In large part, this was because on the second occasion he was not neatly swinging back to "figuration," pendulum style, a phenomenon that might simply have perplexed and dismayed some of his avant-garde supporters while pleasing his more conservative enthusiasts of years past. Rather, he appeared to have veered wide of any aesthetically comprehensible formal dialectic inasmuch as his new "cartoon"-derived work struck many as wholly out of character with any of his previously known artistic identities, while, in the view of others, veering perilously close to the vulgar commercial imagery favored by Pop painters half his age.

In truth, though, Guston was reconnecting to his earliest mentors: comic strip masters such as the African American creator of the nationally syndicated *Krazy Kat*, George Herriman, whose work Guston had copied from the papers as a boy.[1] It was Herriman and his colleagues in the "funny pages" who pioneered the uniquely antic graphic idiom subsequently latched onto by Robert Crumb, Art Spiegelman, and others who led the "Comix" revival of the 1960s. More than a few critics assumed that Guston was aping them rather than mining a rich, deep but long-neglected seam in his own imagination.

But he was—although, in keeping with his profoundly unsettled nature and ambivalent sensibility, he refused to deploy the tropes of cartooning "just for laughs." Instead, he used them to address the most wrenching aspects of contemporary American life and of his personal reality. In that spirit, he began his last creative period delineating deliberately heavy-handed still lifes of the tools of his painterly trade found in his studio. He was also commenting in jarringly slapstick manner on the violence in American streets outside that safe haven—violence that heralded and ran through the presidency of Richard Nixon, to whom he devoted an astonishing series of caricatures,

Plate 19 Philip Guston, *The Painter*, 1976, oil on canvas, 74 × 116 in. (188 × 294.6 cm). Seattle Art Museum, Gift of the Friday Foundation in honor of Richard E. Lang and Jane Lang Davis, 2020.14.11.

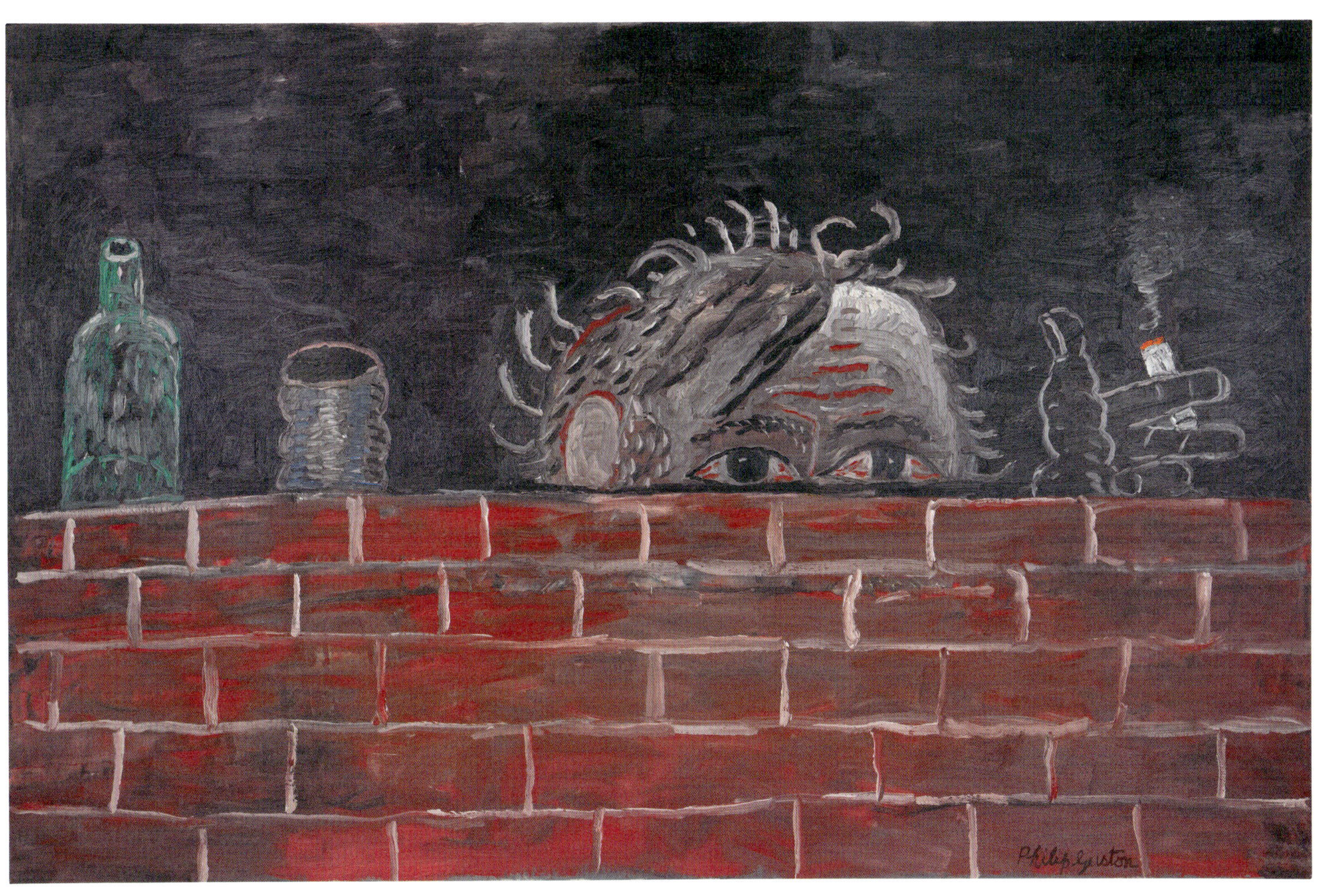
Philip Guston

which constitute his only foray into cartooning for its own sake in the public sphere.

Most notable of his frankly—yet anything but one-dimensionally or programmatically partisan—political works were those in which Guston reprised the iconography of his radical anti-lynching tableaux of the 1930s featuring hooded members of the Ku Klux Klan. When Klansmen returned in the 1970s, they came across as a crew of bumbling "hooded" thugs or variations on the Keystone Kops emanating from the dark side. Guston's purpose was not to make light of these still-dangerous marauders—far from it. He had, in part, been prompted to revisit them by the resurgence of the Klan during the civil rights movement and by the murderous role it had played in the 1963 bombing of Sixteenth Street Baptist Church in Birmingham, causing the deaths of four Black girls attending Sunday services.

To that extent, fear, loathing, and outrage are at the core of all of Guston's late Klan imagery. In this context, the cartooning style he had adopted might seem to be at odds with the depth and seriousness of the artist's convictions, but indicates that something else is at issue as well. Namely, these works mark an uneasy effort to bear witness to the horrors the Klan perpetrated, and to their demonic stupidity, from inside rather than from outside their cohort. Guston's point of view constitutes an ethically courageous admission that "we" are more like "them" than most of "us" would like to believe, that the Klansmen's weaknesses, prejudices, brutality, and cowardice are also an ineradicable part of "our" human nature. In their sheer absurdity—which is where the ridiculous element of these lampoons comes into play—they remind us that the ultimate common denominator of our human condition is rooted in our schizophrenia, our split personalities, and our capacity for inflicting pain and suffering, as well as in being good, our dignity and abjection, and our probably tragicomic fates.

In the highly polarized 1960s and 1970s, such extreme, self-revealing masquerades were exceedingly rare in a sharply divided, which-side-are-you-on nation. Now, perhaps, people have a keener appreciation of how hard it can be to tell the good guys from the very bad guys or, for that matter, to be absolutely sure on which side of that line one is standing. For Guston, who had long been guarded about his heritage, crucial insight into the anomalies of ethnic and racial identity had been provided by the Russian Jewish writer Isaac Babel. As an official Soviet journalist, Babel rode with and reported on his own hereditary enemies, the Cossacks, who made up much of the Red Cavalry fending off the counterrevolutionary White armies but who, in the not-so-distant-past, had terrorized the Jewish communities of the shtetl.

Being and doing evil thus became the subtext for the Klan pictures. In these images, Guston broke ranks with those who were all too quick to absolve whites from the harm done to Black people in this country on the assumption that only obvious, night-riding villains hidden under white sheets were to blame for systemic racism in the United States.

Guston knew better. Accordingly, he painted artists in hoods at their easels limning self-portraits (fig. 76). It was a bold, brave decision whose ramifications reach into the twenty-first century. When art is judged to be before its time, it usually implies that the work bears the traces of stylistic precocity, of being in advance of a raft of work with which it shares obvious formal traits. But art can also be ahead of its time in thematic ways as well. As recent events have proved, we as a nation remain far from dispelling the shadow that the heritage of racism has cast over us all—a heritage that Guston symbolically acknowledged in his choice of hooded "protagonists."

Despite this prescience, fundamental misunderstandings of Guston's intentions in overtly political works of the 1930s as well as of his concerns in the late 1960s and early 1970s led to a woefully misguided delay in the tour of an international retrospective of his career in 2020.[2] In short, art "discourse" and public appreciation of the tenacity of racist attitudes in the United States inspired a basic misreading of his Klan imagery, rendering them temporarily taboo. That taboo, and the debate it triggered over the decision to postpone the Guston exhibition, coming as it did in the waning days of President Donald Trump's administration, oddly served to assist in correcting overdetermined interpretations of his work. This, in turn, prompted an overdue rethinking of deep-seated biases in contemporary art discourse—not least the canard that Abstract Expressionism signaled a widespread retreat from politics among artists. To whatever degree that shift applies to other members of Guston's New York School cohort, his own later work doubled back on the commitments of his

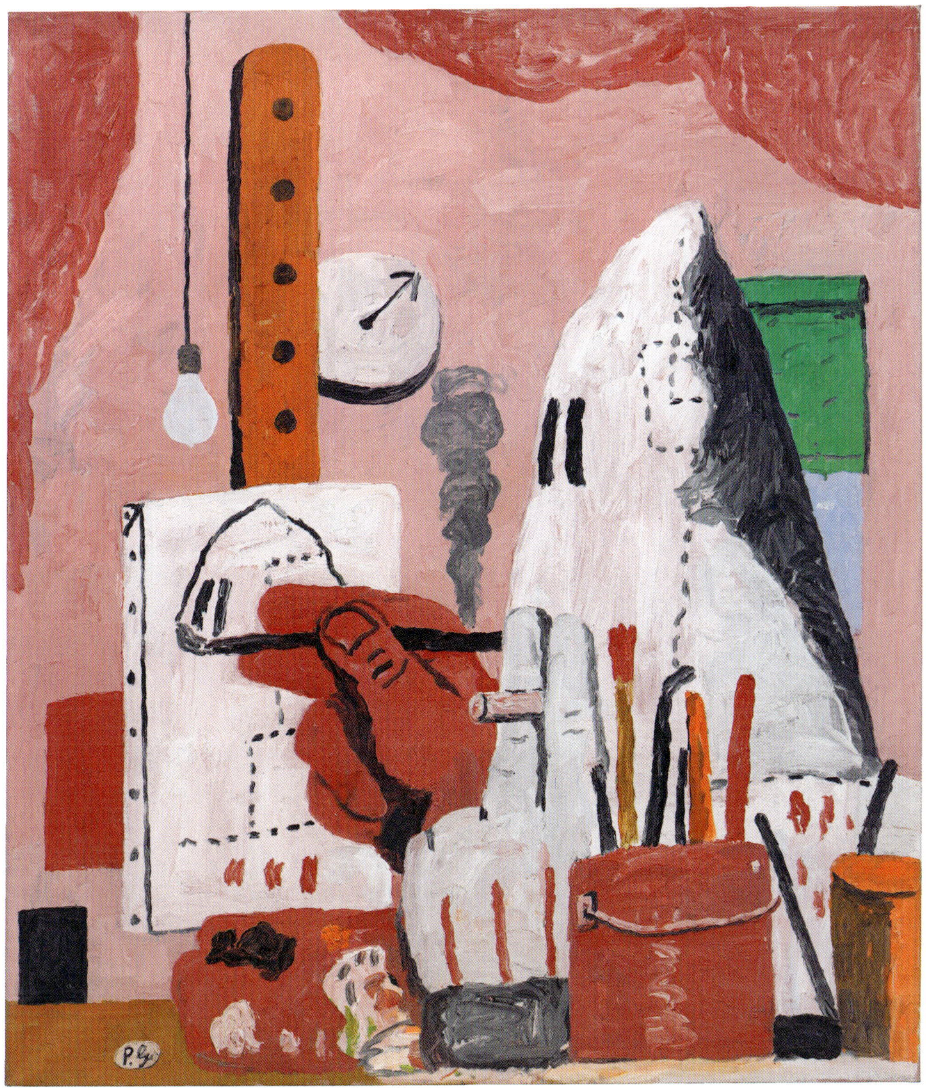

Fig. 76 Philip Guston, *The Studio*, 1969, oil on canvas, 48 × 42 in. (129.1 × 106.7 cm). Private Collection.

politically radical years and cast them in a fresh and disabused but, for all that, still more passionate light.

That light was dark if not explicitly nocturnal. And it became more so while the 1970s wore on—and wore him down—even as Guston's self-questioning cut ever closer to the bone. With his own studio as the main stage of the psychological, social, and philosophical dramas that he played out in blunt but always spontaneously speculative strokes, the costuming, decor, and supporting cast changed and evolved. By mid-decade, Klansmen had all but vanished from his work, and their intrusive menace—the riotous world invading the inner sanctum of his artistic vocation—was replaced by that of densely massed, stamping feet in hobnailed boots and shoes.

Thus, if in *The Studio* (1969) we have a depiction of "the artist" as a hooded brute explicitly erasing the division between "them" and "us" referred to above, and if in *Bad Habits* (1970, fig. 77) we have similar Klan figures

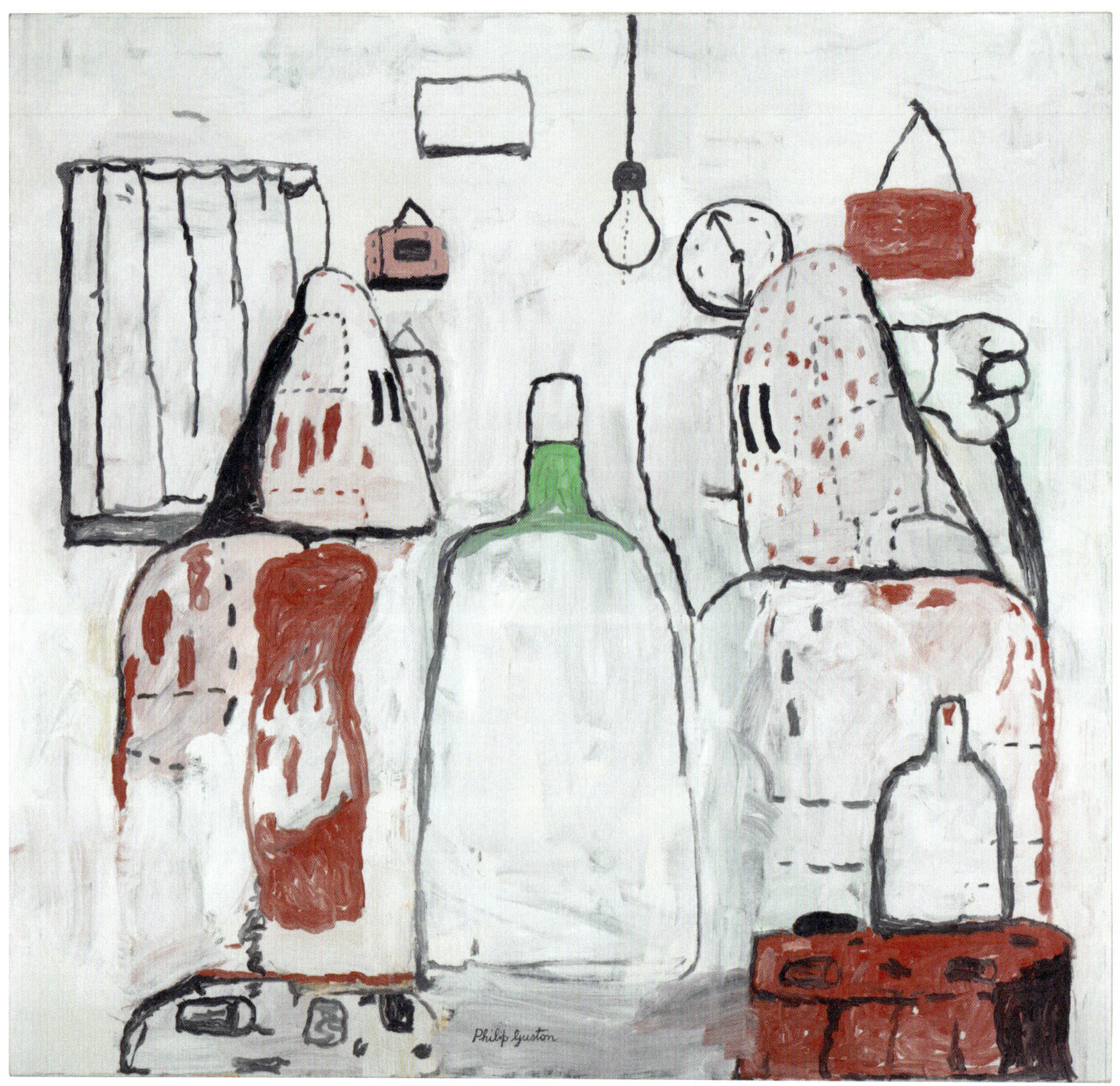

Fig. 77 Philip Guston, *Bad Habits*, 1970, oil on canvas, 73 × 78 in. (185.4 × 198.1 cm). National Gallery of Australia, Canberra, 1981.3050.

interspersed with gigantic liquor bottles effectively equating solitary drinking with the lonely, hallucinatory intoxication of painting, in *The Painter* (1976, plate 19) the comic exaggeration is gone, and we are presented with a stripped-down version of the artist's plight. Cut off and sealed in by yet another iteration of the masonry wall motif Guston had deployed since the 1930s, a grizzled, balding head rises just above the tiers of bricks, its forehead furrowed and its eyes bloodshot. A cigarette-wielding hand brackets the desperate visage to one side, and to the other, an empty fifth of spirits and a tumbler are arranged atop the bricks. One is almost moved to sing, "Ninety-nine bottles of Scotch on the wall . . ."

To be sure, hard drinking is part of the macho myth of Abstract Expressionism, but directly or indirectly it killed or contributed to the premature deaths of many of that tendency's leading exponents, starting with epically, self-destructively drunk Jackson Pollock and continuing on through the suicidally alcoholic Mark Rothko, the habitually thirsty but more genteel Robert Motherwell, and the otherwise bibulous sculptors Tony Smith and David Smith, to mention only a handful of the greats. That said, on the authority of Rudolf Burckhardt, the filmmaker and photographer who took pictures of their work for *Art News* and various galleries, one can say that booze generally did not overtake these artists until they had begun to experience a measure of material success and to have "careers" that required hanging out with collectors who paid the bar bills, all of which ultimately added to their anxieties.

To that degree, the "critique" of Abstract Expressionism by contemporary historians and commentators by and large lacks pathos, given the details left out of current retellings by those fed up with the artists' legend. From inside the prison constructed around him and fellow inmates confined by circumstances including fame and ill-founded hero worship, Guston portrayed his own solitary confinement and alienation in raw, unromantic, antiheroic, and essentially unforgiving terms.

Ironically, he did so at the "peak" of his artistic creativity, which he reached while in internal exile in upstate New York, far from the center of the New York City–based art world that had formerly lionized him. Of all their peers, only Guston and de Kooning fully developed and deployed a "late manner." And, without a doubt, it was the canvases created during that final phase that have in the long run secured Guston's pivotal place in the pantheon of internationally renowned painters of the late twentieth century's "postmodern" era. Nevertheless, they were, in fact, the work of a perpetually anguished modern artist who, in a period governed by competing aesthetic ideologies, was never comfortable being a rule-bound *modernist*. Viewed from that angle, he perfectly fits the description of the type of artist that de Kooning referred to when he said, "Some painters, including myself, do not care what chair they are sitting on. They do not want to 'sit in style.'"[3] Guston was likewise too restless to sit pat, no matter what the rewards, and, as a result, drove himself hard to the very end. In 1980, he died suddenly of a heart attack. He was only 66.

NOTES

1 Herriman's Krazy Kat character first appeared in his strip *The Dingbat Family* in the *New York Evening Journal*, July 26, 1910. The paper published the inaugural *Krazy Kat* vertical daily strip on October 28, 1913. Crucially, the full-page Sunday *Krazy Kat* comic premiered in the paper's arts and drama section on April 23, 1916, exposing Herriman's work to a much broader readership than it might have had in the comics section. According to biographer Patrick McDonnell, this event sparked the strip's wide popularity. See Patrick McDonnell, *Krazy Kat: The Comic Art of George Herriman* (New York: Harry N. Abrams, 1986).

2 See, for example, Julia Jacobs and Jason Farago, "Delay of Philip Guston Retrospective Divides the Art World," *New York Times*, September 25, 2020, http://www.nytimes.com/2020/09/25/arts/design/philip-guston-exhibition-delayed-criticism.html; Sarah Cascone, "Philip Guston's Daughter and Other Critics Speak Out against Four Museums' Decision to Postpone a Major Retrospective on the Artist," *ArtNet*, September 25, 2020, http://news.artnet.com/exhibitions/philip-guston-retrospective-postponed-1910658; "Open Letter: On Philip Guston Now," *Brooklyn Rail*, September 30, 2020, http://brooklynrail.org/projects/on-philip-guston-now/; and Murray Whyte, "What Museums Can Learn from Philip Guston and His Frank Take on 'White Culpability,'" *Boston Globe*, January 6, 2021, http://www.bostonglobe.com/2021/01/06/arts/what-museums-can-learn-philip-guston-his-frank-take-white-culpability/.

3 Willem de Kooning, "What Abstract Art Means to Me," lecture, What Is Abstract Art symposium, Museum of Modern Art, New York, February 5, 1951, http://www.dekooning.org/documentation/words/what-abstract-art-means-to-me.

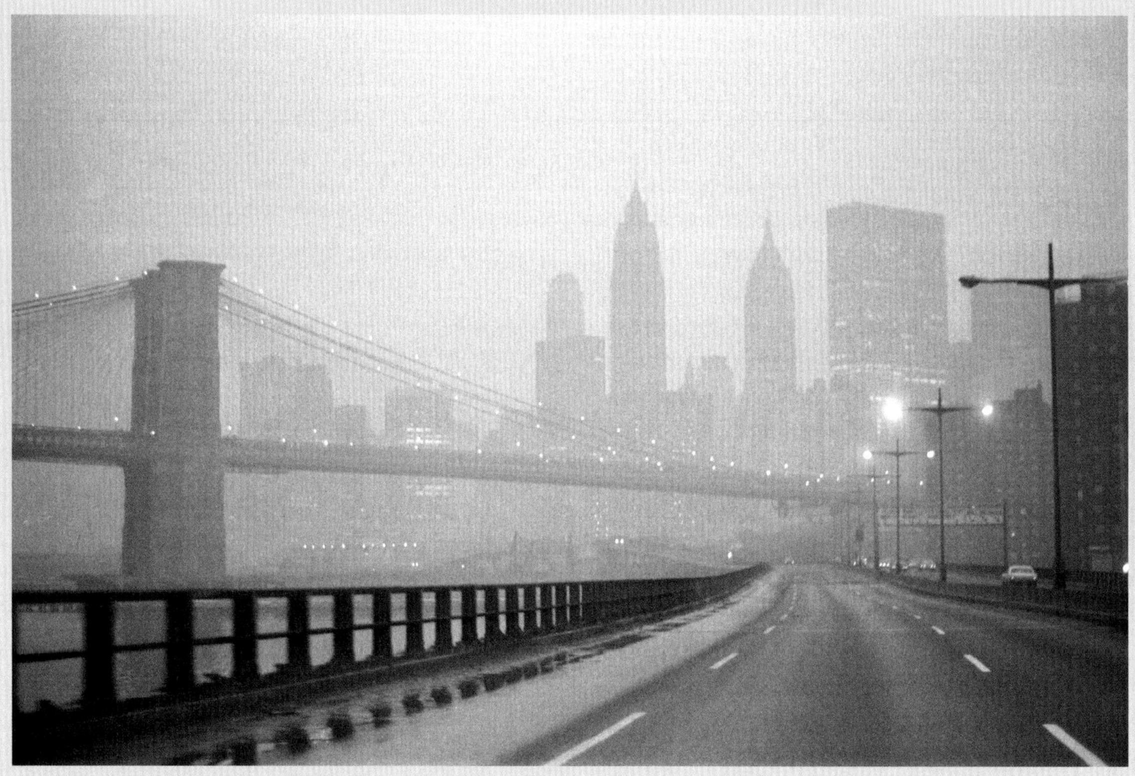

MEMORIES OF THE NEW YORK ART WORLD, AS SHARED WITH CAROL VOGEL

When Jane and Richard Lang were collecting during the 1970s and 1980s, New York was *the* destination for art lovers. This passionate group descended on the city from all parts of the globe to peruse galleries and museum exhibitions, to visit artists' studios, and to socialize. When the Langs went to New York, they would regularly host informal cocktail parties at the Carlton House, inviting their friends from the art world, among them collectors, curators, art dealers, and artists. One evening, guests included Andy Warhol, who came with his business manager, Fred Hughes, along with the artists Michael Heizer and Walter De Maria, dealers Stephen Mazoh, Robin Graham, Xavier Fourcade, and Richard Bellamy, the collector Kathy Johnson, the photographer Tina Freeman, and the ever-popular Jerry ("The Walker") Zipkin.

The art world was a fervent, cozy community of which the Langs were much-loved members. They joined museum groups traveling around the country and the world with like-minded friends, getting behind-the-scenes tours of art wherever they happened to be, visiting museums and galleries as well as private and princely collections. They were also generous donors—of their time, art, and knowledge—supporting many arts organizations and always opening their home to collectors, writers, students, scholars, and artists.

Many who knew the Langs remember those days fondly and shared their memories in early 2021.

The Museum of Modern Art's International Council was like a big family where great friendships are still formed, and the glue was everyone's interest in art. Richard Lang first joined in 1973. In her letter of recommendation, Virginia [Jinny] Wright wrote, "He began buying paintings two years ago. He acquired a first-rate Kline, Rothko, Gottlieb and a really great Motherwell among other things of good quality. Both [he and Jane] seem really committed to art and have demonstrated their civic conscientiousness and for these reasons he seems like the perfect candidate."

The first International Council trip the Langs took was to the Netherlands and Belgium in 1974. One afternoon, there was a reception at the official residence of King Baudouin and Queen Fabiola of Belgium. A note in the itinerary book for that meeting read: "Dress for ladies: gloves, no pantsuits or bare arms; dark suits for men."

Carol Coffin
Executive Director,
Museum of Modern Art International Council

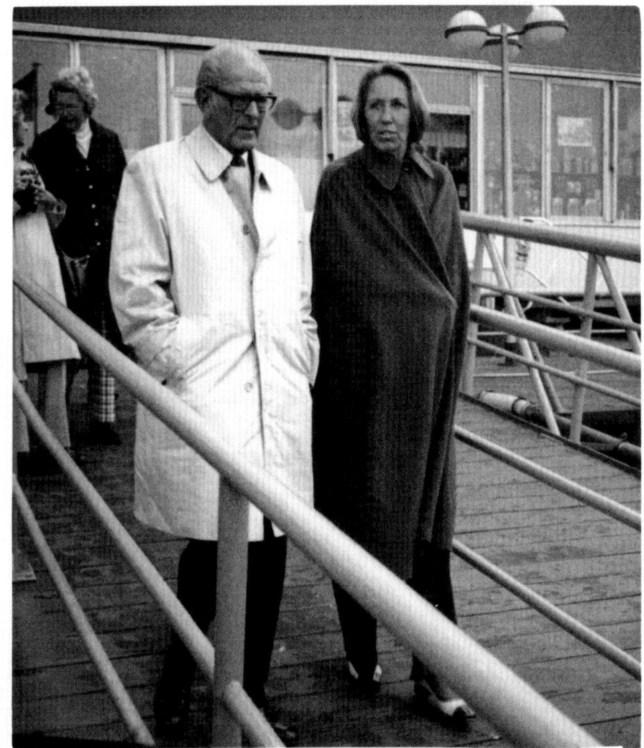

Richard and Jane Lang disembarking in Rotterdam while traveling with MoMA's International Council, 1974.

In the 1960s and early '70s, the art world was just a handful of collectors who would come to New York several times a year to see museum and gallery shows and to buy art. It was far less cutthroat in those days. The collectors took their time and really thought about what they were buying. When somebody came from Chicago and I had seen an interesting show at Leo Castelli's, it was normal just to say, "You've got to see that show." And Ivan Karp at Castelli would do the same for us.

It was the Scull auction in 1973 that really changed everything. Suddenly, contemporary American art had international value on the auction market.

Arne Glimcher
Pace Gallery, New York

In the 1970s and '80s, every day you'd go for lunch at either Les Pleiades on East 76th Street or La Goulue, which in those days was on 70th Street, and you'd see everybody—collectors, dealers, museum curators and directors. I took the Langs to lunch there too.

Stephen Mazoh
Stephen Mazoh & Co., Inc., New York

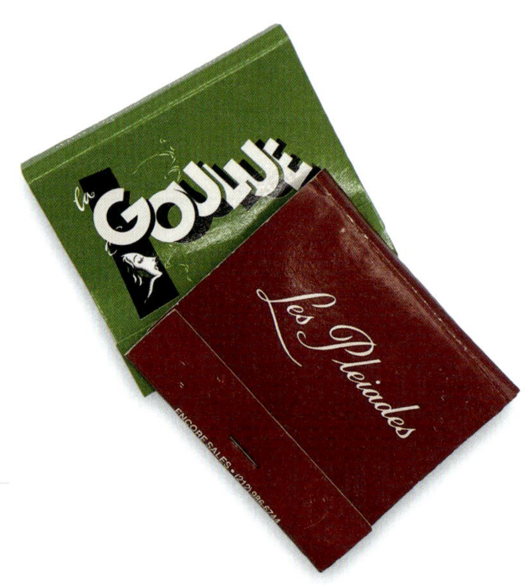

Matchbooks from Les Pleiades and La Goulue in New York.

I sold the Langs an early Cubist Giacometti when they came to see me in London. It was a difficult piece; you really had to know your art to appreciate it. The Langs were a charming couple. They didn't want to gossip about the art world. They only wanted to talk about art. In those days, all the American collectors would come and really look at pictures. The difference between the art world in London and the art world in New York was enormous back then, and Americans were very different to do business with than, say, the Brits or the French. They were all very gracious and very curious.

Thomas Gibson
Thomas Gibson Fine Art Limited, London

Established in 1980, the National Committee of the Whitney Museum of American Art, which Jane and Richard Lang joined, was the Whitney's version of the Museum of Modern Art's International Council, but it was intentionally smaller and included only American collectors. The group met every spring for a weekend in New York and somewhere else every fall.

We spent a lot of time on buses en route to visiting collectors, and once in Seattle there was a celebration of some sort for Jane Lang. We had a party on the bus, and people were wearing grass skirts and dancing the hula while the bus was moving. When the committee traveled, a collector from wherever we were would host a dinner on Saturday night, and on Sunday we'd go on an outing. I remember being in Seattle, where Jane was the host, and visiting Dale Chihuly's studio, which was really fascinating because we got to watch him blow glass.

Jane was a great addition wherever we went. She was knowledgeable, fun, but also terribly irreverent. Many people, like the Langs, were members of both the National Committee and the International Council. They couldn't see enough great art or have enough interesting adventures.

Jennifer Russell
Former Associate Director,
Whitney Museum of American Art

In the late 1960s and early ’70s, there was no sense of art being purchased for its asset value. People mostly bought their art because they liked what they saw. Jane Lang was very intuitive, and Richard was very decisive. He either liked something or he didn’t, and that was it.

I met the Langs when I was working at Marlborough in the 1970s. I had sold a Francis Bacon painting to a collector—an important portrait of Henrietta Moraes. About two years after I sold it, the owner got into trouble and asked me to sell it for him. So, I called Dick and said I had this very good Bacon for sale. And he said, “Well, I’m coming to the city,” so we got together for lunch and the first thing he did was put down six transparencies of Bacons on the table. “You have a lot of competition, David,” he said. Every dealer in London and New York knew he wanted a Bacon, and they all were sending him transparencies—that’s how easy it was to get something back then. He put down six images, then shuffled them around, and asked me, “Which one should I take?”

I said, “Don’t ask me, you have to make your own decision.” He ended up buying mine [plate 15].

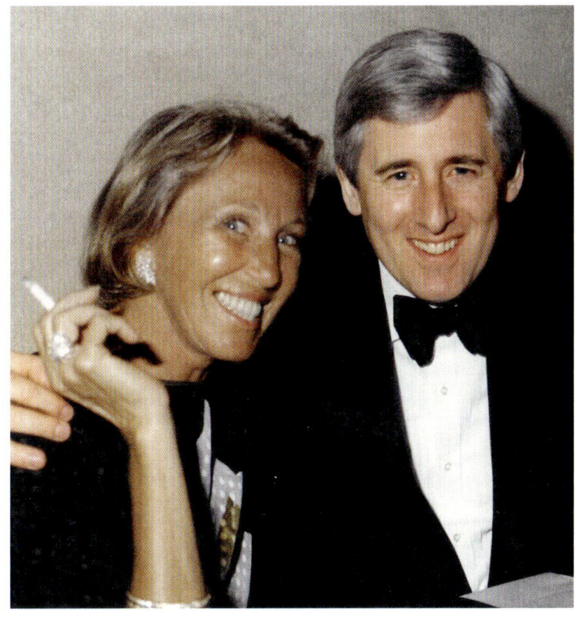

Jane Lang and David McKee in New York, ca. 1977.

As a child, Jane studied ballet. Her lifelong love of dance prompted her interest in Franz Kline. [Kline’s own interest in ballet, centered on Vaslav Nijinsky, was because his wife had been a ballet dancer in London.] Jane asked me if the famous black-and-white abstract titled *Nijinsky* [1950] would ever be available. It belonged to Muriel Newman in Chicago, in her great collection of Abstract Expressionist paintings, which she bequeathed to the Met. However, a few years later, we represented the Franz Kline Estate. As a result, I had a relationship with David Orr, Kline’s first patron, who owned Kline’s well-known portrait of Nijinsky as Petrushka. Because the Langs had previously bought Kline’s *Painting No. 11* [plate 5], he agreed to sell them his haunting Nijinsky [now at Yale University Art Gallery]. So Jane’s interest was covered!

David McKee
McKee Gallery, New York

I opened my own gallery at 32 East 57th Street in 1971. Back then you could see almost every important exhibition on 57th Street from Park to Fifth Avenues. What I always remember about Jane Lang Davis was that she had three Alice Trumbull Masons, which she acquired herself. I always thought of Mason as an artist’s artist, yet Jane had them hanging in her home.

Joan Washburn
Joan Washburn Gallery, New York

If you think about the difference between collectors then and collectors now, there was more time. People would come in; they'd look at things. Collectors like the Langs loved to sit around and talk about art, and eventually you'd make a deal—but it took longer. Back then, collectors liked to live with what they bought.

William Acquavella
Acquavella Galleries, New York

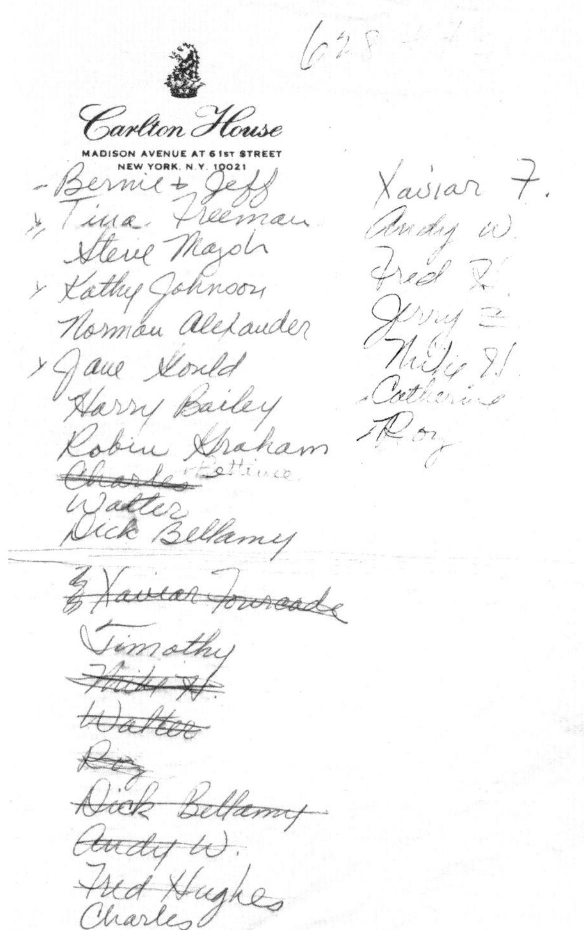
Carlton House
MADISON AVENUE AT 61ST STREET
NEW YORK, N.Y. 10021
Bernie + Jeff
Tina Freeman
Steve Mazoh
Kathy Johnson
Norman Alexander
Jane Gould
Harry Bailey
Robin Graham
~~Charles~~
Walter
Dick Bellamy
~~Xavier Fourcade~~
Timothy
~~Walter~~
~~Roy~~
~~Dick Bellamy~~
~~Andy W.~~
~~Fred Hughes~~
Charles
Xavier F.
Andy W.
Fred H.
Catherine
Roy

Guest list written by Lyn Grinstein for a party in Jane Lang's suite at the Carlton House in New York, late 1970s.

The art world was a lot of fun in the 1970s and '80s. It wasn't about money; it was about relationships, and it was about the art. Just imagine people jumping in and out of cabs with Rothkos under their arms. That was what it was like. Yes, collectors were competitive. It was like a game of poker. There were real stakes.

There were parties all the time and everyone knew everyone else. Every year, my mother and Dick would rent a suite at the Carlton House on Madison Avenue where they would gather their friends for cocktails. Andy Warhol, an artist with whom she and Dick were friendly, was always in attendance. The hotel art offended Andy, so one year he arrived with one of his 1964 Shot Marilyns and hung it over the fireplace, replacing the ugly painting that was there. When the party was over, he took it down, tucked it under his arm and left.

Lyn Grinstein
Daughter of Jane Lang Davis

Opposite: Contact sheet of photographs taken in November 1976, during Andy Warhol's visit to Seattle on the occasion of the opening of his exhibition *Andy Warhol: Portraits* at the Seattle Art Museum. The three images in the top row show Richard and Jane Lang's garden, taken during Warhol's visit to their Medina home. The remaining photographs were taken at Seattle's Pike Place Market, with SAM Curator of Modern Art Charles Cowles leading Andy Warhol, Stephen Mazoh, Tina Freeman, and others on a tour through the iconic marketplace. Iris & B. Gerald Cantor Center for Visual Arts at Stanford University; Gift of the Andy Warhol Foundation for the Visual Arts, Inc.

DATE: ASSIGNMENT: FILE NO:

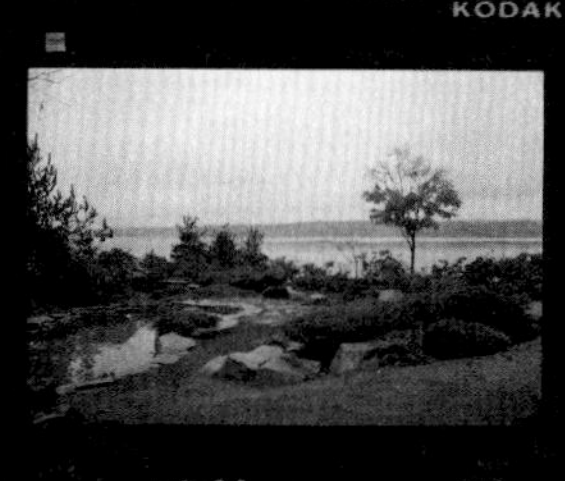
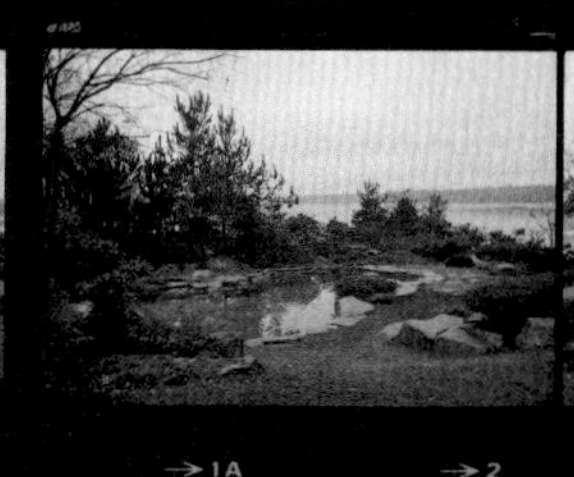
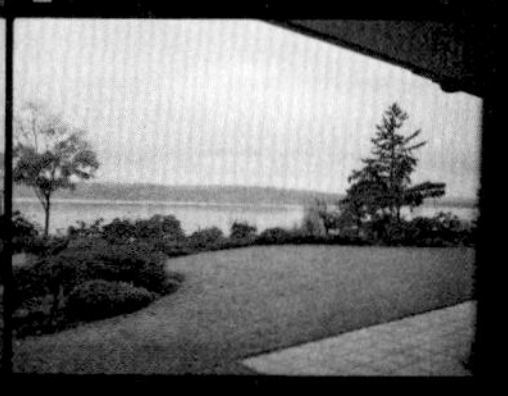
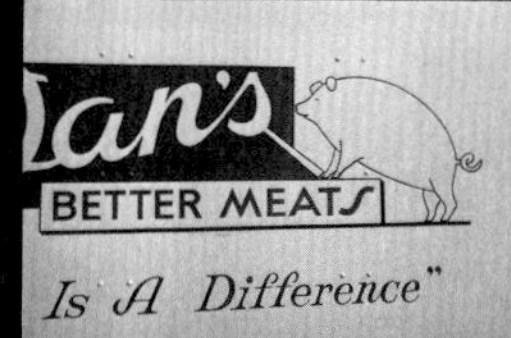

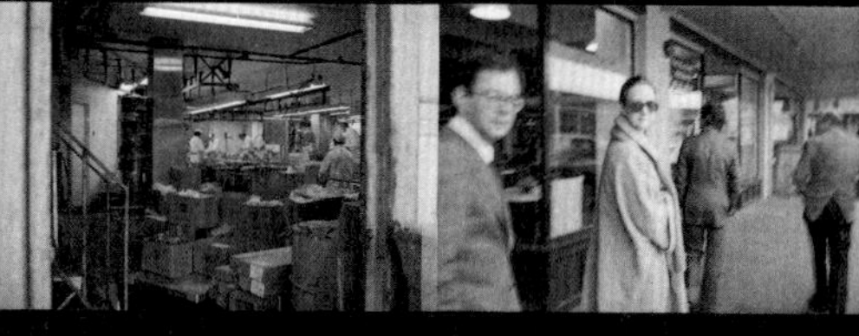
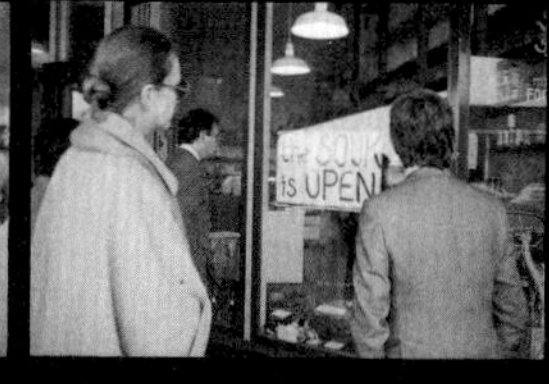
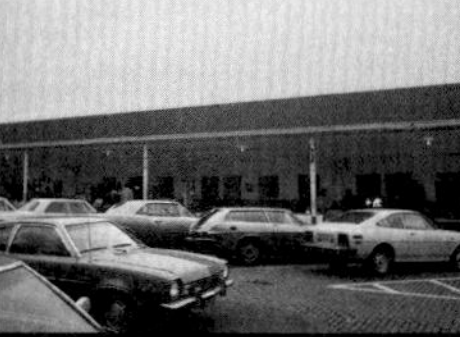
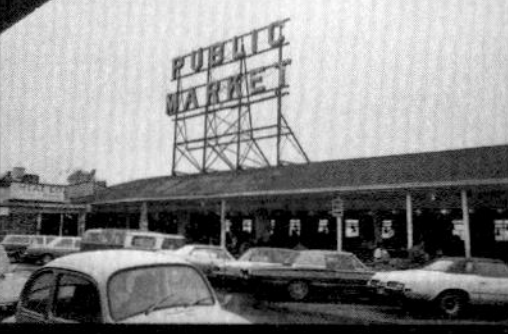

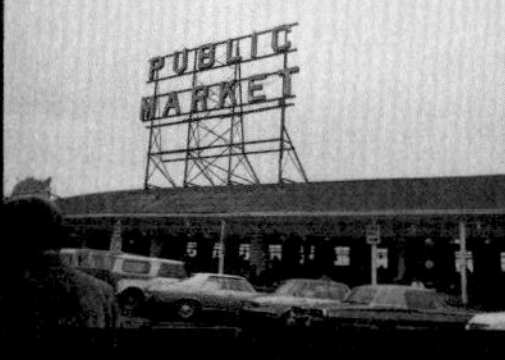

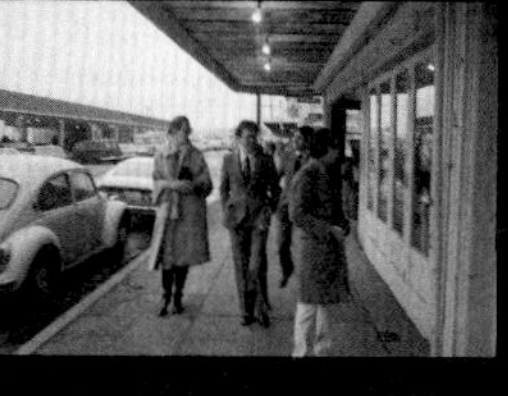
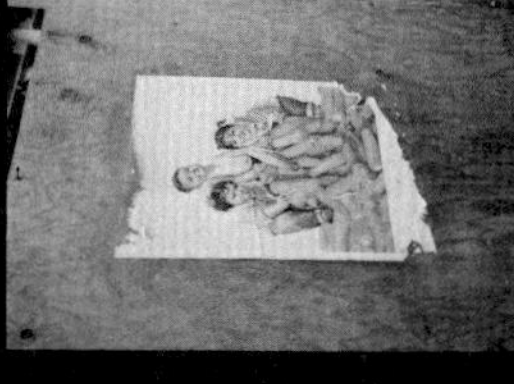
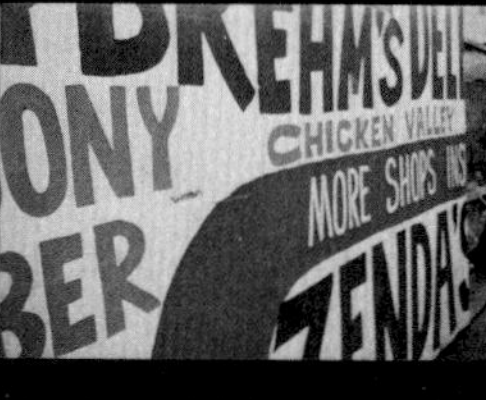

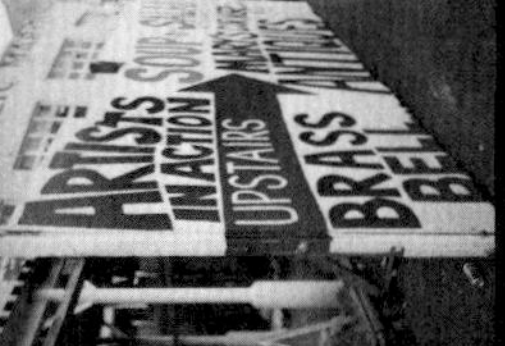

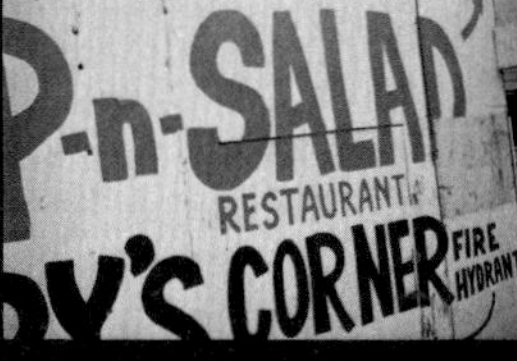

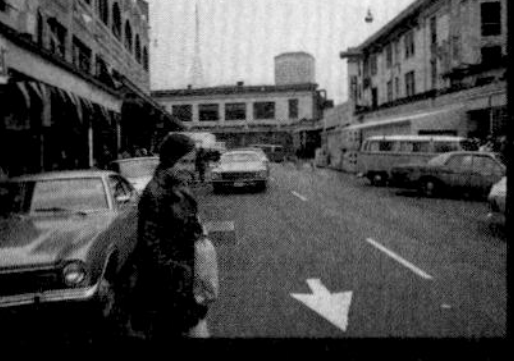
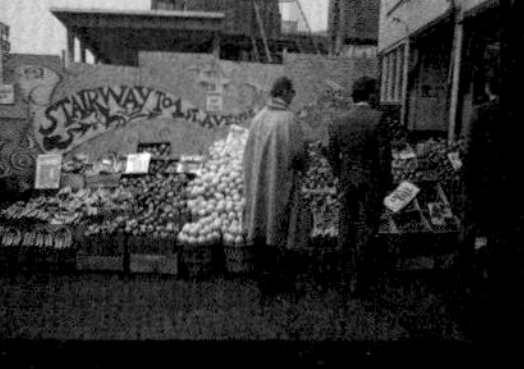
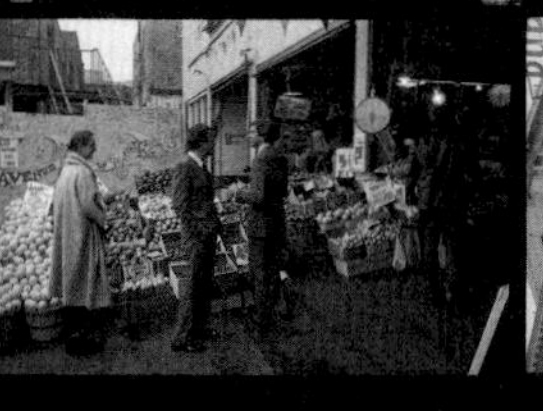
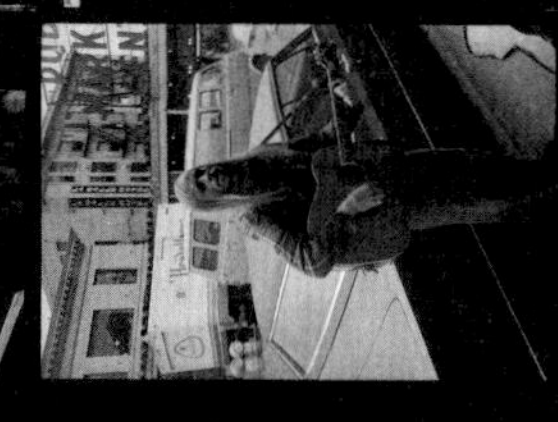
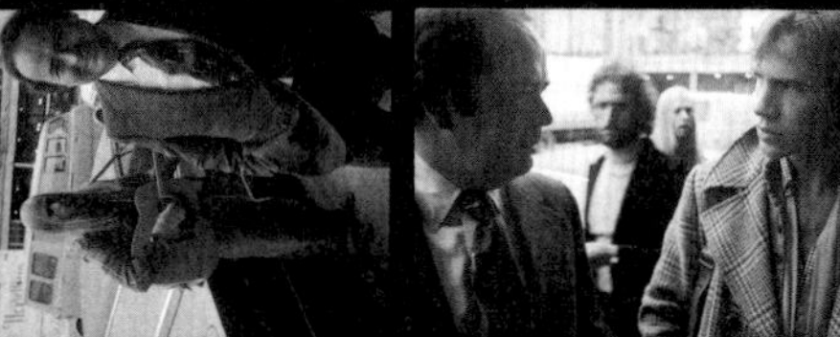
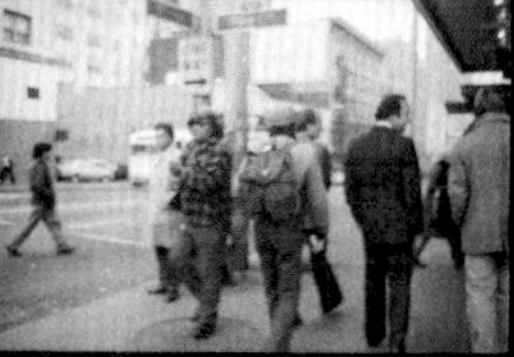
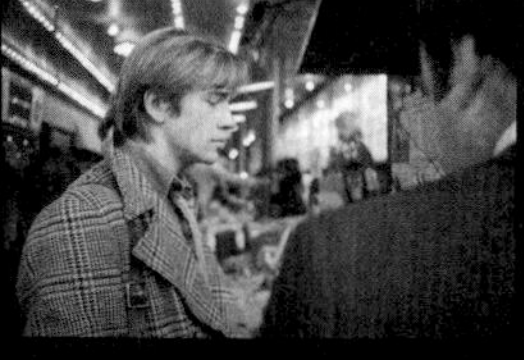
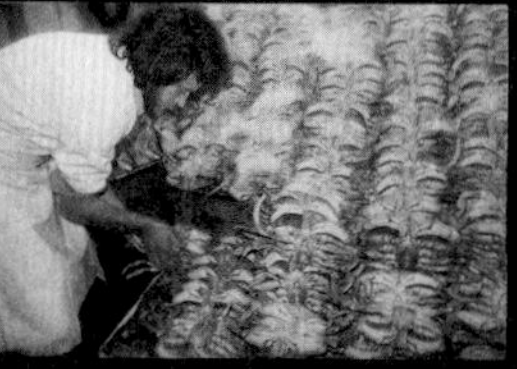
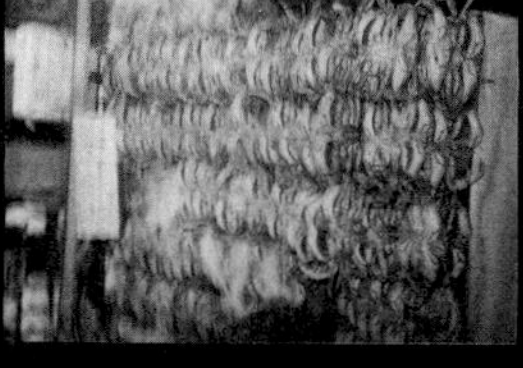
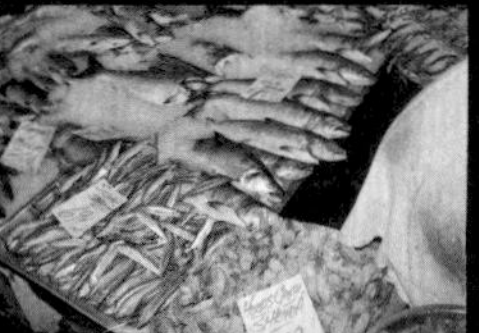
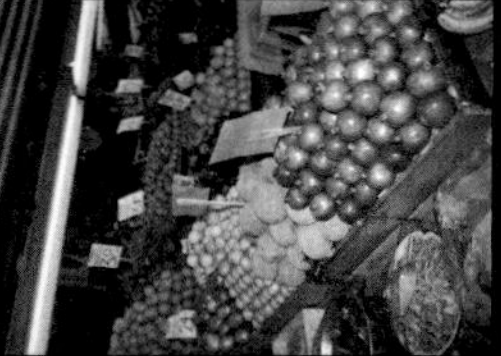
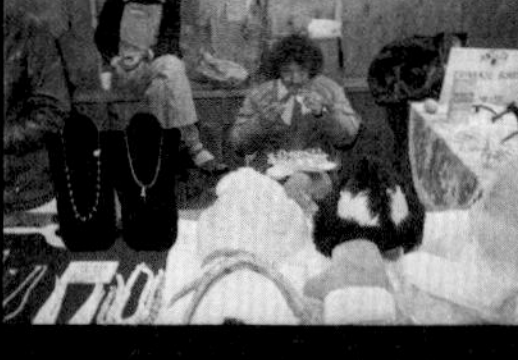
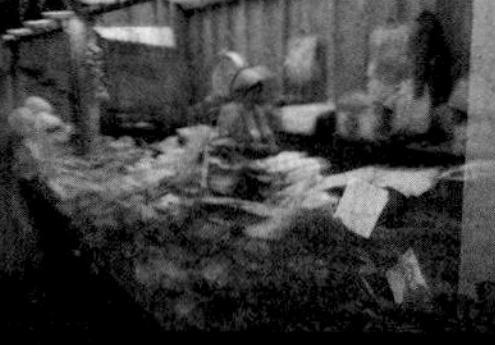
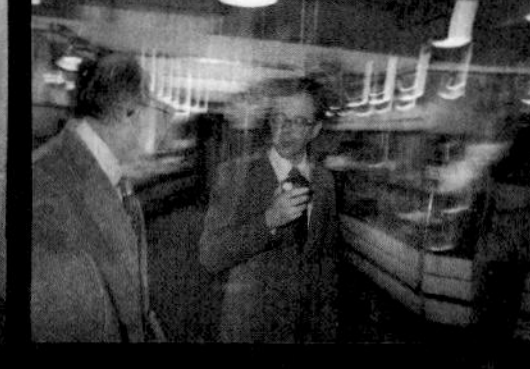
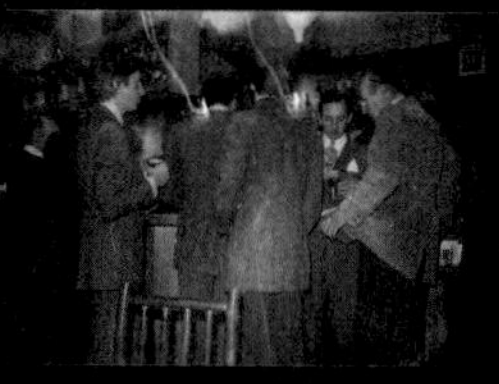
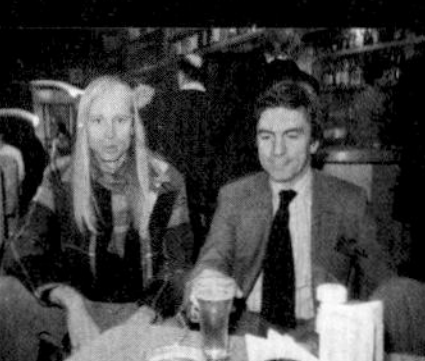
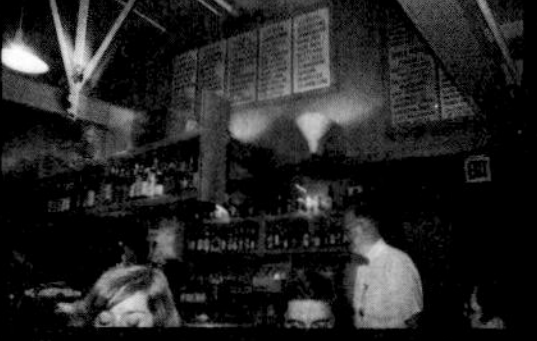
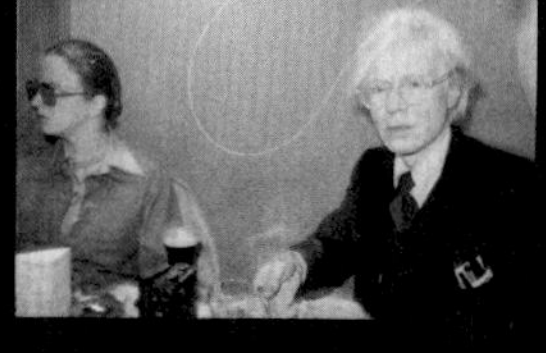
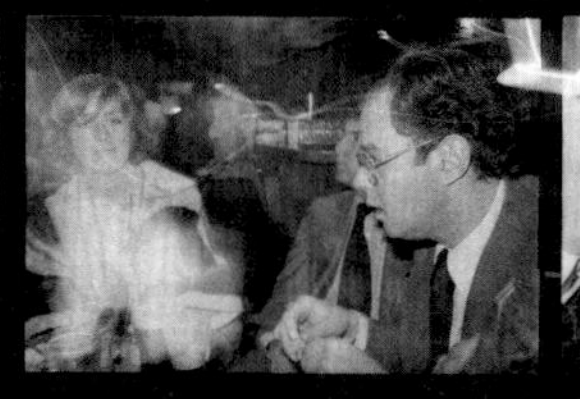
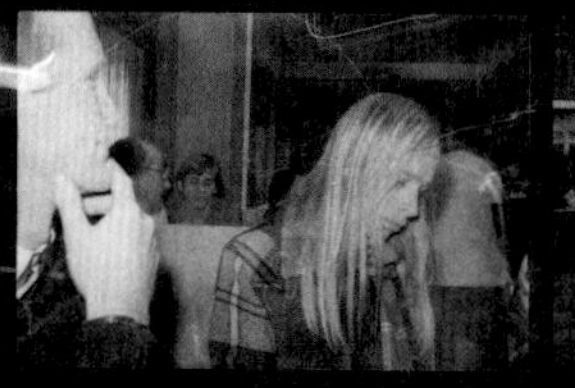
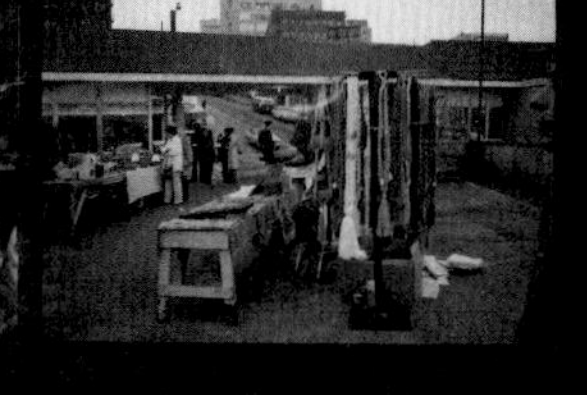

CHRONOLOGY
BUILDING THE COLLECTION, 1970–1982

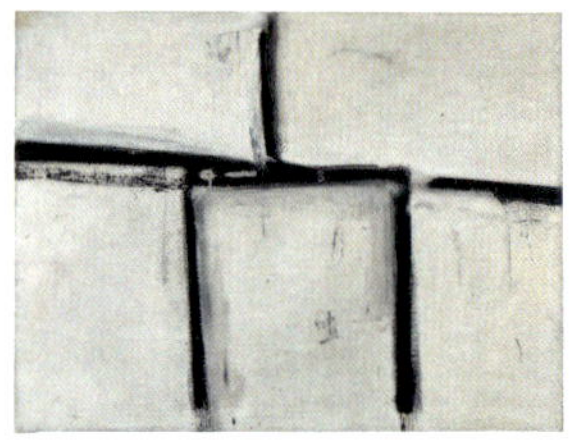

Franz Kline, *Painting No. 11*, 1951
Acquired November 13, 1970

Mark Rothko, *Untitled*, 1963
Acquired May 18, 1972

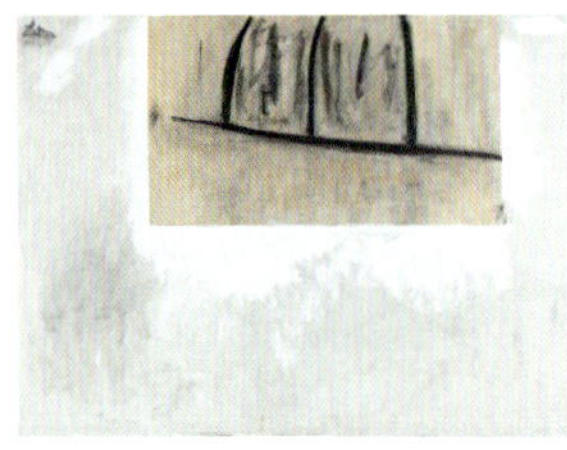

Robert Motherwell, *Before the Day*, 1972
Acquired October 12, 1972

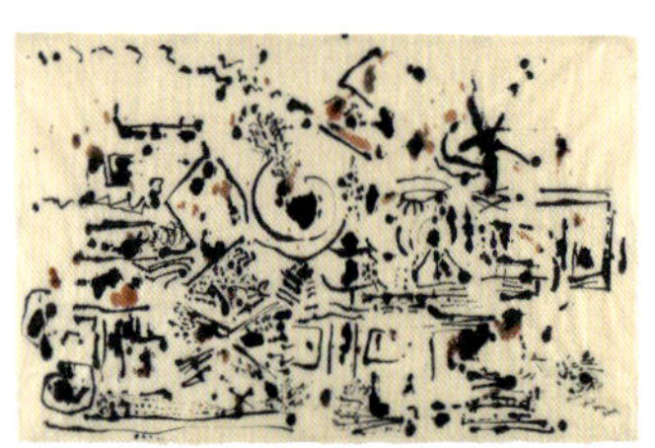

Jackson Pollock, *Untitled*, 1951
Acquired March 29, 1974

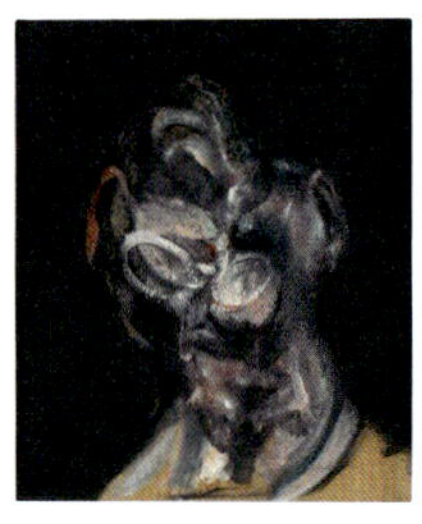

Francis Bacon, *Portrait of Man with Glasses I*, 1963
Acquired October 24, 1974

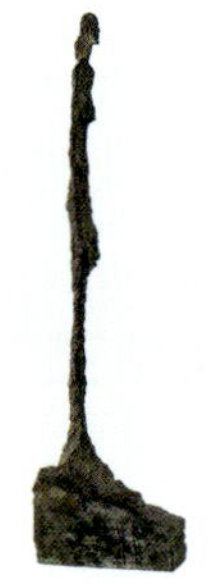

Alberto Giacometti, *Femme de Venise II*, 1956
Acquired January 2, 1975

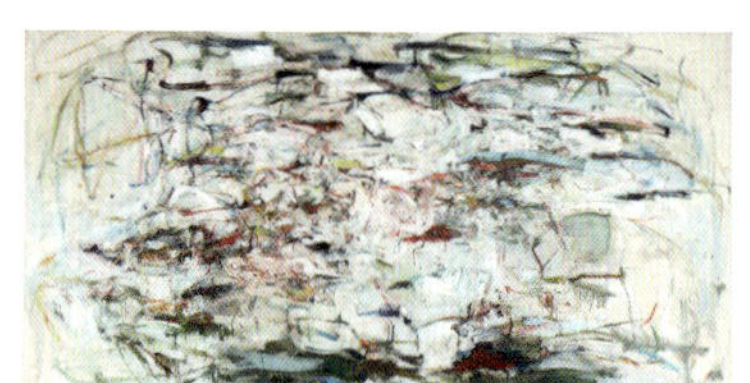

Joan Mitchell, *The Sink*, 1956
Acquired September 12, 1977

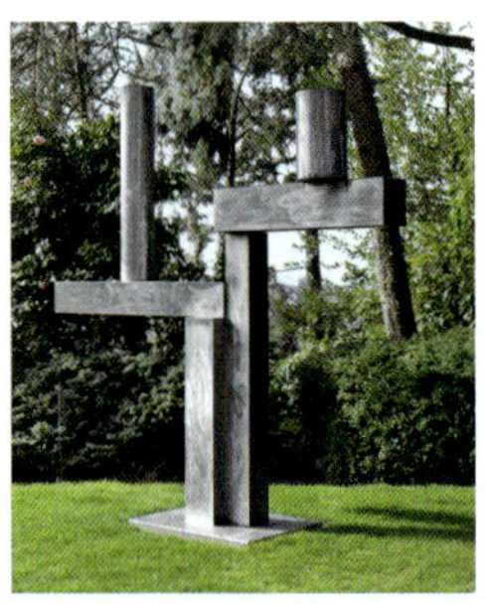

David Smith, *Cubi XXV*, 1965
Acquired February 22, 1978

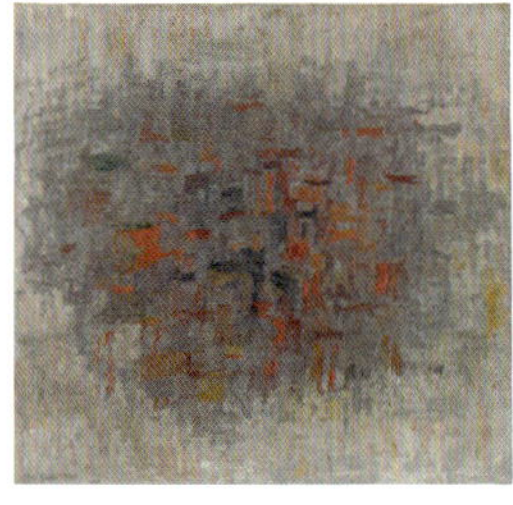

Philip Guston, *To B.W.T.*, 1952
Acquired February 14, 1979

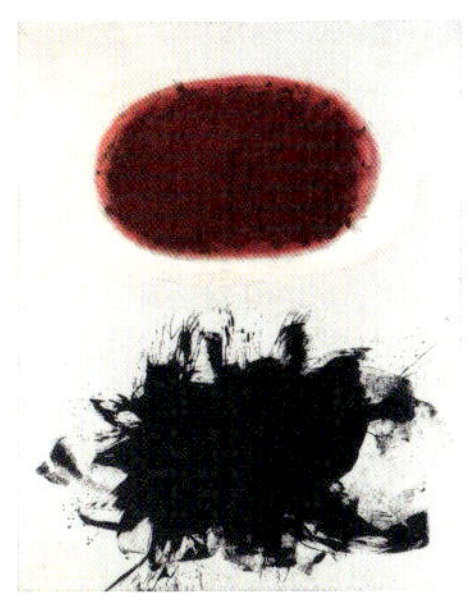

Adolph Gottlieb, *Crimson Spinning #2*, 1959
Acquired December 11, 1972

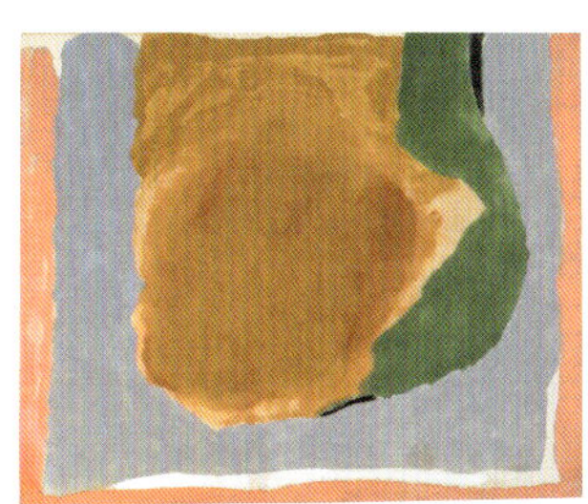

Helen Frankenthaler, *Dawn Shapes*, 1967
Acquired April 26, 1973

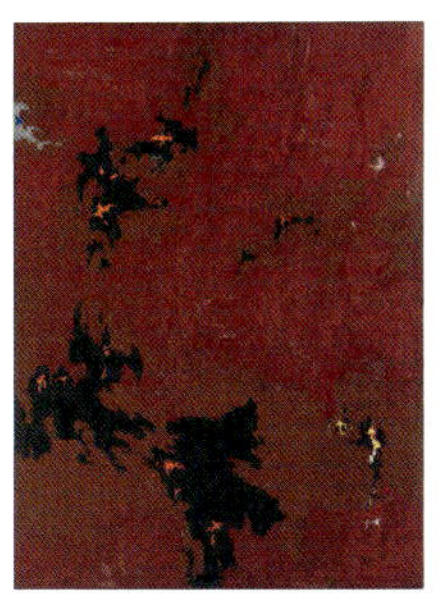

Clyfford Still, PH-338, 1949
Acquired November 10, 1973

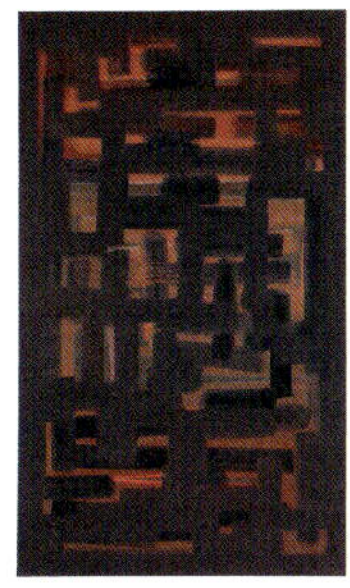

Ad Reinhardt, *Painting, 1950*, 1950
Acquired January 8, 1974

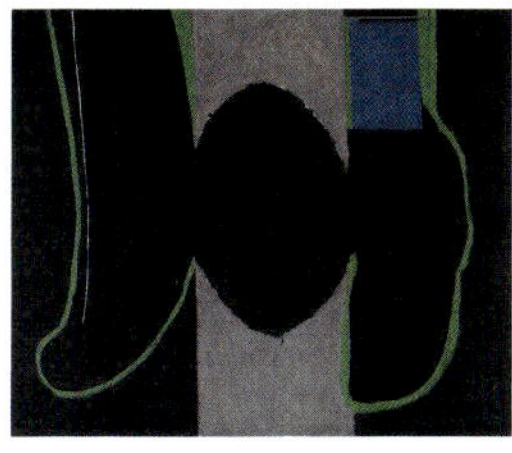

Robert Motherwell, *Irish Elegy*, 1965
Acquired November 7, 1975

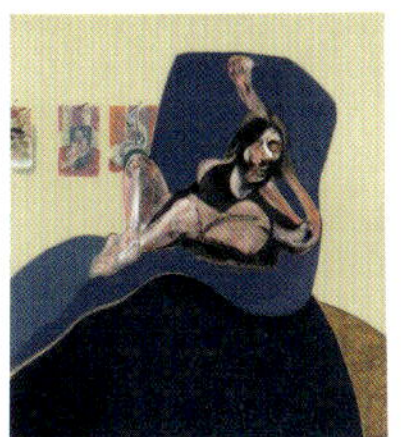

Francis Bacon, *Study for a Portrait*, 1967
Acquired November 20, 1976

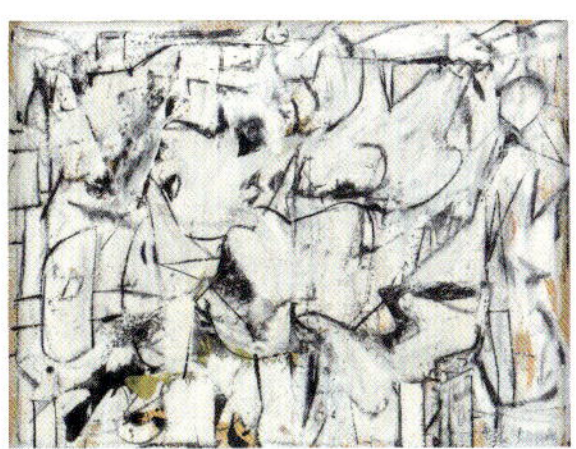

Willem de Kooning, *Town Square*, 1948
Acquired December 6, 1976

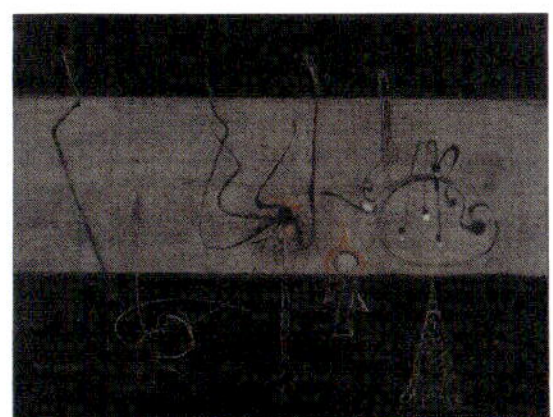

Mark Rothko, *Untitled*, ca. 1945
Acquired November 12, 1980

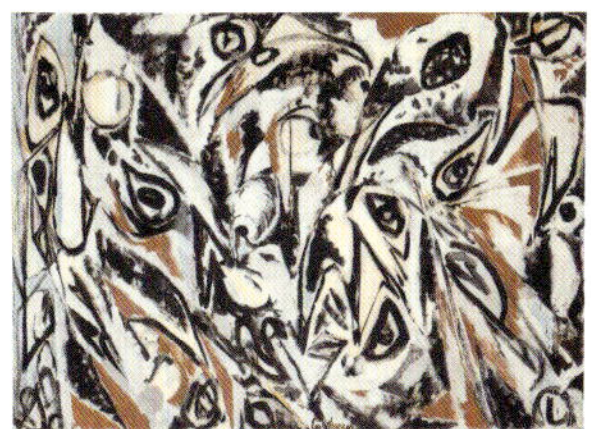

Lee Krasner, *Night Watch*, 1960
Acquired November 19, 1981

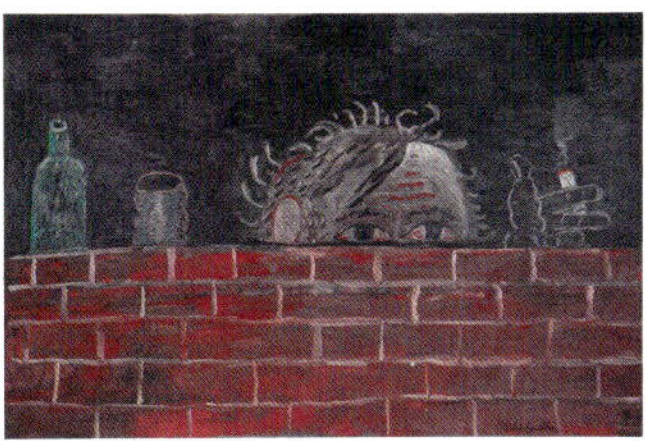

Philip Guston, *The Painter*, 1976
Acquired February 1, 1982

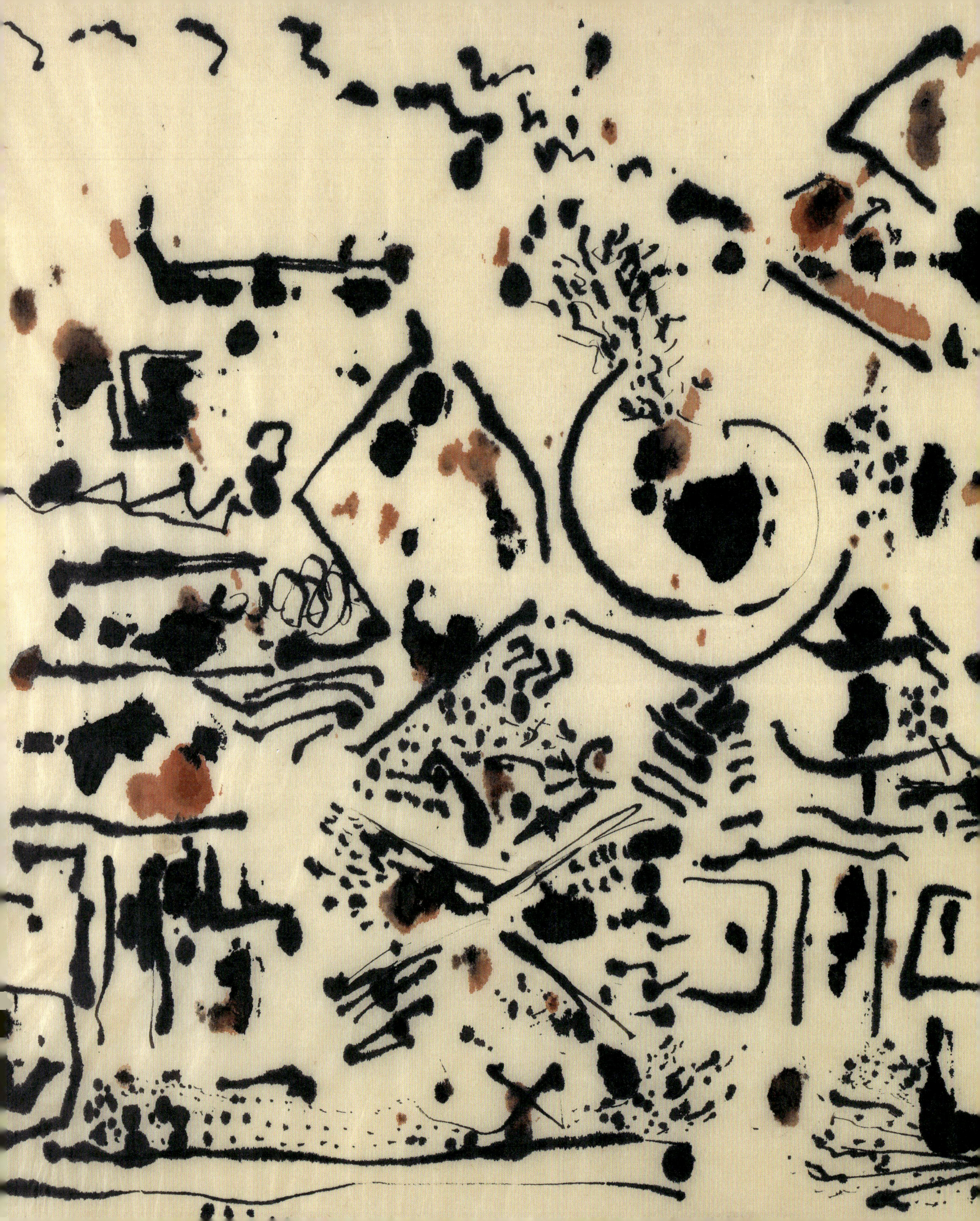

EXHIBITION CHECKLIST

All works are in the collection of the Seattle Art Museum, Gift of the Friday Foundation in honor of Richard E. Lang and Jane Lang Davis, except where noted otherwise.

Francis Bacon

British, b. Ireland (1909–1992)
Portrait of Man with Glasses I, 1963
Oil on canvas
14 1/16 × 12 1/16 in. (35.7 × 30.6 cm)
Dated and inscribed, on reverse: Portrait of Man / With Glasses Version I / 1963
2020.14.6
PLATE 12

Provenance

The artist
[Marlborough Fine Art, London]
Private Collection, New York
[Sotheby Parke-Bernet, New York, *Post-War and Contemporary Art*, Oct. 24–25, 1974, sale no. 3684, lot no. 528]
Acquired from the above by Jane and Richard E. Lang, Seattle, 1974
Friday Foundation, Seattle, 2018
Seattle Art Museum, 2020

Exhibitions

London, England, Marlborough New London Gallery, *Francis Bacon*, July–Aug. 1963
Seattle Art Museum, *The Richard and Jane Lang Collection*, Feb. 2–Apr. 1, 1984; cat. no. 2, pp. 12–13, reproduced (as *Portrait of Man with Glasses*)
New York, Robert Miller Gallery, *". . . a room with a Soutine, Neel, Hockney, Freud, Ensor, Guston, Morley, Bacon, Kossoff, Basquiat and de Kooning,"* Dec. 4–29, 1990
Norwich, England, Sainsbury Centre for Visual Arts, *Francis Bacon in the 1950s*, Sept. 26–Dec. 10, 2006; cat. no. 5. Traveled to Milwaukee Art Museum, Jan. 29–Apr. 15, 2007; Buffalo, Albright-Knox Art Gallery, May 5–July 30, 2007; cat. no. 43, reproduced (as *Man with Glasses*)

Francis Bacon

British, b. Ireland (1909–1992)
Study for a Portrait, 1967
Oil on canvas
61 × 55 in. (155 × 139.8 cm)
Dated and inscribed upper right, on reverse: Study for a Portrait / July 1967
Signed and inscribed on stretcher: PLEASE - KEEP - UNDER - GLASS - / FRAncis Bacon
2020.14.7
PLATE 17

Provenance

The artist
[Marlborough Fine Art, London]
[Marlborough-Gerson Gallery, New York]
Mr. and Mrs. Joseph Bernstein, New Orleans
[David McKee Gallery, New York]
Acquired from the above by Jane and Richard E. Lang, Seattle, 1976
Friday Foundation, Seattle, 2018
Seattle Art Museum, 2020

Exhibitions

Liverpool, England, Walker Art Gallery, *John Moores Liverpool Exhibition 6*, Nov. 23, 1967–Jan. 21, 1968; cat. no. 14 (as *Study for a Portrait*, July 1967)
New York, Marlborough-Gerson Gallery, *Francis Bacon: Recent Paintings*, Nov. 11–Dec. 7, 1968; cat. no. 5, pp. 32–33, reproduced
London, England, Marlborough Fine Art, *A Selection of 20th Century British Art, Cunard Marlborough London Gallery on Board Queen Elizabeth 2*, May 1969
Pittsburgh, Museum of Art, Carnegie Institute, *Pittsburgh International*, Oct. 30, 1970–Jan. 10, 1971; cat. no. 13, p. 16, reproduced
New Orleans Museum of Fine Art, *New Orleans Collects: A Selection of Works of Art Owned by New Orleanians*, Nov. 14, 1971–Jan. 9, 1972; cat. no. 377, reproduced
Four Contemporary Masters: Giacometti, Bacon, de Kooning, Dubuffet. Organized by the International Program of the Museum of Modern Art, New York, under the auspices of the International Council at the Museum of Modern Art; traveled to Caracas, Venezuela, Museo de Bellas Artes, Apr.–May 1973; Bogotá, Colombia, Museo de Arte Moderno, May 30–June 28, 1973; Mexico City, Mexico, Museo de Arte Moderno, July 19–Aug. 24, 1973; São Paulo, Brazil, Museu de Arte de São Paulo, Sept. 13–Oct. 7, 1973; Río de Janeiro, Brazil, Museu de Arte Moderna, Oct. 15–Nov. 4, 1973
Seattle Art Museum, *The Richard and Jane Lang Collection*, Feb. 2–Apr. 1, 1984; cat. no. 3, pp. 14–15, reproduced
Washington, DC, Hirshhorn Museum and Sculpture Garden, *Francis Bacon*, Oct. 12, 1989–Jan. 7, 1990. Traveled to Los Angeles, Los Angeles County Museum of Art, Feb. 11–Apr. 29, 1990; New York, Museum of Modern Art, May 24–Aug. 28, 1990; cat. no. 32, reproduced
Seattle Art Museum, *SAM at 75: Building a Collection for Seattle*, May 5–Sept. 9, 2007

Helen Frankenthaler

American (1928–2011)

Dawn Shapes, 1967

Acrylic on canvas

Signed and dated lower right: Frankenthaler / '67

77¼ × 94½ in. (196 × 240 cm)

2020.14.5

PLATE 16

Provenance

The artist

[Locksley Shea Gallery, Minneapolis]

Acquired from the above by Jane and Richard E. Lang, Seattle, 1973

Friday Foundation, Seattle, 2018

Seattle Art Museum, 2020

Exhibitions

Montreal, Québec, Galerie Godard Lefort, *Helen Frankenthaler*, Feb. 13–Mar. 4, 1971

Minneapolis, Locksley Shea Gallery, *Helen Frankenthaler*, Jan. 15–Feb. 3, 1972

Seattle Art Museum, *American Art: Third Quarter Century*, Aug. 22–Oct. 14, 1973; cat. no. 22, pp. 67–70, reproduced

Seattle, Henry Art Gallery, University of Washington, *Art in America: Washington Collections—Color, Color, Color: American Painting*, Jan. 26–Mar. 7, 1982

Seattle Art Museum, *The Richard and Jane Lang Collection*, Feb. 2–Apr. 1, 1984; cat. no. 9, pp. 22–23, reproduced

Tacoma Art Museum, *What Is Real? American Art 1960 to 1975*, Mar. 19–June 19, 1994

Pullman, Museum of Art, Washington State University, *Art and Context: The '50s and '60s*, Sept. 29–Dec. 15, 2006; no cat. no., p. 68, reproduced

Alberto Giacometti

Swiss (1901–1966)

Femme de Venise II, 1956

Bronze

Overall: 47⅜ × 5¾ × 12⅞ in. (120.2 × 14.8 × 32.7 cm)

Edition 6/6

Signed and inscribed on base: Alberto Giacometti 6/6

2020.14.8

PLATE 9

Provenance

The artist

[Galerie Maeght, Paris]

[Sidney Janis Gallery, New York]

Acquired from the above by Jane and Richard E. Lang, Seattle, 1975

Friday Foundation, Seattle, 2018

Seattle Art Museum, 2020

Exhibitions

New York, Sidney Janis Gallery, *Picasso to Pollock: Two Generations*, 1967; cat. no. 37, reproduced

New York, Sidney Janis Gallery, *Giacometti-Dubuffet*, 1968; cat. no. 5, reproduced

New York, Sidney Janis Gallery, *Twentieth Century European Art*, 1970; cat. no. 41, reproduced

Seattle Art Museum, *Alberto Giacometti: Sculptor and Draftsman*, July 27–Sept. 3, 1978. Organized by the American Federation of Arts; traveled to Purchase, Neuberger Museum, State University of New York; Wichita, Kansas, Edwin A. Ulrich Museum of Art, Wichita State University; Sarasota, Florida, John and Mable Ringling Museum of Art; Austin, University Art Museum, University of Texas; Denver Art Museum; Columbus, Ohio, Columbus Gallery of Fine Arts; Oklahoma City, Oklahoma Art Center; Jacksonville, Florida, Jacksonville Art Museum; Newark Museum (*Femme de Venise II* shown in Seattle only)

Seattle Art Museum, *The Richard and Jane Lang Collection*, Feb. 2–Apr. 1, 1984; cat. no. 11, p. 25, reproduced

Los Angeles, David Tunkl Fine Art, *Definitive Moments of the 20th Century*, Sept. 20–Oct. 8, 2001

Seattle Art Museum, *SAM at 75: Building a Collection for Seattle*, May 5–Sept. 9, 2007

Adolph Gottlieb

American (1903–1974)

Crimson Spinning #2, 1959

Oil on canvas

90 × 72 in. (228.7 × 182.9 cm)

Signed, dated, and inscribed lower left, on reverse: "CRIMSON SPINNING #2" / Adolph Gottlieb / 1959 / 90" × 72"

2020.14.9

PLATE 10

Provenance

The artist

[Galerie Rive Droit, Paris]

Private Collection, Paris

Mr. and Mrs. Harry Sherwood, Beverly Hills, via 1965 auction

[Marlborough Gallery, New York]

Acquired from the above by Jane and Richard E. Lang, Seattle, 1972

Friday Foundation, Seattle, 2018

Seattle Art Museum, 2020

Exhibitions

Los Angeles, Los Angeles County Museum of Art, *New York School: The First Generation, Paintings of the 1940s and 1950s*, June 16–Aug. 1, 1965; cat. no. 35, reproduced p. 98

Seattle Art Museum, *American Art: Third Quarter Century*, Aug. 22–Oct. 14, 1973; cat. no. 23, pp. 14, 98, reproduced

Seattle Art Museum, *The Richard and Jane Lang Collection*, Feb. 2–Apr. 1, 1984; cat. no. 13, p. 27, reproduced

Seattle Art Museum, *SAM at 75: Building a Collection for Seattle*, May 5–Sept. 9, 2007

Philip Guston

American, b. Canada (1913–1980)
To B.W.T. [previously known as *Painting No. 3*], 1952
Oil on canvas
48 × 51 in. (122 × 129.2 cm)
Signed lower left: Philip Guston
Dated and inscribed upper right, on reverse: No. 3, 1952
Signed and inscribed upper left, on reverse: Philip Guston / 112 E. 12 St. / N.Y.C.
2020.14.10
PLATE 7

Provenance

The artist
[Egan Gallery, New York]
[Sidney Janis Gallery, New York]
Mr. and Mrs. Leonard M. Brown, Springfield, Massachusetts
[Acquavella Contemporary Art, New York]
Acquired from the above by Jane and Richard E. Lang, Seattle, 1979
Friday Foundation, Seattle, 2018
Seattle Art Museum, 2020

Exhibitions

Baltimore Museum of Art, *Abstract Expressionists*, Mar. 3–29, 1953; no cat. no., reproduced (as *No. 3*)
Iowa City, Art Building and Iowa Memorial Union, State University of Iowa, *Then and Now: American Painting in the 1930s and 1950s*, June 13–July 31, 1954; cat. no. 40, reproduced (as *Painting No. 3*)
Utica, New York, Munson-Williams-Proctor Arts Institute Museum of Art, *Italy Rediscovered: An Exhibition of Work by American Painters in Italy since World War II*, Mar. 6–27, 1955; cat. no. 22, reproduced (as *Painting No. 3*)
New York, Sidney Janis Gallery, *Philip Guston: Recent Paintings*, Feb. 6–Mar. 3, 1956
New York, Museum of Modern Art, *12 Americans*, May 30–Sept. 8, 1956; no cat. no., reproduced p. 37
New York, Solomon R. Guggenheim Museum, *Philip Guston*, May 3–July 1, 1962. Traveled to Amsterdam, the Netherlands, Stedelijk Museum, Sept. 20–Oct. 15, 1962; London, England, Whitechapel Gallery, Jan. 16–Feb. 17, 1963; Brussels, Belgium, Palais des Beaux-Arts, Mar. 1–24, 1963; Los Angeles, Los Angeles County Museum of Art, May 22–June 30, 1963; cat. no. 18, pp. 23, 41, reproduced p. 56
Waltham, Massachusetts, Rose Art Museum, Brandeis University, *Philip Guston, A Selective Retrospective Exhibition: 1945–1965*, Feb. 27–Mar. 27, 1966; cat. no. 7
New York, Metropolitan Museum of Art, *New York Painting and Sculpture: 1940–1970*, Oct. 18, 1969–Feb. 1, 1970; cat. no. 109, reproduced p. 170
New York, Acquavella Contemporary Art, [group show], Dec. 1978–Jan. 1979
San Francisco Museum of Modern Art, *Philip Guston*, May 15–June 29, 1980. Traveled to Washington, DC, Corcoran Gallery of Art, July 20–Sept. 9, 1980; Museum of Contemporary Art Chicago, Nov. 12, 1980–Jan. 11, 1981; Denver Art Museum, Feb. 25–Apr. 26, 1981; New York, Whitney Museum of American Art, June 24–Sept. 13, 1981; cat. no. 20, p. 57, reproduced pl. 10
Seattle Art Museum, *The Richard and Jane Lang Collection*, Feb. 2–Apr. 1, 1984; cat. no. 14, pp. 28–29, reproduced
Northampton, Massachusetts, Smith College Museum of Art, *Dorothy C. Miller: With an Eye to American Art*, Apr. 19–June 16, 1985; cat. no. 22
New York, David McKee Gallery, *Philip Guston: Paintings from the Fifties*, Apr. 22–June 3, 1995; cat. no. 6, reproduced
Bonn, Germany, Kunstmuseum Bonn, *Philip Guston: Gemälde 1947–1979*, Sept. 2–Nov. 1, 1999. Traveled to Stuttgart, Germany, Kunstverein Stuttgart, and Ottawa, Ontario, National Gallery of Canada (*To B.W.T.* shown in Bonn only); no cat. no., reproduced p. 69
Modern Art Museum of Fort Worth, *Philip Guston*, Mar. 30–June 8, 2003. Traveled to San Francisco Museum of Modern Art, June 28–Sept. 27, 2003; New York, Metropolitan Museum of Art, Oct. 27, 2003–Jan. 4, 2004; London, England, Royal Academy of Arts, Jan. 24–Apr. 12, 2004; cat. no. 31, p. 39, reproduced pl. 32

Philip Guston

American, b. Canada (1913–1980)
The Painter, 1976
Oil on canvas
74 × 116 in. (188 × 294.6 cm)
Signed lower right: Philip Guston
2020.14.11
PLATE 19

Provenance

The artist
Estate of the artist
[David McKee Gallery, New York]
Acquired from the above by Jane and Richard E. Lang, Seattle, 1982
Friday Foundation, Seattle, 2018
Seattle Art Museum, 2020

Exhibitions

Waltham, Massachusetts, Rose Art Museum, Brandeis University, *Aspects of the 70s: Mavericks*, May 22–June 29, 1980; no cat. no., reproduced
New York, David McKee Gallery, [inaugural exhibition], Oct.–Nov. 1981
Seattle Art Museum, *The Richard and Jane Lang Collection*, Feb. 2–Apr. 1, 1984; cat. no. 16, pp. 31–32, reproduced
Berlin, Germany, Martin-Gropius-Bau, *American Art in the 20th Century: Painting and Sculpture 1913–1993*, May 8–July 25, 1993. Traveled to London, England, Royal Academy of Arts, Sept. 16–Dec. 12, 1993; cat. no. 227, reproduced
Modern Art Museum of Fort Worth, *Philip Guston*, Mar. 30–June 8, 2003. Traveled to San Francisco Museum of Modern Art, June 28–Sept. 17, 2003; New York, Metropolitan Museum of Art, Oct. 27, 2003–Jan. 4, 2004; London, England, Royal Academy of Arts, Jan. 24–Apr. 12, 2004; cat. no. 103, p. 63, reproduced pl. 103
Seattle Art Museum, *SAM at 75: Building a Collection for Seattle*, May 5–Sept. 9, 2007

Franz Kline

American (1910–1962)
Painting No. 11, 1951
Oil on canvas
61 × 82¼ in. (155 × 208.9 cm)
Signed and inscribed upper right, on reverse:
FRANZ KLINE / EGAN GALLERY / N.Y.C
2020.14.12
PLATE 5

Provenance

The artist
Estate of the artist
[Marlborough-Gerson Gallery, New York]
Acquired from the above by Jane and Richard E. Lang, Seattle, 1970
Friday Foundation, Seattle, 2018
Seattle Art Museum, 2020

Exhibitions

New York, Egan Gallery, *Franz Kline*, 1951
New York, Whitney Museum of American Art, *Franz Kline, 1910–1962*, Oct. 1–Nov. 24, 1968. Traveled to Dallas Museum of Fine Arts, Dec. 17, 1968–Jan. 26, 1969; San Francisco Museum of Art, Feb. 21–Mar. 30, 1969; Museum of Contemporary Art Chicago, Apr. 12–May 25, 1969; cat. no. 47
Seattle Art Museum, *American Art: Third Quarter Century*, Aug. 22–Oct. 14, 1973; cat. no. 33, pp. 18, 99, reproduced
Washington, DC, National Collection of Fine Arts, Smithsonian Institution, *America as Art*, Apr. 30–Nov. 7, 1976; cat. no. 328, reproduced p. 274
Seattle Art Museum, *Franz Kline: The Color Abstractions*, Sept. 27–Nov. 25, 1979. Organized and exhibited by the Phillips Collection, Washington, DC; traveled to Houston, Institute for the Arts, Rice University, and Los Angeles, Los Angeles County Museum of Art (*Painting No. 11* shown in Seattle only)
Seattle Art Museum, *The Richard and Jane Lang Collection*, Feb. 2–Apr. 1, 1984; cat. no. 25, pp. 38–39, reproduced
Houston, Menil Collection, *Franz Kline: Black and White, 1950–1961*, Sept. 9–Nov. 27, 1994. Traveled to New York, Whitney Museum of American Art, Dec. 16, 1994–Mar. 5, 1995; Museum of Contemporary Art Chicago, Mar. 25–June 4, 1995; cat. no. 6, p. 112, reproduced p. 41
Seattle Art Museum, *SAM at 75: Building a Collection for Seattle*, May 5–Sept. 9, 2007

Willem de Kooning

American, b. the Netherlands (1904–1997)
Town Square, 1948
Oil on paper mounted on Masonite
17⅜ × 23¾ in. (44.2 × 60.3 cm)
2020.14.2
Signed lower right: de Kooning
PLATE 2

Provenance

The artist
Leo Castelli, New York
Mr. and Mrs. Ben Heller, New York
Acquired from the above by Jane and Richard E. Lang, Seattle, 1976
Friday Foundation, Seattle, 2018
Seattle Art Museum, 2020

Exhibitions

Arts Club of Chicago, *Ben Shahn, Willem de Kooning, Jackson Pollock*, Oct. 2–27, 1951; cat. no. 22
East Hampton, New York, Guild Hall, *Fourth Annual Invitation Exhibition by Regional Artists*, July 24–Aug. 12, 1952
Venice, Italy, XXVII Venice Biennale, United States Pavilion, *2 Pitorri: de Kooning, Shahn; 3 Scultori: Lachaise, Lassaw, Smith*, June 19–Oct. 17, 1954. Organized by the Museum of Modern Art, New York; cat. no. 65, p. 395 (as *La piazza della città*)
New York, Whitney Museum of American Art, *The Museum and Its Friends: Eighteen Living American Artists Selected by the Friends of the Whitney Museum*, Mar. 5–Apr. 12, 1959; no cat. no., p. 47 (as *Village Square*)
Cleveland Museum of Art, *Paths of Abstract Art*, Oct. 5–Nov. 13, 1960; cat. no. 94, reproduced (as *Village Square*)
The Collection of Mr. and Mrs. Ben Heller. Organized by the Museum of Modern Art, New York; traveled to Art Institute of Chicago (as *The Ben Heller Collection of Paintings of the School of New York*), Sept. 22–Oct. 22, 1961; Baltimore Museum of Art, Dec. 3–31, 1961; Cincinnati, Contemporary Arts Center, Jan. 22–Feb. 25, 1962; Cleveland Museum of Art, Mar. 13–Apr. 10, 1962; San Francisco, California Palace of the Legion of Honor, Apr. 30–June 3, 1962; Portland, Oregon, Portland Art Museum, June 15–July 22, 1962; Los Angeles, Los Angeles County Museum of Art, Sept. 5–Oct. 14, 1962; no cat. no., reproduced (as *Village Square*)
Willem de Kooning. Organized by the Museum of Modern Art, New York; traveled to Amsterdam, the Netherlands, Stedelijk Museum, Sept. 19–Nov. 19, 1968; London, England, Tate Gallery, Dec. 5, 1968–Jan. 26, 1969; New York, Museum of Modern Art, Mar. 5–Apr. 26, 1969; Art Institute of Chicago, May 17–July 6, 1969; Los Angeles, Los Angeles County Museum of Art, July 29–Sept. 14, 1969; cat. no. 34, pp. 62–63, reproduced
Pittsburgh, Museum of Art, Carnegie Institute, *Willem de Kooning, Pittsburgh International Series*, Oct. 26, 1979–Jan. 6, 1980; cat. no. 10, p. 41, reproduced (award shared with Eduardo Chillida)
New York, Whitney Museum of American Art, *Willem de Kooning: Drawings, Paintings, Sculpture*, Dec. 7, 1983–Feb. 26, 1984. Traveled to Berlin, Germany, Akademie der Künste, and Paris, France, Musée National d'Art Moderne (*Town Square* shown in New York only); cat. no. 169, reproduced p. 166
Seattle Art Museum, *The Richard and Jane Lang Collection*, Feb. 2–Apr. 1, 1984; cat. no. 5, pp. 17–18, reproduced
Seattle Art Museum, *Willem de Kooning in Seattle: Selected Works from 1943 to 1985 in Public and Private Collections*, Nov. 2, 1995–Mar. 3, 1996; no cat. no., reproduced (as *Townsquare*)
Seattle Art Museum, *SAM at 75: Building a Collection for Seattle*, May 5–Sept. 9, 2007
New York, Museum of Modern Art, *Willem de Kooning: A Retrospective*, Sept. 18, 2011–Jan. 9, 2012; no cat. no., reproduced pp. 209, 244, figs. 1 and 9

Lee Krasner

American (1908–1984)
Night Watch, 1960
Oil on canvas
70 × 99¼ in. (177.8 × 252.1 cm)
Signed bottom center: Lee Krasner
2020.14.4
PLATE 11

Provenance
The artist
[Howard Wise Gallery, New York]
[Pace Gallery, New York]
[Robert Miller Gallery, New York]
Acquired from the above by Jane and Richard E. Lang, Seattle, 1981
Friday Foundation, Seattle, 2018
Seattle Art Museum, 2020

Exhibitions
New York, Howard Wise Gallery, *Exhibition of Recent Paintings by Lee Krasner*, Nov. 15–Dec. 10, 1960
South Hadley, Massachusetts, Dwight Art Memorial, Mount Holyoke College, *Women Artists in America Today*, Apr. 10–30, 1962; cat. no. 29, reproduced
New York, Pace Gallery, *Lee Krasner Paintings, 1959–1962*, Feb. 3–Mar. 10, 1979; no cat. no., reproduced
Roslyn Harbor, New York, Nassau County Museum of Fine Art, *The Abstract Expressionists and Their Precursors*, Jan. 17–Mar. 22, 1981; no cat. no., pp. 52, 54, reproduced fig. 54
Museum of Fine Arts Houston, *Lee Krasner: A Retrospective*, Nov. 28, 1983–Jan. 8, 1984. Traveled to San Francisco Museum of Modern Art, Feb. 9–Apr. 1, 1984; Norfolk, Virginia, Chrysler Museum, Apr. 26–June 18, 1984; Phoenix Art Museum, Aug. 23–Oct. 7, 1984; New York, Museum of Modern Art, Dec. 20, 1984–Feb. 12, 1985 (*Night Watch* shown in Houston, Norfolk, Phoenix, and New York only)
Seattle Art Museum, *The Richard and Jane Lang Collection*, Feb. 2–Apr. 1, 1984; cat. no. 29, pp. 42–43, reproduced
Tacoma Art Museum, *What Is Real? American Art 1960 to 1975*, Mar. 19–June 19, 1994; no cat. no. (as *Nightwatch)*
Seattle Art Museum, *Seattle Collects Paintings: Works in Private Collections*, May 22–Sept. 7, 1997; no cat. no. (as *Nightwatch*)
Lee Krasner. Organized by Independent Curators International, New York; traveled to Los Angeles, Los Angeles County Museum of Art, Oct. 10, 1999–Jan. 2, 2000; Des Moines Art Center, Feb. 26–May 21, 2000; Akron Art Museum, June 10–Aug. 27, 2000; Brooklyn Museum of Art, Oct. 6, 2000–Jan. 7, 2001; no cat. no., pp. 159, 164, 218, reproduced pl. 74
Seattle Art Museum, *Elles: SAM: Singular Works by Seminal Women Artists*, Oct. 6, 2012–Feb. 17, 2013

Joan Mitchell

American (1925–1992)
The Sink, 1956
Oil on canvas
54⅝ × 111¾ in. (138.7 × 283.9 cm)
Signed lower right: J. Mitchell
2020.14.15
PLATE 8

Provenance
The artist
[Stable Gallery, New York]
[Ferus Gallery, Los Angeles]
Mr. and Mrs. Abe Adler, Los Angeles
[Adler Gallery, Los Angeles]
Acquired from the above by Jane and Richard E. Lang, Seattle, 1977
Friday Foundation, Seattle, 2018
Seattle Art Museum, 2020

Exhibitions
New York, Stable Gallery, *Joan Mitchell*, Mar. 3–22, 1957
Saint Louis, Givens Hall Gallery, Washington University, *Thirteen American Painters*, 1958
Seattle, Henry Art Gallery, University of Washington, *Art in America: Washington Collections—An American Tradition: Abstraction*, Dec. 4, 1981–Jan. 17, 1982
Seattle Art Museum, *The Richard and Jane Lang Collection*, Feb. 2–Apr. 1, 1984; cat. no. 31, pp. 44–45, reproduced
Pullman, Museum of Art, Washington State University, *Art and Context: The '50s and '60s*, Sept. 29–Dec. 15, 2006; no cat. no., p. 38, reproduced
Seattle Art Museum, *Big Picture: Art after 1945*, July 23, 2016–May 16, 2021 (*The Sink* on view Nov. 20, 2018–May 16, 2021)

Robert Motherwell
American (1915–1991)
Irish Elegy, 1965
Acrylic on canvas
69½ × 83¾ in. (176.5 × 212.8 cm)
Signed lower left: RM
2020.14.1
PLATE 14

Provenance
The artist
[Knoedler Contemporary Art, New York]
Acquired from the above by Jane and Richard E. Lang, Seattle, 1975
Friday Foundation, Seattle, 2018
Seattle Art Museum, 2020

Exhibitions
Providence Arts Club, *Critics' Choice: Art since World War II*, Mar. 31–Apr. 24, 1965; cat. no. 48, reproduced p. 35
New York, Museum of Modern Art, *Robert Motherwell*, Sept. 30–Nov. 28, 1965. Traveled to Amsterdam, the Netherlands, Stedelijk Museum, Jan. 7–Feb. 27, 1966; London, England, Whitechapel Art Gallery, Mar. 18–Apr. 17, 1966; Brussels, Belgium, Palais des Beaux-Arts, May 5–June 5, 1966; Essen, Germany, Museum Folkwang, July 2–Aug. 14, 1966; Turin, Italy, Museo Civico, Galleria d'Arte Moderna, Sept. 27–Oct. 30, 1966; cat. no. 87, reproduced p. 71
San Francisco Museum of Art, *Robert Motherwell: Works on Paper*, Feb. 20–Mar. 18, 1967. Organized by the Museum of Modern Art, New York; traveled to Durham, North Carolina, Duke University; Minneapolis, University of Minnesota; Saint Joseph, Minnesota, College of St. Benedict; Salt Lake City, University of Utah; San Antonio, White Memorial Museum; Tampa, Library Gallery, University of South Florida; Houston, Contemporary Arts Association; Baltimore Museum of Art; Bloomington, Art Museum, Indiana University; Boulder, University of Colorado; Riverside, University of California; Sacramento State College (*Irish Elegy* shown in San Francisco only)
Toledo Museum of Art, *Paintings and Collages by Robert Motherwell*, Nov. 2–Dec. 7, 1969. Traveled to Seattle Art Museum, Jan. 9–Feb. 15, 1970; Palo Alto, California, Stanford University Art Museum (as *New Works by Robert Motherwell*), Apr. 14–May 17, 1970; cat. no. 15
Seattle, Henry Art Gallery, University of Washington, *One Night of Color*, Feb. 6, 1981
Seattle, Henry Art Gallery, University of Washington, *Art in America: Washington Collections—An American Tradition: Abstraction*, Dec. 4, 1981–Jan. 17, 1982
Buffalo, Albright-Knox Art Gallery, *Robert Motherwell*, Oct. 1–Nov. 27, 1983. Traveled to Los Angeles, Los Angeles County Museum of Art, Jan. 5–Mar. 4, 1984; San Francisco Museum of Modern Art, Apr. 12–June 3, 1984; Seattle Art Museum, June 21–Aug. 5, 1984; Washington, DC, Corcoran Gallery of Art, Sept. 15–Nov. 4, 1984 (*Irish Elegy* not shown in Los Angeles); cat. no. 44, p. 127, reproduced p. 85
Seattle Art Museum, *The Richard and Jane Lang Collection*, Feb. 2–Apr. 1, 1984; cat. no. 33, pp. 46–47, reproduced
New York, Solomon R. Guggenheim Museum, *Robert Motherwell*, Dec. 3, 1984–Feb. 3, 1985; cat. no. 27

Robert Motherwell
American (1915–1991)
Before the Day, 1972
Charcoal and acrylic on canvas
72½ × 96⅝ in. (184.1 × 245.3 cm)
Signed and dated upper left: RM 72 / 30 August
Signed and dated upper right, on reverse: 30 August 1972 / Robert Motherwell
2021.1.1
PLATE 18

Provenance
The artist
Acquired from the above, via Lawrence Rubin Gallery, New York, by Jane and Richard E. Lang, Seattle, 1972
Friday Foundation, Seattle, 2018
Seattle Art Museum, 2021

Exhibitions
New York, Lawrence Rubin Gallery, *Robert Motherwell*, Oct. 21–Nov. 8, 1972; cat. no. 7
Seattle Art Museum, *American Art: Third Quarter Century*, Aug. 22–Oct. 14, 1973; cat. no. 43, pp. 19, 100, reproduced
Düsseldorf, Germany, Städtische Kunsthalle Düsseldorf, *Robert Motherwell*, Sept. 3–Oct. 10, 1976. Traveled to Stockholm, Sweden, Stockholm Galleriet Kulturhuset, Nov. 12, 1976–Jan. 9, 1977; Vienna, Austria, Museum des 20. Jahrhunderts, Mar. 8–Apr. 11, 1977; cat. no. 40, reproduced p. 109
Paris, France, Musée d'Art Moderne de la Ville de Paris, *Robert Motherwell: Choix de peintures et de collages, 1941–1977*, June 21–Sept. 20, 1977; no cat. no., reproduced
Edinburgh, Scotland, Royal Scottish Academy, *Robert Motherwell: Paintings and Collages, 1941–1977*, Oct. 15–Nov. 27, 1977
Seattle, Henry Art Gallery, University of Washington, *Art in America: Washington Collections—An American Tradition: Abstraction*, Dec. 4, 1981–Jan. 17, 1982
Seattle Art Museum, *The Richard and Jane Lang Collection*, Feb. 2–Apr. 1, 1984; cat. no. 34, p. 48, reproduced

Alice Neel

American (1900–1984)
Richard Lang, 1978
Oil on canvas
50 × 35 in. (127 × 88.9 cm)
Signed lower left: Neel / '78
Gift of Jane Lang Davis, 87.46
PAGE 29

Provenance
Commissioned from the artist by Richard E. Lang, Seattle, 1978
Seattle Art Museum, 1987

Exhibitions
Seattle Art Museum, *The Richard and Jane Lang Collection*, Feb. 2–Apr. 1, 1984; cat. no. 35, reproduced p. 45
Seattle Art Museum, *Collection Highlights: 1945 to the Present*, Sept. 12, 1996–June 1, 1997
Seattle Art Museum, *First Person Singular*, May 31, 2001–Mar. 17, 2002

Jackson Pollock

American (1912–1956)
Untitled, 1951
Black and colored ink on mulberry paper
24¾ × 39¼ in. (63 × 99.7 cm), irregular
Signed, dated, and inscribed lower right: For Clem / 1951 / Jan. 16 / Jackson Pollock
2020.14.13
PLATE 6

Provenance
The artist
Clement Greenberg, New York, gift of the artist
[Mrs. Virginia Kondratief, Dwan Gallery, Los Angeles]
Mr. and Mrs. J. O. Lambert, Dallas
[Janie C. Lee Gallery, Houston]
[André Emmerich Gallery, New York]
Acquired from the above by Jane and Richard E. Lang, Seattle, 1974
Friday Foundation, Seattle, 2018
Seattle Art Museum, 2020

Exhibitions
São Paulo, Brazil, Museu de Arte Moderna, *IV Bienal do Museu de Arte Moderna*, Sept. 22–Dec. 31, 1957; cat. no. 21, p. 201
Jackson Pollock: 1912–1956. Organized by the International Program of the Museum of Modern Art, New York, under the auspices of the International Council at the Museum of Modern Art; traveled to Rome, Italy, Galleria Nazionale d'Arte Moderna, Mar. 1–30, 1958; Basel, Switzerland, Kunsthalle Basel, Apr. 19–May 26, 1958; Amsterdam, the Netherlands, Stedelijk Museum, June 6–July 7, 1958; Hamburg, Germany, Kunstverein Hamburg, July 19–Aug. 17, 1958; Berlin, Germany, Hochschule für Bildende Künste, Sept. 3–Oct. 1, 1958; London, England, Whitechapel Art Gallery, Nov. 5–Dec. 14, 1958; Paris, France, Musée National d'Art Moderne – Centre Pompidou, Jan. 16–Feb. 15, 1959
Los Angeles, Dwan Gallery, [group show], June 11–July 7, 1962
New York, Museum of Modern Art, *Jackson Pollock: Works on Paper*, 1968; cat. no. 45 (exhibition brochure); p. 90, reproduced pl. 91
New York, Museum of Modern Art, *Jackson Pollock: Drawing into Painting*, Feb. 4–Mar. 16, 1980. Traveled to Oxford, England, Museum of Modern Art, Apr. 1–May 13, 1979; cat. no. 59, reproduced p. 78
Seattle, Henry Art Gallery, University of Washington, *Art in America: Washington Collections—An American Tradition: Abstraction*, Dec. 4, 1981–Jan. 17, 1982
Seattle Art Museum, *The Richard and Jane Lang Collection*, Feb. 2–Apr. 1, 1984; cat. no. 36, pp. 50–51, reproduced
New York, Museum of Modern Art, *Jackson Pollock*, Nov. 1, 1998–Feb. 2, 1999. Traveled to London, England, Tate Gallery, Mar. 11–June 8, 1999; no cat. no., p. 289, reproduced pl. 202
Liverpool, England, Tate Liverpool, *Jackson Pollock: Blind Spots*, June 30–Oct. 18, 2015. Traveled to Dallas Museum of Art, Nov. 20, 2015–Mar. 20, 2016; no cat. no., reproduced pl. 122

Ad Reinhardt

American (1913–1967)
Painting, 1950, 1950
Oil on canvas
60 × 36 in. (152.5 × 91.5 cm)
Signed and inscribed on backing board, center right: Reinhardt; lower right: Brown Windows
Inscribed on reverse, upper left: B. PARSONS; upper center: TOP
Signed and inscribed on stretcher: ReinHaRDt 1950 / 1951 SHOW
2020.14.14
PLATE 4

Provenance

The artist
Estate of the artist
[Marlborough Gallery, New York]
Acquired from the above by Jane and Richard E. Lang, Seattle, 1974
Friday Foundation, Seattle, 2018
Seattle Art Museum, 2020

Exhibitions

New York, Betty Parsons Gallery, *Ad Reinhardt: Recent Oil Paintings*, June 4–23, 1951
New York, Betty Parsons Gallery, *Ad Reinhardt: Twenty-Five Years of Abstract Painting*, Oct. 17–Nov. 5, 1960; no cat. no., reproduced (as *Painting*)
New York, Marlborough Gallery, *Ad Reinhardt*, Mar. 2–23, 1974; cat. no. 44
Seattle Art Museum, *The Richard and Jane Lang Collection*, Feb. 2–Apr. 1, 1984; cat. no. 37, pp. 52–53, reproduced

Mark Rothko

American, b. Russia (now Latvia) (1903–1970)
Untitled, ca. 1945
Oil on canvas
22½ × 30⅜ in. (57.1 × 77 cm)
Signature incised lower left: Mark Rothko
2020.14.3
PLATE 1

Provenance

The artist
[Betty Parsons Gallery, New York]
[Rose Fried Gallery, New York]
Dr. and Mrs. Joseph M. Krimsley, New York
Mrs. Joseph M. Krimsley, New York
[Christie's New York, *Contemporary Art*, Nov. 12, 1980, sale no. 5019, lot no. 12]
Acquired from the above by Jane and Richard E. Lang, Seattle, 1980
Friday Foundation, Seattle, 2018
Seattle Art Museum, 2020

Exhibitions

New York, Betty Parsons Gallery, *Mark Rothko*, Mar. 3–22, 1947
New Directions in American Painting. Organized by the Poses Institute of Fine Arts, Brandeis University, Waltham, Massachusetts; traveled to Utica, New York, Munson-Williams-Proctor Arts Institute Museum of Art, Dec. 1, 1963–Jan. 5, 1964; New Orleans, Isaac Delgado Museum of Art, Feb. 7–Mar. 8, 1964; Atlanta Art Association, Mar. 18–Apr. 22, 1964; Louisville, Kentucky, J. B. Speed Art Museum, May 4–June 7, 1964; Bloomington, Art Museum, Indiana University, June 22–Sept. 20, 1964; Saint Louis, Washington University, Oct. 5–30, 1964; Detroit Institute of Arts, Nov. 10–Dec. 6, 1964; cat. no. 48 (as *Untitled*, ca. 1946)
Seattle Art Museum, *The Richard and Jane Lang Collection*, Feb. 2–Apr. 1, 1984; cat. no. 39, p. 54, reproduced
Seattle Art Museum, *Seattle Collects Paintings: Works in Private Collections*, May 22–Sept. 7, 1997; no cat. no.
Seattle Art Museum, *SAM at 75: Building a Collection for Seattle*, May 5–Sept. 9, 2007

Mark Rothko

American, b. Russia (now Latvia) (1903–1970)
Untitled, 1963
Oil on canvas
69 × 90¼ in. (175.2 × 229.3 cm)
Signed and dated upper center, on reverse: MARK ROTHKO / 1963
2020.14.16
PLATE 13

Provenance

The artist
Estate of the artist
[Marlborough Gallery, New York]
Acquired from the above by Jane and Richard E. Lang, Seattle, 1972
Friday Foundation, Seattle, 2018
Seattle Art Museum, 2020

Exhibitions

New York, Marlborough Gallery, *Masters of the 19th and 20th Centuries*, Apr.–May 1972; cat. no. 50, reproduced
Seattle Art Museum, *American Art: Third Quarter Century*, Aug. 23–Oct. 14, 1973; cat. no. 57, pp. 16–17, 101, reproduced
New York, Solomon R. Guggenheim Museum, *Mark Rothko, 1903–1970: A Retrospective*, Oct. 27, 1978–Jan. 14, 1979. Traveled to Museum of Fine Arts Houston, Feb. 15–Apr. 18, 1979; Minneapolis, Walker Art Center, Apr. 25–June 10, 1979; Los Angeles, Los Angeles County Museum of Art, July 3–Sept. 26, 1979; cat. no. 182, reproduced
Seattle Art Museum, *The Richard and Jane Lang Collection*, Feb. 2–Apr. 1, 1984; cat. no. 41, pp. 56–57, reproduced
Washington, DC, National Gallery of Art, *Mark Rothko*, May 3–Aug. 16, 1998. Traveled to New York, Whitney Museum of American Art, Sept. 10–Nov. 29, 1998; Paris, France, Musée d'Art Moderne de la Ville de Paris, Jan. 8–Apr. 18, 1998; no cat. no., reproduced pp. 200–201, pl. 95
Seattle Art Museum, *Big Picture: Art after 1945*, July 23, 2016–May 16, 2021 (*Untitled* on view Nov. 20, 2018–May 16, 2021)

David Smith

American (1906–1965)
Cubi XXV, 1965
Stainless steel
119¼ × 120¾ × 31¼ in. (302.9 × 306.7 × 79.4 cm)
Signed, dated, and inscribed on base plane: CUBI XXV / David Smith / Jan. 9. 1965
2021.1.2
PLATE 15

Provenance

The artist
Estate of the artist
[Marlborough-Gerson Gallery, New York]
Meshulam Riklis, New York
[Luis Mestre Fine Arts, New York]
Acquired from the above by Jane and Richard E. Lang, Seattle, 1978
Friday Foundation, Seattle, 2018
Seattle Art Museum, 2021

Exhibitions

New York, Metropolitan Museum of Art, *New York Painting and Sculpture, 1940–1970*, Oct. 18, 1969–Feb. 1, 1970; cat. no. 375, pp. 60, 131, reproduced p. 313
Cincinnati, Contemporary Arts Center, *Monumental Art*, Sept. 13–Nov. 1, 1970; reproduced
On loan to Hartford, Wadsworth Atheneum Museum of Art, prior to 1978

Clyfford Still

American (1904–1980)
PH-338 [previously known as *1949-No. 2*], 1949
Oil on canvas
91½ × 68¾ in. (232.5 × 174.5 cm)
2020.14.17
PLATE 3

Provenance

The artist
[Betty Parsons Gallery, New York]
Mr. and Mrs. Milton Fischmann, Saint Louis
Mr. and Mrs. Ben Heller, New York
[Dayton's Gallery 12, Minneapolis]
Acquired from the above by Jane and Richard E. Lang, Seattle, 1973
Friday Foundation, Seattle, 2018
Seattle Art Museum, 2020

Exhibitions

New York, Betty Parsons Gallery, *Clyfford Still*, Apr. 17–May 6, 1950
San Francisco, Metart Galleries, *Paintings by Clyfford Still*, June 17–July 14, 1950
The New American Painting, As Shown in Eight European Countries, 1958–1959. Organized by the International Program of the Museum of Modern Art, New York, under the auspices of the International Council at the Museum of Modern Art; traveled to Basel, Switzerland, Kunsthalle Basel, Apr. 19–May 26, 1958; Milan, Italy, Galleria Civica d'Arte Moderna, June 1–29, 1958; Madrid, Spain, Museo Nacional de Arte Contemporáneo, July 16–Aug. 10, 1958; Berlin, Germany, Hochschule für Bildende Künste, Sept. 1–Oct. 1, 1958; Amsterdam, the Netherlands, Stedelijk Museum, Oct. 17–Nov. 24, 1958; Brussels, Belgium, Palais des Beaux-Arts, Dec. 6, 1958–Jan. 4, 1959; Paris, France, Musée National d'Art Moderne, Jan. 16–Feb. 15, 1959; London, England, Tate Gallery, Feb. 24–Mar. 23, 1959; cat. no. 68 (as *Number 2*), reproduced p. 77
The Collection of Mr. and Mrs. Ben Heller. Organized by the Museum of Modern Art, New York; traveled to Art Institute of Chicago (as *The Ben Heller Collection of Paintings of the School of New York*), Sept. 22–Oct. 22, 1961; Baltimore Museum of Art, Dec. 3–31, 1961; Cincinnati, Contemporary Arts Center, Jan. 22–Feb. 25, 1962; Cleveland Museum of Art, Mar. 13–Apr. 10, 1962; San Francisco, California Palace of the Legion of Honor, Apr. 30–June 3, 1962; Portland, Oregon, Portland Art Museum, June 15–July 22, 1962; Los Angeles, Los Angeles County Museum of Art, Sept. 5–Oct. 14, 1962; no cat. no., reproduced (as *Painting Number 2*)
Seattle Art Museum, *The Richard and Jane Lang Collection*, Feb. 2–Apr. 1, 1984; cat. no. 43, pp. 58–59, reproduced (as *Number 2*)
Washington, DC, Hirshhorn Museum and Sculpture Garden, *Clyfford Still: Paintings, 1944–1960*, June 21–Sept. 16, 2001; cat. no. 19, reproduced
Seattle Art Museum, *SAM at 75: Building a Collection for Seattle*, May 5–Sept. 9, 2007
Denver, Clyfford Still Museum, *Repeat/Recreate: Clyfford Still's "Replicas,"* Sept. 18, 2015–Jan. 10, 2016; no cat. no., reproduced p. 81, pl. 21
Seattle Art Museum, *Big Picture: Art after 1945*, July 23, 2016–May 16, 2021 (PH-338 on view Nov. 20, 2018–May 16, 2021)

Andy Warhol

American (1928–1987)
Jane Lang, 1976
Acrylic and silkscreen ink on linen
Diptych, each panel 40 × 40 in. (101.6 × 101.6 cm)
Signed upper right, on reverse: Andy Warhol
Gift of Mr. and Mrs. Richard E. Lang, 76.47
FIG. 10; PAGE 27 (left)

Provenance

Commissioned from the artist by Richard E. Lang, Seattle, 1976
Seattle Art Museum, 1976

Exhibitions

Seattle Art Museum, *Andy Warhol: Portraits*, Nov. 15, 1976–Jan. 9, 1977. Traveled to Denver Art Museum, Feb. 5–Mar. 27, 1977
New York, Whitney Museum of American Art, *Andy Warhol: Portraits of the 70s*, Nov. 20, 1979–Jan. 27, 1980; no cat. no., p. 137, reproduced p. 89 (with SAM acc. no. 2020.19)
Seattle Art Museum, *The Richard and Jane Lang Collection*, Feb. 2–Apr. 1, 1984; cat. no. 44, reproduced p. 60 (with SAM acc. no. 2020.19)
Escondido, California Center for the Arts, *Narcissism: Artists Reflect Themselves*, Feb. 4–May 26, 1996
Seattle Art Museum, *Collection Highlights: 1945 to the Present*, Sept. 12, 1996–June 1, 1997
Seattle, Henry Art Gallery, University of Washington, *Andy Warhol Drawings, 1942–1987*, July 29–Oct. 8, 2000. Organized by the Kunstmuseum Basel, Switzerland, and the Andy Warhol Museum, Pittsburgh
Seattle Art Museum, *Modern in America*, July 8, 2004–Feb. 27, 2005
Seattle Art Museum, *Pop Departures*, Oct. 9, 2014–Jan. 11, 2015; no cat. no., p. 103, reproduced p. 71 (with SAM acc. no. 2020.19)

Andy Warhol

American (1928–1987)
Jane Lang, 1976
Acrylic and silkscreen ink on linen
Diptych, each panel 40 × 40 in. (101.6 × 101.6 cm)
Signed upper right, on reverse: Andy Warhol
Gift of Lyn and Jerry Grinstein, 2020.19
FIG. 10; PAGE 27 (right)

Provenance

Commissioned from the artist by Richard E. Lang, Seattle, 1976
Lyn Grinstein and Don Hussong, Seattle, 2018
Lyn and Jerry Grinstein, Seattle, 2019
Seattle Art Museum, 2020

Exhibitions

Seattle Art Museum, *Andy Warhol: Portraits*, Nov. 15, 1976–Jan. 9, 1977. Traveled to Denver Art Museum, Feb. 5–Mar. 27, 1977
New York, Whitney Museum of American Art, *Andy Warhol: Portraits of the 70s*, Nov. 20, 1979–Jan. 27, 1980; no cat. no., p. 137, reproduced p. 88 (with SAM acc. no. 76.47)
Seattle Art Museum, *The Richard and Jane Lang Collection*, Feb. 2–Apr. 1, 1984; cat. no. 44, reproduced p. 60 (with SAM acc. no. 76.47)
Seattle Art Museum, *Pop Departures*, Oct. 9, 2014–Jan. 11, 2015; no cat. no., p. 103, reproduced p. 71 (with SAM acc. no. 76.47)

CONTRIBUTORS

David Anfam is senior consulting curator at the Clyfford Still Museum, Denver. His exhibition *Abstract Expressionism* (Royal Academy of Arts, London, 2016–17) was the largest survey of its kind ever held in Europe. Anfam's many publications include *Franz Kline: Black and White, 1950–1961* (Menil Collection, 1994) and the catalogue raisonné *Mark Rothko: The Works on Canvas* (Yale University Press, 1998), now in its sixth printing.

Michael Brenson has written catalogue essays on David Smith for the Museo Nacional Centro de Arte Reina Sofía, the Solomon R. Guggenheim Museum, and the Sterling and Francine Clark Art Institute. He contributed to *David Smith Sculpture: A Catalogue Raisonné, 1932–1965* (Yale University Press, 2021), and his biography of the artist, *David Smith: The Art and Life of a Transformational Sculptor*, will be published in 2022 (Farrar, Straus, and Giroux).

John Elderfield is chief curator emeritus of painting and sculpture at the Museum of Modern Art, New York, where he curated the 2011 exhibition *de Kooning: a Retrospective*; and a senior curator for special projects at Gagosian, New York, where in 2013 he curated *Willem de Kooning: Ten Paintings, 1983–1985*. He also edited the publications that accompanied these exhibitions.

Jack Flam is president and CEO of the Dedalus Foundation and distinguished professor emeritus of art history at the City University of New York. He is coauthor of *Robert Motherwell Paintings and Collages: A Catalogue Raisonné, 1941–1991* (Yale University Press, 2012) and *Robert Motherwell: 100 Years* (Skira, 2015).

Carter E. Foster is deputy director for curatorial affairs at the Blanton Museum of Art, Austin, Texas. His exhibition *Pollock and the Irascibles: The New York School* was accompanied by an extensive catalogue (24 ORE Cultura, 2014).

Catherine Grenier is director of the Fondation Giacometti and former deputy director of the Musée National d'Art Moderne – Centre Pompidou, Paris. She has published extensively on the work of Alberto Giacometti, including the recent books *Alberto Giacometti, L'homme qui marche* (Fondation Giacometti-institut and Fage éditions, 2020) and *Alberto Giacometti, a Biography* (Flammarion, 2018).

Bruce Guenther, a specialist in European and American postwar art, was chief curator and curator of modern and contemporary art, Portland Art Museum, Oregon, until his retirement in 2014. He previously was chief curator of the Museum of Contemporary Art Chicago, and head of the modern art program at the Seattle Art Museum. His recent publications include essays for *Paper: Charles Arnoldi* (Radius, 2017), *Michael C. Spafford: Epic Works* (Lucia | Marquand, 2018), and *Roland Peterson: Works on Paper, 1956–2005* (Studio Shop, LP, 2019).

Martin Harrison has been writing about Francis Bacon since 1999 and edited *Francis Bacon: Catalogue Raisonné* (2016), published by the Estate of Francis Bacon, where he is head of publishing. He coauthored the fourth volume in the series Francis Bacon Studies, *Francis Bacon: Shadows* (Thames and Hudson, 2021).

Sanford Hirsch is executive director of the Adolph and Esther Gottlieb Foundation. He has organized many exhibitions of the work of Adolph Gottlieb, including the 1981 retrospective at the Corcoran Gallery of Art, for which he also contributed to the accompanying catalogue (Arts Publisher and the Adolph and Esther Gottlieb Foundation, 1981).

Norman L. Kleeblatt is an independent curator, critic, and consultant based in New York. He was formerly Susan and Elihu Ruse Chief Curator at the Jewish Museum, New York, where he organized exhibitions on the work of many of the New York School artists, including *Action/Abstraction: Pollock, de Kooning, and American Art, 1940–1976* (catalogue published by Yale University Press, 2009) and *From the Margins: Lee Krasner, Norman Lewis, 1945–1952* (Yale University Press, 2014).

Catharina Manchanda is Jon and Mary Shirley Curator of Modern and Contemporary Art at the Seattle Art Museum, where she curated *City of Tomorrow: Jinny Wright and the Art That Shaped a New Seattle* (2020–21). Her recent publications include *Figuring History: Robert Colescott, Kerry James Marshall, Mickalene Thomas* (SAM / Yale University Press, 2018), and *Pop Departures* (SAM, 2014).

Eleanor Nairne is a writer and curator based at the Barbican Art Gallery in London, where her recent exhibitions include *Jean Dubuffet: Brutal Beauty* (catalogue published by Prestel, 2021), *Lee Krasner: Living Colour* (Thames and Hudson, 2019), and *Basquiat: Boom for Real* (Prestel, 2017). She has contributed essays and criticism to publications including *frieze*, the *London Review of Books*, and the *New York Times*.

Amy Rahn is an assistant professor of art history at the University of Maine at Augusta, where she is director of the Charles Danforth Gallery. She authored an essay for the recent Joan Mitchell retrospective exhibition catalogue (Yale University Press, 2021) and wrote the first dissertation on Mitchell.

Elizabeth A. T. Smith joined the New York–based Helen Frankenthaler Foundation as its first executive director in 2013, following a career as a curator at museums in Los Angeles, Chicago, and Toronto. Her writings on Helen Frankenthaler include an essay in *Abstract Climates: Helen Frankenthaler in Provincetown* (Yale University Press, 2018).

Robert Storr is an artist, critic, and curator based in New York. He was previously senior curator of painting and sculpture at the Museum of Modern Art, New York, and professor of painting and printmaking at Yale University School of Art. His writings on Philip Guston include *Philip Guston* (Abbeville, 1985) and *Philip Guston: A Life Spent Painting* (Laurence King, 2019).

Carol Vogel was a journalist at the *New York Times* for more than thirty years and covered the art world for over two decades, writing the weekly Inside Art column, along with countless articles about museums, galleries, auctions, collectors, dealers, and the art market. She is currently working on a book about the art world for Knopf.

Jeffrey Weiss is an independent curator and critic living in Brooklyn, New York. He has held senior curatorial positions at the National Gallery of Art, Washington, DC, where he organized the 1998 Mark Rothko retrospective exhibition, and at the Solomon R. Guggenheim Museum, New York. Most recently, Weiss was coeditor and coauthor, with Francesca Esmay, of *Object Lessons: Case Studies in Minimal Art* (Solomon R. Guggenheim Museum / D.A.P., 2021).

PHOTOGRAPHY CREDITS

Pages 2, 83: Photo by Spike Mafford / Zocalo Studios. Courtesy of the Friday Foundation. © 2021 The Franz Kline Estate / Artists Rights Society (ARS), New York
Pages 8, 59, 159: Photo by Spike Mafford / Zocalo Studios. Courtesy of the Friday Foundation. © 2021 The Willem de Kooning Foundation / Artists Rights Society (ARS), New York
Page 27: Photo by Paul Macapia / Seattle Art Museum. Artwork © 2021 The Andy Warhol Foundation for the Visual Arts, Inc. / Artists Rights Society (ARS), New York
Page 29: Courtesy of Seattle Art Museum. © The Estate of Alice Neel
Pages 30, 67: Photo by Spike Mafford / Zocalo Studios. Courtesy of the Friday Foundation. © 2021 City and County of Denver, Courtesy Clyfford Still Museum / Artists Rights Society (ARS), New York
Pages 52–53, 55, 133: Photo by Spike Mafford / Zocalo Studios. Courtesy of the Friday Foundation. © 1998 Kate Rothko Prizel and Christopher Rothko / Artists Rights Society (ARS), New York
Page 75: Photo by Spike Mafford / Zocalo Studios. Courtesy of the Friday Foundation. © 2021 Estate of Ad Reinhardt / Artists Rights Society (ARS), New York
Pages 91, 119, 184: Photo by Spike Mafford / Zocalo Studios. Courtesy of the Friday Foundation. © 2021 The Pollock-Krasner Foundation / Artists Rights Society (ARS), New York
Pages 97, 171: Photo by Spike Mafford / Zocalo Studios. Courtesy of the Friday Foundation. Artwork © The Estate of Philip Guston, Courtesy of Hauser and Wirth
Pages 101, 104: Photo by Spike Mafford / Zocalo Studios. Courtesy of the Friday Foundation. © Artist or Artist's Estate
Page 107: Photo by Spike Mafford / Zocalo Studios. Courtesy of the Friday Foundation. © 2021 Alberto Giacometti Estate / VAGA at Artists Rights Society (ARS), New York / ADAGP, Paris
Page 113: Photo by Spike Mafford / Zocalo Studios. Courtesy of the Friday Foundation. © 2021 Adolph and Esther Gottlieb Foundation / Licensed by VAGA at Artists Rights Society (ARS), New York
Page 127: Photo by Spike Mafford / Zocalo Studios. Courtesy of the Friday Foundation. © 2021 The Estate of Francis Bacon. All rights reserved / DACS, London / Artists Rights Society (ARS), New York 2021
Pages 139, 164: Photo by Spike Mafford / Zocalo Studios. Courtesy of the Friday Foundation. © 2021 Dedalus Foundation, Inc. / Artists Rights Society (ARS), New York
Page 145: Jonathan Vanderweit Visual Services. © 2021 The Estate of David Smith / Licensed by VAGA at Artists Rights Society (ARS), New York
Page 153: Photo by Spike Mafford / Zocalo Studios. Courtesy of the Friday Foundation. © 2021 Helen Frankenthaler Foundation, Inc. / Artists Rights Society (ARS), New York
Page 176: Mirrorpix / Getty Images
Page 181: Iris & B. Gerald Cantor Center for Visual Arts at Stanford University; Gift of The Andy Warhol Foundation for the Visual Arts, Inc.
Figs. 1, 3, 4, 5, 9, 12, 44: Photo by Spike Mafford / Zocalo Studios. Courtesy of the Friday Foundation
Fig. 2: Seattle Art Museum
Figs. 6–8, 11, 13, 71, 75; pages 177–81: Courtesy of the Friday Foundation
Fig. 10: Vic Condiotty / The Seattle Times
Fig. 14: Digital Image © The Museum of Modern Art / Licensed by SCALA / Art Resource, New York. Artwork © The Andy Warhol Foundation for the Visual Arts, Inc. / Licensed by Artists Rights Society (ARS), New York
Fig. 15: Photo by Bill Taylor. Artwork © 2021 The Isamu Noguchi Foundation and Garden Museum, New York / Artists Rights Society (ARS), New York
Fig. 16: Image source: Art Resource, New York. Image © The Metropolitan Museum of Art, New York. © 2021 The Pollock-Krasner Foundation / Artists Rights Society (ARS), New York
Fig. 17: Image courtesy of Mildred Lane Kemper Art Museum, Washington University in St. Louis. Artwork © The Estate of Philip Guston, courtesy of Hauser and Wirth
Fig. 18: Digital Image © The Museum of Modern Art / Licensed by SCALA / Art Resource, New York. Artwork with permission of the Renate, Hans & Maria Hofmann Trust / Artists Rights Society (ARS), New York
Fig. 19: Nina Leen / The LIFE Picture Collection / Getty Images
Fig. 20: Image courtesy of the Frances Lehman Loeb Art Center, Vassar College. Artwork © 1998 Kate Rothko Prizel and Christopher Rothko / Artists Rights Society (ARS), New York
Fig. 21: © CNAC/MNAM, Dist. RMN-Grand Palais / Art Resource, New York. Artwork © 2021 The Pollock-Krasner Foundation / Artists Rights Society (ARS), New York
Fig. 22: © 1998 Kate Rothko Prizel and Christopher Rothko / Artists Rights Society (ARS), New York
Fig. 23: Photo by Ben Blackwell / San Francisco Museum of Modern Art. © 1998 Kate Rothko Prizel and Christopher Rothko / Artists Rights Society (ARS), New York
Figs. 24, 26: Photo © Christie's Images / Bridgeman Images. Artwork © 2021 The Willem de Kooning Foundation / Artists Rights Society (ARS), New York
Fig. 25: Image source: http://en.wikipedia.org/wiki/File:Pablo_Picasso,_1910,_Portrait_of_Wilhelm_Uhde,_oil_on_canvas,_81_x_60_cm,_Joseph_Pulitzer_Collection.jpg. © 2021 Estate of Pablo Picasso / Artists Rights Society (ARS), New York
Fig. 27: © 2011 Douglas M. Parker Studio. © 2021 The Willem de Kooning Foundation / Artists Rights Society (ARS), New York
Fig. 28: © 2021 City and County of Denver, Courtesy of the Clyfford Still Museum / Artists Rights Society (ARS), New York
Fig. 29: Katherine Du Tiel / San Francisco Museum of Modern Art. © 2021 City and County of Denver, Courtesy of the Clyfford Still Museum / Artists Rights Society (ARS), New York
Fig. 30: Scala / Art Resource, New York
Fig. 31: Courtesy of David Zwirner Gallery. © 2021 Estate of Ad Reinhardt / Artists Rights Society (ARS), New York
Figs. 32, 33: Courtesy of Michael Rosenfeld Gallery LLC, New York. © Estate of Norman W. Lewis
Fig. 34: Photo by Max Yavno. Courtesy of the Ad Reinhardt Foundation. © Center for Creative Photography, the University of Arizona Foundation
Fig. 35: Digital Image © The Museum of Modern Art / Licensed by SCALA / Art Resource, New York. Artwork © 2021 The Franz Kline Estate / Artists Rights Society (ARS), New York
Fig. 36: Image from Carolyn Christov-Bakargiev, ed., *Franz Kline (1910–1962)* (Skira, 2004), 308
Fig. 37: Image copyright © The Metropolitan Museum of Art, New York. Image source: Art Resource, New York. Artwork © Estate of Charles Sheeler
Fig. 38: Photo by Antonia Reeve, courtesy of the National Galleries of Scotland. Artwork © The Pollock-Krasner Foundation, Artists Rights Society (ARS), New York, and DACS, London, 2018
Fig. 39: Digital image courtesy of the Whitney Museum of American Art / Licensed by Scala. Artwork © 2021 The Pollock-Krasner Foundation / Artists Rights Society (ARS), New York
Fig. 40: Digital Image © The Museum of Modern Art / Licensed by SCALA / Art Resource, New York
Fig. 41: Photo by Rik Klein Gotink. Artwork © 2021 Mondrian/Holtzman Trust
Fig. 42: Courtesy of the RISD Museum, Providence, RI. All rights reserved
Fig. 43: Loomis Dean / The LIFE Picture Collection / Getty Images
Fig. 45: © Musée du Louvre, Dist. RMN-Grand Palais / Christian Decamps / Art Resource, New York
Fig. 46: Photo by Fedele Toscani. Courtesy of the Giacometti Foundation Archives. © 2021 Alberto Giacometti Estate / VAGA at Artists Rights Society (ARS), New York / ADAGP, Paris
Fig. 47: DEA / Archivio J. Lange / De Agostini / Getty Images
Fig. 48: Courtesy of Fondation Giacometti. © 2021 Alberto Giacometti Estate / VAGA at Artists Rights Society (ARS), New York / ADAGP, Paris
Fig. 49: Sergio Martucci / Peggy Guggenheim Collection's Exhibition Archives. Artwork © 2021 Adolph and Esther Gottlieb Foundation / Licensed by VAGA at Artists Rights Society (ARS), New York
Fig. 50: Photo by Rudolph Burckhardt. Courtesy of the Adolph and Esther Gottlieb Foundation, Inc. Artwork © 2021 Adolph and Esther Gottlieb Foundation / Licensed by VAGA at Artists Rights Society (ARS), New York
Fig. 51: Photo by Ian Reeves / San Francisco Museum of Modern Art. Artwork © 2021 Adolph and Esther Gottlieb Foundation / Licensed by VAGA at Artists Rights Society (ARS), New York
Fig. 52: Photo by Irving Penn. © The Irving Penn Foundation
Fig. 53: Photo by Diego Flores. Artwork © 2021 The Pollock-Krasner Foundation / Artists Rights Society (ARS), New York
Fig. 54: Courtesy of the Pollock-Krasner Foundation. Artwork © 2021 The Pollock-Krasner Foundation / Artists Rights Society (ARS), New York
Fig. 55: Digital Image © The Museum of Modern Art / Licensed by SCALA / Art Resource, New York
Fig. 56: Digital Image © The Museum of Modern Art / Licensed by SCALA / Art Resource, New York. Artwork © 2021 The Estate of Francis Bacon. All rights reserved / DACS, London / ARS, New York 2021
Fig. 57: Source: http://commons.wikimedia.org/wiki/File:Pierre_Bonnard_Self-Portrait_with_an_Open_Collar.jpg. Public domain
Fig. 58: © Tate 2017. Artwork © 1998 Kate Rothko Prizel and Christopher Rothko / Artists Rights Society (ARS), New York
Fig. 59: Courtesy of Kunsthaus Zürich. Artwork © 1998 Kate Rothko Prizel and Christopher Rothko / Artists Rights Society (ARS), New York
Fig. 60: Photo by Jordan Tinker. © 2021 Dedalus Foundation, Inc. / Artists Rights Society (ARS), New York
Fig. 61: Artwork © 2021 Dedalus Foundation, Inc. / Artists Rights Society (ARS), New York
Fig. 62: Christian Mueringer / Alamy Stock Photo
Fig. 63: © 2021 The Estate of Dan Budnik. All rights reserved
Fig. 64: Digital Image © 2021 Museum Associates / LACMA. Licensed by Art Resource, New York. Artwork © 2021 The Estate of David Smith / Licensed by VAGA at Artists Rights Society (ARS), New York
Fig. 65: Photo by David Heald. Artwork © 2021 The Estate of David Smith / Licensed by VAGA at Artists Rights Society (ARS), New York
Fig. 66: Munson-Williams-Proctor Arts Institute / Art Resource, New York. Artwork © 2021 The Estate of David Smith / Licensed by VAGA at Artists Rights Society (ARS), New York
Fig. 67: Image courtesy of the Helen Frankenthaler Foundation. Artwork © 2021 Helen Frankenthaler Foundation, Inc. / Artists Rights Society (ARS), New York
Fig. 68: Digital Image © The Museum of Modern Art / Licensed by SCALA / Art Resource, New York. Artwork © 2021 Helen Frankenthaler Foundation, Inc. / Artists Rights Society (ARS), New York
Fig. 69: Digital Image © The Museum of Modern Art / Licensed by SCALA / Art Resource, New York. Artwork © 2021 Succession H. Matisse / Artists Rights Society (ARS), New York
Fig. 70: Collection and digital image © Hugh Lane Gallery, Dublin (Reg. RM98F1A:40). Artwork © The Estate of Francis Bacon. All rights reserved / DACS, London / Artists Rights Society (ARS), New York 2021
Fig. 72: Photo by Jordan Tinker. Artwork © 2021 Dedalus Foundation, Inc. / Artists Rights Society (ARS), New York
Figs. 73, 74: Photo by Steven Sloman © 1983, © 1985. Artwork © 2021 Dedalus Foundation, Inc. / Artists Rights Society (ARS), New York
Fig. 76: Photo by Genevieve Hanson. Artwork © The Estate of Philip Guston, courtesy of Hauser and Wirth
Fig. 77: National Gallery of Australia, Canberra / Bridgeman Images. Artwork © The Estate of Philip Guston, courtesy of Hauser and Wirth

INDEX

Notes: Catalogue entry pages appear in **bold**. Pages with illustrations appear in *italics*. Works of art are given under artists and are listed at the end of each entry.

Published on the occasion of the exhibition *Frisson: The Richard E. Lang and Jane Lang Davis Collection*, organized by Catharina Manchanda for the Seattle Art Museum, opening October 15, 2021.

Generous support for this publication was provided by the Friday Foundation.

Copyedited by Kristin Swan
Proofread by Dianne Woo
Indexed by Kathleen Friello
Designed by Rita Jules, Miko McGinty Inc.
Typeset by Tina Henderson
Printed and bound in Italy by Trifolio S.r.l.

Library of Congress Control Number: 2021937525
ISBN: 978-0-932216-79-3

Published by
Seattle Art Museum
1300 First Avenue
Seattle, WA 98101
seattleartmuseum.org

Distributed by
University of Washington Press
4333 Brooklyn Avenue NE
Seattle, WA 98105
uwapress.uw.edu

Cover: Lee Krasner, *Night Watch*, 1960 (detail, plate 11), oil on canvas, 70 × 99¼ in. (177.8 × 252.1 cm). Seattle Art Museum, Gift of the Friday Foundation in honor of Richard E. Lang and Jane Lang Davis, 2020.14.4.

Frontispiece: Franz Kline, *Painting No. 11*, 1951 (detail, plate 5), oil on canvas, 61 × 82¼ in. (155 × 208.9 cm). Seattle Art Museum, Gift of the Friday Foundation in honor of Richard E. Lang and Jane Lang Davis, 2020.14.12.

Page 9: Willem de Kooning, *Town Square*, 1948 (detail, plate 2), oil on paper mounted on Masonite, 17⅜ × 23¾ in. (44.2 × 60.3 cm). Seattle Art Museum, Gift of the Friday Foundation in honor of Richard E. Lang and Jane Lang Davis, 2020.14.2.

Page 50 clockwise, from top left:

Lee Krasner, Robert Motherwell, and Willem de Kooning with de Kooning's *Town Square* (1948) at the *Fourth Annual Invitation Exhibition by Regional Artists*, Guild Hall Museum, East Hampton, New York, July 1952. Photo courtesy of Guild Hall, East Hampton, New York

Helen Frankenthaler, n.d. Photo by Ernst Haas / Getty Images

Joan Mitchell working on *Bridge* (1957) in her studio at 60 St. Marks Place, New York, 1957. Photo by Joan Mitchell and Rudy Burckhardt. JMFA001_P0509c, Joan Mitchell Foundation Archives. © 2021 Estate of Rudy Burckhardt / Artists Rights Society (ARS), New York

David Smith, ca. 1961. Photo by the artist. © 2021 The Estate of David Smith / Licensed by VAGA at Artists Rights Society (ARS), New York

Ad Reinhardt in *Ad Reinhardt: Recent Oil Paintings*, Betty Parsons Gallery, New York, June 4–23, 1951. Photo by Walter Rosenblum. Courtesy of the Ad Reinhardt Foundation

Jackson Pollock, n.d. Photo by Arnold Newman / Getty Images

Franz Klein (second from left) at his Sidney Janis Gallery opening, New York, March 7, 1960, with Harriet Grossman Janis (front left), William Baziotes (center, obscured), Ethel Baziotes (front right), Mark Rothko (left, third row), Louise Bourgeois (center), and Robert Goldwater (far right). Photo by Fred W. McDarrah / Getty Images

Page 51 clockwise, from top left:

Adolph Gottlieb in his Chelsea studio, New York, February 16, 1962. Photo by Fred W. McDarrah / Getty Images

Lee Krasner, n.d. Photo by Halley Erksine. Courtesy of the Pollock-Krasner House and Study Center, East Hampton, New York

Robert Motherwell, n.d. Photo by Fred W. McDarrah / Getty Images

Clyfford Still in front of *1949-A-No. 2*, 1951. Photo by Hans Namuth. Courtesy of the Center for Creative Photography, the University of Arizona. © 1991 Hans Namuth Estate; Art © Estate of Clyfford Still

Graham Keen, *Artists Alberto Giacometti and Francis Bacon*, July 1965, modern bromide print from original negative, 8 × 9⅞ in. (20.2 × 25.2 cm). National Portrait Gallery, London, Purchased, 2016, Photographs Collection, NPG x199752. Photo by Graham Keen / Topfoto

Dan Budnik, *Mark Rothko 1485 First Avenue Studio, New York, 1964*, 1964; printed 2007, from the series *Picturing Artists*, dye-transfer print on paper, ed. 2 of 10, 20 × 24 in. (50.8 × 61 cm). Kemper Museum of Contemporary Art, Kansas City, Missouri, Bebe and Crosby Kemper Collection, Gift of the Enid and Crosby Kemper Foundation, 2008.08.29. Art and photo © Dan Budnik. © 2021 The Estate of Dan Budnik. All Rights Reserved

Philip Guston. Photo © 1979 Sidney B. Felsen. Artwork © The Estate of Philip Guston, courtesy of Hauser and Wirth

Pages 52–53: Mark Rothko, *Untitled*, 1963 (detail, plate 13), oil on canvas, 69 × 90¼ in. (175.2 × 229.3 cm). Seattle Art Museum, Gift of the Friday Foundation in honor of Richard E. Lang and Jane Lang Davis, 2020.14.16.

Page 184: Jackson Pollock, *Untitled*, 1951 (detail, plate 6), black and colored ink on mulberry paper, 24¾ × 39¼ in. (63 × 99.7 cm), irregular. Seattle Art Museum, Gift of the Friday Foundation in honor of Richard E. Lang and Jane Lang Davis, 2020.14.13.